W9-DHL-698

NEWSPRINT: *Producers, Publishers, Political Pressures*

Newsprint: *Producers, Publishers, Political Pressures*

L. ETHAN ELLIS

Including the text of

PRINT PAPER PENDULUM:
Group Pressures and the Price of Newsprint

RUTGERS UNIVERSITY PRESS
New Brunswick *New Jersey*

Library of Congress Catalogue Number: 60-9691

Manufactured in the United States of America by
Quinn & Boden Company, Inc.

PREFACE

AS A HISTORIAN interested in economic patterns, I have for many years followed the perennial struggle between newsprint manufacturers and consumers over the supply problem. In an earlier volume, *Print Paper Pendulum: Group Pressures and the Price of Newsprint* (1948), I examined the development of a domestic newsprint industry in the United States and showed how this industry, bereft of tariff protection by 1913, largely migrated to Canada. Here there ensued an era of overexpansion of production in the 1920's, resulting in dark days for the manufacturers and easy prices for the newspaper publishers during the depression of the 1930's, both developments being accompanied by severe tensions between the two groups. This account terminated in a period when both parties to the problem were beginning to rally from the buffetings of the depression and before World War II had come to add new elements to the equation.

The following pages chronicle the decades following the termination of the first study. They carry the story through World War II, its aftermath, the Korean crisis, and the developments of the mid-fifties, terminating with the year 1958. Such a study, dealing with a contemporary and seemingly perennial problem, must end on a note of uncertainty. Too many variables must be allowed for, as well as factors now barely discernible which may grow up to shadow the whole scene. This is, perhaps, no good reason for failing to look the present in the eye. That this study has tried to do.

If it has succeeded, the happy result will stem in large measure from assistance rendered me by those familiar with various aspects of the story and custodians of its sources. Grateful mention is here made of organizations and journals which have made available essential material, often to the extent of lending file copies of virtually irreplaceable periodicals: the American Newspaper Publishers Association, the Newsprint Service Bureau, *The Paper Trade Journal* and its editor, John W. C. Evans, and *Editor & Publisher.* I have also profited from correspondence or conversation with the following, though their contributions will not always be found listed in the bibliography: Congressmen Clarence J. Brown and Emanuel Celler, former Congressman Charles A. Wolverton, Senator Warren G. Magnuson, Cranston Williams of the American Newspaper Publishers Association, Charles F. Honeywell of the Newsprint Service Bureau, and Charles E. Moreau of Moreau Publications, Inc. John J. Zima of the Newsprint Service Bureau gave the manuscript a careful reading and has sharpened its statistical and linguistic accuracy at numerous points; the tables which he has compiled form a valuable supplement to the narrative.

The Rutgers University Library and its staff provided the refuge and assistance which relieve much of the drudgery of scholarship, and Mrs. Erma M. Sutton aided materially by completing the typing to meet an early deadline. My wife, Elizabeth Breckenridge, has preserved a remarkable equanimity through this second assault on the newsprint citadel.

L. ETHAN ELLIS

New Brunswick, New Jersey
January, 1960

CONTENTS

Preface v

I. Retrospect and Prospect 3

II. From Depression into War, 1937 to 1939 21

III. War's Alarms 43

IV. Postwar Problems 95

V. The Fifties, First Phase 133

VI The Fifties, Second Phase 191

VII. Summary and Conclusions 229

Statistical Data 240

Notes 244

Bibliography 287

Index 298

Appendix—*Print Paper Pendulum: Group Pressures and the Price of Newsprint*

NEWSPRINT: *Producers, Publishers, Political Pressures*

CHAPTER I

Retrospect and Prospect

THIS IS the author's second approach to the problem of newsprint supply and demand in the United States and Canada. In *Print Paper Pendulum* (1948)[1] he examined the historical development of the newsprint industry and its relations with the newspaper publishers for whom its product constituted the raw material of their own means of livelihood. Here were set forth not only the technical changes whereby the sources of this raw material shifted from rags and straw to cellulose derived mainly from spruce logs but also the economic and political pressures which transferred the bulk of production from the United States to Canada by the middle 1930's. Included, too, was the story of relationships, seldom friendly and often overtly hostile, between producers and consumers. This history and these relationships gave rise to a succession of problems. Recently, the author has been encouraged to follow these problems and patterns through two more decades. But first, a brief recapitulation of the previous story as a setting for the forward narrative.

The latter years of the nineteenth century witnessed a large-scale American application of a pulp paper manufacturing process which had been developed over a considerable period. The process, refined and tremendously speeded up but changed remarkably little in fundamentals, starts with a "furnish" of from 80 to 85 per cent of mechanical or groundwood pulp and from 15 to 20 per cent of chemical or sulphite pulp. The first element is produced by forcing barked logs against grindstones by water or electrical power. From this emerge short, stiff cellulose fibers still combined with other components of the original log. The second element comes from the chemical "digestion" of chipped timber by a process which leaves a residue of long cellulose fibers.

The two are combined in a complicated and expensive machine which first spills the mixture onto a continuous belt of finely woven bronze wire, through which some of the water is drawn off by suction boxes underneath. Thereafter pressure and heat, applied by a succession of felt blankets and metal rollers, remove more moisture and impart a smooth finish before the end product is ready to be slit to proper widths and wound on cores for shipment to the newspaper consumer. Only two real changes have occurred since the process was first perfected: mechanical refinements of the machinery which have made it possible to increase the speed of production from 800 to well over 2,000 feet per minute, and the perfection of a technique permitting substitution of semichemical hardwood pulp as part of the furnish; the latter, however, remains of prospective rather than immediate importance.

The papermaking process has always depended upon the juxtaposition of large amounts of pure water for the production of natural or electrical power and for producing and carrying the two pulps to the machines, and of considerable supplies of cellulose-bearing materials. In the early days of manufacture the chief raw material was spruce; in later years great effort has been expended to develop alternative supplies, and research has demonstrated that almost any form of cellulose, including cornstalks, saw grass, and bagasse, a residue left in enormous quantities after the expression of juice from sugar cane, can be made into newsprint. Despite the possible utility of these materials, however, economic and technical factors have prevented any of them from becoming substitutes for the tree.

With this limitation, two broad approaches to the problem of supply have been explored successfully. The first consists of a process making available various types of resinous trees that grow widely in the southern United States. Here climatic conditions are such that the growth rate is several times as rapid as that in the north or in Canada, and with early harvest the wood is used before resin content has reached its high point. The pioneer research in this field was done by Dr. Charles H. Herty during the twenties and thirties, and his work contributed to the establishment of mills in Texas, Tennessee, and Alabama. The second process consists of a method for producing chemi-groundwood pulp from hardwood, first applied commercially by the Great Northern Paper Company in 1953.[2]

The necessary combination of wood and water was found in various places and in sufficient supply to enable United States mills to service domestic needs until after the turn of the present century. Gradually, however, another combination of increasing demand and dwindling supply generated economic and political pressures which resulted in removal of the tariff from imported newsprint in the years 1909 to 1913. This had at least two significant results. First, the Canadian industry received such a stimulus that it eventually outstripped that of the United States. Below the border a high peak of production was attained in 1926, to be followed by a gradual decline to a low point in 1944, after which the curve started to climb once more. Canadian production passed that of the United States in 1926 and eventually (in 1948) mounted to a point where it furnished 79 per cent of the newsprint used in the United States. The second result, closely related to the first, was that continued protection of other paper grades, plus the expansion of Canadian production of newsprint, encouraged United States newsprint mills to shift production into more lucrative channels. Thus was developed a dependence upon Canadian newsprint which became threatening in times of crisis and galling in times of shortage; but it constituted a pattern very difficult to change. Attempts to rectify this imbalance are a significant part of the subsequent story.

Severe strains preceded and accompanied this northward movement of the industry, strains which recurringly embittered relations between publishers and manufacturers; and neither the passage of time nor sporadic efforts on either side have sufficed to cure them. They were compounded of business practices on the part of manufacturers to secure maximum profits by raising prices, and of counterefforts by exceedingly vocal individual publishers and their highly efficient organization, the American Newspaper Publishers Association (hereafter designated as A.N.P.A.), to moderate the price structure favorably to the consumer. Recurring periods of oversupply, induced by the entry of successive waves of investment capital into the production of newsprint following periods of shortage and high prices, rendered this complicated story still more difficult to unravel. The following pages constitute an attempt to summarize it, beginning in 1897, and in so doing to set forth the pattern of relationships which obtained down to the mid-1930's and the problems which those relationships left unsolved.

On December 31, 1896, John Norris of *The New York World* precipitated himself upon the newsprint scene when he asserted before the House Ways and Means Committee that eastern manufacturers were preparing to raise the price of newsprint by collusive combination through a selling agency. This was the opening gun in a campaign which exerted pressure alternately upon Congress to eliminate protective newsprint duties and upon the Executive Department to attack the industry for alleged violations of the Sherman Antitrust Act. Norris' campaign, in which he enlisted the A.N.P.A., at first reluctantly and then enthusiastically, was initially designed, by varying combinations of assertion, invective, and innuendo, to put the manufacturers in such a bad light that Congress would remove the tariff from newsprint. Despite his testimony before the Ways and Means Committee, the Dingley Tariff of 1897 raised the level of protection. Toward the end of the year, too, prices, which had been lowered by cutthroat competition in a period of oversupply, hardened into a seller's market which facilitated the formation (January 31, 1898) of the International Paper Company. This soon added to its seventeen constituent members until it came to control the bulk of eastern production. Publishers could only view such an organization as an agency for boosting prices; because of the combination, or the demand created by the Spanish-American War, the price went up momentarily, giving Norris a chance to memorialize Congress and country against the exactions of the alleged paper trust. A further price increase in 1899 stimulated the A.N.P.A. to request Congress to study the paper situation, but entry of the Great Northern Paper Company (November, 1901) and other independent producers into the market broke the price, and several quiet years ensued.

A congressional proposal to investigate the high cost of newsprint afforded Norris (now Business Manager of *The New York Times*) and Don C. Seitz of the *World* an opportunity in 1904, acting as individuals and not on behalf of the A.N.P.A., to exploit the antitrust aspects of the situation by attacking alleged collusion between International and the General Paper Company, a combination of twenty-six mills in the Midwest. International's point-by-point refutation of the charges and point-blank denial of collusion shifted the attack to the General Paper Company, against which suit was entered in December, 1904, for violation of the Sherman Act. This litigation resulted in a decree ordering (1906) the dissolution of the company.

A return of high prices in 1907 turned the publishers, now spearheaded by Herman Ridder of *Die New-Yorker Staats-Zeitung*, President of the A.N.P.A., to a double-barreled approach demanding both tariff reduction and observance of the antitrust law. Their pressure was sufficient to induce Theodore Roosevelt, a notorious temporizer in the tariff area, to recommend removal of the duty on wood pulp (not newsprint) in the same message (of December 3, 1907) to Congress which contained his more famous statement that his successor should undertake general tariff revision. By the end of a decade it became evident that of the two vehicles of attack—tariff reduction and antitrust prosecution—the former was the more promising, though the latter was by no means to be abandoned. Meantime, too, the specter of ultimate shortages of raw materials was beginning to rise, and Canadians, realizing that their forests held a treasure essential to satisfying the United States' appetite for news, were beginning to feel that at least the first step in paper manufacture, the making of wood pulp, should be performed north of the border.[3]

The years 1908 to 1913, stormy ones in the history of newsprint, witnessed the triumph of John Norris, Herman Ridder, and the A.N.P.A. in the complete removal of the tariff on that commodity by the terms of the Payne-Aldrich Tariff of 1909, the Canadian reciprocity episode of 1910 and 1911, and the Underwood Tariff of 1913. Both tariff and antitrust aspects were pushed in the congressional session of 1907–1908, with publisher pressure inducing Roosevelt to send a special message (March 25, 1908) repeating his recommendation of the previous December for the free-listing

Before marking a tree for the woodcutter, the forester appraises its maturity, general condition, and location with respect to other trees in the timber limits.

In the southern United States, pine pulpwood is the key raw material for making newsprint. In northern areas, spruce or hemlock or fir may be used.

of wood pulp and expanding it to include a similar proposal regarding newsprint under certain conditions.

A bill introduced by Representative Frederick C. Stevens of Minnesota was designed to implement these twin proposals. Ridder thought he had persuaded Speaker Joseph G. Cannon to permit removal of the duties, but that canny advocate of high protection refused at the last moment to countenance the necessary parliamentary maneuver and took refuge in the time-honored evasive tactic so often characteristic of election years—the appointment of a committee to "investigate" a politically explosive question. This committee, headed by James R. Mann of Illinois, worked until February, 1909, amassing hundreds of pages of testimony covering all phases of the newsprint problem. Its hearings furnished both publishers and manufacturers a sounding board. John Norris hurled arrogant assertions of monopoly (his testimony occupied nearly two weeks of the committee's time), which the manufacturers rebutted with equal vehemence and somewhat greater decorum. The Stevens bill was lost in this shuffle, and Congress went home without positive action.

This lack of results stimulated Ridder to induce John Norris to resign his connection with the *Times* and devote his entire talents on behalf of the A.N.P.A. (despite the fact that that organization was not a unit behind the tariff drive) to the tariff-removal program.

The Mann Committee's final report (February 19, 1909) stressed the inadequacy of native spruce to meet domestic demand, thus admitting future dependence upon Canadian forests. To meet this delicate situation it recommended retention of current duties on the importation of mechanical wood pulp unless the exporting Canadian provinces remitted existing export duties, in which case it might come in duty-free.[4] If this favor should be vouchsafed, the committee recommended reduction of the existing $6-per-ton duty on newsprint to $2. Though designed as a gesture of reciprocity, offering a generous reduction on paper in return for a similar Canadian gesture on pulp, the proposal was looked at north of the border as a move to rob the provinces of vested rights and assured income.

This report shifted the question into the realm of the tariff, on which legislation was already in the making following the election of William Howard Taft, who took office in March, 1909. Without examining in detail the convolutions of the newsprint aspects of the Payne-Aldrich Tariff, suffice it to say that the publishers ran up against a general Republican unwillingness to cut rates. The net result was reduction of the duty on newsprint by only $0.25 per ton, while the duty on Crown-land wood pulp from Quebec was $1.67, as before, and on that from Ontario an additional $0.25. Moreover, it might be necessary to levy, after March 31, 1910, the so-called maximum rates, an additional tax of 25 per cent ad valorem above the regular duties, against any area which unduly discriminated against the United States (this was rendered likely by the prospective action of Sir Lomer Gouin, Prime Minister of Quebec, who threatened to prohibit exportation of Crown-land pulpwood). This levy of maximum rates would raise the duty on newsprint to about $14.50 per ton. Along the way Canada had been antagonized, and the publishers had been dismayed and disappointed, but not completely discouraged; their innings were yet to come.

Between 1909 and 1911 the newsprint question became an issue in international politics as well as in the domestic economy. Publisher pressures finally prevailed, and newsprint went on the free list, first as a side effect of the abortive Reciprocity Agreement of the latter year, and permanently in the Underwood Tariff of 1913.

Newspaper pressure to reduce the rates on newsprint was

only one of many related matters rendering President Taft's lot an unhappy one. Prime Minister Gouin was preparing to ban the exportation of unmanufactured pulpwood from Quebec Crown lands; this meant that operations in huge timber limits that had been acquired by United States interests in the hope of exporting the raw logs would presently be forced to a halt. Moreover, Taft faced the prospect, under the terms of the Payne-Aldrich Act, of having to impose upon Canada the maximum rates. The discussions which averted this unpleasant prospect served to open the larger question of Canadian-American trade relations and led into the reciprocity episode.[5]

During the middle months of 1910 the publishers had sought unsuccessfully to induce the Administration to negotiate a special treaty of reciprocity which would remove duties on pulp and paper in return for Canadian abolition of export restrictions; but Taft's advisers opposed this on the ground that most of the Canadian wood exports came from private rather than Crown lands, and would therefore not be subject to provincial limitations on exports. It was not until early 1911, after the ill-fated congressional elections of 1910 had returned a Democratic House and had drastically reduced the Senate majority, that negotiations began in earnest. The agreement announced January 26 took the form of proposed legislative enactments in each country, in order to evade the two-thirds vote required to put a treaty through the United States Senate. As eventually embodied in legislation, the United States free-listed newsprint and wood pulp produced in Canada from other than Crown-land wood. This provision became effective immediately upon congressional acceptance of the total Reciprocity Agreement, and regardless of whether or not Canada ratified in its turn. Dominion rejection of the agreement followed after a hectic political campaign which ousted the Liberal government of Sir Wilfrid

Laurier which sponsored it, and brought to office a Conservative antireciprocity government headed by Robert L. Borden.

Free pulp and paper, therefore, represented the sole positive contribution of the negotiation, to the delight of the publishers and the corresponding dismay of manufacturers. The practical effect of the Underwood Tariff of 1913 was to permit free entry of newsprint and mechanical pulp from any quarter of the world. John Norris' long battle had been won, and the publishers were momentarily happy; Canadian shipments of newsprint mounted rapidly, the Canadian industry (increasingly financed from below the border) burgeoned, and United States mills began to shift to other and more profitable grades of paper still under tariff protection.

War's alarms soon banished any semblance of normality from the Wilson Administration and in the newsprint area evoked two price crises and an antitrust prosecution. By the end of 1916 a spurt of general business activity had put pressure on the supply of newsprint to a point where publishers of large newspapers were driven into the so-called "spot market," where prices were higher than the normal contract rates.[6] This forced up the cost of newsprint to the small publishers, not protected by contract price stipulations. Thereupon a Senate resolution was passed, calling on the Federal Trade Commission to investigate whether the price increase had resulted from collusion among the manufacturers in violation of the antitrust laws. Earlier charges of antitrust activities were thus brought into sharp focus.

A series of hearings before the Trade Commission afforded publishers, particularly the smaller ones whose raw material had by this time reached hitherto unheard-of prices, an opportunity to attack the manufacturers, and considerable ill-will developed. The Department of Justice presently entered the picture, and a Federal Grand Jury investigation was launched. On March 3, 1917, the Trade Commission roundly condemned manufacturers' practices of recent months, accusing them of restricting free competition. It announced that a price of $50 per ton (the spot market had ranged as high as $140 during the 1916 crisis), f.o.b. mill in carload lots, was adequate to provide manufacturers a reasonable return on their investment; it proposed that manufacturers offer paper at this price and that in return the large publishers release a small percentage of their supply to aid the small-fry papers. Neither side was happy with this arrangement, and while its implementation pended, a New York Grand Jury indictment of seven manufacturers (April 12) threatened its effectiveness.

In the midst of these developments the United States became a party to hostilities, and the consequent war-born prosperity inflated prices once more. The Trade Commission publicly confessed its inability to deal with the newsprint problem but published considerable evidence that the manufacturers were controlling the market to their own advantage. Its proposed remedy was government supervision of production and distribution. This caused some publishers to fear interference with freedom of the press, and a confused and confusing situation resulted. The net result of it all was an agreement of November 26, 1917, whereby procedures under the Grand Jury indictment were terminated after the manufacturers pleaded *nolo contendere* (equivalent to an agreement not to contest the issue—an indication to most observers that their tactics were in no more than dubious accord with the Sherman Act) and paid nominal fines. Their organization, the Newsprint Manufacturers Association, was dissolved as exercising a restrictive influence on trade. Publishers, both large and small, received some relief on price and supply, and a competitive market seems to have obtained through 1918.

An early postwar boom in 1919 and 1920 forced contract

prices as high as $130 in the latter year, though the panic was more a matter of distribution than of total supply. The crisis produced the usual rash of moves for investigation of the manufacturers, mostly at the behest of the harassed small publishers, but no affirmative results emerged, and the total picture showed the larger publishers moderating their earlier hostility toward the manufacturers. By 1921 a recession set prices on a downhill slant which persisted throughout the decade, effectively quieting demands for governmental investigations.

Perhaps the most important immediate aspect of the above, highly compressed story is the divergency in attitude between large and small publishers, with the former shying off from too vigorous governmental interference in the newsprint situation on the grounds that it constituted a threat to the freedom of private enterprise. The long-run results of successive periods of high prices will be noted below.

Although newsprint prices declined during the 1920's, production increased tremendously. This increase was sparked by the insatiable demand of the United States public for news and by wartime high prices for newsprint. As a consequence large amounts of United States and Canadian risk capital were attracted into the Canadian manufacturing industry. Stimulated by provincial authorities anxious to exploit their prime resource, and by the stock promoters so numerous in that ebullient decade, speculators poured money into Canada, and production rose from 800,000 tons in 1920 to 4,000,000 tons in 1930. The decision of the International Paper Company in the mid-decade to embark on an ambitious expansion program hastened a process already well-advanced, and new capital was reported to have entered the Canadian industry at the rate of $3,000,000 a month in 1924. By 1928 overproduction was an admitted fact, and price-cutting became common; early in the year it was estimated that by

August, mill capacity would exceed demand by 1,500 tons per day, and by mid-May the eastern Canadian mills were running at 80 to 85 per cent of rated capacity.[7]

The net result of these maneuvers was to create a productive capacity out of all realistic relation to the potential market. This in turn rendered it extremely difficult for a sales-hungry industry to maintain uniform or adequate prices. This became apparent in 1928, when Canadian International offered a five-year contract to the Hearst newspaper empire at a price considerably below the current level. This threat to the price structure brought the Premiers of Quebec and Ontario into the picture; jointly, they secured some immediate improvement in the price level, but as production continued to rise, their efforts were vain, and the Canadian industry was deeply in the dumps some months before the general debacle of 1929. General bankruptcy resulted, stemming partly from the industry's own failure to police adequately its profit-hungry members against overexpansion of productive capacity, partly from the entry of new and profit-greedy promoters into the field. The net result was complete failure to maintain a workable relationship between production and likely demand. This bitter lesson, indelibly ingrained upon both the United States and the Canadian industry, was to exert a dampering effect on needed expansion after World War II.[8]

The early thirties found the Canadian mills divided into two categories, the International group, which was eating up Quebec spruce, running at full capacity under the Hearst contracts, and others, grouped under the title of the Newsprint Institute of Canada, Ltd. The Newsprint Institute included the major producers other than the International group, the west coast mills, and the Spruce Falls Power and Paper Company, Ltd., which was affiliated with *The New York Times*. It was formed under the aegis of the provincial

Premiers with the objective of controlling and limiting production and allocating orders on the basis of rated capacity. Its mills ran at 85 per cent of capacity in 1929, while those of Internatonial hummed away at over 100 per cent. By the end of 1930 the differential between International and the Newsprint Institute mills was too great to be borne by the latter; the allocation scheme had broken down, and a free market loomed on the horizon with subsequent insolvency for large segments of the Canadian industry. There seemed two possible solutions of the day's evils. One was to let competition establish a price level. This would have meant elimination of the weaker mills, after which the survivors might assume charge of the market and raise prices once more. The other involved carrying on a process of consolidation among the Canadian mills, closing down the high-cost producers and absorbing their valuation into an already swollen capital structure. Neither offered a pleasant prospect.

All mills began cutting prices in 1931, against a background of bankruptcy. This faced the A.N.P.A., hitherto mainly interested in lower costs, with the question of whether it might not be better to stop pushing in this direction, lest demoralization of the industry endanger the security of supply. The year 1932 saw the developments of 1931 repeated —competitive prices continued to remove the weaklings and hamstring the stronger producers, who took refuge in consolidation to save as many units as possible. Neither technique checked the descent into bankruptcy; by September only International and a few newspaper affiliates could look into the future with anything but dread. The tide of consumption turned late in 1933, but increased sales were inadequate to offset loss of income through lower prices. Only in 1935 did conditions take a real turn for the better, as evidenced by increased production and consumption and the announcement of a higher price for 1937. This year of transition, with a new boom apparently preparing and a seller's market in sight, may be taken as the close of the author's previous study, though some slight attention is given to 1937.

This study covered a period during which the major source of publishers' supply shifted from the United States to Canada. It traced a series of pendulum swings in which brief periods of high prices attracted large increments of capital into the manufacture of newsprint. Publishers' attacks on the producers, combined with overproduction, resulted in recurring and longer periods of low price and consequent drought for the manufacturers. Thus was established a pattern of relationships between manufacturer and publisher apparently set in permanent antagonism. It was the author's reasoned conclusion, writing his original study in the late 1940's, that though both parties shared responsibility for this antagonism, the "major responsibility for a lack of equilibrium should be laid at the door of the publishers, whose aggressive leadership and unique position for influencing public policy have given them striking advantages over the manufacturers." There seemed to be occasional glimmerings, however, of a more conciliatory relationship.

A mechanical track loader picks up timber along the right of way.

CHAPTER II

From Depression into War, 1937 to 1939

BEFORE EMBARKING on the newsprint history of the past twenty years, it may be useful to examine some factors that condition the narrative. These affect one or the other, sometimes both sides, of the publisher-manufacturer equation. Some are carry-overs from the earlier day; some modify previous patterns of action.

The account to follow will deal very largely with supply and demand as these determine a market price for newsprint. This price results from the interplay of extremely vigorous protagonists, neither of whom has been willing to let supply and demand operate in the vacuum of entirely free competition. In the words of John A. Guthrie, the foremost academic observer of the newsprint scene, "it is clear that the price of newsprint is not determined by the free interplay of demand and supply. These forces are continually operating, but are controlled and restricted by cooperative and regulative devices which have evolved largely from economic necessity." Active and vocal trade associations look after the interests of producer and consumer; many consumers are also producers, through financial interest in newsprint mills. Except, therefore, for times of extreme stress and business depression, group pressures operate from both sides in attempts to influence price. As one of many congressional investigating committees pointed out, "to the newsprint producers it appears desirable to have the demand for newsprint slightly in excess of the supply, whereas the public interest in a free press requires that there be an available supply of newsprint slightly in excess of the demand. Thus, from the viewpoint of the newsprint industry enough newsprint is too much; but from the standpoint of the public and the publishers, too much newsprint is just enough." [1] Indeed, not a simple problem.

The method of price-setting becomes, therefore, a matter of considerable moment. The characteristic features of the price picture have been price leadership and price uniformity among the leading firms. Price leadership means that one firm (usually a large producer; frequently International Paper Company) announces a price, and the rest of the industry follows more or less promptly. Though the pattern is clear enough, the underlying circumstances have furnished food for endless argument. The crucial point here is whether or not producers' action is taken as the result of collusive agreement, for this would render it subject to suspicion in the United States under the antitrust acts. The evidence being conflicting and voluminous, a brief description of the points of view will suffice for the moment.

Publishers and, on occasion, congressional committees have held that collusion exists. Richard Scudder of *The Newark Evening News* testified to the Magnuson Committee (February 26, 1957) that "the newsprint industry acts in concert, with just enough hesitation to satisfy appearances. . . . While there may not be monopoly in this situation, there certainly is no competition either." And evidence presented to a senatorial committee in 1951 was in its judgment "overwhelmingly convincing that newsprint prices were set by collusive agreement between the mills. . . ."

On the other hand, August B. Meyer, President of the Bowaters Paper Company, when pushed on the matter of uniform prices, denied that the practice was "so strange," pointing out that his firm sold to many publishers who also bought from other suppliers. Neither he nor his rival suppliers, he asserted, could offer the consumer diverse prices: "If we charge our customer more than our competitor was charging his customer, we would put the newspaper completely behind the eight ball. . . ." Mr. Meyer did not, of course, make the obvious corollary remark that offering diverse prices would likewise put the mills in the same predicament. And without affirming or denying the fact of collusion, Professor Guthrie insisted before another congressional committee that in an extremely competitive situation one company's announcement of either an increase or a reduction in price could set an industry pattern without collusion having occurred.[2]

Production costs also apply to both sides of the equation. With labor unionized and unions protected on both sides of the border, it has become more difficult than in earlier years to adjust either the manufacturing or the publishing business to fluctuations in the business cycle by cutting wages or salaries; costs tend to become fixed. For the manufacturer, the cost of developing new production is a serious item, since newsprint production carries one of the highest ratios in industry between plant investment and unit sales. This becomes particularly troublesome when new plants, built at high costs, have to compete with old plants whose lower initial costs have been largely depreciated over the years. On the other side of the fence, the price of newsprint assumes an increasing percentage of total costs as circulation mounts, placing an extra burden on publishers of large newspapers as compared with their smaller brethren.[3]

In recent years, as contrasted with the situation prior to the depression of the thirties, there has developed a pattern of long-term contracts creating obligations extending over periods as long as fifteen years. Since by far the greatest tonnage of newsprint is marketed on a contract basis, such an arrangement tends to stabilize the situation from the standpoint of both buyer and seller. The buyer may rest assured of a predetermined supply in case a sudden upsurge of demand creates a shortage; by the same token, the manufacturer has a market for stated tonnages, barring conditions which reduce consumption generally throughout the newspaper world. So-called price tie-in contracts are also common. In these, without stating a specific price, it is provided that a purchaser will pay the average of that charged by several (usually three) of the price leaders in the field. These features tend, of course, to exert a stabilizing influence on both price and supply, and suggest the possibility of deleterious effects upon competition.[4]

The present situation is also characterized by publisher participation in production through investment in newsprint mills. This can be traced back at least to 1913, when *The Chicago Tribune* had a mill at Thorold, Ontario, and to 1928, when *The New York Times* bought into the Spruce Falls Power and Paper Company at Kapuskasing, Ontario. This participation has become increasingly common in recent years, and large segments of production on both sides of the Canadian border are presently in publishers' hands. The following listing of publishers who owned or partly owned mills in 1950 will point up the extent of this development: *Chicago Tribune* affiliate, the *New York Daily News* (Ontario Paper Company); *Kansas City Star* (Flambeau Paper Company); *Gary* (Indiana) *Post Tribune* (Gary Paper Mills); *Milwaukee Journal* (Peavey Paper Mills); *Detroit News* and Booth newspapers (Michigan Paper Company); a group of United States papers (Great Lakes Paper Company); Spokane, Washington, papers (Inland Empire Paper Company); Hearst interests (Pejepscot Paper Company);

In many areas, logs are brought out of the woods by rail or diesel trucks.

Tractor trains can haul thousands of cords of wood on connected sleds.

a group of west coast papers (Hawley Pulp and Paper Company, renamed Publishers' Paper Company); another group of west coast papers (West Tacoma Newsprint Company); a group of southern papers (Southland Paper Mills, Inc.); another southern group (Coosa River Paper Company). This listing makes it apparent that several Canadian producers and most of the major United States mills, except Great Northern and Crown Zellerbach, were at this point involved with publishers to a greater or lesser degree. A possible complacency on the part of these publishers at supply shortages and market fluctuations may at least be suggested at this point.[5]

The migration of a large proportion of the newsprint industry to Canada occurred, in part at least, in response to United States tariff policy. Directly or indirectly, this brought about several important developments. In the first place, since the Canadian economy was unable to furnish the enormous amounts of investment capital required, a great deal of United States money crossed the border to underwrite Canadian corporations subsidiary, in fact, to United States interests. This binational character of much of the Canadian newsprint industry was to be of no small significance in perpetuating the antagonisms of earlier days. Since newsprint was one of the less profitable lines of the paper industry, the tendency was for United States mills to shift to other lines where tariff protection was still available; Canadian mills, thus prevented from entering this more lucrative side of the United States market, found themselves increasingly confined to making newsprint. The result was a vast increase in Canadian newsprint tonnage, accompanied by a decline in United States production, both absolute and relative to total United States consumption. This trend was reversed only after World War II, at which point began a long, slow climb back toward greater tonnages and recapture of a larger share of the domestic newsprint market. The strains accompanying the downward adjustment and its reversal added considerably to the problems of both publishers and producers.

These problems and tensions have invested the newsprint problem with a very considerable public interest. Through most of the period under review one or another of its aspects has been under scrutiny. This has been initiated occasionally by the Federal Trade Commission, intermittently by the Department of Justice, and almost continually by congressional committees. The activities of these agencies have produced a vast amount of information but have elicited practically no legislative action. They have, however, kept the newsprint question much in the congressional and public eye; and they have occupied a great deal of the time of both publishing and manufacturing executives, as well as of congressional groups. Publishers, particularly of the larger papers, have not attended numerously or with alacrity, though A.N.P.A. spokesmen are always available for questioning. The Canadian producers, though responsible for a preponderance of the product, have since 1947 been protected from interrogation by American authorities; their United States counterparts have been more vulnerable. The net result has been the creation of an atmosphere of tension, about which, because of the proprieties of the situation, there has been little public comment below the border.

To the north, however, there are fewer inhibitions, and an irritated Canadian remarked in the mid-fifties that the "easiest way for an American congressman or senator to get his name into American newspapers is to make some statement—any statement—about newsprint. There is a certain cheap and easy appeal in proposals to make the United States more 'self-sufficient' and 'independent' of foreign suppliers. These arguments are based on nostalgia for a simpler past and an economic isolationism which still persists despite the abandonment of political isolationism by the United States.

. . . The world's undoubted need for wood fibre may make Canadians and Americans alike hesitant before subjecting themselves to unbridled abuse from publishers and politicians in both countries, especially as they have no hope of ever making an undistorted answer to the public; they can easily choose other lines of endeavour within the pulp and paper industry."[6] With these introductory comments, let us now proceed to the chronological story.

Canadian mill prospects were excellent as 1936 moved into 1937. In retrospect, this was said to be the "best year that the pulp and paper industry has experienced since the depression—a year which has seen new financial foundations completed for many bankrupt companies and production consistently maintained on record levels. . . ." The Canadian mills were running nearly at capacity as demand expanded below the border; here mill capacity declined over 43 per cent between 1934 and 1939. The problem, with demand at a good level, was to adjust price into some workable relationship with the overcapitalization which had taken place in the Canadian industry. Prime Minister Maurice Duplessis of Quebec, after consultation with the Ontario authorities and with mill managers and employees, issued a warning (first on January 28 and frequently repeated) that the sudden upturn must not be taken as an excuse for building new mills. As early as February, Charles Vining, President of the Newsprint Association of Canada, predicted an increase from the $43.50 ($42.50, New York) price then obtaining. To offset this possibility, the A.N.P.A. had already (January 7, with frequent repetitions) suggested that its members abandon the hand-to-mouth ordering of supplies which had contributed to shortages in 1935 and 1936, advising that publishers order paper in equal monthly installments over the twelve months, thus building up inventories during the dull summer period against the peak consumption of the latter part of the year and, by filling the warehouses, discourage the mills from price adventures.[7]

On March 19, 1937, International Paper announced that for the first half of 1938 its price would be $50, an increase of approximately 17 per cent. This action was apparently taken after the provincial authorities had exerted some pressure upon the company; it was closely accompanied by a proposal to its stockholders that dividend arrearages be reduced by $40,000,000 and that capitalization be cut by $29,000,000. This combination of increased price and dehydration of the financial structure might well suffice, it was suggested, to write the yearly record in black ink.

Most Canadian companies followed International Paper's lead—a departure from recent practice, since Great Northern had been taking price precedence. The publishing interest at first took only moderate fright at this increase, the A.N.P.A. hopefully opining (March 23) that International Paper's action was so far merely an *announcement* rather than a *transaction,* the inference being that the threat might possibly be staved off. *Editor & Publisher* admitted (March 27) that prices had for years been too low, but complained that the recent jump was too severe. By convention time in April, however, the A.N.P.A. had concluded that it was "incredible" that such a "drastic increase" should be demanded.[8]

By early autumn, 1937, publishers were building up inventories in preparation for the demands of the remaining months of the year and in light of the prospective price increase; in October, it was reported that the average inventory had doubled, to two months' supply, from the 1936 figure. By mid-October, this maneuver, plus the impact of the 1937 "recession," had had an ill effect on both Canadian production and the hitherto booming position of paper stocks on the Montreal Exchange. It is to be noted, however, that instead of cutting price, as had been characteristic in recent years, International Paper cut production and, with the rest of the industry, watched warily to see what Great Northern would do about price.

The wait was not a long one; Great Northern almost immediately announced an increase of $5.50 for the first six months and $7.50 for the second half-year, leaving its New York price at $48, as compared with the Canadian $50, and giving its consumers a six-month advantage over those buying Canadian paper. Matters were stabilized in December, when, after conferences in New York with A.N.P.A. officials, International Paper announced that its $50 price would obtain throughout the year. This announcement followed hard on the heels of an announcement (of November 12, 1937) in the *Melbourne* (Australia) *Herald* that seven Canadian manufacturers had agreed to supply the needs of a group of Australian and New Zealand papers over a seven-year period. The evidence indicates that publisher pressure for a Canadian price reduction was successful only to the extent of inducing International Paper to maintain the $50 price throughout the year, abandoning an earlier threat of a second-half increase, and that Great Northern's announcement of a lower price had not, as in former years, been sufficient to break the general price level. Publisher dissatisfaction, as evidenced by A.N.P.A. publications, was relatively mild, directed mostly at provincial and banking influence allegedly behind the manufacturers' moves, and toward urging consumers to develop alternative sources of supply from abroad and, particularly, from southern sources. The mildness of the complaints may well have reflected well-stocked warehouses.[9]

This year also witnessed considerable progress toward a long-cherished dream of expanding the domestic supply through establishment of an industry based on southern softwood timber. The great advantage here, in addition to lessening dependence upon foreign suppliers, was the rapid growth rate of the trees in the more favorable climate, it being established that loblolly pine attained a diameter of seven inches in a little over a decade, whereas it took fifty years for Canadian spruce to reach a five-inch diameter. The researches of Dr. Charles H. Herty had by this time overcome the problem of the high resin content of the southern softwoods. The problem then became largely one of procuring the necessary capital, steps toward which were initiated at a meeting of capitalists in Dallas (in January, 1937); by mid-December interested parties had invested $1,600,000, the Reconstruction Finance Company had loaned $3,500,000, and only a further $2,000,000 of private subscription was needed to inaugurate construction of a mill at Lufkin, Texas.[10]

The other important development of 1937 centered around circumstances connected with the initiation of one of the many investigations of domestic manufacturers. One of the early movers was John H. Perry, President of the American Press Association and publisher of southern papers. Perry seems to have become incensed when informed by one of his Finnish suppliers that his paper would cost him $9 more per ton in 1938; this, he was told, " 'was the price set by an organization which represents and speaks for practically all the paper manufacturers in the world.' " Further upset by what seemed to him concerted Canadian price increases which were " 'arranged as part of the conspiracy to gouge the American publishers . . . ,' " he consulted various Senators and members of the Federal Trade Commission. According to his own account, the General Counsel of the Trade Commission handed him a consent decree secured in 1917 against numerous producers, and suggested that the way to start an investigation was to induce the Attorney General to instruct the Trade Commission to take steps.

Barges are often used to transport wood to the paper mill located on a waterway.

This boom, towed by a diesel tug, contains about 4,000 cords of wood.

Perry's complaint seems to have triggered action; likewise, the Administration of Franklin D. Roosevelt was concerned during the autumn with monopolistic practices and was sensitive to a proposal made by Senator James D. Pope of Idaho (December 18) asking the Department of Justice to investigate monopoly in the newsprint industry. The inquiry was shortly (in January, 1938) transferred to the Federal Trade Commission, which possessed a power of subpoena which the Department of Justice lacked, and it was instructed to investigate and report back to the department. Thus was launched an inquiry into west coast production.[11]

The year 1938 was without startling developments. It opened with heavy publishers' inventories and a continuing recession and was complicated toward the end by the crisis in Europe. The announced prices held during the first six months, but developments of that period constrained Great Northern, which had announced that it would match the general Canadian level on July 1, to continue at its original, lower figure of $48 for the rest of the year; the result was that a two-level price structure obtained throughout most of the industry, though an occasional publisher was able to contract with Canadian producers on somewhat more favorable terms than the general $50 level. Toward the end of the year International Paper and Great Northern announced simultaneously (November 4) that each would hold 1939 prices at the 1938 level.[12]

This near unanimity on the part of the Canadian industry in cutting production and maintaining price in the face of publisher pressure and of drastically reduced demand was attributable to strong influence exerted by the provincial officials, resulting in the imposition on the mills of a scheme prorating production for the attenuated market. Negotiations opened when seven United States publishers discussed the situation (January 8) with Premier Mitchell Hepburn of Ontario, other provincial authorities, and Canadian manufacturers. Shortly afterward the manufacturers met with the Premiers of Quebec and Ontario.

At some point, not clear from the evidence available, the governmental authorities had concerted and imposed on the producers a prorating and pooling arrangement put into operation through the Newsprint Association of Canada. This scheme was designed to manage production so that no mill would operate at a greater percentage of capacity than the average established for the industry; if one obtained contracts permitting expanded production, it was to transfer tonnage to those less fortunate, so that an equal, if low, level of production could be maintained. By this device the mills kept going at reduced rates but maintained the price level intact; in earlier days, and minus current governmental pressures, such a situation was likely to lead to a price break. The year ended on a somewhat brighter note, a business upturn to the south being reflected in expanded demand, and the industry feeling virtuous in its united front, if not greatly enriched by the year's operations.[13]

The federal inquiry, launched in January and designed to discover through Federal Trade Commission auspices how the consent decree of 1917 against George H. Mead Company and other manufacturers had operated, moved ahead during the year without great assistance from the publishers, whose interest in launching it has already been noted. Efforts were made to collect information via a questionnaire sent to publishers, but these apparently manifested no great alacrity in replying. In fact, the Secretary of the International Brotherhood of Papermakers charged in August that the A.N.P.A. was engaged in sabotaging the investigation, providing the press with what purported to be photostats of an A.N.P.A. bulletin telling publishers that they were not required to answer the Trade Commission's questions on matters dealing with relations between themselves and their suppliers. Despite this obstacle, however, the study was completed and ready for submission to the Department of Justice in early 1939. Meantime had come a development which was to be copied widely and which would exercise a damaging effect on subsequent investigations: International Paper Sales Company, organized in New York in 1929, moved to Canada and was reconstituted as a Quebec corporation, functioning from Montreal as of September 6, 1939. [14]

The year 1939, like 1938, was a quiet one in most respects, despite the alarms which preceded the onset of war in the early autumn. Price held steady, the Canadian industry continued the process of fiscal recovery which had been going on in recent years, United States consumption increased moderately (3 per cent), as did production on both sides of the border (Canadian production was up 9.3 per cent; the United States figure was 14.6 per cent). Enough capital was finally accumulated to warrant dedicating and starting construction (in May) of the plant of the Southland Paper Mills, Inc., at Lufkin, Texas, the first move in many years toward increasing United States production. What looked like an interesting development was the apparent beginning of cooperation between publishers and manufacturers, when Cranston Williams of the A.N.P.A. wrote Royal S. Kellogg of the Newsprint Service Bureau (October 4) suggesting need for coordination in the statistical services rendered by the two trade associations, and inviting the bureau to name a committee to meet with A.N.P.A. representatives to work together in the wartime period. The committee was named, and preliminary discussions occurred.[15]

The most important newsprint development of the year was the investigation of manufacturers, divided between the

Federal Trade Commission and the Department of Justice, which resulted in the indictment of west coast producers on charges of violating the antitrust laws. The Trade Commission inquiry, initiated largely as a result of the activity of John H. Perry, was concerned about the price rise announced for 1938; other complaints had evidently been added to his, though *Editor & Publisher* was not aware of any organized publisher pressure leading to the Department of Justice action.

The Trade Commission rendered its report to the Attorney General in early January, 1939, but it was not given to the public until January 6, 1947. As has already been pointed out, its objective was to study the operation of a consent decree of 1917 enjoining certain producers and marketers of newsprint from concerting to manage prices. As indicated in a release of May 24 by Assistant Attorney General Thurman Arnold, the Trade Commission found that only two of eight individuals and fourteen of forty-seven corporations covered by the consent decree were still in the business of manufacturing newsprint. Moreover, at the time of the decree the United States supplied 75 per cent of its own newsprint needs; with the shift of industry to Canada only 25 per cent of United States consumption was currently produced at home. It concluded, therefore, that conditions had altered so drastically as to render the 1917 decree inapplicable.[16]

On the way to this negative conclusion on the consent decree, however, Trade Commission investigators unearthed interesting evidence in other directions. A Department of Justice release of May 24 pointed out: " 'Some evidence secured by the Federal Trade Commission indicates that concerted action by Canadian manufacturers restrains freedom of competition in the United States newsprint market. Other evidence tends to show that certain United States manufacturers and distributors cooperate with Canadian producers to maintain price in this country. . . .' " The practices singled out in the release were the zone-pricing system, under which price uniformity was imposed within each of the ten zones into which the country was then divided, and the general uniformity of recent price increases. These, it was asserted, raised such " 'serious questions' " under the anti-trust laws as to warrant a departmental investigation which had then been under way since March, and which, it was announced, had already resulted in the issue of subpoenas to numerous west coast firms for appearance before a Federal Grand Jury sitting in San Francisco beginning June 22.[17]

The Department of Justice approach to the price problem was by way of the injury done the small papers by the alleged practices of the manufacturers, it being pointed out that the small fry could seldom buy by the roll in carload lots—the sort of purchasing pattern on which the contract price was based—but must buy newsprint in sheets on the open market; it was noted that sheet paper cost about 20 per cent more than in the roll, and that the open market price was usually about 10 per cent above the contract figure; moreover, the price in smaller-than-carload lots went up as the size of the purchase diminished. It was calculated that the $7.50 price increase effective in 1938 had resulted in " 'an increase of several times this amount' " to the small newspapers. It was noted, too, that the isolated position of the west coast producers and distributors rendered them relatively independent of the eastern industry. It was also true that a number of west coast producers had Canadian affiliates, affording an opportunity to attack alleged monopolistic practices on both sides of the border.

On July 12, 1939, the Grand Jury returned indictments against Crown Zellerbach Corporation, Zellerbach Paper Company, Pacific Mills, Ltd. (Crown Zellerbach's Canadian affiliate), Hawley Pulp and Paper Company, Inland Empire

Paper Company, and two Canadian firms, Powell River Company, Ltd., and Powell River Sales Company, Ltd., as well as fifteen officials of the various firms, four of whom were domiciled in British Columbia. The charge was that since some indeterminate date in 1935 these had been engaged in practices restraining interstate and foreign trade by a series of meetings at various times and places on both sides of the border at which they engaged in fixing the price of newsprint. Thus was launched a long-drawn-out proceeding which did not culminate until 1941.

The industry's first reaction to the outbreak of war in September, 1939, was an optimistic one. All hands were agreed that the runaway situation which had characterized the War of 1914 to 1918 must not be repeated. The mills took the initiative in an announcement by the Newsprint Association of Canada assuring their consumers that they would be protected against unnecessary price inflation; publishers were urged to buy their supplies in monthly installments and to avoid excessive inventories, which last exhortation was echoed by the A.N.P.A. It was pointed out that Canadian production could be increased by 30 per cent if necessary, and that the exchange situation favored Canada to the extent of $5 per ton. All in all, a note of complacency seems to have pervaded the scene, and only one Cassandra warned that a manpower shortage might alter matters for the worse.[18]

The three-year period just chronicled was one of shakedown and readjustment for an industry just emerging from the depths of depression. It was a time during which considerable progress was made toward a sound financial structure, made possible by a more adequate price and a good demand during much of the time. With matters in relatively good case between producers and consumers, it was a time of relatively easy relationships in this crucial area. Government-wise, the Canadian provinces exerted a strong but not omnipotent control over Canadian production; south of the border, governmental attention was directed, apparently by individuals rather than organized publisher pressure, toward one of a long series of investigations, the end of which was not yet in sight.[19]

tion." He later told the Publishers' Association that Cannon had "practically agreed . . ." to let tariff removal go through. When faced with a specific demand to recognize a motion to suspend the rules and permit passage of a particular measure, however, he bethought himself of the possible political consequences and refused, as he put it later, to be "bulldozed." He took refuge in the introduction of a resolution (April 20; passed with commendable celerity on April 21) proposing a select committee of six to investigate a long series of allegations contained in fourteen "whereases" designed to place the publishers' contentions in an unfavorable light. Republican supporters of the proposed research urged the necessity of knowledge prior to action, there being no consensus about whether the high price of paper was due to the tariff, to combination, or to legitimate increases in production costs. One question raised, pertinent here as through all the discussion, was how a tariff, essentially stable since 1890 and through three successive enactments, could suddenly raise paper prices. Democratic opponents combined ridicule of Republican tariff timidity in a presidential year with accusations of trying to circumvent the "old German devil," head of the publishers, in his desire to put through any one of several proposals slumbering in pigeonholes of the Ways and Means Committee. Thrown in for good measure were bitter attacks on Cannonism, part of the filibustering maneuvers which had characterized most of the month. Thus the "Mann Committee," composed of four Republicans and two Democrats, was launched upon a strenuous career of investigation which lasted until February, 1909, occupied weeks of its members' time, took them upon thousands of miles of travel, and piled up hundreds of thousands of words of testimony upon all phases of the problem.[7]

The story of the events of 1908 should be concluded prior to an attempt to evaluate the committee's work, though this

CHAPTER III

War's Alarms

THE YEAR 1940 was one of gradual adjustment to a wartime situation for the newsprint industry, with price relatively stable, with supply easy, with producer-consumer relations good, and with some beginnings of governmental involvement in the newsprint picture. International Paper led in holding the $50 price throughout the year, followed by the Canadian producers. Great Northern raised its price $1, to $49, and held this level after a tentative gesture toward equaling the Canadian figure; most United States mills followed its lead, as usual. This slight price differential enabled the United States mills to operate at 93 per cent of rated capacity, as compared with 78 per cent for Canada, 94 per cent for Newfoundland, and an 82 per cent continental average. It was suggested that the newsprint price, which was below the general commodity average, was perhaps kept low by the threat of competition from the American south, where Southland Paper Mills, Inc., began production in January; however, after an extensive trip through that area, a veteran Canadian newsprint man reported that " 'we have nothing to fear' " from that quarter. D. C. Everest, President of the American Pulp and Paper Association, warned (January 26) lest higher prices serve as an incentive to increased capacity, which had had disastrous results in the 1930's. Despite the increased operating rate, it was pointed out that a million tons of Canadian producing capacity remained idle at the beginning of 1941, despite the elimination of some 700,000 tons of Scandinavian and German tonnage with which Canadian production normally had to compete.[1]

Before the year's end the industry on both sides of the border began to feel the impact of war. Profits were good, with many companies making payments on deferred dividends, with others entering the dividend-paying class for the first time in years, and with still others casting off the millstone of receiverships. The Canadian industry came into a role of new importance in furnishing precious foreign exchange, adding upwards of $125,000,000 (U.S.) to British Empire funds. This was increased by the favorable exchange situation, which added a Canadian value of about $5 in United States dollars to each ton of newsprint sold below the border. The provincial governments of Ontario and Quebec continued the prorating of tonnage which had been in operation since 1936, distributing manufacturing permits among the mills in accordance with rated capacity; the existence of a number of newspaper-connected mills which were not so restricted, and which could therefore run at full capacity, created difficulties in enforcing this arrangement.

The Cold War erupted into one of higher temperature in the spring and summer, with the invasion of France and the invasion of Norway. This stimulated moves to create production controls in the United States, and by early September, 1940, there was in existence a Pulp and Paper Section within the National Defense Advisory Commission, with D. C. Everest at its head and Charles W. Boyce as his assistant.[2]

The A.N.P.A. repeatedly exhorted publishers to take paper in equal monthly installments, and the manufacturers gratefully concurred. The A.N.P.A. also advised publishers to build up inventories, first at will, then to a ninety-day supply, and finally to a six-month level. These steps were taken under the aegis of a special Committee on Supplies, appointed by the A.N.P.A. board of directors in August; a year later, the committee gave way under the establishment of priorities.[3] The year's most significant development was the appearance of a spirit of cooperation between publishers and manufacturers. Several factors may have contributed to this, among them the war emergency, the improving economic position of the industry, and its self-denying statement of early September, 1939, that Canadian manufacturers would "'meet the wishes of their Government by avoiding any attempt to profiteer and will make every possible effort to maintain stabilized conditions of continuous supply and to discourage methods of buying and selling which might cause a disorderly market. . . .'"

In a totally unprecedented move, A.N.P.A. invited Charles Vining, President of the Newsprint Association of Canada, to attend its annual convention in April. Though unable to come, he made an address which was widely circulated, in which he asserted: "'The Canadian newsprint producer and the American newspaper publisher have not only a mutual dependence but a common responsibility which recent months have made more plain. Part of this responsibility is to strive for honest understanding, confidence and fair dealing in their relations with each other.'" The new year, however, found him viewing matters on a cautious note and reiterating (January 25, 1941) the fact that with a million tons of unused newsprint capacity, the Canadian industry was not out of the woods.[4]

Another dramatic, and much dramatized, development of the year was the first commercial production of newsprint from southern pine. The first two rolls of newsprint to come off the machine of the Southland Paper Company were used, appropriately, to print an issue of the *Lufkin News*, on January 23; by the end of the month the *Dallas News* had received two carloads, and 31,000 tons came off during the year. This marks the end of a long and difficult road and was a tribute to the research persistence of Dr. Herty. It owes a great deal, too, to the faith of publishers of numerous southern papers who risked their capital in a high-cost venture in a time of considerable uncertainty. Finally, the confidence of the Reconstruction Finance Corporation in furnishing a substantial loan of government funds should not be overlooked.

Here was taken the first commercial step toward the establishment of a new phase of the industry and a long stride toward bringing the United States industry back in balance with the Canadian industry—a result, however, to be long deferred by war and other factors. A number of elements contributed to making this initial adventure a success and hence an incentive to the erection of other mills in the region. The rapid growth of the raw material in the south, as compared with more northerly regions, was important, as was also the fact that the new machine was of latest design, making more efficient operation possible. Distances to the market were shorter than from either the northeastern United States or the Canadian mills. This situation combined with the zone-pricing system to enable this mill and its successors in the region to charge the same for the shorter hauls as the more distant mills did for the longer, thus piling up so-called "phantom freight" to its own advantage.[5]

The record shows very little progress in the prosecution of the west coast producers. The Canadian companies which had been indicted took two steps to alleviate their difficulties, moving in February to have the indictments quashed on the ground that their activities were outside the jurisdiction of the United States and, when unsuccessful here, urging Premier T. D. Pattulo of British Columbia to persuade the

Dominion government to intervene with Washington; no positive results accrued, however.[6]

The address of Wendell Berge, Special Assistant to the Attorney General of the United States, to the American Pulp and Paper Association (in mid-February) carried an obvious threat to any price-controlling practices in which the industry might be indulging or which it might contemplate. Noting a recent revival of interest in the enforcement of the fifty-year-old Sherman Act, Mr. Berge sang a paean to the free enterprise system and issued a warning about possible questionable activities on the part of trade associations. The present problem, he pointed out, was one of " 'keeping business organizations which are technically separate and ostensibly competitive from getting together through one subtle device or another to effectually eliminate real competition between them. . . .' " The ultimate criterion, he pointed out, was the matter of attitude: " 'Are they seeking to expand production and distribution at lower costs so that an ever increasing body of consumers can purchase a greater volume of goods at lower prices; or are they seeking to restrict production, regiment distribution, raise prices and corner the profits for that little group that is fortunate enough to belong to the club?' "[7]

During 1941 the price-production-consumption complex remained on a relatively even keel, though by the end of the year producers' self-restraints on both sides of the border were beginning to weaken in the face of increasing costs which ate deeply into the margin the exchange differential accorded the Canadian mills. It was pointed out on occasion that the price of newsprint was lagging behind generally increasing price trends. Papers reporting to the A.N.P.A. indicated an increase of 3.2 per cent in consumption over 1940; neither the United States nor Canada showed a corresponding increase in production, the figures being 0.1 per cent and 0.2 per cent, respectively. The Canadian price remained firm at $50 through 1941 and the first quarter of 1942. In mid-December International Paper announced an increase to $53, effective April 1, 1942; governmental regulations, to be noted below, rendered this move ineffective. Meantime, Great Northern went up $1 per ton during the last quarter of 1941, bringing its price to the $50 Canadian level; St. Croix Paper Company, a smaller United States manufacturer, held to $49 through 1941, but went to a par with the other United States producers in 1942.

Thus for the first time in several years United States prices were on a common level in the first quarter of 1942. Great Northern's increase of the last quarter, however, was looked upon as encouragement for similar action by the Canadian mills, and may have influenced International Paper's announcement. This increase, be it noted, applied only to sales in the United States, a ceiling having been placed (as of November 17, 1941) on Canadian wages and prices, controls being vested in the Wartime Prices and Trade Board (WPTB).[8] It should also be pointed out that the proposed increase created no great stir among United States publishers.

Producer-consumer relations continued good, perhaps under the influence of continuing price stability. The *Toronto Financial Post* remarked on April 26, 1941: "'For the first time in years there is relatively little interest in Canadian newsprint. This lack of interest is due to the fact that American publishers are satisfied with the way the policy of the Canadian manufacturers is working out. When the war started, the mills decided on price stability, and newsprint is one of the few major commodities which has not advanced in price. . . . The American Newspaper Publishers Association has been particularly active in working for a better understanding. It has urged the publishers to estimate their requirements closely, spread deliveries evenly throughout the year and in other ways has been helpful not only to its own members but also to the newsprint manufacturers.' "

The same journal, remarking (May 3) on Vining's invited appearance before the spring convention of the A.N.P.A., pointed out: " 'This was an unprecedented action. It was the first occasion an outside person had been invited to attend a session of the publishers' convention—one of the most exclusive affairs of its type held in the U.S.' " Vining himself asserted on this occasion: " ' "In providing the raw material for a free American press, the Canadian newsprint industry has a partnership in the American way of living, in American business and home life, in the preservation of our similar political institutions and of our common liberties of conduct, thought and speech. To Canadian producers the maintenance of dependable continuous supply becomes a serious necessity." ' " By mid-year, however, an ominous small cloud had appeared on the horizon. This was the lack of water-borne transport for newsprint under the increasing wartime pressure on shipping facilities. This shift of newsprint from shipboard to the more expensive rail carriage would in its turn exert pressure for price increases and so tend to lessen the temporary warmth in producer-consumer relations.[9]

Some notice should be given to two of the year's developments below the border. First of these was an approach toward controls, a slow and hesitant progress perhaps reflective of the gradualness of American awakening to the emergency so dramatically brought home by the Pearl Harbor tragedy and United States entrance into the war in December. In the newsprint area the first step apparent from the record was a meeting to which the Paper and Pulp Division of the Office of Production Management (OPM) invited one hundred and thirty-nine representatives of the newspaper, magazine, book publishing, and printing industries

(July 29). Here it was proposed that the respective industries nominate members of three divisional committees, to be formed by the Paper and Pulp Division after governmental scrutiny of the nominees; there was also projected the formation of an over-all Pulp and Paper Products Defense Committee to advise the OPM on broad policy questions.

The OPM announced on August 20 the formation of the divisional committees, representing, a. pulp, paper, and paperboard; b. paper products; and c. printing and publishing, which last was eventually charged with responsibility for distributing the available supply. This stage of organization apparently placed consumers and producers under the same supervisory machinery. As late as October 4, 1941, Norbert A. McKenna, then Chief of the Pulp, Paper, Printing, and Publishing Branch of the OPM, was pointing out to the joint industries that they constituted the only segment of the industrial economy not under complete governmental domination—the only segment " 'given the opportunity to demonstrate the effectiveness of self-management under government leadership. . . .' " By mid-month, however, now designated somewhat less broadly as Chief, Pulp and Paper Branch, Division of Civilian Supply, McKenna was speaking of an industry advisory committee whose activities were likely to include recommendation of production practices and standards. No further organizational changes seem to have occurred during 1941.[10]

The second development marked the culmination of the Federal Trade Commission–Department of Justice investigation of the west coast manufacturers. In May, 1941, four of the companies (one Canadian) and two of the individuals who had been indicted in July, 1939, pleaded *nolo contendere* and paid fines totaling $30,000. Those paying fines were Crown Zellerbach Corporation, Powell River Sales Company, Ltd. (representing mills in British Columbia), Hawley

Pulp and Paper Company, an Oregon producer, Inland Empire Paper Company of Washington, and individuals connected with the two first-mentioned firms. Plea and payment terminated the government's action for alleged violation of the Sherman Act without formal judgment of guilt or innocence; the plea, however, carried strong implications that company trade practices were not all they should have been. Years later, counsel for Crown Zellerbach suggested to the Celler Committee (which in 1950 conducted extensive hearings addressed to the allegedly monopolistic aspects of newsprint manufacture) that the practices of 1937, on which the indictment had been largely based, were embarked upon in light of government exhortations to cooperation under the National Industrial Recovery Act; at any rate, he argued, the antitrust aspects of business were less prominent then than a decade later. Mr. Celler reminded him with some asperity that no newsprint code had been signed under NIRA and that anyway that ill-fated experiment had been outlawed in 1935. The episode, here concluded, bears considerable similarity in detail, if not in scope, to the 1917 proceedings discussed in Chapter 1.[11]

The year 1942 was one in which intergovernmental cooperation appeared on a considerable scale, to a large extent supplanting the unofficial situation described above whereby the Canadian mills had absorbed increasing costs without corresponding price increases, to the consumer's considerable advantage. The cooperation produced important policy developments in the area of price, production, and consumption; it did more to detract from than to enhance the good producer-consumer relations recently prevailing.

The price maneuvers of late 1941 contributed their own share to this decline in good relations. It will be recalled that International Paper had announced an increase of $3 per ton on its product, to become effective April 1, 1942. This produced a prompt reaction below the border. On January 8 the Office of Price Administration (OPA) held an exploratory meeting with several " 'representative publishers' " to " 'survey the possible effects on the American newspaper industry' " of the proposed price increase. In addition to furnishing the OPA with cost data, the publishers were asked to determine whether current revenues could absorb prospectively increased costs of raw material without curtailing newspaper size or advancing newspaper prices. Later in the month (the 29th) representatives of the OPA and of the Canadian WPTB began joint price discussions in New York City.

These were evidently inconclusive, for on March 26, just before the new price was to become effective, the OPA issued Temporary Maximum Price Regulation 16, which "froze" the price at the current $50 port price level for sixty days after April 1, with the announcement that a permanent price ceiling would be set prior to the expiration of the temporary period. From somewhat scanty evidence it appears likely that a change in the personnel of the OPA representatives in the joint committee was responsible for the reversal of an original disposition to permit the increase, on the ground that the publishers could not sustain increased costs; in any case, this action appears to be a reversal of earlier and private OPA assurances to the producers that "it was the function of a price-fixing system to set a price that would maintain the production of an essential commodity." [12]

Canadian reaction was prompt, the A.N.P.A. *Newsprint Bulletin* quoting the *Toronto Financial Post's* complaint (April 13) that the action, attributed to the OPA without recognition that WPTB officials had participated in it, was tantamount to application of American price-fixing on a Canadian product. It was pointed out that export trade had been specifically excepted when Canadian price ceilings were established—a deliberate action, designed to protect the supply of foreign exchange. Now the freeze, if continued, would help to dry up this source of needed dollars. International Paper promptly started a backfire, informing its customers (March 31) that, with the recent curtailment of water transportation, costs had risen to such a point that some price relief was essential to the industry.[13]

On April 25, the Pulp and Paper Branch of the War Production Board (WPB) issued a policy statement promising to seek recommendations from the industry, through organized committees, when formulating production regulations. Three days later Leon Henderson, OPA Administrator, issued a less reassuring statement continuing to an unnamed future date the price level of October 1 to 15, 1941 (that is, $50, New York port), the order to become effective on May 11. Thus opened a period of uncertainty for the Canadian mills, now beginning to be beset by higher costs of wood, wages, and transportation, by a drop in United States consumption, and by fears of imminent curtailment of power supplies and a shortage of manpower in the woods.[14]

Canada made the next policy move, in September, when a WPTB order proclaimed an allocation system to be managed by R. L. Weldon as Newsprint Administrator. This was eventually to involve an elaboration on the prorating scheme, long in effect above the border, whereby mills would be assigned production quotas. An attempt was to be made, moreover, to move newsprint manufacture to areas best suited for wartime operations, leaving the electrical "grid" system of central Canada free for production of other items increasingly essential to the war effort, particularly aluminum; a great eater of electricity, aluminum used eight times as much power per ton of output as did newsprint.

To take care of the dislocations caused by this shift, a newsprint pool would be created into which the entire Canadian output would be channeled. Thus some mills might be entirely closed, but would continue to receive payments for tonnage delivered under their own contracts but manufactured by other mills where a surplus could be economically provided. The principal reasons then given for this drastic rearrangement were the sharp decline in United States demand (consumption for 1942 was 3.8 per cent below that of 1941), diversion of power to other aspects of the war effort, and limitations on the supply of pulpwood, which in turn were connected with the problem of manpower for the armed services and for other war industries. The pattern here forecast was the first Canadian application of a policy of production concentration to a non-war industry, and it was expected that it would be applied in due course to other segments of the economy.[15]

The next step was the joint WPB–WPTB order (M-241 below the border) of October 30, 1942, implementing the September announcement. This had been forecast three days earlier in a gingerly statement by Donald M. Nelson of OPM to the Newspaper Industry Advisory Committee (established meantime, and composed of representatives of both small and large publishers). To soften the threat of possible curtailment of supply and rationing, which he held over publishers' heads, he proposed that they themselves be left in charge of allocating the reduced supplies. The order itself froze production on both sides of the border, effective November 1, at the average operating rate for the six-month period from April through September just past. This was intended to cut North American production by a figure variously estimated at from 9 to approximately 11 per cent below the 1941 level; it was reported that this would permit the United States mills (which had been running nearly at capacity) to operate at more favorable levels than the Canadian, which had been running at a low rate for some time. Inventories were to be held to a ninety-day maximum.[16]

The Canadian mills were doubly restive, with production controls succeeding the failure of their spring move for higher prices. Their United States counterparts promptly fell in line, and the OPA was soon besieged for price relief.[17] Completion of the production-consumption cycle seemed more important to the government planners, however, and they resisted the pressure for the time being. The result of negotiations conducted during December was WPB Limitation Order L-240 (issued on December 31 and effective immediately), complementing the earlier order curtailing production, and implementing a warning issued nearly a year earlier by Norbert A. McKenna of the WPB (January 27, 1942) that production of newsprint was "'using too much critical materials, too much transportation and too much labor for the war program. The publishers of America should be on notice that they can expect rationing.'"

The order was currently justified on the ground that manpower and other shortages were expected to reduce the 1943 pulpwood cut to 20,000,000 cords, as compared with the 25,000,000 cut in 1942. The order was drafted with the objective of achieving a reduction of approximately 10 per cent in over-all consumption, with an escape clause designed to place the heaviest burdens on the large publishers, leaving the small fry in a relatively easy position (which they maintained throughout the war period). Its basic provision was establishment of a consumption quota for 1943 permitting use, quarter by quarter, of an amount of paper equal to that used in producing net paid circulation in the corresponding quarter of 1941, plus a 3 per cent addition to cover spoilage. The year 1941 was taken as a base period in order not to penalize publishers who had since embarked upon voluntary measures to conserve their raw material. Frequently emphasized during the succeeding years was the fact that WPB regulations made no attempt to specify the use to which assigned tonnages should be put, leaving this important matter to the judgment of individual publishers.

This formula "followed, almost precisely, the recommendations of the representatives of the newspaper industry itself . . . ," who had since October been in consultation with WPB officials through the Newspaper Industry Advisory Committee. Small publishers were protected by a provision to the effect that the limitation order should not apply to any newspaper which in the base period consumed twenty-five tons per quarter or less. This was adopted on the suggestion of Edward Anderson of Brevard, North Carolina, a member of the five-man Subcommittee of the Task Committee charged with making recommendations to the Advisory Committee. The order represented a compromise between voluntary newspaper action and strict government rationing. Though it acknowledges the necessity of some regulation, still it is remarkable for the extent to which it left the establishment of basic regulation of consumption to the industry to be regulated; indeed, an A.N.P.A. pronouncement of August 11, 1943, after the order had been in effect over six months, pointed out that it was "more a matter of self-regulation than allocation. . . ." The subsequent story will bear on the results of this liberal governmental approach to a wartime problem.[18]

Newsprint became fully involved in wartime problems in 1943. Pressures in the areas of price and supply contributed to a deterioration in the good relations between producers and consumers which had characterized the earlier war years. Increasing activity by government administrative agencies further complicated the scene. These, bedeviled by conflicting demands upon increasingly scarce matériel and manpower, were not always in close touch with each other; nor, so bedeviled, were they always sensitive to suggestions. Canadians, moreover, were beset by similar problems, given a particular twist by the importance of newsprint in their wartime economy; they tended, not unnaturally, to desire greater returns and to resent intimations that their efforts might be more productive. Congress likewise entered the picture in 1943 by establishing the Boren Committee, which was designed to stimulate supply, but moved in so many directions as to agitate all the other elements of the situation. Under all these circumstances, tensions and confusions developed at a great rate. In an effort to separate out the principal elements of the story, the following account will devote itself successively to questions of price, supply, and investigation, but attempt in so doing to relate each to the others.

Agitation from both sides of the border resulted in two price increases during 1943, the first announced in February, effective April 1, the second announced in July, effective September 1; each carried a $4 increase, making the final price $58. Neither one, nor the two together, satisfied the manufacturers. Neither drew publishers' protests, a hitherto unique phenomenon, in this writer's experience.

Representatives from both sets of manufacturers were on the OPA's doorstep early in January, 1943, the Canadians reportedly asking for an $8 increase as compared with a more modest request of from $3 to $5 from the south. The Canadian mills, under pressure, furnished the OPA with hitherto sacrosanct cost figures, and after repeated conferences the first $4 increase was announced on February 27, the effective date changed to March 1, for all companies except St. Croix, which deferred its increase for another month. Probably as a means of allaying the unconcealed Canadian disappointment (apparent within twenty-four hours) at the modesty of the increase, it was promptly announced that the matter was not closed and that discussions were continuing. *Editor & Publisher* editorialized philosophically (March 6): "The present increase will break no newspaper; neither will reasonable rises in the future, if they are made after careful consideration of every factor, properly spaced, and announced in time to give publishers opportunity to adjust their working plans. . . ." The same journal later (April 5, 1947) explained acceptance of successive OPA price increases on the ground that publishers were "anxious to protect their supply in a highly competitive field and thought a higher price might prevent diversion of tonnage to other markets where price control was not effective." [19]

By May and June manufacturers were back asking for another increase, with United States mills seeking from $5 to $6; in mid-June the Canadians were reportedly losing about $3 per ton on their product, and in July they let it be known that they would like a $6 raise. After protracted meetings, which took the negotiators to Washington, Ottawa, and Montreal, a more modest jump of $4 was announced on July 26, effective September 1. It was suggested that this double increment would restore the earning capacity of the manufacturers to about the level of 1942, which had been a reasonably lucrative one for them. Thus came to an end one of the longest periods of price stability in the history of the newsprint problem.[20]

Questions of supply moved rapidly to center-stage against the price background sketched above. Key to this situation is the operation of Order L-240 (designed to reduce consumption by approximately 10 per cent from a 1941 base) in relation to a currently reduced supply of paper and a threat of further curtailment due to manpower shortages in the woods above and below the Canadian border. A prime factor was the unwillingness, or inability, of United States publishers, particularly of the larger papers, to comply with the order's provisions. This problem of supply, with its overtones of economic and political pressures and its obbligato of investigation, contributed substantially to the deterioration of consumer-producer relations already initiated by Canadian disappointment at inability to secure greater price increases.

The statistics as presented by A.N.P.A. and the Newsprint Service Bureau show that both consumers and producers burned the candle at both ends, and that the candle itself was of smaller dimensions than in 1942, though greater than had been feared might be the case. The picture, briefly, is as follows.[21] Over-all North American production was at 70.5 per cent of capacity, down 8.7 per cent from 1942 and lower than in any year since 1938, with Canadian production holding up better than that in the United States and Newfoundland. Canada and Newfoundland together turned out 3,219,000 tons in 1943, and shipped to *all destinations* 3,273,000 tons, or 54,000 tons more than were made. Mill stocks on hand at the end of 1943 amounted to 105,000 tons, as against 159,000 at the end of 1942—a reduction of 54,000 tons. Under the self-policing provisions of Order L-240, publishers reporting to A.N.P.A. reduced consumption by only 4 per cent as compared with 1942, and 7.7 per cent (instead of the stated 10 per cent) from the 1941 base on which L-240 was predicated. They achieved this excess of consumption by drawing on their stocks on hand to the tune of 112,000 tons, reducing their inventory to fifty-two days' supply.

Matters started on an optimistic note, with *Editor & Publisher* commenting favorably (January 2, 1943) on the work of the Newspaper Industry Advisory Committee, which was said to have "created and maintained in Washington a friendly atmosphere between government officials and the newspaper business and knocked out completely the notion that newspapers might be 'controlled' by government through print paper allocation. . . ." It was soon apparent, however, that the initial formula was not going to take care of the problem of supply. The smaller newspapers, very numerous but using only about 5 per cent of the total tonnage, were protected by the terms of L-240 exempting papers consuming not more than 100 tons annually; the so-called metropolitan press, using upwards of 85 per cent of the total tonnage, was for some time taken care of by an overliberal policy of appeals for "ex-quota" tonnage in addition to the amounts allowed by L-240. In the middle, and increasingly uncomfortable, were about nine hundred papers with daily circulation ranging from 5,000 to 25,000; by early February J. S. Gray, former President of the Inland Daily Press Association, was bringing their plight to the attention of W. G. Chandler, a newspaper publisher and currently Director of WPB's Division of Printing and Publishing, and to Donald J. Sterling, general adviser to Donald M. Nelson on printing and publishing matters.[22]

Crisis developed in early February, 1943. On the basis of available information Chandler recommended to the WPB on February 5 the imposition of an additional 10 per cent cut in consumption, to become effective April 1; this was apparently based on Canadian reports to the WPB of a prospective reduction of 20 per cent in the winter wood harvest. This proposal had evidently already reached congressional ears, and played a considerable part in a situation, compounded of economic and political factors, which produced the creation of the so-called Boren Committee. It was also public property by February 9, the day after indignant congressmen began buzzing around the ears of WPB authorities. On February 15, the same day the papermakers proclaimed the existence of plentiful manufacturing capacity, the Pulp and Paper Division formally recommended the cut to the WPB. In other words, both publishers and manufacturers

The woodpile at a southern paper mill.

At one large newsprint mill, wood is stored in huge ponds to prevent decay and deterioration. It is removed when needed by orange peel grapples.

The pulpwood stacker at a large northern mill.

opposed the cut, though for hardly identical reasons. Informed sources were by this time aware that there was plenty of wood cut and available for current production; the real problem lay in the extent to which the current winter cut would suffice for operation of the mills (and hence of supply to publishers) in months ahead. With a meeting of the Newspaper Industry Advisory Committee scheduled for February 20 to canvass the situation, the Canadian Newsprint Administrator arrived in Washington on the afternoon before with reports to the effect that Canadian wood prospects looked better than originally anticipated; this optimism was based upon an unusually open season and an unexpectedly large output of logs per man. The immediate result was an announcement on February 20 that no cut in consumption was immediately necessary. Longer-run results included injection of the newsprint question into politics in the United States, publishers' charges that Canadians had threatened production cuts in order to secure a price increase, and the natural Canadian resentment of these charges.[23]

Though an immediate emergency was averted, continued overconsumption and the specter of shortages continued to plague all hands. Disturbing first-quarter consumption figures drew from Donald Gordon, Chairman of the Canadian WPTB, a strong statement on April 16 indicating that continued delivery of the agreed monthly quota of paper was predicated on the " 'definite premise' " of an effective consumption cut of 10 per cent. Since the actual cut was only half that amount, it was apparent that the self-policing policy, crowded by advertising and circulation pressures, was only half-effective. Chandler, on behalf of the WPB, announced on May 19 that the newspaper situation was " 'serious.' " By mid-summer several approaches to solving this disturbing problem were in preparation, while overconsumption continued merrily.

On July 5, the WPB, on recommendation of the Newspaper Industry Advisory Committee, amended Order L-240 by putting in effect immediately for the third quarter, already well under way, a further 5 per cent cut in consumption. Twenty-six states north of North Carolina and east of the Rockies were instructed to reduce inventories from seventy-five to fifty days; the remaining areas, due to distance from supply sources, might hold to the higher inventory. In mid-July, effective August 1, publishers were directed to cease ordering newsprint in excess of the amounts to which they were entitled under L-240; they had recently been ordering tonnages ranging from 12 to 13 per cent above the 210,000 tons a month Canada had bound herself to supply.

At the end of June, Linwood I. Noyes, President of the A.N.P.A., wrote Lyle E. Boren urging congressional support in obtaining Treasury Department redefinition of the term "standard newsprint" so as to permit importation of so-called "30-pound paper," to supplement the 32-pound weight normally in use and subject to free entry under the tariff laws. It was hoped that use of this lighter paper would stretch the wood supply and so increase available tonnage. This project, to be pursued with considerable diligence by the publishers, and finally adopted as governmental policy, awakened no great enthusiasm among the mills and probably resulted in little actual economy, if any.

By early July the A.N.P.A. had appointed a Pulpwood Committee with the objective of seeking ways and means to increase supply; and Walter M. Dear, its Chairman, was emphasizing the need for more wood and lining up newspapers to put on a drive for increased pulpwood production in twenty-seven states east of the Rockies. Likewise, means of applying various pressures to Canada were being prepared —pressures not likely to be found acceptable by a neighbor as deeply involved in war as the United States. Among these was an A.N.P.A. release of July 12, 1943 hinting delicately how the Dominion should manage its manpower policies: ". . . publishers feel that if sufficient manpower is provided in Canada, there can be a reasonably adequate supply of newsprint, but the supply from Canada will diminish unless Canada takes steps to assure a greater wood cut. While United States publishers recognize that it is Canada's own responsibility to fix her manpower policies and execute her war program, disquieting reports continue to reach United States publishers about a considerable amount of manpower being taken from cutting wood into Army service. . . . In addition, in Canada agriculture or farming is a basis for deferment from military service but pulpwood cutting is not classified as a basis for deferment from Canadian military service. . . .

"If the policy is pursued by the Canadians of not taking any special steps to maintain the volume of woodcutting because of the manpower situation and the supply of newsprint from Canada to the United States is allowed to dwindle, it can be seen that the Canadians will be making frequent visits to Washington demanding further increases in newsprint prices. . . ." United States draft officials late in July declared woodcutting an essential occupation, assuring its practitioners extra consideration in requesting occupational deferments. Lyle E. Boren, Chairman of the congressional committee bearing his name, shortly held meetings with the domestic manufacturers which stressed the manpower problem, and was soon (in mid-August) on his way to carry the same message to Canada.[24]

By this time the A.N.P.A. was in a state of fright lest mounting shortages bring about real rationing at the hands of government instead of the self-policing policy of L-240. In a masterpiece of understatement its *Bulletin* pointed out (August 11) that "it is not believed they [the publishers] favor allocation of the type generally used today by government" and suggested that stringent allocations were "so dangerous that every newspaper should make known its views without hesitation to WPB. . . ."

Responding to pressure, Canadians too began to develop some of the sense of urgency manifest below the border. The pulp and paper producers issued a release on August 6 emphasizing the need to maintain production and delivery rates in the interest of international comity and the Canadian economy, and urging that prisoners of war be put into the woods, as well as farmers and other rural workers in slack seasons; this use of war prisoners was already in the program stage in the United States.

The government made haste slowly, however, on the matter of draft deferment for woodsmen, since this major decision had to be geared into a number of other demands on the available manpower. The A.N.P.A.'s board of directors had preceded the Boren Committee to Canada, telling Dominion producers of United States efforts to improve production and continuing the pressure for Canadian efforts in the same direction.

To the south the American Pulp and Paper Association likewise issued a bulletin (August 17) pointing up the urgency of increased pulpwood cutting, emphasizing the action of the War Manpower Commission in declaring woodcutting an essential activity, and suggesting pointedly that draft boards take cognizance of this ruling in passing on individual cases.[25]

September brought several developments. The Advisory Committee (after stormy sessions of its Task Committee and of the full body, lasting the best part of a week) admitted early in the month that fourth-quarter quotas would exceed deliveries by over 72,000 tons. It pointed out two ways of meeting this shortage: a. by an immediate and drastic cut of

14.5 per cent to take up the entire slack; or b. by making a less drastic cut, with the difference to be furnished by eating into stocks on hand. It recommended the second alternative, to be embodied in a 5 per cent cut for the fourth quarter, combined with reduction of inventory to take care of the difference.

This in effect indicated the committee's willingness to eat its cake, in the hope that the measures already under way to maximize production in Canada and the United States would provide more before the supply was exhausted. The WPB accepted the industry's recommendation, formalizing the 5 per cent cut order on September 28, to become effective on October 1. Meantime, however, it was brought out that the operation of WPB machinery had resulted in awards of large extra tonnages to metropolitan newspapers, and steps were taken to correct such abuses in the future. Personal visits and telephone calls were no longer to be acceptable methods of seeking ex-quota grants—all requests were to be made formally and in writing. Later in the month this stricter approach was embodied in a supplement to L-240, drawn up in the WPB. This was imposed upon the publishers, some of whom apparently received it without conspicuous enthusiasm. By this time, it is fair to say, the operation of L-240 had become the object of considerable concern and no little criticism.[26]

On September 18, prior to the reassembling of Congress, Donald M. Nelson of the WPB wrote publicly to Chairman Lyle H. Boren of the House Committee predicting further drastic curtailment of supply and quoting Harold D. Boeschenstein, a trouble shooter brought in to straighten out the newsprint supply bottleneck, as saying: "'I [Boeschenstein] would be less than honest if I were not to say that we are confronted with a much more drastic curtailment in 1944 than anything we have experienced up to now.'" Nelson himself placed squarely on the Newspaper Industry Advisory Committee the responsibility for approaching the shortage problem circuitously by eating into inventories rather than facing it head-on by sharp curtailment of consumption. On receiving reports that up to September 1 the publishers had curtailed only 4.5 per cent instead of the expected 10 per cent, Boren reportedly asked, " 'What is the use of issuing 1943 new year's resolutions when you haven't used up your 1942 resolutions? It looks to me like you need more cooperation rather than more orders.' " When he replied formally to Nelson (September 30), however, he pointed up the danger to the press of curtailed supplies, and insisted that his committee would not " 'accept the inevitability of further curtailments without closest consideration of all the facts and without being convinced that every proper thing which CAN be done IS being done to maintain the supply of newsprint for newspapers.' "

At a hearing on October 8 he and his committee sharply interrogated Dr. A. N. Holcombe, Chairman of the WPB board which passed on appeals for extra tonnage, and elicited from him the opinion that a stricter policy in passing upon metropolitan papers' appeals would have resulted in cutting consumption close to the figure contemplated in the original L-240. The October 16 issue of *Editor & Publisher* carried a slashing attack on the Advisory Committee's stewardship of its trust, written by one of its own members, S. E. Thomason, a publisher of Chicago and Tampa, Florida, papers. He charged that " 'an intolerable situation exists in the control and distribution of a seriously diminished and diminishing supply of newsprint, *for which intolerable situation our Committee is more than partially responsible.*' " He documented amply the fact that nearly four hundred out of approximately eight hundred papers really affected by the order had applied for and received extra tonnage during the first three quarters of the year, condemned the secrecy with which appeals procedures had been carried on, and demanded early and drastic further amendment of L-240.

October witnessed a new emphasis on the lightweight paper approach to the problem of dwindling supply. The A.N.P.A. entered a plea before the Boren Committee (October 11) to secure Treasury Department redefinition of standard newsprint so as to permit entry of the lighter grade. Boren, whose committee had meantime visited Canada, reported that he found no enthusiasm among the manufacturers there, but rather considerable skepticism as to whether its use would result in net savings. Royal S. Kellogg opposed it on behalf of the Newsprint Service Bureau, arguing that the lighter weight necessitated use of a higher proportion of more costly sulphite pulp and slower operating rates on the machines, with a net result of from $4 to $5 increase in cost per ton. It was finally agreed that a committee of manufacturers would be designated to study the problems and possibilities involved in use of the lighter article.

Plans for 1944 began to take shape, with the Newspaper Industry Advisory Committee listening (October 19 and 20) to pessimistic reports of production prospects on both sides of the border and coming up with a recommendation for consumption cuts in the first quarter of 1944 involving a sliding scale less generous than the 1943 allotments, and based on 1943 consumption rather than the 1941 figures underlying L-240. So difficult had the situation become that Boren felt called upon to appeal directly to President Franklin D. Roosevelt. In a letter of October 27, 1943, he pointed out the existence of plentiful capacity, manpower, and transportation to take care of publishers' needs; he pointed to his committee's success in persuading the War Manpower Commission to declare woodcutting an essential industry, but chided Selective Service for failing to pay adequate attention to this ruling when passing on individual requests for deferment; he pointed out how his committee had " 'in a diplomatic way' " tried to call Canadian attention to the " 'importance of newsprint and paper in our national economy and war effort and to the benefit that would be derived from maintaining an adequate number of workers in the Canadian woods . . .' "; and he urged the President to use his good offices " 'with our Canadian friends in obtaining their cooperation in increasing pulpwood and paper production in that country.' " Roosevelt replied diplomatically (November 11), calling attention to the difficulty of gearing together all the diverse elements of the war effort, and pointing out success in arranging the importation of 3,500 Canadian woodcutters for work in United States forests. A letter of October 16 from Paul Kellogg of the Newsprint Association of Canada to President Linwood I. Noyes of the A.N.P.A. evidenced rising irritation at charges by some United States publishers that " 'Canadian newsprint manufacturers have failed in their obligations to their good customers on the other side of the line.' " These charges, said Kellogg, showed " 'a complete disregard, or lack of knowledge, of the actual facts of the case.' " He pointed out, moreover, that Canadian shipments in 1942, Canada's third war year, were 617,000 tons above those in 1939, and would be 16 per cent over the 1939 figure in 1943. He concluded: " 'I submit without any apology that Canada's performance during the time of war has been superb. . . .' " The long months of pressure were beginning to bring some retaliation.[27]

The supply problem continued to occupy attention through the autumn and early winter. United States pressure for more manpower in the Canadian woods also continued, and bore some small official fruit when at the end of October the Dominion selective service authorities placed pulpwood cutting on a somewhat higher priority classification. In mid-November the Advisory Committee recommended that the WPB set the consumption level for the first quarter of 1944 at 23 per cent below the 1941 base (the 1943 base proposed in October was abandoned for some unexplained reason). This cut of 13 per cent in addition to the 10 per cent presumably operative in 1943 boded ill for the publishing industry, but was based on the prospect that Canadian shipments would be cut from 210,000 monthly tons to 182,000. About a month later, under the stimulus of suddenly brightening production prospects, Canada announced that she could furnish 200,000 tons per month, only 5 per cent under the 1943 figures. Thereupon it was announced that the WPB would buy the 18,000-ton difference during the first quarter and stockpile it for distribution in the second half of 1944. This year of exceeding difficulty with supply ended on a note of publisher exasperation with this proposal, and efforts to get it rescinded.[28]

The other important development of 1943 was the establishment of the subcommittee of the House Committee on Interstate and Foreign Commerce, headed by Congressman Boren of Oklahoma and usually mentioned under his name. Thus was instituted what was to become one of the principal features of the newsprint situation, and consequently of this narrative—a long succession of congressional investigatory proceedings, launched under impetus of the wartime emergency, and continued long after its termination.[29] Brought into being largely as a result of newspaper pressure, the committee's origins were not devoid of political overtones. It devoted itself intensively to questions of conservation and supply, to the matter of a possible shift to the production of lightweight paper, to urging producers on both sides of the border to greater effort, to acting as a watchdog on the war production authorities, and generally to increasing the amount of newsprint available to the press of the United States.[30]

Initial impetus for the Boren Committee seems to have been connected with a resolution introduced by Representative Charles A. Halleck of Indiana (February 3) proposing that the Interstate and Foreign Commerce Committee be directed to investigate matters "with respect to contemplated requirements with respect to the labeling, production, marketing, and distribution of articles and commodities. . . ." This was specifically oriented toward the problem of grade labeling, and generally based on the unhappiness in some quarters at increasing governmental involvement in the operation of the national economy; as introduced, it made no mention of the problem of newsprint supply. However, in his remarks during the same day, Mr. Halleck announced that he wanted to know why the order curtailing consumption of newsprint (L-240) had been issued, and opined: "A spotlight in the hands of a congressional committee is the only weapon we seem to possess to safeguard the freedom of the press and the Nation's economic and business structure. . . ." Representatives Fred Bradley and Paul W. Shafer of Michigan, a lumber-producing state, chimed in to support his arguments.[31]

Whether Halleck knew of the likelihood of another cut in consumption is not clear from the record. At any rate, by February 8, forty Republican congressmen from wood-producing states were waiting upon Arthur G. Wakeman, Director of WPB's Pulp and Paper Division. Though Wakeman informed his interrogators that there would be no cut in consumption prior to the end of the quarter, Bradley, who had called the conference, insisted that he had been " 'reliably informed' " of a further cut of 10 per cent, and told reporters that the proposed action was " 'the first step in setting up a dictatorship. . . . These bureaucrats are trying to set up a collective state in this government so that the people will read and hear only what they want them to read and hear. . . .'" This outburst was still ringing in WPB ears when it admitted (February 9) that the congressmen had been well informed that a cut was likely.[32]

On February 15 Bradley introduced a resolution to investigate governmental motives in curtailing the use of paper; this was not acted upon, but its substance was incorporated in the Halleck Resolution by the Committee on Rules, for when the latter was reported to the House on March 25, the newsprint investigation was included. Meantime, of course, the proposed cut had been averted, but the impetus for investigation carried over, and debate on the Halleck Resolution afforded its author and several colleagues an opportunity to make remarks obviously intended for public consumption. Halleck intimated that prompt action in congressional circles had staved off the additional cut; though the earlier story has approached the same facts from a somewhat different angle, the possibility of congressional influence should not be neglected. The Resolution passed on April 12, and the Boren Committee was born. A brief account of its activities will be given here, at the risk of some repetition of the previous story of supply.[33]

After devoting considerable attention to the grade-labeling aspects of its assignment in the early summer, the committee went to New York in August for discussions of the manpower and pulpwood supply questions with interested parties. The group then journeyed to Canada on invitation of the Department of External Affairs. During the course of its visit, which was shepherded by the Newsprint Administration of the WPTB, it exerted pressure for increased production, followed by the recommendations of the Pulp and Paper Industry that woodcutting be made essential and that more manpower be sent to the woods. Back home in September and October, committee irritation began to be apparent both with the Canadians and with various domestic administrative agencies. The Nelson–Boren exchange, mentioned above, indicated dissatisfaction with current efforts at conservation, asked a number of specific questions as to what was being done, and wound up on a sarcastic note to the effect that if the WPB was unable to furnish the answers, perhaps it could tell the committee where they might be found.

Boren commented caustically (at a hearing on October 11) on a letter of September from Paul V. McNutt, Chairman of the War Manpower Commission, to Cranston Williams of the A.N.P.A., refusing a request to put newsprint manufacturing on the list of essential activities warranting draft deferments, though production of pulp, paper, and shipping products had been so favored. Boren pointed out that his committee had warned McNutt's agency in mid-August of the need in this quarter, and said that he was "greatly surprised" that McNutt "would write a letter at this late date showing yet a complete lack of information on this subject and apparently no disposition to learn what the facts are. . . ."[34]

Hearings in October elicited considerable information on current and past procedures, and further manifested committee irritation. Harold D. Boeschenstein, Director of the WPB's Products Control Bureau, bore the brunt of interrogation on October 7, attempting to point out that the manpower problem had to be attacked as part of a larger picture, but admitting that relatively slight progress had been registered toward its solution. The following day Dr. A. N. Holcombe, Chairman of the Appeals Board which passed on publishers' applications for extra tonnage, was led to admit that this matter had been handled overliberally; and Boren, although insistent that the committee was averse to "allocations" (that is, to a tight rationing system) was openly critical of the way in which large publishers had evaded Order L-240 by way of the appeals procedure.

Further sessions of the hearings, which occupied much time in October and November, were enlivened by the Thomason letter of October 12 blasting the administration of L-240; the committee devoted themselves to various aspects of the problem, especially to the manpower and lightweight paper questions. The year's activity culminated in the exchange of late October between Boren and the President. All in all, it is but too clear that problems of supply, with consequent repercussions in the field of investigation, had left relations between consumers and producers in much less favorable light by the end of 1943.[35]

Despite war's pressures, the Canadian industry entered 1944 in "the best shape in its history," financially speaking. Since the end of 1937 the fifteen leading pulp and paper manufacturing firms had increased cash and security holdings from $8,250,000 to over $50,000,000, had upped their working capital from about $29,500,000 to almost $96,500,000, and had reduced bank loans from about $22,000,000 to $3,500,000, and aggregate funded debt from $168,500,000 to less than $131,000,000. Organizationally, the Newsprint Association of Canada and the Canadian Pulp and Paper Association created in October a Joint Executive Board to deal with common problems. Production-wise, Canadian mills, running at 94 per cent capacity in 1944, increased their output by 8,985 tons over the 1943 figure, while those in the United States produced less than in any recorded year since 1900.

The year witnessed a considerable increase in Canadian overseas shipments (384,000, as compared with 267,000 tons in 1943), a development noted with trepidation in United States consuming circles. Price, be it noted, remained stable throughout the year, due to a number of factors, among which were strong publisher pressure against increases, a Canadian tax structure which would have tended to nullify any possible gains from higher prices, and, possibly, a desire on the part of the Canadian mills to cultivate customer good will by restraint in this area.[36]

The year 1944 opened with the level of supply in some doubt, Canada having announced ability to provide 200,000 tons a month, as against her earlier estimate of 182,000, and the Washington authorities having proposed that the difference be placed in a stockpile. The uses to which this would be put were variously interpreted by different agencies—one proposal being that it be held on government account for use during the second half of the year, another (the Department of State) proposing that it be used to permit other American republics to establish a ninety-day inventory of newsprint, a figure considerably higher than that currently effective in the United States, and still a third suggesting its conversion to boxes and wrapping paper. These brought publishers to their feet and the Boren Committee into further activity late in January. By this time the Boren group was recognized as a watchdog of newspaper interests, F. M. Flynn of the *New York News* writing Boren (January 25) of publishers' " 'comfort in the knowledge that this committee stands available to make certain that no more than the absolute minimum of wartime restrictions are imposed upon newspaper operations.' " Announcement of the various alternatives mentioned just above exercised the publishers, and Donald Nelson spent considerable time on February 14 trying to reassure the Advisory Committee on the stockpiling matter, supposedly telling the group that "it was all right with him if the publishers wanted to use the newsprint as fast as they could get it . . ." and giving it figures indicating that the likelihood of stockpiling was fading in the face of increased Canadian production estimates. The WPB promised (January 14) that any government purchases would not be exported, but retained for domestic use.[37]

The Boren Committee opened a series of hearings on January 25, 1944, directing its attention first to the questions of stockpiling, manpower, and lightweight paper. On the first matter, Arthur R. Treanor of the WPB again tried to reassure the group on the unpleasant stockpiling matter, asserting that the surplus tonnage would be left in newspaper hands during the first two quarters and would not be stockpiled, but used to take care of the extra leap-year demand and to rebuild inventories. These demands, he pointed out, would leave only 1.3 per cent of estimated deliveries to take care of the drastically curtailed appeals program now set up under Order L-240 as amended on January 13, 1944. Other witnesses pointed up the manpower shortage and urged application of further pressure for its augmentation, both above and below the border. The Chairman pointed out that, acting on committee instructions, he had introduced a bill permitting entry of lightweight paper of narrower width than presently permitted under tariff regulations as interpreted by the Treasury Department; this, he said, had been made part of pending tax legislation, and would doubtless go through without further ado.[38]

With price removed temporarily from the field of contention, and with problems of supply less controversially important than in 1943, the lightweight paper question occupied major attention during the first half of the year. The story was one of United States pressure for 30-pound paper, to achieve increased yardage and so greater consumption, and of stout Canadian resistance, at first overcome and later recognized as valid. The Canadians, while admitting the possibility of manufacturing the lighter grade, adduced arguments against the shift. These centered around three points,

A paper mill in the South.

two of which dealt with matters of production. In the first place, though the lighter weight produced 6⅔ per cent more yardage per ton, this was accomplished at such an expense in lowered machine speed that the hourly production was cut by 11 per cent in tonnage and 4⅓ per cent in yardage. In the second place, adaptations had been made to the manufacture of the 32-pound article making it possible to stretch output 4 per cent by adding filler and decreasing the content of the more expensive sulphite pulp; this could not be done with the lighter paper. Finally, purveying the two types of paper to consumers would necessitate complicated adjustments to avoid inequities between users of the two grades.[39]

During February, Senator Arthur H. Vandenberg aided in the passage of Boren's measure to permit duty-free entry of 30-pound paper as part of a revenue measure. The Dominion authorities, however, promptly forbade manufacture of the commodity prior to May 1, to give time for careful study of the problem. Perhaps hoping to influence a favorable recommendation, the OPA on April 1 set a price for the new article $4 higher than for the standard grade, and on April 20 it was announced that it might be manufactured, sold, and used during an experimental period covering May and June. Publisher pressure was effective, and large amounts were ordered from Canada in May, amounting to about 50 per cent of the Dominion production; it apparently met with publisher approval, and despite dislike of the change, Canadian mills felt compelled to continue in order to meet competition from United States mills. In June, however, Canadian producers enforced their views on the American consumer, resulting in discontinuance of the experiment. In mid-month a Task Committee of ten publishers spent three days in Montreal at the request of the WPB.

It reported (June 22) that experience had borne out the Canadian prediction of reduced output if the machines were turned to the lighter product, and practically recommended discontinuance of its manufacture. It insisted, however, that more favorable conditions of wood supply might restore a situation in which a return to it might be feasible; a drought in Canada was momentarily hindering movement of cut logs to the mills, while in the southern United States an excess of rain was interfering with the harvest. Publishers were permitted to continue use of 30-pound paper after July 1, but if they did so, were ordered to reduce their tonnage allowance under L-240 by 6¾ per cent, which would in effect place them level with those using the heavier paper. This elimination of a consumption differential, plus Canadian resistance, resulted in an end of the experiment.[40]

By autumn, with the continental invasion several months old, and with premature visions of war's end, postwar problems began to loom large on both sides of the border. Replacement of worn equipment and a restoration of competition began to occupy increasing attention.[41] The months present a curious mixture of optimism and pessimism as to the possibility of lightened restrictions, with the latter attitude coming to the fore as the year ended. In early September the Boren Committee was reportedly considering an investigation to determine whether the end of the war in Europe might ease such burdens. By September 20, however, Boeschenstein was warning that high demands for paper would continue for at least ten months after European victory had been achieved. On September 28 the Newspaper Industry Advisory Committee recommended to the WPB that controls be continued after VE-Day " 'until every newspaper in the United States is assured of an adequate supply of newsprint, or until the industry through its committee shall advocate a change or discontinuance.' " This, it will be noted, contained no definition of the words "adequate supply"; moreover, the alternative recommendation would leave removal of controls to the discretion of the industry itself.[42]

Toward the end of October governmental authorities on both sides of the border approached the matter of relaxing controls. Canada spoke through C. D. Howe, Minister of Reconstruction, and Donald Gordon, Chairman of the WPTB. The latter, pointing out that controls had hitherto worked reasonably well, nevertheless insisted that the real testing time was still ahead; he directed the bulk of his message toward the necessity of holding prices to their autumn, 1941, levels as a means of avoiding an inflationary spiral. In the United States the approach was on a somewhat lower governmental level, and was a much more specific one. On October 24, 1944, W. G. Chandler submitted to the WPB the report of a Task Committee assigned to make recommendations for the relaxation of L-240. Admitting that there were no present facts to justify relaxation of wartime restrictions "'to any degree,'" the Task Committee nevertheless made several particular recommendations, one, that a gradual readjustment of the quota figures be made as supplies became increasingly plentiful and, most important, "'That Order L-240 be discontinued as soon as government restrictions in effect in the U.S. and other countries on the production of print paper have been discontinued or relaxed sufficiently to permit a total production for U.S. consumption at a rate equivalent to that of 1941.'" The committee called attention to the fact that it had been under some pressure, which it had resisted, to propose a change in L-240 which would give large consumers, who had taken a greater reduction in supply under L-240 than their smaller brethren, a corresponding advantage in increased allowances when the tide began to turn.[43]

The Task Committee recommendation apparently stirred up considerable controversy when presented to the full Newspaper Industry Advisory Committee, some members asserting that its position differed sharply from the September 28 proposal that controls obtain until an "adequate supply" was in sight. WPB representatives, however, took the position that the Task Committee recommendation was an *interpretation* of the words "adequate supply," and it was adopted. Boeschenstein pointed out: " 'Once production reaches the rate of 1941 consumption, it would be difficult for WPB to justify the retention of controls over the distribution of newsprint. . . .' " On the strength of its investigations, the WPB informed the country (October 31) that no relief from restrictions was in sight before the middle of 1945, and by mid-December the agency was gloomily predicting that this half-year would doubtless witness " 'an increasingly tight newsprint supply situation. . . .' " And, to the north, the year ended on a rather minatory note, with Paul Kellogg, General Manager of the Newsprint Association of Canada, asking for an early end of WPTB regulations and indicating that, operating under the " 'uneconomic and unnatural' " pooling arrangements, the Canadian industry had stretched every nerve to keep production going, while during the five war years the selling price of its product had increased only 14 per cent, as against a rise of 90 per cent during a similar five-year period at the time of World War I. The signs, on the whole, were not too promising as the year ended.[44]

Supply problems loomed large during the first half of 1945. The monthly Canadian delivery quota remained at 200,000 tons as the year opened, but from this, plus what the United States could furnish, various government agencies took larger and larger quotas to supply newly liberated areas on the continent of Europe. This meant that the earlier pessimism on supply was well founded; severe pinches developed during the first two quarters. To take up the slack somewhat, and at the same time avoid cutting the consumption quotas, Order L-240 was amended (March 24), requiring publishers to reduce their monthly orders for the second quarter by 6 per cent, a restriction which was lifted for the third quarter.

The situation brightened somewhat by mid-May, and the Canadian mills offered to deliver 215,000 tons monthly during the third quarter, an offer increased by a further 5,000 tons on June 6. Publishers ordered heavily and beyond their quotas, however, and to offset this the WPB ordered (May 31, to be effective June 1) a reduction of inventories to thirty days in the northeastern states and fifty days in the southern and southwestern sections. Thus, by eating into their capital, the publishers were able to continue consumption on an even level pending the emergence of an easier supply situation. In the midst of this story, with little fanfare and with very little adverse comment from the press, the OPA, on petition of United States producers and after consideration of their earnings in the last quarter of 1944, increased the price of newsprint on March 30 by $3, to $61, New York.[45]

The question of making and using lightweight newsprint, reopened by the publishers, was carefully considered and answered in the negative. When the Canadian producers were approached on the matter, Charles Vining, President of the Newsprint Association of Canada, readily agreed, but declared that neither side should develop undue optimism. At his suggestion a joint committee was appointed to canvass the possibility of producing 30-pound paper during the second half of 1945. The Newspaper Industry Advisory Committee considered on April 18 information gathered by the A.N.P.A. from publishers (purchasers of about 54 per cent of the total tonnage consumed in the United States) who had used the lighter article in 1944. The experience, according to report, was "'not generally distinguishable from results on 32-lb. stock, and all agreed that the minor differences were offset by the increased yardage. . . . The discontinuance of 30-lb. newsprint in 1944 caused considerable regret. . . .' " Conferences held in Canada in early June made it clear that the Canadian mills were willing to go back to producing it.

However, the same sessions canvassed the question of the larger monthly tonnage of 220,000, mentioned above, and the Canadians made it clear that the two proposals were incompatible, that is, that lightweight paper and increased tonnage could not both be achieved. The choice thus lay between more yardage and more tonnage; the Canadians " 'were emphatic that with present conditions and outlook for the future in mind, the continued production of 32-lb. paper would best serve U. S. newsprint users. . . . It was concluded that your Committee would not recommend the production and use of 30-lb. newsprint at this time.' " The exploratory sessions had made it possible to present technical reasons why the production of mixed grades of paper was undesirable; the Canadian offer of greater tonnage of the heavier paper supplied the clincher, and the proposal was abandoned. The easier supply situation made possible, as of July 1, the first amelioration of Order L-240 since it was first promulgated: the adoption of a complicated sliding scale which permitted many publishers to use more newsprint during the fourth quarter—in effect so liberalizing the allowances as to leave 90 per cent of weekly papers free of all consumption controls.[46]

A minor flurry occurred in March, 1945, when Representative Francis Case of South Dakota introduced a resolution calling for a study of means whereby the United States might be made self-sufficient in the production of newsprint and other grades of paper. He was quoted as saying: " 'When a supplier fails its best customer in an emergency, the customer should plan a more dependable source for the future. . . .' " Mr. Boren deflected the lightning by suggesting that his committee could doubtless carry on the necessary investigation. Though the main object of Case's wrath was apparently a recent reduction in Canadian shipments of pulp, rather than newsprint in particular, the episode afforded Vining an opportunity to refute the charges in a letter pointing out that during five years of war (1939 through 1944) "'Canada has not only maintained the pre-war normal flow of pulp and paper supply for the United States but has provided United States consumers with substantial increases of pulpwood, pulp and newsprint. Compared with the five pre-war years of 1935–1939, the average annual INCREASES of wartime supply from Canada have been:

"'pulpwood, increased by 25 percent
pulp, increased by 88 percent
newsprint, increased by 14 percent
Measured in cords of wood, the above increases represent a combined total increase of 33 percent. . . .'"

A spokesman for the American Pulp and Paper Association suggested that Case's conclusions were "'based on faulty or inadequate information. . . .'" Using a somewhat different statistical approach, he noted that in 1943 Canada shipped 112 per cent of the average of the five-year prewar period and that the reduction in tonnage shipped in 1944 was due to United States use-restrictions and the demand for pulp rather than finished paper. He took somewhat violent fright, moreover, at Case's suggestion that government aid be enlisted to encourage an increase in domestic production, insisting that there was plenty of capacity already in existence, and that private capital could be relied upon to carry out any necessary expansion when the time came.[47]

As hostilities moved to actual termination during the summer and early autumn, questions of actual and ultimate supply loomed large, along with the possible effects of the removal of controls. By mid-August both government and publishers were concerned lest overoptimism develop about immediate increases in supply, and were moving to secure both immediate and long-range increases in production. Immediately, the A.N.P.A. sought to lighten restrictions on newsprint production and the channeling of pulp into other than newsprint products. Both the A.N.P.A. and the WPB cautioned consumers against hoping for early increases after VJ-Day, the former on August 14 and the latter in a full-dress warning on August 17, asserting: " 'No increases in supplies of newsprint are in sight at the present time,' " a situation aggravated by the fact that European production was so far below par that no newsprint could be expected to cross the Atlantic, and the further fact that several small United States mills had moved into other grades.

Three days after controls were lifted from all other grades of paper, L-240 was tightened (August 27) to establish consumption quotas for all non-newspaper users of newsprint. The long-run aspects were approached via a task group, which during late August and early September studied the possibilities of increasing domestic production. Its report, presented and discussed on September 10 and 11, was a gloomy one. Its analysis of the future showed that the 1945 capacity of 981,000 tons was likely to drop to 613,000 by 1948. It painted a dark picture of the industry under the OPA, asserting that since the inauguration of governmental controls in 1942 " 'the wartime increases in wood, labor and other manufacturing costs have accelerated the diversion from newsprint to other grades of paper. Practically all mills which have ceased production of newsprint are still in production on more profitable grades. . . . Manufacturers who have diverted production from newsprint to other grades are unlikely ever to reconvert and now appear to be permanently lost to newsprint production. . . . There is no indication that any United States manufacturer is planning to increase facilities for production of newsprint. . . . It is our conclusion that there is no basis for expecting any material increase in United States newsprint production. . . .' " Finally it urged cooperation of congressional committees, the WPB, producers, and consumers in trying to increase production under " 'a plan free from wartime Government controls.' " [48]

Meantime, the movement to suspend controls had gathered momentum despite portents of immediate and long-run supply shortages. As early as August 20, J. A. Krug, Chairman of the WPB, announced removal of all but about forty controls, while leaving newsprint under governmental jurisdiction; the decontrol of all other grades of paper (August 24), just prior to tightening controls on newsprint, has been mentioned in the preceding paragraph. By September 1, in fact, newsprint was practically the only commodity left under controls. In the light of this wholesale abandonment of wartime regulations, the Canadian WPTB wrote the WPB (August 31) urging that L-240 be left in effect until the end of the year so that the Dominion agency, which had fought the war in close cooperation with the WPB, could keep its transition to peacetime economy in similar step.

When this was discussed at the Newspaper Industry Advisory Committee meetings of September 9 and 10, J. Hale Steinman of the WPB pointed out that at an earlier meeting in Montreal he had signed a memorandum agreeing to continue controls until the end of the year, though he had told his Canadian opposite numbers that the decision could not be binding upon his WPB superiors. At this point the Canadians apparently waved a club under American noses, threatening that if L-240 were revoked earlier than proposed, they might start selling paper to South America, where demand was at a high level, and to their own publishers, currently severely rationed. In the light of these facts the Advisory Committee voted on September 11 and 12 (just as the Newsprint Industry Advisory Committee was viewing the supply situation with gloomy alarm) for decontrol on December 31, despite the recognition that " 'Basically, there still exist today many of the factors which created the necessity for L-240. . . .' "

It went on to urge those under the Order's jurisdiction to take " 'immediate action consistent with the Anti-Trust Laws, looking toward a program by industry for dealing with the problems which will surely arise. . . .' " By September 21, in light of increasing possibility that the Order might be revoked, Cranston Williams was solemnly adjuring publishers to exercise self-control when the glad day came, lest a " 'wild scramble' " for the available supply result in establishment of " 'government control . . . which would not be healthy for the public or the newspapers. . . .' " He warned his constituents that "neither the government nor the ANPA manufactures any newsprint—what happens is in the hands of the publishers and the manufacturers." Thus pressure without planning had resulted in a decision to decontrol; the next problem was to plan for the event.[49]

To bridge the gap, and in the light of the Newspaper Industry Advisory Committee's recommendation for decontrol, the A.N.P.A. appointed (September 27) a committee whose functions would be to "bring about an increase in the production of newsprint available for United States newspapers and to see that no newspaper suspends publication because of lack of newsprint." Recognizing that any combined operations would prove delicate under the antitrust laws, it was emphasized that "no pool of newsprint will be available to be shunted about on the basis of what any committee or publisher might desire to do. . . ." Matters remained largely in suspension during October, but on November 1 Steinman let it be known that policy would depend largely upon the attitude of the publishers; he pointed out that these had it within their power, subject to the limitations of the antitrust laws, to continue the principles of L-240. The following day Williams circularized all United States dailies, reporting that on the basis of A.N.P.A. studies it appeared that the only alternative to a runaway market was voluntary self-limitation during the first half of 1946 in restricting deliveries on the pattern of a somewhat liberalized L-240, and asking whether publishers would pledge themselves to such a self-denying program.[50]

At an important meeting on November 15 the Newspaper Industry Advisory Committee voted to remove controls on December 31, following a report of " 'generally favorable' " replies to Williams' proposal of voluntary self-discipline. It was then voted to call a meeting on November 28 to consider adoption of a plan already elaborated by the New England Daily Newspaper Association whereby publishers agreed to contribute a maximum of 3 per cent of their total tonnage to be doled out to papers in imminent danger of suspension for want of newsprint. It was hoped that matters could be put in train in such a way that other regional and state associations might copy this scheme. The scene then shifted to the Boren Committee, which on November 16 listened to publisher opposition to decontrol.

The spokesmen were headed by Gene Robb of the Hearst interests who had cast the only negative vote in the Advisory Committee. Robb exhibited little faith in the proposed A.N.P.A. attack on the distribution problem since, as he alleged, "a few large users stated they would not accept it." Thus, he said, the smaller newspapers and mushrooming war cities were left unprotected and the press generally left subject to rationing by the mills themselves; his interest preferred continued controls by experienced administrators to the inevitable chaos thus preparing. The tender solicitude of the Hearst interest for the small publisher did not escape the notice of the Boren group, and sharp questioning of Robb and two west coast newspaper representatives elicited the information that Crown Zellerbach had cut fourth-quarter deliveries to customers in the Los Angeles area by 20 per cent. William L. Daley expressed the fears of members of the National Editorial Association (NEA), the trade association of the weekly press, lest decontrol injure their supply position, but was countered by Clarence J. Brown, a member of both the NEA and the Boren Committee and a publisher of small papers. After the hearing Boren wrote the Civilian Production Administration (CPA) (November 17) expressing continued belief in decontrol, and asking for an early policy statement.[51]

The next step was a meeting of state and regional publishers' associations, assembled in New York on November 28 at the invitation of the A.N.P.A.'s newsprint committee. Those present listened to a series of questions and answers propounded by the A.N.P.A., designed to cast aspersions on the WPB's handling of wartime supply problems and to play up the manufacturers' willingness to try for equitable distribution of an admittedly short supply during the crucial months of 1946. After the meeting the A.N.P.A. circularized to the daily press a promise on behalf of those present: "The newspapers of the United States will see that no newspaper suspends publication for lack of newsprint, . . ." through state and regional organizations operating on the pattern of the New England Daily Newspaper Association. This of course meant the substitution of the New England Plan of specific remedy for distress cases for L-240's scheme, which established a quota system for the larger papers and provided a free supply of up to 100 tons per year for the small fry; it continued to leave the bulk of supply available to the large papers and made the smaller papers dependent upon a dole in case of need.[52]

On December 4, the Newspaper Industry Advisory Committee presented its plan for voluntary distribution of newsprint to government officials and repeated its previous request for decontrol. The decontrol order was drafted by mid-month, but its promulgation was delayed for several days, being announced on December 21. Until the last minute there was apparently trepidation on the part of government officials as to the fate of the smaller papers in a free market, but assurances of the large papers that they would look after their smaller brethren won the day. Some remnants of controls remained, however, in the retention of inventory and price regulations. Moreover, CPA officials requested the Advisory Committee to continue subject to call at need, and specifically threatened to reinstitute controls should the voluntary scheme show signs of failure. Decontrol, of course, gave no promise of ample supply, and a gloomy editorial note may be quoted as a conclusion of this portion of the story: "Make no mistake about it, the newsprint picture for U.S. publishers is dark. It is accentuated by optimistic publishers who refuse to believe what they are told.

"We are *not* going to have enough tonnage in the first six months of next year. . . ." [53]

To this chronicle of war may be added a brief footnote of price history. Rumors of a price increase, current as early as October, materialized on December 6, 1945, when the OPA announced a $6 increase, to $67, New York, as of December 11; this became effective, however, on January 1, 1946, since December deliveries were already under contract. This substantial increase was apparently recommended by the Newspaper Industry Advisory Committee in spite of the extra burden it entailed on publishers, and may be taken as an earnest of their realization that a crisis in production impended. It was widely interpreted as a means of checking the flight from newsprint on which United States mills had embarked so vigorously and which Canadian producers were apparently willing to consider. It serves as a good bridge to carry the story of wartime shortages over to peacetime difficulties.[54]

This account of the events of a turbulent period has detailed significant developments in the newsprint story. Publishers weathered the storm reasonably well, though curtailed somewhat in their operations and subjected to particular stresses in areas where troop concentrations and mushrooming war industries put strains on established newsprint quotas. By and large, the small publishers were better off than the large ones; the extra pinch of shortages in metropolitan areas undoubtedly helped build up pressure for decontrol and support for the New England Plan, which left the small papers more vulnerable in periods of drastic shortage.

Manufacturers in Canada did well, after a period of short labor supply; a favorable exchange rate and a hungry market enabled them to continue and complete the process of consolidation chronicled in Chapter II. They came through, in fact, in better condition than ever and, with expandable productive capacity available, could face the new period with some equanimity. To the south, returns on newsprint were less good, and this fact, plus war-born demands for other paper products, stimulated a flight from newsprint which was to persist for some time. It would probably not be amiss to suggest that in the newsprint area one of the most important consequences of the war period centered around this question of supply, with its problems of whether, and how, Canadian production would be increased, and of whether, and how, the decline in United States production could first be halted and then reversed.

There were important developments, too, in the area of

producer-consumer relations. The period opened in an atmosphere of relative urbanity, but degenerated with the events of 1943 into an antagonism which was to decline somewhat but remained close to the surface. Another element was added to this compound by the appearance of the first of a long series of congressional investigative bodies. The Boren Committee, in its earnest desire to provide paper for the United States press, was not above applying an occasional goad to the Canadian productive machine, a treatment not likely to be forgotten above the border. All in all, with questions of booming demand and short supply, of incipient ill-feeling between producers and consumers, and with the possibility of investigation hovering over the industry north and south, the problem of gearing the newsprint producer-consumer complex into the postwar economy looked to be an interesting one.

Inside some wood rooms the logs are cut into short lengths by huge circular saws. The cants are then ready for the debarking operation. Trees cut while the sap is running can be peeled in the forest.

CHAPTER IV

Postwar Problems

THE IMMEDIATE postwar period was one in which a suddenly rising demand strained an elastic but not indefinitely expandable supply, a time when, as a contemporary observed, no publisher had to suspend for lack of newsprint, but when on the other hand no publisher had as much as he wanted.[1] The ultimate problem was one of "balancing productive facilities with long-range demand" within a price framework of maximum stability; all three factors contained disturbing elements. Immediate demand was great, but its growth rate was uncertain. The matter of productive facilities gave much food for thought; the similarity between the current situation and the one obtaining after the War of 1914 to 1918 was not lost on producers. The memory of idle capacity in overexpanded mills in the thirties, resulting partially from overoptimistic mill-building in the twenties, conduced to caution on the part of Canadian producers.

To the south, the high capital cost of new equipment, and consideration of the greater profits to be extracted from other pulp and paper operations, left interest in expansion at a modest level, despite Cassandra warnings against overdependence upon foreign suppliers. The publishers, under pressure of would-be advertisers and subscribers, became increasingly starved for paper. This hunger found them caught between a stubborn Canadian reluctance to build new mills (plus an almost complete refusal to undertake new construction in the United States) and what seemed to them a Canadian-led procession of price increases producing swollen profits on one side of the border and unduly increased costs on the other. It will be the purpose of this chapter to examine the resulting tensions which, accompanied by continued congressional investigatory activities, raised irritation to a high pitch.[2]

All hands marked time during the early months of 1946, watching adjustment of producers and consumers to the peacetime situation, in which consumption controls had been removed, but in which price and inventory controls were still effective. With wood and labor now plentiful, production mounted rapidly, the North American output increasing 21.6 per cent in the first quarter, as compared with 1945. Publishers consumed the supplies faster than they were shipped, making up the difference by devouring inventories, and by April storm warnings were up on this front.[3]

Continuance of governmental controls agitated matters during the early months. President Harry S. Truman made the first move, asking Congress (January 21) to extend beyond June 30, 1946, the life of the Price Control Act administered by the OPA, and of the Second War Powers Act under which the Civilian Production Administration (CPA) controlled publishers' inventories. This cleared the way for development of policy relative to controls. Before the end of February domestic manufacturers had approached the OPA about a price increase; on April 11, however, the Newsprint Industry Advisory Committee abandoned what had apparently been a move to increase the price by $6 per ton and formally requested the OPA to suspend price controls entirely. The A.N.P.A. urged publishers to communicate their wishes on the subject, but no immediate action ensued.[4] Shortly afterward (April 16) it was announced that the CPA had decided to retain inventory ceilings "indefinitely," despite a Newspaper Industry Advisory Committee recommendation of the previous December that they be abandoned.

This decision resulted in a session of government representatives with this Advisory Committee on April 22 at which the publishers reiterated their request for decontrol on the ground that retention of ceilings served no good purpose and might be harmful. J. Hale Steinman, now Chief of the CPA's Printing and Publishing Division, felt that since manufacturers and the press associations had functioned effectively in distributing existing supplies, there was no great need for continued controls; on the other hand, no harm would come from their retention. His superior, John D. Small, Administrator of the CPA, called attention to the likelihood of an inventory scramble if Congress removed price controls; in such a case inventory ceilings might be the only hedge against an inflationary situation. After all this, Small refused to abandon controls for the moment.[5]

Mid-May brought ominous reports of imminent supply shortages, due to actual and impending strikes in areas closely connected with the industry; shortly afterward Robert M. Fowler, spokesman of the Canadian newsprint industry, wrote the A.N.P.A. (May 29) that Canadian production for the year was likely to outstrip previous predictions by 10,000 tons per month. He made it clear, however, that there was no guarantee that the extra tonnage would come to the United States, in view of the " 'demands of world markets in which short supply is becoming increasingly critical. . . .' " This thinly veiled threat was followed promptly by an OPA announcement (of June 4) refusing the earlier request of the domestic mills for removal of price ceilings on the ground of insufficient evidence of need. Rapid action ensued.

Fowler journeyed to Washington to talk with OPA Administrator Paul Porter concerning Canadian needs, as did

United States publishers; and apparently a tentative agreement was made to permit the Canadian mills a $4 increase. Such a move, it was thought, would at once afford relief to Canadian producers and stimulate production, and apparently the publishers were willing to put up with the one in order to secure the other; perhaps their concern was more particularly with the fear that Canadian tonnage would be diverted from the United States to other markets where it could command a price of $125 as compared with the OPA ceiling of $67.[6] At any rate, producers and consumers for the moment found common ground in support of a better price.

Toward the end of May, also, increasing production dissipated CPA Administrator Small's insistence upon retention of inventory ceilings. As of July 1 the regulation was changed from the current rate of thirty days' supply in the east and fifty days' in the south and west (that is, a specific number of days) to "'a minimum practical working inventory.'"[7] The legislation covering price ceilings went out of existence on the same date, prior to implementation of the agreement to give the Canadian mills the relief they had been seeking earlier in the month.

While Washington debated the re-establishment of price controls, Canada acted. On July 5 the Dominion placed its dollar, previously at a 10 per cent discount, on a par with that of the United States. The Canadian mills, which had been realizing $73.80 in Canadian funds for the sale of their product at the $67 (New York port) OPA price, found their income correspondingly depleted. Abitibi Power and Paper Company, promptly followed by other Canadian and United States mills, increased its price to correspond to the new exchange pattern, taking care to inform its customers that this action was merely an equalizing adjustment and had no relation to the real price increase the publishers had been supporting before the OPA prior to that agency's dissolution.

The whole maneuver became abortive when a new law (signed July 25) restored price controls for a year, automatically restoring the $67 New York port price. The incident had, however, served to dramatize the threat of diversion of supplies and nerved the A.N.P.A. to further action to influence the new OPA to approve a real price increase.[8]

This pressure began almost immediately, Cranston Williams urging his constituents to help save the market from the disruption bound to follow failure to provide the industry with a better return. His intimations of intra-agency differences as to what should be done were borne out by the OPA's obviously interim action of August 8 permitting manufacturers to ship paper on an "open billing" arrangement under which sales could be made subject to establishment of a final price—a tacit promise that something was in the wind. The United States producers added their word to the A.N.P.A.'s, recommending an increase on August 13. The net result was an OPA announcement of August 22 upping the price by $7, to $74, New York port. The increase was admittedly granted on the basis that " 'Canada and Newfoundland . . . are receiving increasing pressure from their overseas customers for increased tonnage at a considerably higher price than the ceiling hitherto existing in the United States. . . .' "

The agency announcement, however, indicated a long-range objective as well: " 'For almost twenty years United States newsprint production has been declining, at times very rapidly. It is the intent of this action to check this decline, and, if possible, to reverse the trend so that in future emergencies United States newspapers may look to United States newsprint producers for a greater portion of their requirements.' " From the Canadian standpoint it will be noted that the OPA ruling merely rounded out to an even figure the $6.80 increase the northern mills had proclaimed in July, and netted them an effective increase of only 20 cents per ton in view of the loss caused by the dollar revaluation. Both mills and publishers soon voiced dissatisfaction at this slender relief, and by mid-September the A.N.P.A. was sponsoring a meeting (held on September 18 and 19) with Canadian manufacturers, after which Fowler hinted strongly (September 28) at the great self-restraint which led Canadian producers to supply the United States markets in the face of vastly higher prices to be secured elsewhere; strong statements appeared at the same time pointing to the possibility of increasing Canadian production by 250,000 tons a year within a short period, predicated on adequate price and stability of demand. In the face of these pressures, the OPA announced that no price increases were in the immediate offing.[9]

Turning to a longer-range proposal than a mere price increase, the A.N.P.A. combined forces with the Boren Committee in early October to push a reluctant OPA toward a complete removal of price controls at the earliest possible moment. Committee hearings of October 2 and 3, held at the request of the A.N.P.A., were an unpleasant experience for Fred C. Holder and Robert F. Nelson of the OPA. Boren had asked the agency to come prepared with plans for decontrols. These were not forthcoming; indeed, Holder indicated his belief that the current price was sufficient for Canadian needs, and that outside demands would not lead to diversion of newsprint from the United States. He was attacked sharply on this point by Fowler, who had been invited to attend and who repeated earlier insistence that outside demand was urgent, asserting that Canada could market an additional 350,000 tons if she wished to go back on her commitments to the States. He also pointed delicately to the fact that Canadians could get $20 a ton more for pulp than for newsprint, while avoiding the extra manufacturing process, to say nothing of the possibility that they could derive larger profits by converting their mills to other grades of paper.

Members of the committee were quite sharp with the OPA men, asking point-blank whether it was or was not their intention to follow the congressional mandate to decontrol as promptly as possible. When pressed, they admitted that the OPA had no regularly constituted advisory committee representing the press and that the agency had held no formal discussions with the publishers, though one was scheduled for the following week. Moreover, OPA representatives insisted, the publishers had in no organized manner asked for a price increase, and one would not be granted without such request. When pushed further, they said that the necessary discussions prior to a decontrol order would take from four to six weeks. The committee insisted that this was too long, and moved on October 4 for prompt decontrol, passing the request directly to the President.

The hearings brought into sharp focus the possible relationship between a price increase and production increases. The publishers shared this feeling, Cranston Williams assuring the committee of his conviction that an increase would increase supply, but would not result in a runaway market. Fowler, on behalf of the mills, insisted that only a price incentive would bring increased production. The committee adopted this position as its own, its resolution insisting that decontrol would not unleash a price spiral, but would contribute to stability of supply. This unanimity of producers and consumers was remarked by Royal S. Kellogg of the Newsprint Service Bureau, who testified: "It is the most unique situation that I have ever seen in the newsprint and newspaper publishing industries of North America, when, for the first time on record, the newspaper publishers have joined with the manufacturers in an effort to get a price for newsprint paper that will insure the adequacy and permanency of the supply. I say it is an absolutely unique situation that never before has taken place. . . ."

The OPA bowed to this unanimity to the extent of approving on October 11 a price increase of $10 per ton, to $84, New York port, but refused for the time being to decontrol. The announced ground of the action, which was taken despite the definite imbalance between demand and supply, was to avert the danger of diversion of newsprint away from the United States to other markets. The final step, the abandonment of controls, taken with little fanfare and realizing the joint objective of publishers, producers, and the Boren Committee, was announced on November 9, 1946, and took place the following day. Thus at long last the market was in a position to find its own level of supply and demand.[10]

Important developments marked 1947. Production entered a phase of expansion which was to last through 1950, outstripping that of 1946 in both Canada and the United States by 7 per cent. Consumption pressed sharply on this stepped-up supply, and serious distribution problems emerged. With the general adoption of long-term contracts between mills and large consumers, and with demand entering an acute phase, the supply problem placed the small publishers, not protected by contracts, in an unenviable position. It will be recalled that Order L-240 of the wartime regulations had exempted small publishers from quotas, securing their supply at the expense of large users of newsprint, who had to curtail consumption according to a government-determined scale. With the substitution of the New England Plan for L-240, the small fry found that their mounting shortages could be ameliorated only by appealing to their larger brethren for a dole, or by purchasing in the spot market. Here they found themselves competing with larger and wealthier rivals who, also pushed for raw material, were buying odd lots where they could. The result was a fantastic increase in spot market prices, with figures as high as $250 per ton being bandied about. This situation, apparent toward the end of 1946, became acute in early 1947 and generated numerous investigative approaches.[11]

Early in December, 1946, the Department of Justice was reportedly scanning the newsprint situation, and by the end of the month a Newsprint Consumers' Emergency Committee, representing some two hundred publishers and printers of small newspapers, was expressing alarm at monopolistic aspects of the situation, and was reported to be preparing to request a congressional committee to ration newsprint. Its concern arose out of failure to secure renewal of 1946 contracts with jobbers, with whom, rather than with the mills, most small papers were forced to deal.[12] Congressional response was reasonably prompt, and took several directions. In the House a resolution introduced by Representative Clarence J. Brown of Ohio, a former member of the Boren Committee, and passed on February 26, 1947, addressed itself to the long-range problem of increasing the available supply of newsprint, with immediate attention to correction of current maldistribution of the existing supply.

It was avowedly established to carry forward the work of the wartime Boren Committee. In the Senate matters were complicated by an organizational change whereby James Murray of Montana relinquished chairmanship of the Special Committee to Study Problems of American Small Business. During the later days of his tenure he took several steps to point toward monopolistic operations in the manufacturing industry and to recommend an "'immediate, full-scale study'" of the existing shortage. He was quoted as declaring that "'the vise-like grip of monopoly-big-business newsprint manufacturers upon the 15,000 small newspaper publishers of the country' " was endangering freedom of the press. This pressure ultimately resulted in hearings by a continuation of Murray's committee, operating through a subcommittee headed by Homer Capehart of Indiana.[13]

A dearth of boxcars further complicated the situation, and by mid-February the A.N.P.A. was reporting, somewhat defensively, that its own check on reported shortages indicated that "there are now no instances of United States newspapers being without a newsprint supply where the publisher and the mills deal directly." The mills were urged to keep jobbers' supplies at least up to the 1946 level, and were complimented on filling gaps in the market caused when United States mills diverted production to other grades of paper. Between the lines can be read a growing awareness of the difficulties faced by the small publishers.[14]

Soon both Houses of Congress were busily investigating, and their efforts were supplemented presently by a Grand Jury inquiry. The Senate was first in the field, hearings by Capehart's subcommittee opening on March 4. The chairman's preliminary statement announced that while the current shortage constituted the most urgent matter for consideration, it was only one of multiple pressures affecting the situation, all of which his committee was determined to investigate. The hearings, though oriented definitely toward the plight of the small publisher, developed a considerable fund of information on the general newsprint problem. Edward M. Anderson of the National Editorial Association (a small-paper trade association) complained of shortages at the committee's first session, but was unable or unwilling to name a single jobber who had discriminated on price; moreover, he was singularly ill-informed concerning the existence of a so-called black market in newsprint and was disinclined to project specific remedies for current evils.

These came from Charles Helfenstein, a succeeding witness who sorted his objectives into short-, middle-, and long-run remedies. The long-run aim should be to increase production in the United States and Alaska; the middle-run to persuade mills to reconvert to newsprint and urge small purchasers to organize for joint contracts with jobbers; for the short-run his principal proposal was the establishment of a board made up of one representative of the NEA, one from the A.N.P.A., one each from the jobbers' and manufacturers' trade associations, and one from the Department of Commerce. This would in effect act as a ration board to see to it that during 1947 and 1948 the weeklies, the small dailies, new newspapers, trade, racial, and fraternal publications, and foreign-language papers would share the available supply according to a fixed percentage scheme to be determined in advance; he intimated that if six months' trial of such a scheme proved unsuccessful, a restoration of L-240 would be desirable. He was followed by Charles E. Moreau, a publisher of small papers in New Jersey, who somewhat reluctantly named a paper which he believed had bought paper in the spot market at $165 per ton.

Cranston Williams upheld the A.N.P.A.'s handling of the current situation, asserting vigorously that no newspaper had been forced to suspend for lack of newsprint if supplied by direct mill contacts; he pointed out that distress cases arose among those publishers who were forced to deal with jobbers, and insisted that there were actually very few such cases at the moment, though all publishers would like more paper. In spite of uniform pricing, he denied the existence of monopoly, according to his definition of the term, in the producing industry.

There followed testimony by numerous representatives of

trade, religious, fraternal, labor, and racial publications, most of whom had their supplies from jobbers, urging relief even to the extent of restoration of government controls. On March 6, Philip M. Hauser, on behalf of the Department of Commerce, drew a gloomy picture of future supply prospects. The United States, he pointed out, was "unlikely" to revive manufacture of newsprint on a large scale; indeed, 169,000 tons of potential production had been eliminated through the transfer away from newsprint in 1946. Moreover, prospects for expansion in Canada were "not great." Robert E. Canfield of the American Pulp and Paper Association suggested that small-fry needs could easily be supplied if large publishers would set aside a small percentage of their contract tonnage, but doubted whether such a scheme would pass scrutiny under the antitrust acts.

An important witness on March 11 was Fowler, now President of both the Canadian Pulp and Paper Association and the Newsprint Association of Canada, but insistent that he appeared as an individual rather than as an official representative of Canadian newsprint interests. Denying that an over-all shortage existed, he insisted that the immediate problem was one of distribution, which could be handled within the publishing industry itself, but could not be handled on his side of the border as the Canadian mills were fully under contract and had no free paper to reshuffle; he believed government rationing to be the only alternative to a distribution scheme. This he opposed, arguing that reimposition of government controls would result in reduction of Canadian exports to the United States. For the long pull he advocated measures to bring world-wide idle capacity back into production as rapidly as possible. He had figures to back up his belief that existing capacity was "adequate for any reasonable projection of world supply." [15]

Capehart's first positive move was to call a meeting in

Washington for March 14, 1947. Issuing a statement that the early hearings had " 'revealed conclusive evidence of diversion of appreciable quantities of newsprint to unusual channels—and at prices which would exclude the smaller publisher,' " he gave it as the committee's conviction that " 'our first and quickest solution is to seek the cooperation of the larger users and producers of newsprint in a concerted sharing effort—sponsored and approved by Government.' " When the group assembled, it was composed mainly of publishers of large newspapers; large producers of newsprint were conspicuously absent. Capehart appealed to the body "for a voluntary offer from the larger users of newsprint to share a small percentage of their consumption with smaller publications." Cranston Williams asked for a closed session of the publishers to "decide what offer they were prepared to make."

Whatever enthusiasm they may have had for a pooling scheme was dampened when Wendell Berge, representing the Department of Justice, "stated frankly that the possibility of antitrust prosecution existed in any cooperative plan that would control the distribution of available supply, in any proportion. Objection would come from those who were denied assistance or could not be served under the plan. Mr. Berge would not commit the Department on whether sanction could be given to such a voluntary plan, without legislative action. . . ." A substitute was found in the appointment of a voluntary committee of A.N.P.A. members which would investigate current distress cases and report back to the Capehart group. After some further sessions the senatorial committee recessed to give the A.N.P.A. group an opportunity to develop an approach to the problem.

Its report, rendered on March 26, reaffirmed the publishers' earlier offer to do all within their power to relieve bona fide small newspapers, but indicated their inability to extend this offer to include civic, fraternal, labor, and religious publications. It recommended a cooperative approach in the appointment of a committee to consist of manufacturers, jobbers, magazine publishers, and newspaper publishers, since the problem involved too many elements to be susceptible of solution by any one of them. The Capehart Committee adopted this recommendation and called a meeting of interested parties for April 9, presenting to the session its own plan for a voluntary organization. Continued fears of antitrust action hindered acceptance of the proposal, and Capehart and three of his colleagues introduced a bill giving temporary authorization for transfer of newsprint among publishers despite the antitrust laws. Meantime, the only recourse of distressed publishers was continued dependence upon the ministrations of the press associations to individual distress cases.

The committee concluded its immediate activities with an interim report on May 1, which brought out the interesting fact that whereas 95 per cent of the newsprint consumed in the United States was sold on direct contract between mills and publishers, 90 per cent of the small papers were forced to rely upon jobbers, whose contracts with the mills covered the remaining 5 per cent of total consumption. Most of the increased production of 1945 and 1946 had gone to the large publishers, with the small fry being held by the jobbers to their 1945 level of purchases, or to even lower figures. The committee repeated its earlier recommendation of a publisher-manufacturer-jobber committee to act as distributor of pooled contributions, conditional of course on the passage of immunity legislation such as was already before the Senate. It also proposed that the Federal Trade Commission investigate evidence that jobbers were diverting supplies from regular customers for sale at exorbitant prices. Finally, it recommended speeding up efforts to increase supply in the

United States and in Alaska. On the whole, study of the Capehart investigation seems to warrant the conclusion that existing distribution methods were operating fairly efficiently for most segments of the press, though the smaller publications which during the war had been largely free from regulation now felt the pinch.[16]

As an interlude to the story of investigations came a price increase of $6 per ton, bringing the cost of newsprint to $90, New York port. This was announced on March 21 by Canadian International, followed promptly by Abitibi, while the Capehart Committee was in recess and while the Brown Committee and Department of Justice investigations, to be mentioned shortly, were in preparation. It brought invidious comment from the publishers' side of the fence, it being more than insinuated that the mills were taking advantage of the current situation to charge all the traffic would bear. *Editor & Publisher* suggested pointedly that, barring prompt and acceptable explanations of the action, the industry would "destroy much of the valuable goodwill it has built up with customers in the past few years." Some Canadian producers were said to question not only the necessity of a boost but also its wisdom, following as it did so closely on the heels of a Senate investigation. The A.N.P.A. printed financial statements showing that Canadian mill earnings in 1946 had increased sharply over 1945 and earlier years; Fowler retorted warmly and somewhat sarcastically, admitting the facts, but accusing the A.N.P.A. of conveniently forgetting the years when paper sold at depression prices, and the war years when government controls kept increases at levels barely compensating for increasing costs. He declared that the Canadian mills were standing by their contracts and doing their best to take care of " 'publishers small and large left stranded by diversions of U.S. newsprint mills to other products,' " and asserted that the distress evidenced before the Capehart Committee was largely caused by jobbers and decline in United States production. He concluded: "'As far as Canadian producers are concerned, there is no price advantage favouring the larger purchaser over the smaller. . . .'" Both the A.N.P.A. and the Southern Newspaper Publishers Association warned members against spot market buying which would endanger price stability.[17]

The House had also been active in newsprint matters, authorizing in January a committee whose functions would be oriented toward increasing supplies and adjusting current maldistribution. This group, known as the Brown Committee, held executive sessions for some weeks, in the course of which it studied and reviewed the testimony given before the Capehart Committee. This was followed by private conferences with representatives of publishers' organizations and with individual publishers. The next step was distribution of a questionnaire, to be returned April 15, to mills and dealers in the United States, Canada, and Newfoundland. In May and June eight days of public hearings elicited information from publishers and manufacturers. Thus was launched the first head-on attack on the problem of new supply, as distinguished from that of redistributing the existing short rations. The questionnaire inquired pointedly whether mills had terminated contracts with United States consumers since January 1, 1946, whether they had taken on new customers, and whether they had maintained even treatment of all United States customers (that is, had not discriminated for or against). Dealers were asked whether they had sold paper at higher than the contract price, and whether they had terminated contracts or taken on new customers.

The committee held sessions in New York in the summer and moved to Canada in the autumn, holding sessions in

Toronto in early October which developed a good deal of information and brought to light the possibility of further price increases. The committee also gave Fowler an opportunity to point out that Canadian supply had invariably been brought into line with United States demand, and that there was no reason to feel that this situation would not continue to obtain. An interim report, rendered July 22, 1947, boasted that the committee had been instrumental in bringing about an expansion of production to the amount of 450,000 tons per year; it called attention to the possibilities of further expansion in the southern states, and indicated its intention of investigating development of the newsprint possibilities of Alaskan timber resources. In its final report it gave further particulars on increasing production, both in Canada and the United States, and took some credit for preventing even greater price increases, but opined that, after all was said and done, it was unlikely that supply would catch up with demand either in 1949 or 1950.[18]

Paralleling congressional interest in supply came a third executive approach to the newsprint matter from the standpoint of monopoly; the Department of Justice proceedings of 1917 and of 1939 to 1941 in this quarter have been mentioned above. This time the move was directed against interference with a free United States market on the part of Canadian firms, some of which were wholly subsidiaries of United States concerns. This move was to be aborted by refusal of the Canadian companies to make records available, a refusal supported by Ontario law and viewed with sympathy by Dominion authorities.

The Department of Justice, headed by Tom C. Clark, had late in 1946 inaugurated an inquiry by the Federal Bureau of Investigation into reports contained in complaints to the Federal Trade Commission that Canadian newsprint manufacturers were contributing to a shortage of paper in violation of the domestic antitrust laws. As neither of these inquiries elicited the requisite information on Canadian operations, the Department decided to proceed through a Federal Grand Jury operating in the Southern District of New York State, and toward the end of March, local officials of United States and Canadian companies were issued subpoenas, returnable May 26, for appearance before this body.[19]

The focus of attention turned on the International Paper Company, whose directors, apparently aware of the inquiry, had decided as early as December, 1946, against making available to United States authorities documents physically located in Canada.[20] On April 17 Canadian International instructed its officers to disregard all demands for production of records on the ground that, as a Canadian corporation, it was not subject to the jurisdiction of the United States courts; its general manager was also told to keep Ontario and Dominion authorities fully informed of subsequent developments. Return of the subpoenas was delayed for reasons not entirely clear from the record; however, on the very date (May 26) they were returnable the Canadian Embassy memorialized the Department of State, asking assistance " 'in preventing any undesirable interference with the Canadian companies,' " and Secretary of State George C. Marshall inquired of the Attorney General " 'as to the necessity and desirability of the subpoenas.' " After some further exchanges Marshall indicated (June 19) that he saw nothing amiss in continuing the proceedings.[21]

Action followed promptly. On June 20 the Grand Jury presented the officials of International Paper Company to Judge Henry W. Goddard of the Southern District of New York for refusing to produce papers "belonging to and alleged to be in the physical control of two foreign corporations," Canadian International and Canadian Paper Sales.

Groundwood pulp constitutes about three quarters of the pulp mixture for newsprint. It is made by placing debarked softwood in the magazines of the grinder and forcing the logs under pressure against revolving grindstones.

Chemical pulp, which is necessary to give strength to newsprint, is produced by cooking wood chips and chemicals under pressure in a digester.

At the same time the Canadian corporations moved to set aside the subpoenas. In a lengthy discussion before Judge Goddard the government contended that the Canadian concerns were actually operated and controlled from the United States and by United States citizens.

Contrariwise, International's representatives insisted that the Canadian companies were independent entities over whose records it had no control. Attorneys for both sides were given until July 1 to submit briefs before answering the Grand Jury presentment. On July 21 Judge Goddard denied the motion to set aside the subpoenas, but pointed out that the volume of records under subpoena was so great as to be " 'unreasonable and oppressive,' " and suggested that counsel " 'endeavor to agree upon modifications' "; and he announced that items on which agreement had not been reached might be argued before him on July 24. No action seems to have been taken on this proposal, perhaps in view of rising official Canadian indignation at the course matters were taking.[22]

By September 11, with the subpoenas still returnable, the press announced that the Dominion government was prepared to " ' "make quite sure that United States authorities do not overstep their legal jurisdiction and infringe on Canadian sovereignty. . . ." ' " Two days later the Department of State asserted there was no quarrel with Canada over the matter, it being departmental understanding that an exchange of communications in May (not available to the author) had produced mutual understanding. Attorney General Clark, however, felt impelled to tell the press (September 22) that current action was only exploratory, that his Department had no thought of " ' "persecution" ' " of Canadian firms, and that a recent personal visit to Ottawa at which he had had conversations with the Dominion Ministers of Interior and of Justice had produced no formal Canadian complaints.[23]

With the Canadian companies still recalcitrant, the Department of Justice considered contempt proceedings against them in order to bring matters to a judicial termination. Before taking this drastic step, however, it consulted the Department of State, and was informed that although the investigation had " 'aroused considerable concern in Canada' " the matter of contempt proceedings was " 'a legal matter for the determination of the Department of Justice.' " This thinly veiled hint to go slowly resulted in sending agents of the Department of Justice to Ottawa for conferences with the Canadian manufacturers. These, according to Clark, " 'permitted inquiry into factual situations relating to the complaints under consideration. The information supplied to our representatives at these meetings covered the immediate problems, insofar as the subpoenas addressed to Canadian corporations are concerned. . . .' "

While things were still in this indeterminate state the provincial government of Ontario presented a bill, which presently became law, making it a criminal offense to comply with any judicial process emanating from extraprovincial authorities for removal of records of provincial business concerns—a piece of legislation which in the future would greatly limit the investigatory function below the border. As a culmination of the whole episode, the Attorney General of the United States announced (November 22) withdrawal of the subpoenas, though insisting that the Grand Jury would continue its investigation of the industry. It seems apparent that industrial reluctance, provincial and Dominion irritation, and Department of State caution combined to thwart this third governmental attempt to stigmatize the industry for monopolistic tendencies.[24]

Supply and price issues again became intermingled toward

the end of the year. In early October, W. G. Chandler visited Canada on behalf of the A.N.P.A.'s special committee on newsprint. Here he heard Fowler's exposition of the current state of the Canadian industry, indicating among other things that the Dominion planned a capacity expansion of only 100,000 tons for 1948, as against a considerably higher estimated United States demand. Pointing out that price was now close to the danger point from the publisher's standpoint, he urged each party to a policy of caution: Publishers, he said, should frankly tell their suppliers of their difficulties; the latter should seriously consider more rapid expansion of productive facilities.

Such advice, cautiously given as it was, had little effect. Canadian producers had already determined to avoid a rapid plant expansion such as had wreaked disaster after World War I and stood committed to expansion of production by speeding up existing machinery rather than by building new mills; this decision was to remain firm for years to come. On price, moreover, they were less convinced than publishers that an optimum situation had been reached, and on December 4 Abitibi announced an increase of $6, to $96, New York port, effective January 1, 1948; this was followed promptly by Canadian International. This action came on the heels of an earlier promise by Consolidated Paper Company to hold the price level through February, 1948, and introduced the possibility of a multipriced product, particularly when Great Northern announced (December 26) that its current price of $87.50, New York port, would stand for the present.[25]

A final development of 1947 deserves brief mention. This is the emergence into greater prominence of Alaska as a source of paper—which would be at once effective in relieving consumers from dependence upon Canadian suppliers and freeing the United States industry for operations along more lucrative lines. Several factors operated as limitations on production of paper in this area. First, the distance of the raw material from the markets tended to raise costs to a prohibitive level and to introduce the possibility that government subsidies might be necessary to induce production. This was re-enforced by a ruling of the Forest Service of the Department of Agriculture, placed in administrative control over the vast timber resources of southeastern Alaska, to the effect that raw timber could not be exported, but must be processed in the Territory; the intention was to bolster the Alaskan economy by introducing industrial operations, but the result was to contribute further to costs of possible production. Government power to dispose of the forests, moreover, was clouded by the necessity of persuading the aboriginal inhabitants to surrender acknowledged claims. Under all these circumstances, the plans for exploitation which had gathered some headway in the 1920's fell into abeyance during the depression and wartime periods, and it was only with postwar shortages, the reluctance of Canadian mills to move into the breach to increase United States supply, and the preference of United States mills for other branches of production that Alaska moved again into the limelight.[26]

With one eye on the postwar situation, the Forest Service in 1944 issued a prospectus describing Alaskan opportunities and outlining contract terms. This was widely circulated and aroused some interest, but nothing concrete materialized. In 1946, however, J. A. Krug, then Secretary of the Interior, made a trip to Alaska and returned with glowing reports of its potentialities. By March of 1947 investigations were under way and the Forest Service was in communication with interested parties. The failure of the Capehart Committee to develop a real solution of the newsprint problem sharpened the problems created by the forthcoming boom in the newspaper field and the reluctance of Canadian manufacturers to meet the rising needs of publishers; and by June the Forest Service, at the request of a west coast group, had drawn up sample agreements for development of Alaskan resources. In July and August, Congress passed a resolution authorizing sale of timber in the Tongass National Forest, and the Forest Service advertised for bids, to be opened October 1, for purchase of timber in the Petersburg area. The money received would be impounded, pending culmination of negotiations for surrender of aboriginal rights. In September, however, the sale was postponed until February, 1948, and in the following month it was announced that one of the two interested concerns had abandoned the idea of newsprint manufacture and was reorienting its interest in the direction of pulp making. Thus by the year's end considerable activity had resulted, but nothing concrete had been accomplished; an unanswered and probably unanswerable query is the extent to which the agitation for Alaskan production was a stalking-horse to induce greater productive activity in Canada.[27]

The year 1948 opened with newsprint supply and demand considerably out of balance, but during the first quarter and for the rest of the year it began to move toward an equilibrium. During these early months Canada and Newfoundland found it possible to export greater tonnage to the United States because European austerity programs forced some purchasers to discontinue normal buying of North American newsprint. Canadian capacity, too, was rated as increased by 128,000 tons from 1947, instead of the 100,000 predicted toward the end of that year. The price picture was confused during the early part of the year, with a reported spread of as much as $8.50 per ton between top and bottom contract figures. This condition, which was leveling off by April 1, afforded *Editor & Publisher* opportunity for ironic comment

(January 10) anent the recent Grand Jury investigation which had been "trying to uncover monopolistic practices within the newsprint industry, including price fixing.

"If ever proof was needed that the government agency was on a wild goose chase, it is the hodgepodge pattern now appearing in the newsprint price picture." With less pressure of demand upon supply, the tempo of investigation tended to moderate somewhat.[28]

In April and May it began to appear, according to trade association publications, that the supply situation was considerably eased; some cautious comment indicated the possibility that a buyer's market might be in the offing.[29] This relatively quiet situation was disturbed in May by several domestic and foreign complications, though none developed immediately into great importance. A new judge, sitting in the Southern District of New York, threatened to revive the moribund Grand Jury investigation of monopoly among the manufacturers. John W. Clancy denied (April 28) the petition of Consolidated Paper Sales, Ltd. (formerly St. Maurice Valley Paper Company, Ltd.) to quash the subpoena demanding submission to the Grand Jury of the records of its New York office. Judge Clancy held that the activities of Consolidated Sales' Vice President, David W. Sherman, constituted "doing business" in New York State.

Although nothing of importance eventuated, the action continued to dangle a Damoclean sword over the Canadian producers' heads. Of greater possible importance, though again producing no immediate results, was a decision of the United States Supreme Court banning multiple basing-point delivered-price systems in the cement industry. This encouraged the Federal Trade Commission to hope that the same prohibitory principle might be applied to the zone-pricing system so long applicable to newsprint deliveries, whereby all publishers buying newsprint under contract in a given geographical zone paid identical prices, regardless of their supplier or their own distance from the mill. This matter furnished ground for congressional committee consideration in the later year, but at the moment produced nothing more than animated discussion.[30]

A price rise, forecast as early as June 28 and announced on July 21, to become effective August 1, forms an interlude in the narrative at this point. Though a Canadian mill sent up the original trial balloon, it was Crown Zellerbach, a west coast mill, which assumed price leadership, announcing a $4 increase to $100, New York port. Rising costs, as usual, constituted the chief assigned reason. It was pointed out repeatedly that price had consistently lagged behind costs since decontrol; the Canadian mills suggested that spiraling prices had left them so far behind that if newsprint were brought abreast of the current United States commodity price index, it would fetch $122. It may be pointed out, however, that there was surprisingly little complaint on the part of publishers and that the approach of a demand-supply equilibrium reached a point where President John H. Hinman could report to a meeting of International Paper's stockholders (May 11, 1949) that "'the so-called seller's market came to a close, so far as most of the paper industry was concerned, during the latter part of 1948. . . .'"[31]

Two newsprint developments occurred in September. The first was a meeting at Milwaukee, one of an annual series going back to wartime sessions under OPA auspices. This one was attended by some thirty-five United States publishers and twenty-five Canadian producers, and was devoted to a mutual consideration of problems of supply and demand. The publishers presented the mill representatives with the results of a questionnaire distributed to 801 members of the A.N.P.A., and eliciting 550 replies. Four hundred and thirty-five papers projected expansion totaling $113,782,343.39 over the proximate two-year period, and indicated their willingness to negotiate long-term (five- to ten-year) contracts for 472,583 additional tons of newsprint. Publishers projected a demand for 6,201,000 tons, which the Canadian mill representatives confidently predicted they could supply through existing speed-up methods. Their spokesman, Fowler, said these estimates were too low, since they failed to take into account an enormous backlog of orders and unfilled demand in 1947, the year on which the study was based. It may be pointed out that both parties were in error; by June, 1950, Charles E. Moreau was telling the Celler Committee that at current rates the consumption in 1950 would probably come within 250,000 tons of the projected demand of a decade later, and that 1951 might well see demand for the full estimate for 1960. Being wise after the event, it would appear that neither publishers nor manufacturers proved good prophets and that their joint inability to pierce the veil contributed largely to subsequent tensions.[32]

September's other development was a new approach to the problem of monopoly via the basing-point decision. William Simon, general counsel of the Senate Subcommittee on Trade Policies (a subcommittee of the Committee on Interstate and Foreign Commerce), told the Milwaukee meeting that, following the judicial precedent of the Cement Institute case, the Federal Trade Commission had concluded that the zone-pricing system practiced in the newsprint industry was illegal and that the only legal approach to the problem was a return to the f.o.b. mill system which, it will be remembered, was prevalent before International pioneered the zone-pricing system in the later 1920's.

Such action presaged trouble, since other industries would doubtless object to such drastic revamping of their selling practices, and it was Simon's judgment that Congress must embark on a legislative remedy before prospective confusions could be remedied. Shortly afterward the Trade Commission issued (October 12) a policy statement on "geographic pricing practices," which failed to command the unanimous support of its members. Almost simultaneously the Trade Policies Subcommittee, headed by Senator Capehart, announced that it would hold hearings in preparation for a legislative approach. And by December 9, while the Capehart hearings were in progress, Trade Commission agents "invaded" the Chanin Building, where most of the paper trade associations were domiciled, in search of information contained in files dating back as far as 1935, on which to base an attack on zone-pricing practices in the general paper industry.[33]

Hearings by the Capehart Committee preceded and overlapped the Federal Trade Commission incursion, but produced no positive action during the year. They were attended by representatives of both publishers and manufacturers, who alike decried the calamitous results sure to flow from disturbing the *status quo*. Under date of November 30 the Newsprint Service Bureau presented a brief replying to a committee questionnaire in which it pointed out that the zone-pricing system was forced on the mills by the necessity of competing for the business of "very strong buying groups" which insisted upon "equality of treatment," and that enforced return to f.o.b. mill pricing would work to the advantage of foreign producers, particularly those located near water transportation, and would thus tend to decrease total United States production. Many domestic manufacturers, it was averred, would be so adversely affected as to be unable to remain in business, and the domestic industry would thus be forced to give up much of the small share (16 per cent) of the domestic market which it had hitherto succeeded in retaining.[34]

On December 6, Charles E. Moreau spoke on behalf of

publishers of small papers who would, he argued, be seriously disadvantaged by a reversion to f.o.b. mill pricing. The change, he suggested, would be accompanied by destruction of the existing contract system; the larger publishers, with greater bargaining power, would inevitably come out ahead in making new deals with mills in favorable geographic locations, leaving the small publishers, particularly those in the south and west, to pay the resulting high freight rates. He denied the validity of one of the principal arguments in favor of abandoning zone-pricing—that is, that it would result in dispersion of the industry—since in the case of newsprint, location was more than usually dependent upon the location of raw material. His proposed remedy for existing difficulties was a congressional enactment legalizing and regulating zone-pricing.

Toward the end of the hearings a spokesman for the American Pulp and Paper Association asserted that the industry could not remain in business without the power to meet the price competition prevailing in any given area. He also recommended that the legislative picture be clarified, but in such a way as to " 'permit freedom of action by any individual manufacturer to sell his product on the basis that best suits his competitive needs, and that the general adoption, without collusion, of any system of selling by manufacturers of paper shall not be in violation of such laws.' " After receipt of these variant proposals, the committee adjourned on December 8, to be reorganized under other leadership in the new Congress convening in January, 1949.

Prospects of an Alaskan newsprint industry received a blow in the early year. On January 30 the Capehart Small Business Committee (not the group referred to in the preceding zone-pricing discussion), after three of its members had junketed to Alaska for personal observation, reported discouragingly. Numerous factors were adduced to offset the advantages of the enormous natural resources of the Tongass National Forest: danger to the fishing industry, inadequate housing, high labor and shipping costs, and dearth of power sites in proper juxtaposition to timber stands. Moreover, under existing regulations, the Forest Service had no authority to require that Alaskan timber be devoted to any particular end product. Under these circumstances, there was no guarantee that development of an Alaskan wood pulp industry would increase the supply of newsprint to the United States; indeed, given the status of "practical timber and lumbering operations, the great bulk of these stands of timber can be manufactured profitably only into a pulp product." The best the committee could recommend, therefore, was that the smaller publishers band together in cooperative effort to establish an Alaskan newsprint industry—not a particularly fruitful suggestion in view of the very considerable amounts of capital required to establish a new mill. Immediately discouraging to newsprint prospects was governmental acceptance in early August of a bid by the Ketchikan Pulp and Paper Company for the construction of an Alaskan mill which, it was generally understood, would manufacture sulphite pulp rather than newsprint.[35]

On the final day of the year the Brown Committee rendered an account of its stewardship, reporting on its survey of previous investigations and the development of its objectives. These were initially to increase both the supply and production of all types of paper within the continental United States, but soon broadened into the more particular task of looking after the immediate needs of consumers threatened with short supply, especially among the smaller publishers. The report complimented both manufacturers' and publishers' associations for their cooperation, and boasted that through these joint efforts "not a single newspaper in the United States was forced to suspend publication at any time during the past 2 years because of lack of newsprint." While announcing the committee's conviction that its activities had been instrumental in preventing an even greater price advance than the $10 increase which had occurred during its lifetime, the report admitted that increases in the price of newsprint had lagged behind those of other staples. The committee's principal contribution to the future of newsprint was expression of the belief that the American south could become the home of a viable industry.[36]

The year 1949 was a relatively quiet one in newsprint affairs. Business generally was not too good, particularly in the early months. Newsprint was in good supply, Canadian production increasing by over 200,000 tons and a buyer's market being "an accepted fact," with Canadian paper appearing in the United States spot market during the first quarter at close to contract prices. Price consequently held steady, at a virtually uniform figure, absorbing rising costs without an increase. Company profits, after a slow start, wound up with ledgers satisfactorily in the black. The principal developments centered around continued interest in zone-pricing practices and in the relation to newsprint matters of a Canadian dollar devaluation which occurred toward the end of the year. This devaluation spiked publishers' hopes, vigorously expressed beginning at mid-year, for price reductions. Finally, word of increasing production, actual or potential, in the United States as well as Canada, began to be a feature of the situation, with Great Northern adding 25,000 tons, with the Southland Paper Company bringing in an additional 60,000-ton machine, and the Coosa River development due to add another 100,000 tons early in 1950.[37]

A development of the early year was submission (February 10) of the final report of the Capehart Committee. Its conclusions and recommendations included the opinion that the prospects of Alaska as a source of increased newsprint supply were "remote" in view of the slight likelihood of enlisting the necessary financing in the "foreseeable future." Greatest hope in this direction lay in the further development of southern production and in the encouragement of processes for de-inking waste papers for conversion into newsprint. For the long run, it recommended that government and industry continue experimentation in the development of alternative sources of supply such as straw, grasses, and bagasse (the residue left after the sap has been expressed from sugar cane).[38]

The problem of zone-pricing received some attention, though no conclusion was reached. On January 5, Senator Edwin C. Johnson, who had succeeded Capehart as Chairman of the Trade Policies Subcommittee, introduced a bill designed to remedy the difficulties caused by the Cement Institute decision by permitting individual sellers to absorb freight costs in order to compete in distant markets. Barring conspiratorial connivance to rig prices, this would enable mills to even their prices to purchasers at varying distances from the point of origin. It also gave the Federal Trade Commission power to order companies to establish f.o.b. mill pricing, and to give purchasers a choice between the two methods. In a report rendered early in March the subcommittee indicated its belief that a uniform requirement of f.o.b. mill sales (that is, a complete denial of the right to absorb freight charges) would result in placing the mills located close to the raw materials at a substantial disadvantage, with corresponding advantage to those located near centers of consumption. Eventually the Senate Committee on the Judiciary reported a bill establishing a fifteen-month period during which mills competing in good faith might continue selling at delivered prices and absorbing freight charges (that is, the zone-pricing system). This passed the Senate (June 1), but was amended in the House (July 7) and failed of passage during the year when the Senate postponed consideration until January 20, 1950.[39]

In January, 1949, the American Newspaper Guild (CIO) launched an attack aimed almost impartially at publishers and manufacturers, charging producers with " 'concerted price-fixing and attempts to restrict output in apparently monopolistic fashion,' " and alleging among other things that this collusion "has not been offset by unified action from the newspaper publishing industry. . . . Large publishers are inhibited from challenging newsprint producers by . . . the absence of leadership on the part of their major organization, the American Newspaper Publishers Association." The A.N.P.A., it was further alleged, had helped producers secure price advances. The A.N.P.A. replied stoutly to these charges (February 24), asserting that the guild document was "slanted" and that the summary, which had been widely distributed, "draws conclusions which are not based on facts." Evidence of collusion to curtail production was denied, and the antitrust laws were pointed to as a barrier against A.N.P.A. advice to publishers on price matters. As for helping producers to get higher prices, this had been a wartime measure designed to provide the mills with sufficient income to dissuade them from converting production to more lucrative grades of paper.

Sam P. Eubanks rebutted this rebuttal on behalf of the guild (March 26), arguing A.N.P.A. indifference to the fact that large newsprint mill capacity remained idle, with no indication that it would be activated in time to prevent recurrent shortages, and charging that the association was more sensitive to the position of the Canadian producers than to domestic efforts at regulation. At its convention (June 27 to

July 1) the guild, charging that although "'tightly controlled distribution gives newsprint manufacturers the power of life and death over newspapers,'" the A.N.P.A. and "'other industrial trade associations, for unpublicized reasons, have failed to take action looking toward release of newspapers from subservience to the newsprint producers,'" called upon Congress to "'conduct an investigation of newsprint prices and newsprint manufacturing profits; and upon the attorney-general of the United States to reactivate antitrust proceedings against the price-fixing corporations dominating the newsprint market; and upon the several agencies of government to initiate projects that will insure the early development of the forest resources of Alaska as a perpetual source of substantial quantities of newsprint.'" [40]

With the mid-year, increasing productive capacity combined with the likelihood that the current "readjustment" might turn into a "recession" to suggest the possibility that the price reductions which had occurred in the wood pulp market might extend themselves to newsprint. By July the spot market had "collapsed," odd lots were obtainable at prices below contract levels, and a Toronto investment house had issued a brochure, *Newsprint Price Outlook,* representing "the thinking of manufacturers and others in the industry," advancing arguments why price should be kept steady. This volume argued that many United States consumers, thanks to Canadian production efforts, which had destroyed the spot market, were already "paying considerably less for their supply than a year or so ago"; it suggested that since the price of newsprint had risen less rapidly than those of commodities in general, it could "logically" be expected to trail them on the down-curve as well; it pointed up the inconsistency of consumers in at once demanding expensive expansion of capacity and lower prices; it noted that newsprint was currently being made from wood cut a year earlier at the "highest costs on record"; and it warned somewhat indefinitely that "consumers might well lose more than they could gain" if prices dropped.[41]

Devaluation of the Canadian dollar in September introduced a new variable into the price equation and furnished much food for comment during the autumn; its general effect, however, was to improve the position of Canadian producers while leaving United States costs unchanged. Devaluation, to the extent of 10 per cent, occurred on September 19. This action followed a pattern already developed by Great Britain and several continental countries and was designed in general to stimulate a trade revival between sterling and dollar areas and in particular to obtain more United States dollars. It naturally occurred to publishers that some of these benefits might be passed along in the form of a price reduction.

Cranston Williams, promptly noting (September 20) that the mills had raised the price by $6.80 following revaluation in 1946, inquired about the prospects of their " 'passing on to their U.S. customers the $10.00 saving which they obtain from their revaluation of the Canadian dollar.' " Such a query contained elements of embarrassment, since failure to reduce prices would subject the mills to charges of riding dollar horses traveling in opposite directions. By the same token, however, price reduction would negate the objective of trade stimulation upon which the action had been based. Manufacturers were equally prompt in deciding not to cut price, Abitibi's notice to customers neatly avoiding the dilemma by stating that the action of 1946 " 'occurred at a time when newsprint price had been artificially restrained by government and when not only the change in Canadian exchange but all other factors clearly and urgently called for upward price revision. Today widespread currency devaluation threatens to jeopardize all of our overseas markets and will undoubtedly affect manufacturing costs to an extent not now ascertainable. Accordingly we are not taking any price action.' "

Several newsprint-connected Canadians likewise hastened to point out that the devaluation made no difference in the dollar cost of paper to United States publishers. It was also argued that devaluation would be of little value to Canadians, since they would have to pay more of their cheaper dollars for such items as sulphur, coal, and freight; the total situation, indeed, might deteriorate under devaluation, in view of the likelihood that Britain would reduce purchases of Canadian paper, which might glut the United States market and so depress prices in the future. For the moment, however, until mill capacity showed signs of greatly outstripping the steady demand, there seemed no call for action. In the light of this situation, the manufacturers, apparently watched sharply by the Ottawa authorities, resisted pressure brought to bear upon them at the annual session with publishers held at Quebec in October, and 1949 ended with prices stable and all hands apprehensive about the future.[42]

This chapter has chronicled a postwar period during which fairly rapid removal of wartime controls, followed by a sharp imbalance of supply and demand, left the larger and contract-protected consumers in fairly good case, but subjected the small fry, hitherto protected by L-240, at the mercy of almost astronomically high spot market prices. This situation spawned a rash of investigations by both the Executive and Legislative Branches. The Department of Justice attack on alleged restrictive practices was inconclusive as to monopoly but produced sharp antagonisms; the work of two congressional committees produced considerable information and made some contribution to the relief of the small papers. None sufficed to relieve the tight situation of supply and demand, which obtained until the final year of the period 1946 to 1949, when they stood in virtual equilibrium without solving any of the real problems involved.

The Canadian industry ended the period in good position to expand conservatively. So far, this approach had been adequate, but succeeding years would indicate its dubious effectiveness in a time of sudden and unexpected demand. On the other hand, United States production was beginning the long slow upward climb which would tend to ameliorate matters. Alaska was considered briefly as a possible source of supply, but no action was taken in the face of heavy costs and unwillingness of either producers or publishers to risk the required capital investment. The period was marked by two manipulations of the Canadian dollar, both of which operated to the advantage of Dominion producers, under circumstances to which the United States consumer could hardly object too strenuously. On the whole, producer-consumer relations were less good than in 1946.

CHAPTER V

The Fifties, First Phase

THE NEW decade opened with the industry both north and south of the border in essentially good position. To the north conservative expansion policies, plus generally high-level operation at good profits, had enabled the mills to consolidate their economic position. Repeated references to conservative expansion policies should not lead to the conclusion that no expansion was taking place; machine speed-ups and new techniques had long been in evidence, and their continued application during the years 1950 to 1955 would increase Canadian production by a total of 17 per cent at an annual average (1950 to 1954) of about 175,000 tons. To the south the tide had turned from a production of 826,000 tons in 1947 to one of just over 1,000,000 tons in 1950; this would be followed by a slow but steady, and percentagewise a very great, increase of 53 per cent by the end of 1955. Neither northern nor southern production, however, sufficed to meet the insatiable demand, and its upsurges, inadequately foreseen by both producer and consumer, gave publishers qualms; their expression opened old sores. A renewal of particularly vigorous investigation in 1950, directed once more toward the monopoly aspects of the problem, did little to assuage these injuries. And finally, wartime conditions created by the Korean crisis had important repercussions on both the domestic and international aspects of the newsprint problem.[1]

Matters moved slowly in early 1950, but soon quickened until the year became one of the most active in recent times. The near-equilibrium of supply and demand made for a quiet market in the first quarter, with Canadian overseas shipments dropping off and with production 35,000 tons below the 1949 level. A sudden upsurge of advertising linage, however, soon brought consumption back to a high point, and the spring months found the Canadian mills operating at or above capacity, a condition which obtained throughout the remainder of the year, so that total production was 102,000 tons (2 per cent) above that of 1949. More remarkable, however, was the increase in United States output, which, boosted considerably by the Coosa River tonnage, exceeded the Canadian figures both percentagewise (11½ per cent) and tonnagewise (104,000).[2] A mild slump in consumption in the early year was counteracted by the emerging Korean crisis, which brought emergency defense problems to the fore. Presently, too, another investigation got under way. All in all, it was an interesting year.

Impetus to investigation developed in January after the sale of the *New York Sun* had inspired Sam G. Eubanks of the American Newspaper Guild to send a telegram, which he followed to Washington for an interview with Emanuel Celler, Chairman of the House Committee on the Judiciary, at which Eubanks demanded a congressional inquiry into the activities of producers whose "'monopolistic control,'" he alleged, was "'a major factor in destruction of newspaper properties.'" At his press conference on January 24, Celler was quoted as saying that the price of newsprint had been "'jacked up'" and that the government should not stand for such "'monkey business.'"

His remarks reportedly leaned heavily on the American Newspaper Guild pamphlet to which reference has been made above. The Canadian reaction was swift and hostile, Premier Duplessis denying the existence of a newsprint cartel, and Fowler retorting sharply (January 25), followed by a restrained letter (of February 28) inviting the Celler Committee to follow the example of the Boren and Brown Committees in traveling to Canada to learn about matters at first hand. Celler was quoted in the press (of February 11) as charging that " ' "This Canadian monopoly works hand-in-glove with a number of American paper and pulp companies. . . ." ' " His somewhat casual reply to Fowler's invitation, indicating that his committee would " 'approach the subject from a perspective not hitherto employed,' " was issued only after he had announced (February 18) presidential authorization to proceed with inquiry into newsprint matters, but had decided first to study the steel indusry. Matters then rested for some weeks.[3]

By early April, just as demand was beginning to freshen after a slow first quarter, the A.N.P.A. began exerting pressure for increased North American production. Cranston Williams, asserting (April 8) that there was nothing to indicate that demand had reached its peak, urged development of new resources in the United States south, and commented on encouraging prospects that Canadian expansion might move away from the current postwar policy of speed-ups and in the direction of new mills. *Editor & Publisher* editorialized fearfully (also on April 8) as to what might happen if overseas purchasers, now kept out of the Canadian market by dollar shortages, suddenly found themselves possessed of viable funds. This was the first of repeated pleas for increasing domestic manufacturing capacity. The A.N.P.A.'s annual convention discussed (April 26) the dangerous situation which would obtain if a free market, with its consequent pressures on inadequate supply, should suddenly appear. Clearly, a general sensitiveness to the matter of supply was developing.[4]

The most vocal concern over this question, however, came, not from A.N.P.A., but from the Inland Daily Press Association. At its Chicago meeting late in May it expressed its fears through a letter addressed to Fowler by its President posing several direct and provocative questions. The questions stemmed from the fact that, with non-dollar countries already inquiring about supplies for the immediate future, Canada might be tempted to turn from the United States to overseas markets, and included the following:

" '1. Will contracts with U.S. publishers and jobbers be honored before overseas commitments which may now be in abeyance are reinstated?

" '2. What immediate plans have the Canadian mills made to take care of both the increased newsprint demand which has developed this year in the United States, and the probable return of some of the overseas market in the second half of 1950 and 1951?

" '3. What long range plans have the Canadian mills made to take care of increased demand due to the growth in population and the aggressive selling campaign by newspapers?' "

This fairly pugnacious approach drew from Fowler a long analysis of recent and current developments which deserves recapitulation at some length as a prelude to the Celler hearings which were about to open.[5] While bristling at the insinuation that newsprint difficulties were attributable to Canadian failures, Fowler counseled a " 'sincere mutual effort' " to avoid the harm that would result from this conclusion. Admitting that relations between producers and consumers had recently deteriorated to a point where public attention was being called to a renewed "feud," he insisted that the only evidence of such had arisen south of the border. He cited the

As the mixture of groundwood and chemical pulp travels along this moving wire screen, water is drawn out by gravity and suction. The sheet of paper is formed by the time the pulp reaches the end of the wire. The dryer section is in the background.

The press section picks up the wet sheet of newsprint from the wire, squeezes out moisture, and passes it into the dryer section.

forthcoming Celler Committee investigation, charging that the Chairman had " 'followed the strangely unjudicial course of making accusations and pronouncing his verdict before hearing any evidence.' " He went on to assert that *Editor & Publisher* had recently attacked the Canadian newsprint industry in a " 'series of false statements' " which the Toronto *Financial Post* had characterized as " ' "one of the most vicious and distorted smear campaigns we have seen in a long time." ' " Finally, he charged that the A.N.P.A.'s criticism of Canadian failure to build any new mills since 1938 begged the question of the great capacity increase achieved by speed-up processes and overemphasized the modest expansion of United States production. He compared current accusations of Canadian remissness with similar charges bandied about in 1943 and 1944, and insisted that one set was as baseless as the other. He concluded that the solution of the problem demanded " 'intelligent cooperation of both our industries and is only impeded by an atmosphere which American sources are again creating.' "

Going on to answer the specific queries posed by Inland, he pointed to drastic reductions in Canadian overseas sales, and promised that Canadian commitments to United States purchasers would be honored in advance of overseas obligations. He pointed out in reply to the second question that concerted *planning* on an industry-wide basis was no more legal in Canada than in the United States, and then asked: " 'Do you mean to suggest that there could, or should, have been "plans" by Canadian mills "to take care of the increased newsprint demand which has developed this year in the United States?" I am sure you know that increased newsprint production even by the method of speeding up machines . . . requires large capital investments and considerable time. In the last six or eight months Canadian producers have been bombarded by U.S. publishers with protests against the present price of newsprint which, apart from all other considerations, would have made any sensible manufacturer hesitate in embarking on new, heavy capital expenditures. These protests, taken at their face value, would make anyone think that American publishers would rather have lower prices than new capacity. You certainly can't have both.' "

He pointed to the fact that at the Quebec conference of the previous autumn the Canadians estimated United States demand in figures which were not disputed by their publisher opposite-numbers, but which failed to meet the current upsurge. Tailoring their production to the modest orders of the early year had resulted in loss of irrecoverable tonnage. Finally addressing himself to the long-range aspect of affairs, he hedged again about making official predictions, but gave it as his impression that manufacturers would be helped by firmer knowledge of what publishers themselves were planning and what needs they themselves predicted; while insisting that United States consumers ought to be better prepared to forecast their own needs than outsiders, he somewhat slyly pointed out that the A.N.P.A.'s 1948 prediction of 1960 needs had already been exceeded. He concluded this section of his document by estimating that, given steady demand, there was no " 'technical reason' " why Canada could not continue for " 'a good many years' " to increase production by annual increments of 200,000 tons, relying wholly on higher machine speeds and entirely apart from building either new machines or new mills.

In reply to a final request for " 'any other information' " he might think pertinent, he dealt with three matters. In the area of capacity expansion, he pointed to Canadian addition of 600,000 tons' capacity since 1946, which had " 'been the salvation of U.S. newsprint consumers. . . .' " He then reprinted a statement from *Editor & Publisher* of May 13 demanding more United States production and concluding: " ' "The Canadian manufacturers show no inclination to build any more [mills]. They intend to keep the publishers in a tight situation" ' "; and citing other statements indicative of departure from early postwar amicability.

On production performance he suggested that Canadian expansion in the previous four years was the equivalent of six new mills of the caliber of the Coosa River development. Dealing gingerly with the price question, he noted recent publishers' demands for reductions and, referring to repeated claims that Canadians were keeping prices high, he stated " 'flatly' " that such accusations " 'are not based on fact,' " and intimated that " 'they constitute a form of self-delusion on the part of the U.S. publishers which is likely to impede them rather than assist, in coping with their acknowledged difficulties.' " He noted that the price had not only not spiraled, as had other commodity prices, but for two years had remained level or, in fact decreased, due to greater production in relation to demand, which had avoided a repetition of the astronomical spot market prices of 1946 to 1948.

Concluding that producer-consumer relationships had not been " 'sensible or reasonable' " except for the early war years and another " 'encouraging interval from about 1945 to the beginning of this year,' " he proposed a " 'conscious, mutual effort to recapture the understanding cooperation that existed between U.S. publishers and Canadian newsprint manufacturers from 1945 to 1949, which has been slipping from our grasp in recent months. This attempt would be no impractical pursuit of an ideal, but would be in the sound, best interests of both industries. It can be of no value to a Canadian manufacturer to have criticism and suspicion from his largest market. It must be equally undesirable for a publisher in the United States to have indignation and resentment developing in his principal source of newsprint supply.

And these attitudes on both sides of the border are so unnecessary.' " Following this eloquent plea and defense, he declined (June 12) to testify before the Celler Committee, which was at last preparing to hold its hearings.[6]

These opened on June 19. Three days earlier the Chairman's news release pointed to previous investigations growing out of recurring shortages, accused foreign governments of "attempting to maintain the price and keep down the supply," and keyed his investigation to an " 'attempt to determine whether present or threatened shortages result from any violation of existing antitrust laws or any world-wide cartels.' " This of course indicated a new tack in the investigatory process, since previous committees had addressed themselves to such matters as price and supply; previous approaches through the avenue of monopoly had been made by the Executive Department of the government. In his introductory remarks on the opening day he gave the committee's objective as one of finding out whether a shortage presently existed, and if so, what its causes might be. He confided his own doubts as to whether, if monopoly existed, it would be susceptible of excision by the domestic antitrust laws, and insisted that his group was "not trying to prove a case. It is trying to ascertain the facts." [7]

Representatives of the publishers figured in most of the first day's testimony, inaugurated by John H. Perry, President of the Western Newspaper Union, Cranston Williams of the A.N.P.A., and William F. Canfield, Secretary-Manager of the Inland Daily Press Association. Their discussion ranged widely over historical matters in the newsprint industry, pricing and supply problems, and the contract practices which had developed in the postwar period. Neither Perry nor Williams approached the monopoly matter in great detail, but committee members drew Canfield into the field, albeit reluctantly and somewhat evasively. He denied that his association believed there was "a lack of competition between newsprint producers," and repeatedly refused opportunities to express a personal conviction that monopoly existed. Under urging he did admit, however, the "possibility" that his constituents might be fearful of reprisals by their suppliers if they testified to such a situation. His principal real affirmation was a belief that zone-pricing eliminated one "very strong . . . element of competition. . . ." In the course of his uncomfortable experience he admitted that he had been disinclined to testify, but insisted that this was because he believed he had little to contribute to the committee's study.[8]

The principal testimony of June 21 was given by Professor John A. Guthrie of the State College of Washington, whose studies gave little support to those searching for monopoly in newsprint. He stated: "The record of prices and profits in newsprint does not, in my opinion, bear out the charge that producers have, over the years, exercised an undue amount of monopoly power. Because of the very nature of the newsprint industry fewness of firms is not undesirable, but rather it contributes to the achievement of greater efficiency and stability and lower costs and prices." Pressed for a definition of "undue monopoly," he agreed that the large mills had apparently gotten together to fix prices, using a zone arrangement "which, in part, restricts competition. But I do not feel that there has been any unusual amount of that. I don't think in an industry of this type you can get away from attempts of that kind completely." He felt, moreover, that in an industry such as newsprint "too much price competition" was undesirable. He concluded that "there is no monopoly on newsprint manufacture in the United States. It has not been brought out." [9]

Hearings continued with considerable regularity through

June 30, at which time Chairman Celler reported publicly his "tentative findings." Exigencies of space compel summary report of the hundreds of pages of testimony gathered during this period. Monopoly (with consequent results in uniform pricing practices) and supply furnish the chief threads, with considerable emphasis on ways and means of persuading the Canadians to increase their output; this was the case, though one of Celler's gambits would hardly have contributed to this result. On June 21, in examining a representative of the Tariff Commission, he called attention to Section 337 of the Hawley-Smoot Act of 1930, which provided penalties when the President found " 'unfair acts in the importation of articles into the United States or in their sale,' " and conferred investigatory powers on the Tariff Commission. The Tariff Commission man admitted that his agency had taken no action since 1947, when Judge Goddard had "called attention to certain unfair trade practices of the Canadian manufacturers. . . ." This led Congressman Celler to exclaim: "I do not know how to characterize that inattention or laxity on the part of the Tariff Commission," and to report the matter to the President. Failure of the Executive to take action is perhaps explainable by the fact that the penalty under the Hawley-Smoot Act was exclusion of the commodity in question.[10]

Despite strenuous efforts on the part of committee and counsel, the grist of evidence on monopoly was conflicting and indecisive. The reader of the testimony comes away with a feeling of unreality, due to the fact that the committee failed to elicit evidence that would prove either the existence or nonexistence of monopolistic practices on the part of Canadian firms selling in the United States. The argument in favor of the existence of such monopoly could not be established from the documents, since these were withheld from committee scrutiny. It was therefore compelled to rely largely, aside from a few assertive statements not backed by evidence, on an argument by analogy, spending a great deal of time and energy endeavoring to prove that common pricing prevailed in Canadian operations in other areas, with particular emphasis upon the so-called "Seven Suppliers" agreement for sales in Australasia; the inference, of course, was that if such policies prevailed in one quarter they did also in another. Some attention was also given to the matter of the "common directorate," in which directors of two newsprint companies served on the board of a third, non-newsprint concern, as a possible "loophole through which otherwise offenders of the antitrust laws might crawl. . . ." On the whole, however, little of a positive nature was developed.[11]

On the other hand, both publishers and manufacturers denied monopoly. Congressman Brown, an old hand at investigation and also a newspaper publisher, told the committee (June 22) that though he was "not naive enough to believe that the manufacturers of any given commodity don't at least cock a weather-eye toward their competitors to see what they are doing. . . . I think that there is no more collusion in newsprint sales than there is in selling shirts or coffee, or anything else. . . ." Charles E. Moreau, spokesman of the small papers, insisted that if a monopoly existed, "it is certainly the strangest that a congressional committee has ever investigated. . . . I doubt if there is actual collusion between the companies to fix prices and control production. I think it is more likely that the smaller companies simply follow the larger in price and other policies. . . ."

Manufacturers' spokesmen, representing Bowater, International, Crown Zellerbach, and Southland, all but the last operating on both sides of the international boundary, unitedly and vociferously insisted that the industry was fiercely competitive. One of the clearest expositions of this viewpoint was that of Archibald R. Graustein, former President of International and currently counsel for Bowater: "It has been said that the prices are fixed by agreement or are 'administered.' . . . I cannot speak from personal experience in the case of most commodities. But . . . I do know that in normal circumstances uniform prices, or substantially uniform prices, can be the result, not of agreement or conspiracy, but the reverse, the result of competition. . . . The bigger the publisher the more insistent he is on paying no more than his competitor. . . ." And James D. Zellerbach pointed out that "As a practical matter, it is impossible for us to maintain a price in excess of our competitors. Our publisher customers are aggressive and well-informed. They see no reason to pay us any more for newsprint than our competitors charge. . . . The reverse of this situation is also true. We see no reason to take a lower price than our competitors, for the quality of our product is as good as theirs. . . ."[12]

Testimony on supply was also conflicting. The Chairman indicated his belief that since "Canada seems to be the only source of real supply," the problem was one of influencing the Dominion mills to greater production, giving it as his judgment that "there is not the assumption of a proper social responsibility . . . on the part of the Canadian industry to provide newsprint for a hungry world." Moreau, on the other hand, believed that the solution lay in construction of mills in the United States to a point where the industry would again become competitive, forcing Canadian construction of new facilities as an alternative to loss of standing in the United States market. Graustein and John H. Hinman, President of International, adduced historical reasons for Canadian reluctance to expand rapidly in the face of a sudden demand such as characterized the current state of affairs. Graustein, moreover, suggested: "They have no duty to us to increase their supply to us if they do not think it in their interest to do so. . . ." And he voiced the conviction that if they concluded adversely on expansion, domestic production could be increased to fill the void. Hinman was confident that stabilization of demand would bring Canadian risk capital into the field for construction of new mills.

One of the few publisher witnesses, Robert L. Smith of the *Los Angeles Daily News*, declared forthrightly that governmental attacks on manufacturers under the antitrust laws had "had a tendency to worsen rather than better the entire situation. . . ." It was his contention that continued uncertainty as to the industry's legal position was responsible for reluctance of risk capital to enter the field, and suggested the desirability of a sort of declaratory judgment procedure on the part of the Department of Justice and the Federal Trade Commission.[13]

At the close of this somewhat inconclusive testimony, Celler delivered (June 30) what he denominated some personal and tentative observations. He took as his basic premise the belief that a competitive situation was essential for the existence of "an adequate and healthy industry for newsprint to supply the needs of this country. . . ." This, in his judgment, did not currently obtain because of certain "troublesome situations" affecting the domestic market. He detailed these sore spots as: a. tie-in contracts according to which the price charged by a particular mill depended upon the average price charged by specified competitors; b. the zone-pricing system; c. coercion of one mill by others on price matters; d. apparent resale price maintenance by the mills; e. long-term contracts. He complained further that firms which claimed to be "hotly competitive" in the United States market operated cooperatively in other areas and that Canadian concerns operating in the United States were able to prevent American examination of their business records; he concluded that the remedy seemed to be increased domestic manufacture. Later in the day he told reporters that it might be necessary to subpoena publishers in order to obtain their point of view.[14]

Further hearings in July produced statements tending to counter some of Celler's tentative conclusions, to emphasize previous denials of price-fixing among manufacturers, and to point up reluctance of publishers to go on record. Prominent among the witnesses was James D. Zellerbach, whose testimony pungently pointed out that while governmental agencies were at perfect liberty to investigate any branch of American business, the expense, time, and uncertainties involved did not conduce to expansion of domestic production of newsprint. On behalf of his company he vigorously denied collusive price-setting, as did Albin R. Caspar of Great Northern—though counsel for the committee brought out somewhat damaging evidence (referred to above) concerning Crown Zellerbach's participation, with other west coast firms, in the proceedings of 1937 leading to the plea of *nolo contendere*.

Celler indicated his own clear belief that publishers were reluctant to testify "because of fear, fancied or actual, of reprisals. We have been up against it to get anybody to come in here to testify as to conditions surrounding the newsprint industry where they are users of newsprint." This was echoed by another committee member who inquired of publishers in order to enlighten his own ignorance, but "could not get one of them to say aye or nay. I do not know why. . . ." On the other hand, Zellerbach denied that his concern would make reprisals, and insisted that he had told Smith to " 'say anything you damn want to say. . . .' "[15]

These lengthy hearings failed to produce conclusive evidence of monopolistic activity on the part of producers, and they were marked by considerable consumer resistance to being drawn into the controversy. The refusal of Canadian

International to be interrogated elicited Celler's personal judgment that legislation should be enacted making foreign corporations doing business in the United States amenable to judicial and congressional processes. Canadian reflections on the episode were reasonably severe, an Ottawa dispatch to the *Paper Trade Journal* asserting that charges that the Canadian industry was curtailing supplies were " 'flatly contradicted. . . .' " The chief concrete result, it was pointed out, was the impression that Canadian dependence on the United States market should be lessened by increasing shipments to other quarters. The *Paper Trade Journal* made uncomplimentary comments upon several of the contentions urged against the Canadian producers, and concluded in favor of a continuation of the present reasonably satisfactory approach to the whole problem.

Meantime the A.N.P.A., as represented by a speech of Cranston Williams at Roanoke, Virginia (July 21, after the outbreak of Korean hostilities), admitted that publishers had contributed to existing difficulties by failing to estimate their needs adequately, and he urged that the problem now was to make proper use of existing supplies rather than push for new production—there being at best a two-year lag between ground-breaking for a new mill and actual production of paper. At the end of August he was congratulating the Canadian mills for their "superhuman effort" to continue production during a railroad strike which decimated shipments and vastly overstrained Canadian storage facilities.[16]

Korean hostilities erupted in late June, in the later stages of the Celler investigation. These found Celler, presently the leading public figure concerned with newsprint matters, still asserting his belief that the Canadian industry was organized and operating under " 'cartel-like' " agreements. He announced the shelving of his investigatory functions for the duration, but indicated that he was preparing a legislative approach to the secretiveness of Canadian producers via a bill compelling foreign corporations to submit to examination of their records as a condition precedent to operations in the United States. He likewise predicted that defense exigencies would lead to government allocation (rationing) of newsprint at an early date, a position which alarmed publishers who had been allowed a considerable degree of self-management during World War II.

There followed a period of uncertainty during which Congress passed the Defense Production Act of 1950, under which by mid-September had been established a committee representing the pulp, paper, and paperboard industry to be advisory to the Secretary of Commerce in the implementation of the law. The act permitted establishment of priorities, allocations, and wage and price controls, and authorized the establishment of incentive programs to encourage increased production in defense-connected industries which were to have a profound influence on expansion of the domestic newsprint industry. An aftermath of the legislation, also important in future months, was a renewal and elaboration of the Hyde Park Agreement of 1941, signed on October 26, 1950, according to which promises were made to gear the two defense economies together by consultation and joint action in the establishment of controls over scarce defense materials such as newsprint. During a period of waiting, Fowler, in addressing a Canadian papermakers' meeting, urged maintenance of friendly Canadian-American relations during the crisis, and pronounced Celler's suggestions of an independent United States industry to be not only impossible but unrealistic.[17]

Two price-connected matters enlivened this period of tentative relations between government and industry. Spurred by a high level of United Kingdom and continental expenditure of economic aid funds in Canada during recent months, a condition which Korean hostilities would be likely to extend indefinitely, the Canadian dollar had appreciated greatly in value. It was no surprise, then, when the Canadian authorities announced that on October 2 the dollar would be revalued—that is, be allowed to find its market level in relation to the United States dollar. This in effect repealed the 10 per cent cut in effect since September, 1949, and the Canadian papermakers were confronted with the problem of how to adjust to this development. As in the revaluation following the war, this was of course injurious to producers of paper, reducing the exchange advantage they had enjoyed since the devaluation of 1949, and encouraging thoughts of price increases which had recently been circulating within the industry. These thoughts were rather promptly implemented when Powell River, not normally a price leader, announced a $10 increase (effective October 16). Abitibi and other mills followed more or less promptly. After a confused period, and following the lead of International, most firms on both sides of the border contented themselves with a $6 increase, effective at various times in November, 1950, though there were occasional deviations from this general level.[18]

The price action stimulated Congressman Celler to propose several remedies. He wrote the Attorney General urging antitrust action against the United States mills if they followed the Canadian example; he proposed to reopen his committee investigation; he talked again of introducing his bill to compel foreign corporations to submit to examination of records prior to receiving permission to operate within the United States; and he threatened to appeal to the President to use his powers under the Defense Production Act to roll back prices in case of a general increase.

By mid-November Canadian reaction to these and other United States developments had crystallized to the point where a reasoned statement in rebuttal was dispatched to the *Paper Trade Journal*. It took off from an earlier proposition that Canadian producers, too dependent upon the United States, should begin diversifying their exports "and not lean almost completely on the vagaries of the United States market," in the face of repeated criticism on grounds of monopoly and price exactions. Attention was called to the burdensome 8 per cent Dominion sales tax; the "insinuation" that an "evil combine" characterized the Canadian industry was denied; current production at over 100 per cent of rated capacity at a level 600,000 tons a year above the wartime figures was noted, as was the fact that wage increases had raised costs appreciably. Finally, it was asserted vigorously that the pattern of similar and concurrent price increases denoted competition rather than combination, concluding that in "any old major industry in Canada, producers are faced with the same problems and use the same methods of solution on prices as in the long-established newsprint industry, though generally less criticisms are heard because of similarity of prices."

The year ended on a note of uncertainty, with the Korean episode unresolved, with defense machinery in process of elaboration, with price temporarily stabilized but at a level which brought continued Canadian complaints of insufficiency, with consumption at a high level, and with supply momentarily fairly adequate but with considerable fears for the future. As events were to prove, 1950 would mark the end of one postwar period of rapid consumption increases. The year 1951 would be marked by entry of the publishing industry into a period of more modest consumption demands, lasting through 1954, in which the needs of the metropolitan press, to the fore in recent years, would be exceeded by those of the small and medium-sized papers. The year, too, would be a year of continued investigation in which the establishment of a new inquiry would accompany reports of previous groups. Its chief problems, however, would be war-connected, and would center around shortage of critical raw materials and complicated maneuvers in the area of price. These facts, however, were not apparent as one year merged into another, and all hands viewed the future with some trepidation.[19]

The new year, 1951, opened on a note of concern over the possibility of a short supply, with its inevitable concomitant of price uncertainty, complicated in turn by possible shortages in essential raw materials—a possibility amply documented by subsequent events. Canadian producers, early in January, were reportedly without definite plans for long-run expansion, partly on the ground that publishers had not as yet developed any techniques for estimating their own future needs. By mid-month Fowler was warning the New York State Publishers' Association that price and distribution controls might appear, with consequent diminution in supply. Backstage he had evidently already been involved in discussions on questions of price and of controls with Michael V. DiSalle of the United States Office of Price Stabilization (OPS); he had apparently promised to notify DiSalle of any Canadian proposal for price increases in time for intergovernmental discussions prior to their imposition. On January 26 the Economic Stabilization Administration (ESA) froze wages and prices in the United States at the highest point they had reached during the base period December 19, 1950 to January 25, 1951, with the undoubted object of preventing generally spiraling prices. This action was taken in the face of considerable demand in the United States for imposition of controls and against the opposition of Canadian participants in the recent discussions.[20]

By early February prospective shortages of newsprint and raw materials had stimulated talk of rationing. Rationing was discounted in high quarters of the government and opposed in publishing circles, where it was felt that the industry might handle its own problems if a way could be found to prevent jobbers from diverting supplies into the spot market; if policing proved necessary, revival of L-240 was preferable to imposition of a real rationing policy.[21] Congressional interest in newsprint, as measured by committee activity, continued high. The House Committee on Interstate and Foreign Commerce heard witnesses on February 7 and 8, by which time one of its members, Lindley Beckworth, had already introduced (February 5) a resolution directing the committee to investigate "actual and contemplated action affecting production or consumption of newsprint. . . ." This was passed in March and resulted eventually in the establishment of a subcommittee headed by Beckworth with functions essentially similar to those performed earlier by the Boren and Brown Committees. On February 2, Senator John J. Sparkman announced that the Senate Small Business Committee would set up a subcommittee, to be headed by Hubert Humphrey of Minnesota, to study the problem of shortages; and on March 6 the House empowered the Celler Committee to continue its investigations. Clearly, the newsprint problem was not to be neglected.[22]

A price flurry occurred on March 6, when Federal Price Administrator DiSalle announced that newsprint was subject to a ceiling price of $106, which would be maintained. Then, in an apparently off-the-cuff statement, he let it be understood that Canadian manufacturers had agreed to this arrangement, which they would assist in enforcing, and that they also understood that failure to hold this price line would result in retaliatory increases in the price of goods exported to Canada from the United States. No direct Canadian reply to this statement has come to the writer's attention, but on April 25, Fowler, speaking before the A.N.P.A. as a representative of the Newsprint Association of Canada, took occasion to vary the tenor of an otherwise friendly and conciliatory address to point out that a government-enforced price ceiling in the United States would operate to void all publishers' contracts with Canadian mills.

With a meeting of a committee of the International Materials Conference scheduled, within a week, to consider needs of newsprint-starved nations, no blueprint was needed to make clear that, once Canadian manufacturers were freed from their contractual obligations in the United States, they could dispose of their product abroad at higher prices than they were then receiving. In view of the fact that Fowler presently entered government service as Director of the Pulp and Paper Materials Branch of the Canadian Defense Production Department, it was inferred in some quarters that his remarks carried a government imprimatur; this gave rise to a question in Parliament, to which Defense Minister C. D. Howe replied that the Fowler address to the A.N.P.A. was made as President of the Newsprint Association of Canada and not as a Dominion official.[23]

The first fruits of congressional interest appeared in a preliminary report by the Humphrey subcommittee. When first established, this group had decided that, instead of embarking promptly upon investigations of its own, it would begin its procedures by studying the voluminous evidence already in the record. The result, announced on May 5, was therefore a distillation of much of the story previously narrated in the present account, resulting in development of certain conclusions. The report admitted frankly that the question of current shortages might be argued in terms of either supply or demand, an argument "as futile as trying to decide whether a size 9 foot is too large for a size 7 shoe, or whether the shoe is too small for the foot. . . ." The committee's momentary concern was therefore to be with determining "how the demand arises, where the supply comes from, and what means are available to reduce the demand or increase the supply," leaving aside for the present the question of implementing means to either of these ends. No good end would be served by reiterating the entire story in the committee's words, since these added little or nothing.

Certain summaries, however, approached sufficiently close to judgments to be worth recounting here. One of these stated in unequivocal language that the evidence submitted to the Celler Committee "was overwhelmingly convincing that newsprint prices were set by collusive agreement between the mills. . . ." Further reliance was placed upon these hearings to support the conclusion that "there is little likelihood that the industry will itself engage in any substantial expansion of productive capacity unless faced with the threat of competition from another source. . . ." The most likely areas for such developments were held to be Alaska and the southern United States, but the opening of operations in these areas seemed unlikely without governmental assistance.

The report concluded by stating the problem in terms legal, economic, and social, and summarizing the suggestions so far made toward its solution. The legal problem, that of dealing with alleged monopoly, was complicated by the foreign location of the bulk of the industry, and seemed an insoluble one. The economic problem was one of persuading manufacturers to cease their flight from newsprint production, of assembling the enormous amounts of risk capital necessary to expand the industry, and of preserving the small

Each of these two giant paper machines can turn out one mile of newsprint more than twenty feet wide every two minutes. In the foreground, the finished, calendered paper is being built up on reels. Behind the calender stack are three large dryer sections (covered by an aluminum hood).

fry of the publishing business in competition with their larger contemporaries. This introduced the social questions of the value of newspapers as against other business enterprises, and of the importance of preserving the small-fry press in an era of increasing consolidation.

There followed a formidable list of thirty-five suggestions for solving these various problems (entirely too long for even summary treatment here). The report concluded by inviting comment on proposed solutions of the problem of equitable distribution of existing supplies, on increasing domestic production, on the possibilities in utilization of new materials and techniques, and on preventing the recurrent shortages which had historically plagued consumers. This was to be the last word from the committee until September, when it was heard from in the form of a questionnaire inquiring from 14,000 publishers as to the price and availability of their raw material.[24]

Mr. Celler, not to be outdone by Senator Humphrey, announced on May 5 that his committee was issuing a "rough copy" of its proposed report on the long investigation of the previous year; this formidable document was formally released on May 28. Its summaries and conclusions dealt with many of the matters already examined in the discussion of the committee's hearings, and a brief recapitulation, emphasizing recommendations, must suffice at this point. It was found necessary to admit that although shortages had prejudiced newspaper publication, they had contributed but little to the actual discontinuance of individual papers: "There is evidence to indicate that newsprint shortages were to at least a slight extent responsible for discontinuance during 1949 of a few newspapers." Criticism was leveled at contract provisions containing end-use restrictions designed to prevent leakage of paper into the spot market; such practices, it was charged, were being carried to such lengths as to constitute attempts to limit the freedom of publishers in the use of their paper.

In spite of testimony to the effect that uniform prices might come from competition rather than collusion, considerable attention was devoted to factors which might have a pernicious influence on price matters, including the zone-pricing system, alleged Canadian efforts at price-setting in markets other than the United States, efforts on the part of Canadian provincial authorities to interfere in price matters on behalf of their own producers, and efforts on the part of the industry to stabilize prices against cuts in time of depression and against undue increases in times of boom. While admitting, as did most of the witnesses appearing before it, that the latter policy had operated to the advantage of publishers, the committee criticized it as a deterrent to the building of new mills on both sides of the border. The committee called further attention to the barrier between Canadian firms and United States judicial process posed by Ontario's Business Records Protection Act; and the efficacy of this barrier in protecting Canadian producers (albeit subsidiaries of United States concerns) from the probing fingers of the antitrust acts was noted unfavorably.

In conclusion, the committee, believing it to be important "that the antitrust laws be vigorously enforced against Canadian as well as American newsprint producers in order to protect the freedom of interstate and foreign commerce," recommended specifically that the Department of Justice should study its report for evidence on "possible agreements fixing prices and allocating markets . . ."; and that the Federal Trade Commission study statistical exchanges between United States, Canadian, and Scandinavian producers' trade associations for evidence of monopolistic tendencies. Asserting that at times the government of the United States had on occasion been among "the greatest abettors of monopoly practices" by countenancing zone-pricing practices during NRA and OPA days, the committee entered an urgent plea that such connivance at illegality cease. Other committees were encouraged to keep a wary eye on government as well as on producers and consumers to prevent stifling competition among the old or the prevention of new sources of supply. Finally, stress was laid on developing new sources of supply and on legislation to minimize the effect of the Canadian law in hampering investigation.[25]

Meantime, toward the end of May, the Beckworth Committee had begun somewhat desultory hearings, which, as repeatedly demonstrated in congressional investigations of newsprint matters, were slow in picking up momentum because of the necessity of bringing uninitiated committee members up to the level of their better informed confreres by repetition of standard and well-known information. Questions of supply of paper and of sulphur were early to the fore, with the latter occupying the committee's attention well into June. This chemical, important in munitions manufacture, was also essential in making sulphite pulp for combination with groundwood pulp into finished newsprint. The proportions required were one ton of sulphite to six tons of groundwood pulp for seven tons of paper, and it was estimated that reduction of the sulphur supply by one ton cut newsprint production by forty-four tons. Well-nigh frantic efforts had been under way to develop alternative sources of supply in both Canada and the United States, but the hearings disclosed the fact that a real problem continued and was likely to become worse with the passage of time.[26]

A price increase of $10 per ton, previously approved by the Dominion government, bringing the New York port price to $116, was announced by Abitibi on June 1 (to become effective a month later) and was followed as usual by other Canadian producers. This action potentially placed the

Canadian manufacturers at a considerable advantage over their United States competitors, since the latter were limited by the price freeze of January 26, a domestic OPS regulation not applicable to imported commodities. The action, accounted for on the ground of increasing costs, was allegedly taken in violation of promises made by Canadian newsprint authorities, involved high-level personages on both sides of the border, and generated no small amount of ill-feeling. Inasmuch as the Beckworth Committee hearings carry much of the story, their disclosures will be amalgamated with other available material as the basis of the following chronological account.[27]

The narrative begins with the January meeting between DiSalle and Fowler mentioned in an earlier paragraph. At this session, according to DiSalle's review of the situation in a letter of June 4 to Fowler, the two agreed that current conditions did not warrant a price increase; Fowler indicated that although Canada had no price controls, he was in a position to hear of any prospective increases, in which case he would inform DiSalle " 'so that we might have the opportunity of discussing it.' " The next step, on May 15, was a telephone conversation between Fowler and staff members of the United States Forest Products Division, prompted by the rumor of a price hike. This, Fowler assured them, was a rumor only; he stated, furthermore (Fowler was now wearing two hats, one as a government official and the other as President of the Newsprint Association of Canada), that he had advised Canadian manufacturers not to increase prices without notifying him, and that if and when such notification occurred, and if circumstances warranted, he would take up the matter with the Canadian government; he further stated that the American authorities " 'would be advised before any increases were put into effect. . . .' " The next step was receipt of news of Abitibi's prospective action, less than twenty-four hours before it was given to the public, and too late for the period of review promised in the January memorandum. DiSalle concluded: " 'We are very disappointed in this approach, which seems to be altogether unilateral. . . .' " He continued on a minatory note: " 'Already some sources are asking why we should control prices on our exports when at the same time we are faced with unlimited increases on our imports. . . .' " And he concluded with a request that Fowler use his good offices to secure a suspension of the Canadian move to give opportunity for a " 'study and review of the situation.' "[28]

If DiSalle's statement of the facts was correct (and the author has not seen the actual memorandum of the January meeting), Fowler's reply of June 12 was not entirely ingenuous. According to his account, he requested Canadian manufacturers in April not to change price levels without clearing with his department; shortly thereafter he was approached by Abitibi with a request for an increase. His discussion with Abitibi demonstrating that the problem was industry-wide, the matter was carried to the Cabinet level, and after careful consideration the Canadian government decided on May 30 " 'that it would not use its emergency powers to interfere with the commercial decision being taken by the Abitibi Power & Paper Co., Ltd. . . .' " This decision was conveyed to DiSalle the following day, with the public announcement following on June 1. He insisted that, since the increase would not become effective until July 1, the United States government and publishers had received a month's notice instead of twenty-four hours, as DiSalle had claimed. If, as Fowler himself indicated, his contacts with Abitibi dated back to shortly after his meeting with DiSalle, it would seem reasonable to conclude that Canadian officials had treated the promise of prior discussion somewhat cavalierly, lending at least some color to the charge that their action made it difficult for United States authorities to maintain the price freeze of January 26.[29] Subsequent events, to be detailed below, tend to confirm this judgment.

South-of-the-border comment was sharply critical. The International Typographical Union complained to the Humphrey Committee that Canadian action presented the United States with a *fait accompli.* United States Defense Mobilization Administrator Charles E. Wilson reported that Canadian Defense Minister C. D. Howe had informed him, prior to the public announcement, of the Cabinet decision that the price increase was justifiable. Senator Humphrey was somewhat less restrained, suggesting that Canada might be brought to heel by a threat to withhold chemicals essential to defense production. Threats of imposing a ceiling price on newsprint were bandied about, bringing a retort from Lester B. Pearson, Canadian Minister of External Affairs, to the effect that Canada, while anxious to cooperate in defense of the free world, was not willing to become a tail to the United States kite; there were also Canadian counterthreats to seek other markets.[30]

The next event in the story occurred on June 12 (just as Fowler was replying to DiSalle), when DiSalle met with a Newsprint Industry Advisory Committee, newly empaneled after the World War II pattern, and later with representatives of the publishers, whose Industry Advisory Committee had been in existence since May 9. The session with manufacturers canvassed the question of price increases for the domestic industry. Discussion centered mainly around the optimum method of computation, and it was generally agreed that a flat, industry-wide increase of from $3 to $5 per ton would be preferable to the method, permissible under current regulations, whereby each mill computed its increase individually; the first, of course, would maintain the existing price structure intact. A later session with twenty-one publishers drew unfavorable comment from the A.N.P.A. because DiSalle excluded trade association representatives and included in the discussion publishers not members of the A.N.P.A., as well as a representative of *Editor & Publisher*. Moreover, DiSalle announced, without taking counsel with his publisher advisers, that he had decided to handle price negotiations with Canada on a government level rather than through industry spokesmen. The publishers, however, were apparently able to dissuade him from what seems to have been his original intention of establishing a price ceiling, for after the double sessions he announced that there would be no price action until he had talked with Canadian officials.[31]

There followed a variety of approaches to the price problem, none of which seemed particularly viable in view of the strong Canadian position of the moment. A successful attack on the proposed price increase would drive Canadians into production of pulp and the more profitable grades of paper. Canadian officials, therefore, stood pat and tended to disregard retaliatory threats from below the border. Neither did they view with great alarm the possibility of price ceilings, which, they held, would end the obligation of their contracts and free them to sell paper in more lucrative markets.

The A.N.P.A. adopted its own approach as a supplement to that proposed by government officials, and announced (June 19) that its board of directors would invite manufacturers from both sides of the border for discussions (planned for July 6) which it was hoped would ease the situation. Frederick Mears, long connected with Great Northern, told the Beckworth Committee that it would be unwise to push Canadians too hard on price matters, in view of United States needs for 2,000,000 cords of wood a year, subject to Canadian export restrictions, and for the seasonal labor of woodcutters, whose temporary exodus the Dominion could also prevent.

Arthur R. Treanor, a former publisher now connected with the government, repeated to the same group the warning that a rollback of prices would void Canadian contracts, though in his judgment world markets could absorb little of the Canadian product thus freed for sale. He had, he said, secured promises of assistance from large metropolitan papers in case of hardship caused by developing shortages. G. J. Ticoulat, another government official, repeated this warning against a price rollback, both to the Beckworth Committee and to his own agency superiors. Arthur Hays Sulzberger, publisher of *The New York Times,* on a visit to Canada, opposed government pressure to secure reductions, but asserted mildly that the Canadian increase was too great. Eric Johnston, United States Price Stabilizer, visited Canada to discuss general economic integration, but refrained from particular price talks on the ground that DiSalle would come later for that express purpose. The latter, in a last-minute effort, telephoned Fowler on June 28, but failed to make any dent on Canadian insistence on the increase. Finally (June 30) the Canadian producers declined the A.N.P.A.'s invitation for a July discussion on the ground that time for the necessary preparation was lacking. Thus passed the month of June, without any effective counter to the Canadian move, which became effective on July 1 as scheduled.[32]

The Canadian example was too good to resist, and on July 20, Crown Zellerbach informed its customers of an increase, effective August 1, putting its price on a par with that of the Canadian mills. Though an official denied that the matter had been cleared with the OPS, that agency noted that on June 30 the company had filed the necessary information on increasing costs, entitling it to the increase under General Manufacturers' Ceiling Price Regulation 22. Other mills qualified similarly, and on August 8 the Newsprint Industry Advisory Committee recommended to the OPS that any forthcoming regulation of prices should take the form of a " 'flat dollar and cent increase over the prices established . . . under the General Ceiling Price Regulation, which governed the sale of this commodity . . . when that regulation was made effective January 26, 1951.' " This was of course in effect a request that the OPS up the ceiling price to the Canadian level of $116. The question of a ceiling price on what consumers should pay brought up the mooted problem of a ceiling on imported newsprint. This was passed on to the publishers, who were supposedly better able to advise on this point, but it was pointed out the price of lower-cost Canadian paper had always governed that of the domestic product.[33] Thus the long controversy over price had been settled favorably to the Canadian position, with the United States industry taking advantage of domestic regulations to qualify belatedly for the same benefits.

During the summer the matter of increasing the domestic supply of newsprint began to assume greater prominence. On July 30, Senator Joseph C. O'Mahoney of Wyoming, using the cartel-monopoly approach, urged antitrust investigation. More significantly, he suggested: " 'The time has come for the publishers of the United States to consider what they are willing to do to promote the production of newsprint within the boundaries of the United States by manufacturers who will not associate themselves with . . . cartel practices.' " Treanor, appearing before the Beckworth Committee on September 27, noted that whereas at the time of his previous appearance there had been no applications to the NPA for permission to construct newsprint manufacturing facilities, now five concerns were interested in constructing mills to produce 160,000 to 170,000 tons a year. This interest was manifested by filing of applications for accelerated tax amortization of the high-cost properties to enable them to compete with older and partly or entirely depreciated mills.

By October the committee had progressed to the point of considering whether there was a sufficient shortage of newsprint to justify the release of scarce materials for its alleviation. On November 23 clearance was given for the consideration of applications for certificates of necessity, without commitment as to the priorities still necessary for the acquisition of machinery. Statistics accompanying the announcement indicated that estimates of the 1952 supply, including imports, fell 344,000 tons short of meeting the estimated demand, a figure which it was estimated would increase to a deficit of 494,000 tons in 1953 unless facilities for new supply were added. This action partially opened the way for construction of new capacity to take care of the expected deficit, and passed on to the Office of Resources Expansion the problem of deciding whether to grant certificates of necessity to the five firms whose applications were still pending. The year ended without final clearance as to tax amortization, after which, of course, the accredited firms must still grapple with the problem of obtaining scarce materials. An important beginning, however, had been made toward increasing domestic production.[34]

The publisher-manufacturer session, postponed from July by Canadian reluctance, took place in New York on October 3 and 4, constituting the first formal A.N.P.A. conference with Canadian producers on production problems. An important event of this meeting was the submission of a brochure compiled by Dr. Charles W. Boyce, the A.N.P.A.'s economic consultant, *Newsprint Now and in the Next Decade*. The Canadians presented figures to show that their expansion-by-speed-up technique had added 1,000,000 tons' production in six years, and would provide 305,000 additional tons in the coming two years. Boyce's figures indicated that the United

States would need 7,500,000 tons in 1960, an amount the Canadian industry could not be expected to provide. His estimates called for expansion of North American capacity by an average of 3 per cent per year, a problem the solution of which *Editor & Publisher* failed to see in any proposed construction south of the border; it editorially tossed the ball to Canada: "The Canadian manufacturers in the past have said to U.S. publishers: 'Tell us what to expect in your industry so that we can make our plans.' Well, here it is. What are the plans?" The Canadian reply was issued in the form of a December report by the Newsprint Association of Canada. Whereas the Boyce forecast spanned a decade, the Canadian prognostication stopped with 1953 and, by inference, indicated the belief that Boyce's figures were too high; if Canadian production followed the Newsprint Association of Canada pattern, and if United States consumption followed the Boyce predictions, the obvious discrepancy could be avoided only by construction of larger domestic facilities.[35]

It remains, finally, to complete the tale of the Beckworth Committee's work for the year. In September the group gathered in New York for a session with publishers, after which the Chairman pointed out that publishers were suffering from diversion of Canadian newsprint to Europe and diversion of pulp to other more profitable products; he hinted at, but did not definitely advocate, the balancing of increased exports of now-scarce sulphur against increased imports of newsprint; he insisted, however, that both sides were approaching the matter in an amicable spirit. The committee then followed what was by this time the traditional pattern of a journey to Montreal and the Canadian producing areas prior to presenting its interim report on October 3. This document directed its attention principally to the results of the Canadian trip, coming up with the conclusion that the current supply situation was "at best none too easy. . . ." It pictured the Canadian manufacturers as still "convinced that speed-up of machines has by no means been exhausted, . . ." since current average speeds varied from 1,100 to 1,200 feet per minute, and many were running as high as 1,700 feet; with only 20 per cent of the machines having been speeded up, the possibilities of extending this technique were looked upon as adequate to meet publishers' projected demands. Under these circumstances, Canadians remained reluctant to put new money into newsprint, preferring to build pulp mills, of which ten new examples had appeared since the war as against only one new newsprint mill, presently under construction in British Columbia. The committee, on the whole, had gained a reasonably optimistic picture of the Canadian newsprint scene.[36]

The year 1951 was thus one when emergency-born threats of paper and sulphur shortages spawned new investigations and created new irritations. It was also a year when complicated price maneuvers, accompanied by threats of retaliation, generated further ill-will but failed to shake the strong Canadian position. Finally, the later months witnessed the appearance of the first attempt of publishers to forecast demand over the long run as a means of stimulating production on both sides of the border, and the beginning of moves designed to use the defense emergency as a device for affording those interested in developing the domestic industry some help, via tax favors, in surmounting the hurdle of the high cost of mill equipment.

During 1952, while prices took a further jump, considerable attention was devoted to increasing the domestic supply through the defense-connected devices mentioned in preceding paragraphs. Continental production continued at above rated capacity (102 per cent) for the sixth consecutive year, that of the United States increasing by 2 per cent and that of Canada by 3.1 per cent. United States consumption, though still on a high plane, leveled off during the first ten months of the year. Canadian shipments to the United States, therefore, increased only 1.1 per cent, while United States mills delivered 2.9 per cent less paper to their local customers than in 1951, but increased overseas shipments by 275 per cent. The net result was a period of high but less explosive consumption, of large exportation, and of stockpiling by domestic users.[37]

Demand eased during the early year, and a good deal of attention was devoted on both sides of the border to the matter of future supply. With respect to measures by which the privilege of rapid tax amortization was extended to the newsprint industry during 1951, by mid-February, 1952, Bowaters Southern Paper Corporation had received a certificate allowing rapid tax write-off of 45 per cent on a mill valuation of $47,915,000 for construction of facilities in East Tennessee; four other applications were then pending, and before the year was over certificates had been granted to ten concerns for construction of new capacity to the extent of 751,000 tons a year to be completed by January 1, 1956. On January 25, Fowler's annual report to the Canadian Pulp and Paper Association painted an optimistic picture of long-range paper trends, but contained a cautionary note against repeating the errors of management which had contributed to the disastrous conditions of the 1930's. On February 1 he released the text of a statement indicating the Canadian newsprint industry's plans for expansion of its own capacity. This was prepared by the industry at the instance of the Department of External Affairs, which in turn had been asked (during the preceding December) by the United States Department of State whether the Canadian industry had established future production goals.[38]

This statement was given careful attention by a meeting of A.N.P.A. directors with representatives of the Newsprint Association of Canada in Montreal (February 7 and 8), an aftermath of the October, 1951, conference in New York at which the Boyce prognostications had been presented for the manufacturers' scrutiny. In part at least the Canadian reply to the publishers' projection of their own needs, it confined its attention to the proposals of existing manufacturers, taking no account of the entry of new concerns into the industry. It indicated that the Canadian industry had *planned* a production capacity increase of 914,000 tons by 1960, bringing its total capacity up to 6,161,000 tons as of that date; it indicated further that *potential* tonnage increases could bring the total up to 6,977,000 tons.

These figures were avowedly designed to counter the claim made in the United States that the limit of expansion by speed-ups had been reached. In neither case, however, did they provide the amount of tonnage (8,700,000; 7,000,000 for United States needs alone) called for by the Boyce projection. This discrepancy marked, of course, the conviction of the Canadian producer that United States publishers need not expect him to " 'take a 10-year projection of potential newsprint requirements as a basis for specific planning of his capacity expansion, any more than one would expect a publisher to proceed with pressroom expansion on such a basis.' " The document concluded, however, on a confident note, assuring publishers that the Canadian industry would " 'continue to be resourceful in providing supply.' "

On April 7 the Humphrey Committee rendered its official report, which embodies an unusual approach to the investigatory function as described in this study. It will be recalled that the committee's original report was based upon study of previously gathered material. It had been the plan, then, to hold hearings, but due to the busyness of the members it was decided to rely instead upon information gathered by means of a questionnaire distributed to some 14,000 publications of all sorts throughout the country; advice was also solicited from governmental agencies and other sources. The questionnaire elicited replies from over 500 weekly and 1,000 daily publications, the results of which were distilled into the report.[39] The evidence gathered led the committee to conclude that the fundamental problem was that of satisfying the needs of the small papers, which would never be in a secure position until assured of an adequate supply—a state of affairs unlikely to obtain in the near future.

An interesting feature of the document was a point-by-point refutation, offered by Crown Zellerbach and International Paper, of many of the committee's contentions as contained in the Preliminary Report. Crown Zellerbach, denying the prediction of continued scarcity, refused to accept the committee's unjustified "'foregone conclusion'" that the only remedy needed was greater production capacity. It contended that the evidence of recent years was not sufficient to underwrite a prediction of a long-run upward trend of consumption, which in turn would justify increased capacity. It suggested that higher advertising rates, which it hinted might be a good idea, might well cut down the demand for paper. It denied the Celler Committee's contention that the large papers were hindered from testifying because of their fear of contract reprisals from their suppliers, that the mills favored large as against small publishers, that the newsprint industry had fled to Canada in order to escape the antitrust laws, that prices were collusively controlled, and were adjusted at a level sufficiently low to discourage new capital from entering the industry, and that only governmental action would remedy existing difficulties; finally, the fundamental bases of the committee's approach to the matter in terms of social values was challenged, and Crown Zellerbach's own remedies were put forward.

These involved the necessity of realizing that since the main production area was and would remain in Canada, the consequent interdependence of the United States publisher and the Canadian producer was so intimate as to render it desirable to remove their relations from the area of direct negotiation and place them upon the plane of " 'intergovernmental cooperation.' " Again, said Crown Zellerbach, it must be recognized that since expansion of supply in a heavy industry such as newsprint was not an overnight matter, a firm conclusion that the real remedy was governmental action to stimulate the United States industry to new efforts must be preceded by and predicated upon accurate statistical analyses such as had recently been set under way by the west coast manufacturers through the agency of a research agency connected with the Leland Stanford, Jr., University. Further, instead of interfering artificially with price in the supply-demand equation, why not let these matters find their natural economic level; if price is high, new money would come into the industry, and existing mills would also make good profits. Still further, it was urged that governmental agencies desist from investigating the paper industry in order that it might pursue its economic function of turning out newsprint for the hungry presses. Finally, it was pointed out that a relatively small diversion of tonnage from the large papers, which, incidentally, were not getting all they wanted, would provide amply for the small fry, whose fate was being so loudly bemoaned.

International's critique started from the premise that the committee's report " 'very inaccurately summarizes the voluminous material on which it is based, as a result of misdirected emphasis, omission of relevant material, false inferences, and failure to weigh evidence judicially.' " It proceeded to refute the contention that existing conditions jeopardized the establishment of new newspapers, though admitting that it might be difficult for a large paper to secure contracts for the necessary tonnage. It questioned the suggestion that demand was likely to continue to grow along the recent trend line by pointing to the lightened demand which in 1949 and 1950 left many machines idle and caused publishers to slack off on orders for paper—which they soon wished was in their warehouses. It denied that the mills favored the large purchasers at the expense of the small, and asserted that the long-term contracts, which the committee had criticized, were desirable from the standpoint of both producer and consumer. It denied, too, the committee's " 'bald' " assertion of price-fixing, mainly based, as it had been, upon the Celler Committee hearings, whereas that Committee's recent report had " 'made only highly qualified claims to this effect. . . .' " Like Crown Zellerbach, International denied holding down prices to discourage new production; it scouted the possibility of certain prediction that demand would continue to keep up with and might even outpace supply; and finally, it insisted that private capital was entering the industry at a considerable rate, and could be relied upon to continue to do so in answer to " 'any reasonably demonstrated assurance of a future demand for their output at competitive prices. . . .' "

The report also contained an approach to the problem from the standpoint of the professional economist. Professor Guthrie, referred to in these pages as the foremost scholarly student of the newsprint problem, made a statement generally underwriting the desirability of attracting private capital into the industry, as stated by the committee's Preliminary Report. He added, moreover, that such entry could

After the reel of paper has been formed, it is fed onto the rewinder to be slit into newsprint rolls of the width and diameter ordered by the publisher.

be stimulated only by a price sufficient to justify high current costs of construction, which in turn would enable old and partly or largely depreciated mills to make handsome profits and would substantially increase publishers' expenses, a solution " 'unpalatable' " to most of them. He concluded that the only solution he could see was government subsidy or higher prices all-round: " 'In my opinion, higher prices for newsprint, for newspapers, and for newspaper advertising will bring about a solution to the present shortage and will require a minimum of Government regulation and control.' "

Rumors of price increase, followed by the fact, occupied no small attention during 1952. As early as February 18 the Beckworth Committee was told that some Canadian manufacturers were considering a raise. Three days later Fowler and an aide journeyed to New York and informed a representative of the OPS that studies were under way which might result in governmental approval of a higher price, but that opportunity for discussion would be given prior to any action. On February 27 a representative of the Office of Defense Mobilization (ODM) informed Ellis Arnall, Director of the OPS, of the Canadian situation and advised the latter to telephone Fowler. This conversation, with Fowler's deputy, denied Canadian intent to increase price, but promised consultation. There also appears to have been contact between Charles E. Wilson and C. D. Howe, Canadian Minister of Defense, on a still higher echelon. On March 5, Beckworth requested Arnall to confer with Canada before a price elevation became effective, and to inform his committee prior to any discussion of the matter with the Canadian authorities.

By early May, *Paper Trade Journal* was commenting on the current dullness of the market as an "adjustive" period—a less frightening term, it hoped, than "recession." This situation of comparative calm was broken when, on May 15,

Abitibi informed its customers that in view of " 'press reports that the Canadian Government has decided not to prevent an increase in the price of newsprint,' " they might look forward to an increase of $10 per ton, effective June 15, making the price $126 per ton, New York port. This was necessitated, said the communication, by the " 'fact that the net return to us from the sale of newsprint has been reduced by about $20 per ton due to increased costs of labor, materials, pulpwood and freight and the depreciation in value of the American dollar.' " This action was followed, as usual, by other Canadian firms. This time, it appears, the form of consultation had been observed, but Arnall presently (June 5) let it be known that there had been no more than "token observance" of the agreement.[40]

Editor & Publisher took the unusual step of publishing (May 24) excerpts from publishers' comments, including " 'terrifying,' " " 'shocking,' " " 'A matter of greed, not of need,' " " 'great mistake,' " " 'embarrassing burden,' " etc., with only an occasional " 'somewhat justified,' " and " 'we'll survive.' " The Beckworth Committee met promptly (May 26) to hear testimony from representatives of the OPS, NPA, and A.N.P.A., but developed no "new approach" beyond that of the publishers' representatives, who, it was reported, advocated no action beyond Price Administrator Arnall's fruitless complaint to the Canadian authorities.

The following day the Celler Committee also interrogated government officials, including men from the Departments of State, Justice, and Commerce, and the Reconstruction Finance Corporation. The problem of price ceilings apparently came up at one or both of these sessions, but was opposed by publishers from fears of retaliation through cutting of supply or other devices. Arnall informed his interrogators that Canadian authorities had once more acted upon the basis of the exchange situation, this time due to the appreciation of the Canadian dollar, which had caused a loss of $6 Canadian on each ton of newsprint. The committee commissioned H. B. McCoy, Director of the Office of Industry and Commerce in the Department of Commerce, to conduct an investigation, reporting within two months; he was a. to study the obstacles hindering further expansion of production within the United States; b. to consult with domestic interests desiring to enter the field with a view to enlarging production; c. to cooperate with the Bureau of Standards in testing new sources of production; d. to cooperate with publishers' groups in an effort to coordinate any measures these were taking to increase production; and e. to coordinate the work to this end being done by other governmental agencies. It soon came out, too, that most United States production was eligible for increases within the price ceiling structure then in effect, and domestic mills were soon at work making the calculations necessary to establish higher prices for their own product.[41]

The price developments just chronicled were preceded and accompanied by several proposals for investigation. Congressman Celler had written the Attorney General on February 19 asking, on behalf of the small publishers, that the Department of Justice investigate collusion among the producers to increase price, but was told (February 20) that since 90 per cent of United States consumption came from Canada, where the government had no jurisdiction, the department was powerless to manifest an effective interest in the price situation. Early in April, Celler introduced a bill requiring foreign corporations to furnish books and records when subpoenaed in antitrust cases. In May, just prior to announcement of the new price, he inquired of the A.N.P.A., via a letter to Cranston Williams, whether that trade association would like to be invited to testify at proposed hearings on the bill. The A.N.P.A.'s advice was that those willing to testify should make contact with either Williams or Celler.

After the price increase, Senator Herbert R. O'Conor of Maryland proposed (May 19) that the Celler Committee investigate the matter from the antitrust angle. He was quoted as desiring to " ' "bring home to the Canadian authorities the resentment aroused in all sections of the United States by this drastic display of intent to cash in on the fact that America is so thoroughly dependent on its Canadian sources of newsprint supply." ' " He commented further on the deleterious effect of the action on normally good Dominion-United States relations, and played up the danger to the small press inherent in Canada's action which would, he asserted, " 'sever the one remaining link of thousands of farm dwellers of the nation with what is going on in the world. . . .' " Representative Francis Case of South Dakota joined Senator Edwin C. Johnson of Colorado in introducing (May 27) a resolution calling for a joint congressional committee which, unlike most of its predecessors, would not hold hearings, but would study the evidence already available and come up with concrete recommendations for action designed to increase the domestic production of newsprint. Proposed avenues of investigation included exploring the use of new resources, exploiting the Alaskan situation, amendment of Reconstruction Finance Corporation regulations to facilitate loans to old and new concerns seeking capital, and encouragement of the formation of newspaper cooperatives to enter the manufacturing industry. Like many other proposals, the resolution remained buried in committee files.[42]

The only other development of moment during 1952 was an investigation by the Pulp, Paper and Paperboard Division of the NPA. Its representatives met successively in June with delegations from the manufacturers and the publishers. These meetings and other studies resulted in a report rendered in October which will be summarized below. At the first meeting (on June 18) the manufacturers were not encouraging as to the possibility of increasing domestic production, due to the industry's poor ratio of high investment costs to low rates of return. They were inclined to blame the government for some of the trouble, through current policies of removing large tracts of timber from possible profitable exploitation through a. making the Olympic Peninsula in Washington a National Park, and b. forcing local processing of any timber cut in the Tongass National Forest of Alaska. There was a preponderance of opinion to the effect that "there should be no specific drive for expansion in the United States beyond the level which would come about naturally as a result of basic economic developments," a polite way of saying that a price increase was the surest way to attract new money into the industry.

When the publishers met (on June 26), attention was called to the fact that, whereas the Defense Production Administration had in November, 1951, set a goal of 494,000 new tons a year, to date only 375,000 tons of this amount were in sight; the group, however, favored continuing the larger production goal. Like the manufacturers, publishers were not enthusiastic about affirmative governmental assistance in obtaining new production, but recommended further study of the possibilities of the Olympic Peninsula and Alaska as sources of new supply. They were no more than lukewarm as to their own willingness to finance new domestic sources. Though some difference developed within the group, there was no great enthusiasm for extending government aid beyond the current (and not yet fully used) device of rapid tax amortization—this on the usual ground that governmental involvement " 'might affect the independence of the newspaper business.' "[43]

The Celler Committee held a hearing (October 2) at which H. B. McCoy, in presenting the NPA report referred to in a preceding paragraph, took occasion to go over some of the work of his division in exploring the possibilities of new supply. He was most enthusiastic, on the basis of pilot plant and publishers' tests, concerning the possibilities of utilizing bagasse as a source of newsprint, being careful, however, to point out that any statements made were subject to considerable further investigation. He reiterated the manufacturers' reasons for a conservative attitude toward domestic softwood supply, high unit cost for building of new mills to be placed in competition with established units, and the greater profits realizable from other lines of paper production.[44]

During October, also, Fowler made a significant address to the Inland Daily Press Association (October 13) in which he urged more cooperation between publishers and manufacturers, arguing that his constituents had made greater efforts to explain their problems than had publishers, and urging the latter to take more pains to spell out the exact nature of their problems. This chiding of the publishers, however, was accompanied by a rather stirring plea for cooperation, Fowler asserting that " 'there is a fundamental identity of interest between the business of manufacturing newsprint and the business of publishing newspapers, and . . . there cannot be conflict and friction and misunderstanding between the two industries, for any substantial period, without serious injury to both.

" 'In recent years I think that both publishers and newsprint manufacturers have come to see more clearly that their enterprises are dependent on each other. Moreover, some of them have begun to realize that each needs to know more about the business problems of the other. . . .' " In addition to this plea for cooperation, the year's end saw predictions of both price increases and production cuts as a remedy for the obviously soft market produced by the approximate balance between supply and demand.[45]

The year 1953 was a quiet one in the newsprint world. Supply and demand were in delicate equilibrium, a condition not conducive to adventures on either side of the producer-consumer equation. The North American industry operated at 98.7 per cent capacity, with an output 28,000 tons below 1952, when the operating ratio was 102.4 per cent of capacity. By using inventories, United States publishers were able to consume 2.6 per cent more newsprint than in 1952, despite the modest drop in production. The A.N.P.A.'s Newsprint Committee reported to the annual convention in April, 1953: " 'Supply and demand for newsprint are in more even balance. . . . As of today, the ANPA knows of no publishers of a newspaper lacking a sufficient supply and adequate inventory of newsprint. . . .' " And a year later the same committee, though constitutionally wary of optimistic attitudes toward supply, could say that " 'there is now no immediate cause for alarm as to newsprint supply, . . .' " though insistent that such could develop from very slight dislocations of the existing situation. Looking back on 1953, the Newsprint Association of Canada could remark that " 'the abnormal bulge of post-war demand for newsprint has been digested. . . .' "[46]

The House continued its investigatory activities, transferring this function to a subcommittee of the Interstate and Foreign Commerce Committee, where it had been lodged in several earlier Congresses, and assigning the Celler Committee, which for some years had been active in this area, to the sole function of rendering a final report (which appeared on September 14). This transfer apparently produced some irritation on the part of the Judiciary Committee, which attempted in June to regain some influence in the matter by requesting the Department of Commerce to study the industry with a view to furnishing information useful in an antitrust approach to the newsprint problem. With matters in such a stable situation, there was little incentive to real agitation, and the Commerce Committee, though given an appropriation, did little or nothing toward investigating the matters entrusted to it: a. current and prospective consumption of newsprint; b. possibilities of additional supply through use of "'alternate materials'"; c. governmental policies as to export and import of newsprint; and d. the adequacy of supply, particularly for the small press.[47]

The Celler Committee's final report may be mentioned briefly here while the investigatory aspects of 1953 are under consideration. The report took off from the current equilibrium of supply and demand. It then summarized the committee's previous approach to the subject by referring to the plight of the small publishers and the antitrust implications which, in the committee's view, were inherent in the structure of the industry. A survey of production trends was followed by a reasonably gloomy prediction as to the likelihood that new Canadian production would be sufficient to meet the projected demand. Some comfort was taken, however, in the fact that a domestic production program was well under way; indeed, it may be pointed out parenthetically that the sources for the year contain considerable information apropos this increasing domestic potential. Some attention was paid to the price-production dilemma, it being pointed out that whereas a high price served to discourage demand, a lower price would increase requirements; present prices were not sufficiently high to entice new capital into the industry.

On the whole, though supply and demand were temporarily in balance, "the economic picture of the future was far from reassuring unless positive steps were to be immediately taken to obviate some of the difficulties described above. A long-term solution to the newsprint problem depended upon the ability to solve the pricing-production dilemma as well as overcome other obstacles to further newsprint expansion such as shortages of raw materials." It is interesting to note that only one of its considerable list of recommendations for future action dealt with matters which could be connected with the relation of the industry to the antitrust laws, the purpose for which the committee had originally been established; all the rest dealt in one way or another with matters related to the problem of increased supply. Thus ended the extensive labors of a hard-working committee, whose activity brought out a greater amount of information than any of its predecessors or successors within the period of the present study, but which made a much less significant contribution in the area for which it was originally constituted.[48]

Long before the Celler report, just mentioned, Fowler had attempted, in a speech of March 24 to the Town Hall Forum in New York, to build a backfire to cut off the protests emanating from south of the border concerning United States dependence upon a "foreign" source of supply, and the proposals to use government assistance, new materials, and tax concessions as a means of alleviating the alleged danger. Complaining at recent " 'statements by a number of your politicians, supported by some of your publishers,' " he insisted that Canada had hitherto proved herself a " 'reliable source for U.S. expanding needs,' " and remarked rather pointedly that failure to continue purchasing Canadian newsprint would by just so much reduce the Canadian market for United States exports.[49]

The mid-year period saw some easing in production schedules as consumers turned to living off their inventories; an occasional change in price was announced, with publishers profiting mildly by the ample supply available, and becoming more demanding as to the quality of the product; by the same token, manufacturers above the border were cautioned to cut costs in view of the current situation. By the autumn, storm warnings were flying at some mastheads lest current policies of parsimonious purchasing and of consuming stocks on hand result unfavorably in a time of possible shortage growing out of greater consumption at the end of the year. At the usual autumn meeting of the A.N.P.A.'s directors with their Canadian suppliers (December 8) the latter reported that they were in a position to meet all demands for 1953 and "'that projects to increase production would continue to go forward for several years after 1954, all of which would maintain the Canadian position of being able to take care of U.S.A. requirements.'" The year, on the whole, had been a quiet one, with no significant price adjustments and considerable diminution of the investigatory spirit below the border.[50]

The year 1954 was also a quiet one in the newsprint domain, a calm perhaps reflecting a bearish attitude toward the national economy in general. The year opened with economists considering the possibility of a recession, which, if not actively checked, might easily turn into a downward spiral. These circumstances, modified upward only slightly and toward the end of the year, had their influence upon the publishing industry, where consumption of newsprint leveled off to a point where the papers reporting to the A.N.P.A. registered a gain of only 0.3 per cent over the 1953 figures.

At the same time continental productive capacity was increasing by about 300,000 tons a year, a third of which was developed south of the border, where total production, topping a million tons, was the highest since 1930. This represents, of course, the first fruits of the drive conducted for some years by the A.N.P.A. and various governmental agencies for greater domestic production as a means to end the long-run dependence upon Canada which had exercised so many in the United States.

Immediately, however, manufacturers were faced with the problem of disposing of the extra tonnage, aggravated by the fact that when, late in the year, domestic consumption took an upward turn, publishers met their increasing need for paper by drawing upon inventories rather than increasing orders to the mills. The mills solved the problem largely by peddling the excess tonnage in the spot market or selling it overseas, where demand continued heavy and where the exchange situation had improved somewhat. The year ended with both publishers and manufacturers, by and large, resting fairly comfortably and without any real inkling of the explosive situation which was to develop in the early months of 1955—a commentary, it may be added with the wisdom of hindsight, upon the prognosticating capacity of the professionals in both publishing and manufacturing areas.[51]

With matters in this somewhat indeterminate state, there were few important developments in the newsprint area in 1954. Only three need passing mention. One of these was occasional evidence of price concessions, particularly on the spot market, an almost inevitable consequence of a plethoric supply situation.[52] A second was evidence of continued investigatory interest, though this was held to a rather modest level, amounting to presentation (on August 5) of a second and substantial report by the Business and Defense Services Administration (BDSA) of the Department of Commerce to the House Committee on the Judiciary; this report concentrated on the prospects of expanding production by the use of hardwoods, as its predecessor had been based in considerable measure on the use of bagasse as a new source of supply. Despite the fact that Great Northern was already in the market with a paper based on hardwood, the report was fairly tentative in its recommendations, insisting that considerable experimentation must still precede a final determination of its commercial value. The report commented more optimistically on the prospects of increased supply through expansion of existing facilities for manufacture of paper from the traditional softwood varieties, and pointed out that certificates of necessity had been granted since 1951 for plants which would expand production by 586,000 tons a year; most of these plants were already completed or under construction.[53]

Finally, repeated evidence of actual or potential increases in supply permeated the literature of the year. This took the form of expanded facilities for established firms, of entry of new firms into the supply picture, particularly Bowaters Southern Paper Corporation, which delivered its first newsprint on July 20, 1954, and of talk of further new mills in the south. In the first category, a Great Northern machine using mixed hard- and softwoods was in full production by the end of the year, with contract negotiations for a second under way; their combined capacity was estimated at 400 tons a day. Southland, Coosa River, and Crown Zellerbach were also reportedly considering additional tonnage.

The most substantial single addition to the supply picture was furnished by the entry into production on July 20 of the $60,000,000 mill at Calhoun, Tennessee, constructed with combined British and American capital by Bowaters Southern Paper Corporation, to deliver an output of 130,000 tons a year; it was to supply over 100 southern papers formerly dependent upon the Bowater mills in Newfoundland. Finally, and despite Canadian assurances of ability to supply the United States market, optimistic promoters were encouraging southern publishers to invest in a mill project in Arkansas, and International, long absent from the United States newsprint picture, was denying that it intended converting a southern kraft mill to newsprint production. It would thus appear that, despite a momentary lull in consumption, the drive for new production was beginning to bear its fruit in the United States. The stage, indeed, was being well set for the explosion of 1955 ff., which it will be the task of the final chapter to describe.[54]

The period 1950 through 1954 opened with the industry on both sides of the border in good position to undertake the rapid and continuous expansion of production which was to characterize these five years. Under pressure of publishers and government, and assisted by tax concessions on the part of the latter, United States production grew both via new mills and expansion of old facilities; the Canadian pattern continued to confine itself to the latter method. The impact of renewed hostilities in Korea upon increased production in the United States must not be forgotten. Canadians, secure in their primacy in the United States market, maintained price leadership and carried newsprint to a high level of $126 per ton in 1952; here a buyer's market kept it during the remainder of the period. Some efforts, not too successful, were made to forecast consumers' future needs; some stress was laid, without appreciable effect, upon the desirability of cooperation between producers and consumers in this important area. Congressional committees continued active, with the figure of Mr. Celler dominating the scene for much of the period, and with those of Capehart, Humphrey, and Beckworth sharing part of the spotlight. The monopoly approach undertaken by the Celler Committee did not, it must be noted, achieve the affirmative results hoped for by its sponsors. The continuing inquisitiveness manifested by this and other committees did, however, produce an increasing restiveness on both sides of the border at the pertinacity of the investigatory process and resulted in some exacerbation of feelings between producers and consumers which were hardly soothed by occasional attempts at conciliation. The period ends with a quiet market, with supply, both actual and potential, seemingly well abreast of current or prospective demand, and with virtually no indication of a drastic change in the current situation.

Some newsprint is shipped by water and truck to the newspapers.

CHAPTER VI

The Fifties, Second Phase

THE YEAR 1955 introduces a period when questions of newsprint supply and demand continued prominent. Productive capacity was exceedingly high, in response to diverse pressures, and at the outset the market suddenly and unexpectedly expanded. Successive tensions resulted. The first of these came about because of difficulty in stretching a rapidly expandable supply to cover an even more elastic demand. Next a downward dip in the national economy caused decreasing consumption and left the producers with excess productive capacity on their hands—a familiar swing of the pendulum in the newsprint story, and one which, as in earlier days, caused trouble.

The developments that characterized the first quarter of 1955 were almost completely unforeseen and nothing short of startling. Consumption of newsprint in 1954 (6,163,000 tons) had almost exactly duplicated that of 1953 (6,143,000 tons). Publishers, generally believing that a temporary plateau had been reached, told their suppliers late in 1954 that they would need approximately the same tonnage for 1955. Then, and suddenly, there occurred an upsurge of demand which by the end of the year had increased advertising linage by 10 per cent, circulation by 1.3 per cent, and newsprint consumption by 384,000 tons (6.3 per cent). These changes resulted from shifts in population into the west and south, producing heavy advertising increases in those areas, and from a return of business confidence in the newspaper as an advertising medium, following television's recent heavy inroads on newspaper revenue.[1]

Consumption shot up month by month during the first quarter, papers reporting to the A.N.P.A. using 5.6 per cent more in January, 5.7 per cent more in February, 9.6 per cent more in March, and 7.1 per cent more for the quarter than for corresponding periods in 1954; it continued at a record level during the remaining quarters, with November's consumption being 9.9 per cent above that of 1954. The increase in consumption for this single year was greater than the overall increase for the years 1951 to 1954, inclusive, and placed a corresponding strain upon production facilities. The mills, although virtually without warning of the inflated demand, proved equal to the task; it was made somewhat easier by some enforced devouring of publishers' inventories.

North American production was reportedly up 7.6 per cent over 1954; the most significant figure, however, was a 28 per cent increase in production by United States mills, reaching a total of 1,550,000 tons, the highest in history except for 1926. This was made possible, of course, by the diverse approaches to the postwar supply situation: speeding up of old machinery, addition of new machines in existing mills, and production from new mills. Heightened interest in additional facilities preceded and accompanied the boom. In January, before the upsurge could have been more than conjectural, International Paper Company announced plans for its first entry into United States newsprint production in approximately thirty years, through a plant to be located at Mobile, Alabama. The same firm presently shifted one of its existing mills back to newsprint; and, significantly, by spring Canadians were beginning to talk in terms of new mill construction as well as of higher production by speed-ups and new machines—a new phenomenon in the postwar scene.[2]

The newsprint situation evoked some congressional interest, manifested before the boom in consumption and continued parallel with it. On February 25 the House authorized the establishment of a subcommittee of the Committee on Interstate and Foreign Commerce, eventually headed by Arthur G. Klein of New York. It addressed itself to the double problem of the adequacy of immediate and long-range supply, operating first through hearings opening on March 15 and resulting in a report of May 26 to the House, and later, during the recess of Congress, through fact-finding journeys to several producing areas.[3] At the March hearing, R. C. Flom of BDSA assured the committee that supply and demand were in good balance and should so continue through 1956. When it reported to the House, however, the committee was somewhat more conservative in its forecast, refusing to predict adequate supply beyond the current year, and pointing out "that beyond the immediate future there was nothing in the outlook that would lend any assurance that newsprint users would continue to get all of the newsprint they might want." Committee delegations took advantage of the summer recess to visit London to study the continuing effects of British controls on newsprint, to visit Alaska to explore the Japanese wood pulp operations proposed for that area, as well as Alaskan newsprint potentialities, and to explore the timber and mill resources of the southern United States.

With demand on an upward spiral and with a spot market appearing in May, it was only natural that price should become a factor, as it presently did. In the light of rumors already circulating, President R. W. Slocum warned A.N.P.A. members that although the association had no control over price, its individual members were in a position to influence the situation through frank warning of suppliers that a price increase would force publishers to economize by buying narrower rolls and by increasing subscription and advertising rates, all of which would reduce the tonnage sold by the mills. In presenting the newsprint report to the A.N.P.A. convention (April 27) he said: " 'There was a day when I thought we had better be silent when these rumors are around. Not now. Newsprint manufacturers have seen some evidence of the conditioning process, and I think to say nothing at this time is a mistake. But I think it should be done with the greatest seriousness, the greatest endeavor, to convince these people that it will not be to their interest. . . . I believe these people, certainly most of them, basically, want to cooperate with us and we do them a service as well as ourselves if we talk to them frankly and fairly about it. . . .' " Following this warning, the A.N.P.A. canvassed all suppliers (April 27), inquiring as to their intentions on price, following which at least one producer denied the likelihood of an increase " 'in the foreseeable future.' " At about the same time one mill representative told *Editor & Publisher* that publishers seemed more concerned about higher prices than manufacturers.[4]

Although price matters remained stable for the time being, some excitement was created during the summer by Dr. Louis T. Stevenson's article of July 4 in *Paper Trade Journal*. In this he ventured the surmise that increasing domestic production might stabilize and even reduce the volume of imports necessary to sustain the domestic demand. His contention was based upon the fact that consumption, 1949 to 1953 inclusive, had remained stable at 75 pounds per capita. If consumption remained stable through 1960, he argued that new domestic production then in sight was likely to "increase as fast as the consumption during the period to 1975."

This was promptly and vigorously controverted in an article in the *Toronto Financial Post* (July 9, reprinted in *Paper*

Trade Journal July 25). There it was argued that Stevenson had underestimated United States demand, as proved by the experience of very recent months, and that Canadians would still remain in competition for any increase in the volume of United States business. Perhaps the significant point here was the admission of the possibility that a competitive situation might develop between Canadian and United States producers. The matter rested with Dr. Stevenson's rebuttal, in which he contended that the future would see Canada more and more selling its growing production in overseas markets, while United States production met the increase in domestic need. He based his argument in considerable measure upon the fact that the economics of the current situation had prompted International, Bowater, and Great Northern, " 'no novices in this field,' " to step up United States production.[5]

By mid-summer rumors of price increases began to accompany talk of a "gray" or high spot market, with publishers expressing fears and manufacturers denying intention to take steps, but at the same time refusing to promise continence in this area if a competitor should make a move. With reports of shortages developing in early October, Sir Eric Bowater told *Editor & Publisher* (October 8) that "increase in the price of newsprint is inevitable and it is necessary right now. . . ." Though his firm had never been a bellwether in price increases, and though he denied sending up a trial balloon on behalf of the industry, his remarks attracted wide attention. Slocum retorted sharply on behalf of the A.N.P.A., asserting publishers' belief that " 'a price increase is neither justified nor wise,' " and exhorting Bowater to talk with some of his customers to discover the likely long-term results of a price increase; he urged his own constituents to " 'be vocal with their suppliers, speaking freely about the problems they face and how the best interests of the suppliers may be affected. . . .' " Editorial attention was also called to the fact that though manufacturing costs had undoubtedly risen, the evidence was incontrovertible that mill earnings were higher than ever in history. Into this welter of conflicting statements came, on October 17, St. Lawrence's announcement of a $5 increase (to $131, New York port), effective November 1 for the final quarter.[6]

Publishers' reaction was prompt and vigorous, with a sharp bead being drawn on the fact that St. Lawrence's profits for the first six months of 1955 were 37.3 per cent above those for the corresponding period in 1954; attention was also called to the fact that the price increase came two days after the mill had announced a $9,000,000 expansion program, and it was charged that the company was asking the publishing industry to finance its expanding plant. On the other hand, *Paper Trade Journal* editorialized: "Newspaper group cries of '. . . dire threat to American liberty . . .' are a little far fetched on this overdue move by producers to meet mounting costs." Alarmed by this untoward development, Congressman Klein called his committee into session in New York for November 1, later changing his approach to a trip through southern producing areas. Abitibi followed the St. Lawrence lead on October 23, and two days later International increased its price by $4. Between these two dates it was announced that the Antitrust Division of the Department of Justice was holding conferences with unnamed producers in an attempt to prevent joint efforts at price increases on the part of the domestic industry.

Public attention was also called at this time to the fact that the Canadian dollar had recently been appreciating to a point where the new price would give Canadian producers an extra "dividend" over the actual figures announced. Mr. Celler, meantime, harping on the oft-plucked monopoly string, reportedly told *Editor & Publisher* that a price investigation would be futile, commenting that the situation remained unchanged since his committee had made recommendations which the newspaper industry had ignored. He continued: " 'A tight cartel operating with the connivance of the Government of Canada holds the whip hand and there isn't a damn thing we can do.' " Representative McCormack, House Majority Leader, telegraphed Secretary of State John Foster Dulles, asking that the government protest to Canada and devise a program " 'that will be protective of the interests of the newspapers of our country.' " Senator Warren Magnuson telegraphed all United States producers (October 27) pointing out that his Committee on Interstate and Foreign Commerce was " 'deeply concerned' " at the increases, and asking their views as to measures to relieve the immediate emergency. Further price increases ensued promptly, with some mills following the St. Lawrence lead, others the lower International pattern, and still others diverging from both. Great Northern postponed operation of its $4 increase until February 1, 1956. Because of tie-in price contracts, the eventual price increase dropped to $4, and became effective only on January 1, 1956.[7]

After the flurry noted just above, the issue changed rather quickly from one of price to one of supply, which became the high note as the year ended. Fowler had warned of the inevitability of this development as early as November 1, when he pointed out that " 'if usage by North American publishers continues at present rates some publishers may be in real distress before the end of the year. . . .' " This proved to be the case, when overordering was complicated by a boxcar shortage, by a strike in one of the Canadian mills, and by failure of some new machines to deliver expected tonnage. By year's end there was widespread reporting of mill cutbacks on deliveries, ranging from 5 per cent to 13 per cent, a situation which was in many instances projected into 1956 deliveries. By December 10, Cranston Williams was reported as saying that "'the industry is confronted with the worst newsprint supply situation ever encountered in peacetime. . . .'"

Looking back over the year, *Editor & Publisher* pointed out that the situation had "been shaping up since last Winter when publishers held back on orders and ate up newsprint on hand while taking care of increased linage, stepped-up circulation and record-breaking special editions." Thus, as 1956 approached, so did the possibility of a new crisis, born of the sudden and well-nigh completely unforeseen spurt in demand which had characterized recent months. True, much new production was on the drawing boards or under construction, but no one conversant with the situation expected it to catch up with demand before some time in 1956, with no prospect of easy supply prior to 1957 and 1958.[8]

The pattern of 1956 bade fair to repeat that of 1955, with demand in the early months running far ahead of supply. Year-end figures supported the early promise of an active new year in both publishing and manufacturing. Newsprint consumption increased by another 5 per cent over the 1954 figures (to a total of 6,800,000 tons), though not as rapidly as in 1955. Advertising linage and circulation were again higher, the first up 2.4 per cent over 1955 (as 1955 had been up 10 per cent over 1954), and the second up 1.6 per cent (as 1955 had been up 1.3 per cent over 1954). The cumulative effect of these increases became apparent as supply tightened during the early year, particularly on the small publishers, many of whom sought assistance from the Department of Commerce in securing tonnage; most papers could have used more raw material during the first half-year had it been available, though this situation tended to ease during the later months as supply began to catch up with demand

and as storm signals, indicating that 1957 might not be as rosy as 1955 and 1956, began to appear toward the year's end.[9]

As usual, such stringency elicited congressional solicitude, with resultant committee activity on several fronts. The Klein Committee was first in the field. Its hearings, opening on January 10, 1956, were held in the light of present and prospectively continuing shortages, particularly on the part of small publishers, and took off from this premise. They moved, also, under the shadow of British re-entry into the newsprint market, rendered imminent by the forthcoming removal of rationing in March, 1956.

While the Klein Committee hearings were under way, Senator Warren Magnuson announced that his Committee on Interstate and Foreign Commerce would hold hearings designed to break the "'Canadian stranglehold'" on the newsprint industry by way of expansion of domestic production, and J. William Fulbright of the Senate Committee on Banking and Currency announced that his group would review and analyze a report submitted by the Department of Commerce to the Klein Committee. Meantime, the A.N.P.A. had already entered a plea (as early as January 5) on behalf of the beleaguered small publisher, thus making known its own interest in his plight. And, by mid-month and obviously under the influence of current developments south of the border, Fowler would be expatiating to a Canadian Royal Commission anent the politically explosive character of the newsprint question, which, he said, gave American legislators their easiest avenue to newspaper headlines.[10]

Officially, Chairman Klein opened the hearings of January 10 on a note of avoiding price matters, important though these might be, in favor of keeping the small publisher in business by stimulating production. Starting from the obvious fact that mills had cut back deliveries, and from the obvious conclusion of the technical witnesses from BDSA that construction under way or planned would end the supply emergency by 1958, he suggested, as an immediate approach to the problem of supply for the small publisher, an increase in advertising rates on the part of the metropolitan press. He opined bluntly: "I must say to the big newspapers of this country that I cannot cry too much for them. I am more concerned about the small newspapers. Some of them may be forced out of business, not because they do not want to pay the price, but because they cannot get it even if they pay the price. But I think if everybody gets together here, we can solve this situation. . . ."

After giving the large publishers an opportunity to digest this particularly unpalatable morsel, Klein called Cranston Williams to testify on January 25, 1956. Williams repeated his previous belief that the expansion planned through 1958 would not meet publishers' demands, and expressed the conviction that mere price increases would not draw capital into new mills, since the present return on investment was more than adequate; the publisher, moreover, should not be expected to bear the brunt of manufacturers' plant expansion, which, in his judgment, was not proceeding fast enough to meet the coming demand. His own remedy was the suggestion that publishers must invest actively in plant construction to meet at least part of their newsprint needs.

Typically wary of government involvement in the supply situation, Williams insisted that private industry would step into the breach if prospective profits were sufficient. He took fright when Klein suggested the possibility of government allocation of supplies to look after the needs of small publishers, and even at the milder suggestion that the big press might voluntarily share with the small fry, taking refuge in the stock statement that no publisher had yet been forced to suspend publication solely because of shortage of paper and, on behalf of his organization, promising to see to it that the small fry got their share. He concluded: "I do not want to see any form of cutback by any newspaper regardless of how much newsprint he has until we are convinced that it is the only way that the small paper can be cared for. . . ."

Most mills expanded production during the spring and early summer while this investigatory process developed; delivery cutbacks still in effect promised to continue into the latter season, and the spot market price of odd lots was up as high as $215 per ton. Announcement of expansion plans came from International (for a second United States mill at Pine Bluff, Arkansas), from Great Northern (at its Maine location), from Abitibi (at Fort William, Ontario), from J. and J. Rogers Company (for a mill at Silt, Colorado), and from a proposed mill in New Brunswick ("the first Canadian newsprint mill in the East since the Thirties"). The only sour note detected in this chorus was announcement that construction of a proposed mill in the Arkansas-Oklahoma area had been postponed due to inability to sign up customers for its potential tonnage.[11]

The A.N.P.A. was less optimistic than the industry about supply. President Slocum's address to the 1956 annual convention (April 25) spoke pridefully of the association's continual support of increased supplies and complimented the manufacturers for the valiant efforts which were furnishing the greatest output in history, despite which, however, a shortage persisted for which " 'no relief is in sight. . . .' " The Newsprint Committee pointed out that publishers were able to meet the demands upon them only by buying overseas paper at high prices and by depleting their reserves, tactics which could tide things over only temporarily until, it was hoped, new production in 1957 and 1958 would become available " 'in the amounts needed. The picture is not optimistic.'" The report concluded: "'It would be incorrect to assure publishers that their newsprint difficulties will shortly be solved. The present picture gives no indication that such is the case.

"'Newspapers should operate on the facts that there is not sufficient newsprint to supply demand; that there seems but little hope that the present lack of balance between supply and demand will not continue at least through 1956; and that the announced speed-ups by the mills will serve only to alleviate and not completely relieve existing shortages.'"

The convention also heard a significant analysis of the situation by Dr. Charles W. Boyce, its newsprint consultant, which was presently embodied in a pamphlet, *The First Five Years: Report on the Decade 1951–1960 of Newsprint Supply and Demand.* Together, address and pamphlet pointed out that at the half-decade demand was running ahead of the trend predicted in 1951 and that although large amounts of new tonnage were in sight, there was no guarantee that these would solve publishers' problems; indeed, "From 500,000 to 1,000,000 tons of capacity in excess of trend requirements should be provided as a cushion to safeguard customers' interests." With this need, coupled with the possibility of increasing overseas demands, he concluded that "as much as 1,000,000 tons more capacity than is now scheduled is needed by 1960." [12]

Before the mid-year, however, Cassandra voices were being raised. As early as May 21, 1956, *Paper Trade Journal,* while confident of the long future, was calling attention to the dangers of short-run overcapacity because of the great amount of new tonnage coming in at the same time; and its editor, John C. W. Evans, was counseling manufacturers to take a long look at plans for new expansion, a warning which was repeated from various angles in succeeding issues.

In mid-August J. D. Zellerbach predicted a state of over-

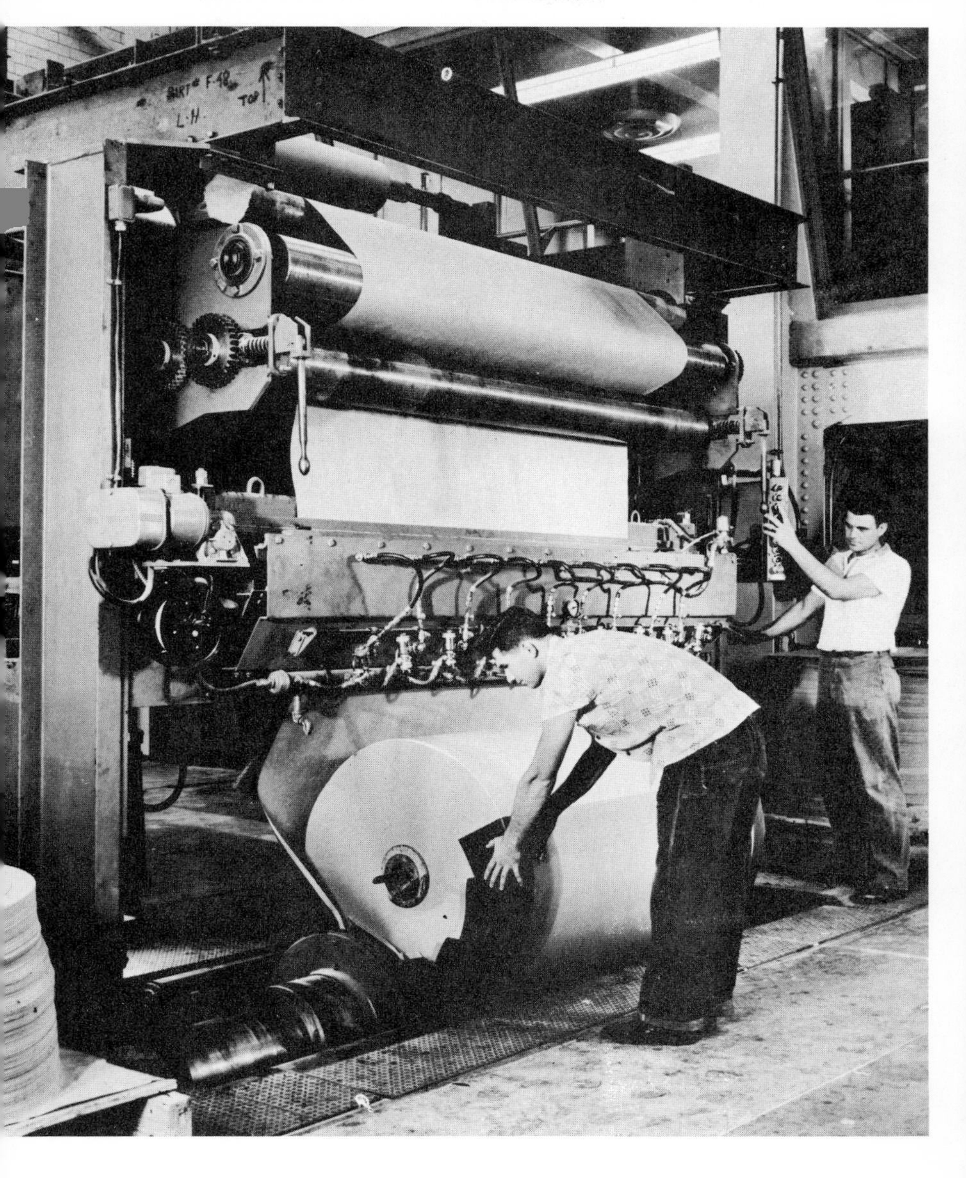

Automatic wrapping machines take over most of the packaging task.

Newsprint is usually produced against orders and can therefore be sent out to customers as soon as it is made. Most newsprint is shipped by rail freight to publishers. The picture shows a typical railroad loading platform at a paper mill.

production within two years, and warned of the danger of a consequent price war. And the Forest Products Division of the Department of Commerce, casting a balance on the first half-year, reported (in September) that "supplies had come into closer balance with demand and allowed a 36,000 tons rebuilding of inventories since the first of the year. . . ." Indeed, by mid-year it was becoming apparent that inventory accumulation and excess capacity would ere long require a period of readjustment within the industry; this prediction became conviction during the last half of 1956.[13]

As summer moved into autumn, attention shifted from supply, now definitely accepted as either presently or prospectively in excess, to price. As if to ward off any move in this area, President Slocum of the A.N.P.A. expressed in April " 'the opinion that current prices should remain stable. Financial statements . . . indicate strong and rewarding manufacturing positions. . . .' " Shortly afterward (May 9) Lord Rothermere, head of important Canadian newsprint interests, was quoted as not anticipating an increase in the near future. By early October, however, the A.N.P.A.'s board of directors was exercised by rumors that mill salesmen were "priming" publishers for a jump, and felt called upon to issue a statement through the association's new President, William Dwight, indicating the conviction that an increase was not necessary in order to maintain profits at a reasonable level. It was pointed out that manufacturers owed the courtesy of discussing mutual problems with their customers, so that the latter might have an opportunity to urge the dangerous effects of increases on the future of consumption. Interestingly enough, this approach followed closely upon the publication by President M. J. Foley of Powell River Sales Company, Ltd., of a brochure summarizing his remarks of the past summer to west coast publishers in which he regretted the ill effects of the manufacturers' failure, prior to the price hike of 1955, to take publishers into their confidence on matters of rising manufacturing costs.

Robert U. Brown, of *Editor & Publisher*, commenting favorably upon the brochure, pointedly called attention to the possibility that better communications between the protagonists might well minimize the "periodic ill-feeling . . . which coincides with newsprint price increases. . . ." Rumors that Powell River was planning an increase prompted the A.N.P.A. to telegraph a direct query to that company, to which it replied that there had been " 'no official statement on price' " but that in the company's best judgment " 'newsprint cannot be isolated from the general upward trend of costs and prices.' " By early December (December 3) Senator Charles E. Potter of Michigan was calling upon John W. Gwynne, Chairman of the Federal Trade Commission, to suggest the possibility of a joint approach to the price problem through cooperation between the commission and its Dominion counterpart, the Restrictive Trade Practices Commission, which might lead to legislative action against price-fixing by both governments. This senatorial interest stimulated activity on the part of the commission, which announced late in the year a study of the newsprint problem as a preface to possible interagency cooperation. It was not, however, until December 31 that Abitibi announced a $4 increase, to $134, New York port, effective March 31, 1957, justified on the grounds of constantly increasing costs which it was no longer possible to absorb.[14]

The year just reviewed was definitely one of transition, during which new supply eased the pressures of the previous twelve-month. With the easing of the supply problem came a corresponding diminution in congressional activity. Toward the end of 1956, rising costs caught up with the manufacturers to a point where one of them felt justified in seeking a higher price, despite the practical certainty of overproduction which faced the industry as a whole. A higher price, too, might help to offset the cost of carrying idle production capacity. Thus the new year found publishers relatively content on supply, but aggravated as to price, with another phase of antagonism in the offing.

The events of 1957 reflected to a considerable extent the year-end prognostications of 1956, colored and modified by unexpected developments in the form of a business recession and, toward the end of the year and carrying over into 1958, a strike in the British Columbia mills which had a minor effect on the production-supply picture. Publisher-consumer relations started under the disturbing influence of the price increase announced just before the New Year, which resulted in the normal and predictable congressional inquiry into newsprint matters, this time by two committees operating almost simultaneously.

As the curve of increasing production crossed the line of decreasing consumption during the second half-year an obviously "growing margin of supply over demand" developed, and the resulting overproduction brought about postponement or cancellation of considerable segments of proposed tonnage increases. North American production increased almost infinitesimally, that of the United States standing at about 6 per cent increase, Canada's down 1.1 per cent, and the over-all figure up 0.4 per cent. United States production attained an all-time high of 1,826,000 tons, improving upon the previous top figures of 1926, and accounting for 25 per cent of the national consumption, as against 18 per cent in 1951. Despite the fact that mills on both sides of the border operated at well below their maximum rated capacity, it was estimated that a "cushion" of 150,000 tons a year (excluding exports) in excess demand would characterize the years 1957 to 1960, inclusive.

Consumption remained high during the first six months, but dropped during the second half-year (while production was declining somewhat) in response to declining advertising activity and the business recession, and at year's end was slightly below the 1956 level—the first year since 1952 which failed to register a gain in this area. These developments found publishers momentarily satisfied with the supply situation, but refusing to become complacent in the face of a momentary excess of productive capacity over demand. The manufacturers were in a somewhat poorer profit position, but still comfortably well off, though the specter of idle tonnage with its attritionary effects on high-investment mills was not a pleasant one.[15]

The parade of price increases, which presently included the United States firms, bore its usual fruit of crimination, justification, and investigation. By the time the sixth major Canadian company had fallen into line in mid-January, President Dwight had announced (January 2, 1957) that the A.N.P.A., "disappointed" at Abitibi's action, was unconvinced of its necessity in view of large industry profits; the action was, he said, particularly ungracious in the light of delivery cutbacks which in 1956 had forced publishers to buy large tonnage in the spot market; he accused the mills of charging all the traffic would bear and of endangering "the goodwill that should exist between manufacturers and their customers." And Cranston Williams had advanced (January 14) what was to become a common theme: " 'So long as there is no cushion of production the publishers are in a strait jacket and at the mercy of the first mill which decides to raise the price.' "

President M. J. Foley of Powell River riposted (January 3) that the $4 increase was overmodest and should instead have been from $8 to $10 to take care of producers' real needs. Bowaters' announcement (of January 14) carried an unusual note of concern: " 'We do hope you will realize that it is distasteful to us to have to increase prices because we know you have very real problems in passing on your additional costs, and the last thing in the world we want to do is to add to your problems. . . .' " The mills, obviously on the defensive, tended to take this line that the increase was being held to a minimum in deference to the problems of their customers and in spite of customer pressure for constantly increased production.[16]

The investigatory process was soon well under way, resulting in considerable discussion and in hearings by two committees; there was talk, too, of an inquiry under the joint auspices of the Federal Trade Commission and the Dominion Restrictive Trade Practices Commission into the possibility of collusive action to increase prices. Informal discussion apparently occurred between the two agencies during January, but a question in the Dominion Commons (January 16, 1957) elicited a government statement that the increase did not warrant investigation, since it was explainable on ordinary economic grounds not necessarily involving collusion.

Congressional action was afoot as early as January 11, when Senator Potter, after conference with Trade Commission officials, asked Senator Magnuson to use the Committee on Interstate and Foreign Commerce, of which he was Chairman, as a vehicle of price hearings. On January 17, Congressman Celler called upon the Department of Justice to take another look at Canadian prices, and suggested the possibility that seizure within the United States of shipments of Canadian-produced newsprint might open the door to antitrust proceedings against the Canadian concerns. On the same day Karl E. Mundt of South Dakota introduced a resolution calling on the Senate Committee on Banking and Currency to investigate price and supply matters.

By January 26, Magnuson had indicated that his committee would open hearings on February 26, and Senator Estes Kefauver of Tennessee had announced interest on the part of his Antitrust and Antimonopoly Committee. Three days later Potter wrote the Secretary of State requesting consideration of the proposal for joint inquiry raised in his earlier communication to the Trade Commission, but was told (February 25) that conversations with the Canadian Embassy led the department to conclude that " 'it would not be useful to press for a cooperative antitrust investigation at this stage. . . .' "

Potter told the Senate that the newsprint supply situation resembled "a colossal spider web spanning the whole of Canada, extending across the United States border and down into our own Southern States. Lurking somewhere within that web is the spider himself. Government antitrust officials have been trying to capture him for years. From 1933 to the present day, he has devoured the profit margin of publishers by sending the price of newsprint up 325 per cent. Like helpless flies, the smaller publishers have been squeezed to death. Larger publishers fight for their lives. . . .

"Some say the spider lurks in Canadian territory. Some say he lives on our side of the border. There is evidence that he operates like a cartel, and the years have produced strong traces of his price-fixing and restraint-of-trade activity. Despite the attention given to newsprint by Federal agencies and congressional committees, he has evaded positive identification." And on January 14, Oren Harris of Arkansas introduced a resolution authorizing the House Committee on Interstate and Foreign Commerce, of which he was Chairman, to investigate questions of production, consumption, and supply. This resolution, passed on February 5, providing the committee with $100,000 for expenses, completes the setting for committee inquiries to be noted in succeeding paragraphs.[17]

Opening the hearings on February 18, 1957, Chairman Harris announced that his committee's purpose would be to develop the current picture and to determine the factors exerting possible adverse influences upon future supply, as a basis for determining the necessity of present and future action. He called somewhat pointed attention to the fact that Cranston Williams of the A.N.P.A. had indicated his inability to attend, but would be invited to a later session.[18] In the absence of A.N.P.A. representation, the principal testimony came from H. B. McCoy, Administrator of the Forest Products Division of the Department of Commerce and a representative likewise of BDSA, who underwent extensive interrogation by committee members as to the current situation. He stated that the function of his agency was a double one, to foster foreign and domestic commerce, and to take steps, under ODM, in relation to the national defense.

His testimony brought out a number of developments which had emerged, with congressional cooperation, from one or the other of these two functions. Among these was the tax amortization program for new units in the domestic industry, authorized by Congress and administered under ODM; here, he pointed out, a defense-connected goal of 571,000 new tons a year had been established, beginning in 1952, of which, however, only 400,000 tons of actual capacity had been added. A second activity, undertaken in response to the committee's request in 1956, was the preparation of an analysis of projected demands in the various grades of paper to the year 1965; this, he reported, would furnish the Department of Commerce with estimates of newsprint capacity for the years 1957, 1958, and 1959, and was well along toward completion. Data would soon be assembled, and he estimated that the report would be available in from sixty to ninety days. He replied spiritedly to committee criticisms of his agency for limiting its activities to the collection of statistics, instead of taking a more active role in stimulating production, by pointing out that its legislative frame of reference gave it neither controls nor cash. It was confined, therefore, to conducting studies, which it had done in the areas of hardwood and bagasse as new sources of supply, and to letting the industry know, as it had also done, its views as to the future outlook.

McCoy refused, moreover, to be as pessimistic as some of his contemporaries on matters of price and supply. Queried by one committee member as to whether he had seen indications of price control by the producers, he replied that he had seen no evidence of such activity, as between United States mills and those of Canada, or between United States and foreign mills. Confronted with the A.N.P.A.'s prediction of January 23 that publishers had "'no prospect of capacity by 1960 to cover unexpected increases in demand such as occurred in 1955 and 1956,'" he agreed that his agency's forecast was "somewhat more optimistic than their estimate. . . ." Under pressure he admitted that his agency was "probably conservative" in its estimates of increasing demand, but defended the mills against pressure to overbuild to take care of such surges as those of 1955 and 1956, since this would entail the expensive maintenance of idle capacity.

He refused to permit committee members to push him into admitting that the industry should be expected to provide publishers with a "cushion," as had been contended in recent A.N.P.A. statements which were picked up in the discussion by one of the committee members, and subsequent exchanges brought out the fact that the steel industry had been impelled to furnish such a cushion only under the spur of presidential insistence. At the conclusion of a long session he gave it as his cautious but reasoned "estimate . . . that the demand will about match the supply, with perhaps some little balances of supply over demand. . . ."

As McCoy stepped down, Chairman Harris opined that the A.N.P.A. picture as portrayed in the January 23 survey "seems to contradict what Mr. McCoy has said" in predicting an adequate supply of newsprint. He concluded: "In view of that, I think it is going to be certainly advisable for someone from the American Newspaper Publishers Association to come before the committee and explain just what they have in mind with this type of criticism in view of the factual information which has been presented here today." It was not, however, until June 3, long after the Magnuson hearings had run their course, that Williams put in an appearance before the Harris group, where he made a fairly careful statement of the postwar price picture, beginning by raising a question as to the conservatism of the Department of Commerce figures.

He pointed to the difficulty faced by publishers, in sharp competition with each other, in dealing with price increases levied by "producers not actually in competition with each other," indicated his belief that the Canadian mills were lagging behind their production potential, although improving in this respect, and gave it as his judgment that the end of increasing capacity by speed-ups had about been reached. He did not, he said, recommend any action with respect to price, but insisted that his function was to convince anyone who would listen of the needs of his industry for more and more newsprint.[19]

The committee assembled again on June 17, 1957, to receive the Department of Commerce report, prepared largely by W. LeRoy Neubrech, which had been promised at the

Conscious of its responsibility to preserve and expand the nation's forest
the newsprint industry has for many years practiced good forest manage
ment, growing more trees than it cuts. In the picture tiny pine seedling
are being planted. Other methods include seeding by plane, and wood
cutting practices which foster and encourage natural reforestation.

February session. This was labeled as the first departmental study prepared for public use which analyzed projected future supply and demand, not in terms of specific forecasts for a particular year, but as statistical projections based on predetermined assumptions; both supply and demand projections, it was suggested, should be re-examined every two years and adjusted for intervening changes. This had previously been submitted to both producer and consumer groups, both of which agreed that "the analysis seemed to be adequate and competent," while giving room for individual differences of interpretation. It indicated that "a growing margin of supply over demand" was indicated for 1957, 1958, and 1959. Publisher comment, so far as it is available, was remarkably mild in tone.[20]

The Magnuson Committee hearings opened February 26 under a broad program of proposed investigation, the Chairman asserting his group's interest in restrictions on manufacture or distribution, in timber supplies, in newsprint in Alaska, in the adaptability of new materials to newsprint manufacture, in recent price increases, and in greater cooperation between producers and consumers. He hoped to probe the problem of cartelization of the Canadian industry, spoke in a somewhat discouraged vein about the inability of the Department of State to make headway against Canadian price increases, and paid his particular respects to the small publishers, presumably worse hurt than their larger compatriots by recent increases.[21]

Cranston Williams was the first witness. He examined the production situation statistically, quoting figures to show that proposed additions on both sides of the border would bring North American capacity to 9,500,000 tons by 1960, "exactly balancing expected demands," but not providing any reserve capacity to care for sudden emergency. Publishers, he contended, were entitled to relief from a situation in which they might at any time be forced into the spot market for their necessities. He concluded that, to avoid being kept in a "tough, tight, high-price situation, we must have a minimum of 500,000 tons additional capacity beyond that now announced" to take care of prospective demand in 1960.

Several executives of domestic mills joined in protesting the Williams analysis and in presenting evidence in other directions. G. J. Ticoulat, now Senior Vice President of Crown Zellerbach, allowing for an adjustment of Williams' arithmetic, which he asserted was incorrect, challenged his conclusions, asserting on his own part that 1960 would see a minimum of 500,000 tons of extra capacity, and might see an additional 750,000. He denied emphatically holding any conversations with his competitors on price, and argued stoutly that increasing costs, which he could not at the moment document, had been responsible for the recent price increase.

Albin R. Caspar, Vice President of Great Northern, went at length into increasing costs which had forced his company in recent years to double its investment in order to increase production by 40 per cent. As a result, Great Northern found it necessary to operate at close to capacity in order to keep fixed costs within bounds. August B. Meyer, President of Bowater, insisted that new production in sight by 1960 would provide the cushion demanded by Williams, and Stuart Kay, Vice President of International, saw no reason to think that prospective capacity would not take care of increasing demands in the immediate future. He spoke with some asperity of the "one-way street" involved in the A.N.P.A.'s demand for stand-by capacity which, he pointed out, left publishers free to reduce purchases, while leaving manufacturers with partially idle plants. Unlike the usual manufacturing witness, he gave figures to show that International's cost, before interest, of manufacturing newsprint and shipping it to the United States had since June 15, 1952, risen $12.10 per ton (6.3 per cent), "running slambang full with all the stops out," as against price increases of $8 over the same period.

Fowler, speaking personally and not for the Newsprint Association of Canada, of which he was still President, furnished a statement which was read into the record asserting, in contravention of the Williams-A.N.P.A. position: " 'There is not today, and there has not been for several months, any shortage of newsprint in Canada or the United States,' " and, barring unforeseen circumstances, " 'there will not be any shortage of newsprint, anywhere, during the next 3 years.' " He held, also, that sufficient stand-by capacity would be available for some time to meet sudden surges in demand. His conclusions were upheld over a limited area by the results of a survey conducted by an agency of the University of Wisconsin and covering twelve midwestern states, indicating that a balance of supply over demand of from 3 per cent to 6 per cent was likely to persist for a three-year period opening in 1957.

An interesting and somewhat unusual development was the appearance of an individual publisher, Richard Scudder of *The Newark Evening News*, breaking a lance in favor of the plight of the large publishers, who, he argued, were in worse position than the small fry, who usually received the bulk of commiseration. His position was based upon the argument that as circulation increased, so did the proportionate cost of newsprint in the total operation. It was his conclusion that the most profitable papers were those with circulation between 30,000 and 50,000, and that at least three "giants" stood to lose $1,000,000 each during the year as a result of the price increase.

One further but abortive approach to investigation based on the law-violation angle came out of the Magnuson hearings. Earl W. Kintner, General Counsel of the Federal Trade Commission, suggested two possible approaches in his testimony of February 28. The first was by asking Congress to instruct the Trade Commission to make an economic survey of the industry such as had been made repeatedly in the past, and most of the materials for which were already available. This, he pointed out, might develop evidence of violations which "could be subject to corrective action by the Commission or by the Department of Justice." Another and perhaps more fruitful avenue might be "another industrywide legal inquiry," designed mainly as a probe into law violations as opposed to the discovery of economic facts.

When he indicated that his agency had neither funds nor staff to make the second approach, Senator Magnuson, who was also a member of the Appropriations Committee, virtually instructed his agency to increase its asking budget so as to provide for an inquiry, despite Kintner's admission that the last previous investigation failed to turn up evidence of a conspiracy to fix prices. Eventually (March 25) a resolution was introduced in the Senate authorizing a Trade Commission probe into newsprint matters, but it was blocked repeatedly by Senator Allen J. Ellender of Louisiana on the double ground that several similar inquiries had got nowhere, and that a particular resolution was unnecessary, as the Trade Commission already had the power to make the move; a resolution would simply afford the agency an opportunity to come to Congress with a request for added funds.[22]

Over-all, the Magnuson hearings brought out unusually vigorous representations from the industry in response to the A.N.P.A.'s demand for a cushion of stand-by tonnage. More emphasis than usual was placed on advancing industrial costs, with more disclosures in this area than the normally close-mouthed manufacturers were willing to make. Statistics, too, appeared to be on the side of the mills. Indeed, the

A.N.P.A.'s demand for a cushion appeared a trifle hollow when it became increasingly apparent that the cushion was actually in existence and was likely to be a factor in the situation for some time to come.

Matters tended to find a level during the spring and summer of 1957, with supply admittedly in excess as against a softening demand and with production continuing high (particularly in the United States, where the first six months' output exceeded that of any previous year by 13.8 per cent) despite the beginning of cutbacks during the summer. Mill profits dropped as decreasing demand and idle capacity ate into the fat. Various efforts ensued, on both sides of the border, to offset this unfavorable situation. In an address of March 3 to the American Pulp and Paper Association, Ticoulat suggested that the industry must change its basic philosophy from emphasis on production to stress on marketing, investigating potential sales areas, and tailoring production facilities to these, rather than building facilities first and then seeking purchasers.

Later in the spring a number of Canadian mills united in establishing the Newsprint Information Committee, operating out of New York to promote better understanding of the producer's point of view on the part of both public and consumers of his product. Generously, one of its sponsors announced, the committee would direct its efforts toward improving public knowledge of the problems of consumers as well as producers. By mid-summer some Canadian mills were trying to meet the situation by increased overseas shipments and by concealed price cuts in the Latin American market, achieved by absorbing freight and insurance costs and by accepting payment in United States dollars (which during much of the period stood at a varying discount of up to 5 per cent, as compared with the Canadian dollar). In September, indeed, it was reported that the exchange situation was costing the Canadian mills from $6 to $8 per ton on New York sales. Despite all these devices, however, the profits of the Canadian mills dropped an average of 20 per cent during the first half-year of 1957.

As this generally favorable supply picture was developing, the A.N.P.A. continued its pressure for more production. Dr. Charles W. Boyce supplemented the appearance of his third study of the newsprint scene by an address to the annual convention (April 24) in which he characterized the postwar period as one in which there had at no time been " 'a really adequate supply. . . .' " His survey, however, concluded with the estimate that supply would exceed demand by about 2 per cent in 1960. As publishers' confidence in adequate supply generally mounted, little evidence of complacency was permitted to appear and pressure for an adequate cushion over current demand continued for some time. Complaints against high prices continued to be heard, but there was some tendency to shift the pressure from price to quality. Privately and individually, publishers admitted that shortages were unlikely for several years, and as the months moved along, there was a lessening of demand for higher production.[23]

The third and final quarters of 1957 produced unmistakable signs of recession, somewhat euphemistically denominated by one writer in the paper field as a " 'prolonged sideward movement' " in the economy. By this time drastic cutbacks had resulted in the scrapping or postponement of 5,000,000 tons of planned capacity for the paper and board industry as a whole. Production continued at a lower level, with the Canadian mills operating in September at 91.1 per cent of capacity, as contrasted with 105.4 per cent the year before. Despite lower production, reduced consumption enabled publishers to increase their October inventories to fifty days' supply, as contrasted with the normal forty-five days' stock on hand. Under these circumstances, pressure for price reduction brought some concessions on spot transactions, though the contract price level remained unaffected. The year ended with Canadian optimism for the long-run still high, and with Fowler reported as recognizing philosophically that some surplus capacity " ' "should be regarded as a normal situation likely to obtain throughout all industry in the immediate and foreseeable future." ' " General adjustment to the current facts of life seemed to be the order of the day.[24]

The year 1958 was a peculiar one in many ways. An overproductive industry, which was still bringing in new tonnage, faced a market which during the first six months consumed less than normal and then registered only a modest upturn from the recession, which apparently reached its depths about mid-year. As a result of these combined circumstances, there was relatively little pressure on either price or production. Relations between publishers and manufacturers created no unusual problems, the former having ample supplies and the latter being mainly concerned with minimizing their loss of profits from high-cost plants idled by the recession. Perhaps the chief development, then, was the appearance of a new gambit in the investigatory area, an outgrowth of events of 1957.

The year opened on a conciliatory note, with Cranston Williams complimenting the Canadian mills (January 22) on the production increases which would eliminate such shortages as occurred in 1955 and 1956. From north of the border, Fowler rationalized the existing plethora of capacity, telling the Canadian Pulp and Paper Association (January 31) that the industry had at last accomplished " 'what we set out to achieve; and what we were right to try to achieve. We have created an excess of capacity to serve our markets, which, in our economic system, those markets were entitled to have. We can now look after sudden surges of demand as we ought to be able to do.' " With the recession still an active factor, consumption remained relatively stable, on a considerably lower scale, during much of the year. January use was down 5.3 per cent from the 1957 level and that for the first quarter was down 5.8 per cent. A steady downward curve in consumption reached the bottom in July; the August figures registered the first gain in fourteen months, and by the end of the year the "deficit" had been cut to only 4 per cent below 1957 levels. In the light of such obvious plenty, no voice could be raised in complaint, and the hardiest criers of short supply were forced to admit that there was ample capacity in sight to take care of any possible demands through 1960.

Against this comfortable state of affairs, the mills had to contend with the problem of high-cost capacity standing idle —to the extent, in late July, of a million tons. As if to compound the difficulty, new production continued to come in, with International's new Arkansas plant and new machines at Great Lakes, Coosa River, and other mills, pouring added tonnage into the market. With rated capacity up approximately 7 per cent over the 1957 level, the mills were forced to operate at 84 per cent of capacity, well below their maximum, with consequent ill effects on the industry's profit balances. All in all, it was a period when the manufacturers could well look to the possibility of a rosier future to right some of the ills of the unpleasant present; a few souls, indeed, had the hardihood to look far ahead to the day when new capacity, rather than better sales, would be the problem.[25]

The principal development of 1958 was an investigation by the Federal Bureau of Investigation on behalf of the Department of Justice, begun toward the end of 1957 and resulting in a report of May 9, 1958, by the department to President Dwight D. Eisenhower and to the Congress. Like numerous previous investigations, it was directed largely toward the possibly monopolistic aspects of the operations of United States concerns which controlled or were affiliated with Canadian producers and which, through their binational character, were able to evade antimonopoly legislation on both sides of the border. Like several preceding investigations, it unearthed and recapitulated a great deal of information, much of it repetitious of previous aspects of the present story; it is, indeed, the best brief survey of what might be called the "monopoly-charge" approach that has come to the author's attention. Like several of the earlier investigations, however, it was compelled in the end to return a verdict of "not proven" with respect to the charges which constitute the gravamen of its plea.[26]

It will be recalled that efforts were made during 1957 to have the Trade Commission look into the "legal," as contrasted with the "economic," aspects of the industry, and that these had been brought to naught by parliamentary objections. By October, however, FBI agents were approaching publishers armed with a letter from Victor R. Hansen, Assistant Attorney General in charge of the Antitrust Division, which reportedly asked their cooperation in an inquiry " 'into possible violations of the Federal antitrust laws with respect to the newsprint industry. . . .' " The letter pointedly indicated: " 'This is not an investigation of publishers.' " The inquiry was apparently confined to the affairs of United States companies which controlled or were affiliated with Canadian concerns. It was conducted under Section 708(e) of the Defense Production Act of 1950 which directed the Attorney General to review the administration of the act. Senator J. William Fulbright, in reporting the document to the Congress on behalf of his Committee on Banking and Currency, pointed out that the current review was "for the purpose of determining any factors which may tend to eliminate competition, create or strengthen monopolies, injure small business, or otherwise promote undue concentration of economic power in the course of administration of the act."

Starting from the fact that ownership and location of this basic industry crossed national lines, the Attorney General's report moved immediately to the "elusive" problem of "the situs of the corporate control and policymaking" of the industry. It listed as "Apparent manifestations of competitive inadequacy" uniform prices maintained by the zone-pricing system and long-term contracts which by price tie-ins and end-use restrictions minimized the competitive element in the industry. It continued: "Each of these items taken singly raises substantial doubt of the competitive functioning of the industry which cannot be resolved with the investigative tools at hand. Taken together with detailed associative activities of the industry giving ample opportunity for collusion, that doubt is reinforced. The industry vigorously denies collusion, but with equal vigor denies access to the records which might dispel the doubt."

There followed a considerable description of manufacturing processes and of price, supply, and production matters, after which the document returned to the "functional ties which blur geographical and jurisdictional distinctions, and tend to weld the separate entities into a stable and cooperative whole. . . ." Here appeared at once the "international character of certain of the major corporate families" which "have become effectively binational and are thereby able to adapt themselves internally to reduce the effectiveness of adverse Government action. . . ." International's organizational scheme was detailed as an example of this phase of affairs.

After some attention to Fowler's adverse observations on the political aspects of the newsprint situation, contained in the Canadian Pulp and Paper Association's recent submission to the Royal Commission on Canada's Economic Prospects, attention was called to Ontario's Business Records Protection Act of 1947, with its obstacles to adequate United States investigation of company records domiciled in the Province of Ontario. There followed a summary of previous antitrust investigations involving newsprint manufacturers, going back to 1904 and running through Trade Commission procedures against Crown Zellerbach and International for alleged violation of Section 7 of the Clayton Antitrust Act (which have not been treated here because their principal immediate interest centered on other grades of paper).

Considerable attention was then devoted to price in relation to competition, taking off from the initial premise that price behavior "creates considerable doubts as to the competitiveness of the industry" and describing at length the pattern of price establishment which had resulted in by-and-large uniformity of price in normal times. Here attention was also given to the zone-pricing system, which, together with price leadership, had resulted in an "almost complete lack of price competition, a lack which has persisted for a number of decades. . . ." Admitting that long-run prices would doubtless tend to find a level in the case of a highly standardized product such as newsprint, the report found it difficult to "explain short-run, simultaneous price movements and price identity among numerous mills in widely-scattered locations and with widely differing costs. . . ." Next was examined the possible contribution to price uniformity of long-term contracts, desired by both publishers and manufacturers for somewhat different reasons.

In view of all these factors, there was raised "the possibility that agreement among the producers is responsible for their identical prices and their simultaneous price changes. . . ." After retailing the Celler Committee's inability, in 1951, to find "'direct evidence of price-fixing in the American market,'" the report echoed the Celler findings by announcing that the current "survey has been unable to uncover direct evidence of agreement among producers either in Canada or the United States to fix newsprint prices in the United States. The producers have vigorously denied the existence of any such agreements. They are equally vigorous, however, in asserting that the most relevant data on individual company costs and records pertaining to establishing prices, cannot be made available for inspection. Consequently, no firm conclusion is possible as to whether agreements presently exist in the industry to fix the price of newsprint in the United States." Evidence was then reviewed to support the conclusion that price-fixing agreements existed with regard to sales of other grades of paper in Canada and with regard to sales of newsprint in other than United States markets, and a somewhat negative conclusion was reached: "To establish that all these [prices] are the results of impersonal market forces requires more evidence than has been made available." Some attention, finally, was given to long-term contracts as a possible factor in minimizing competition, with the conclusion that there was "no clear evidence" that commerce in newsprint was necessarily dependent upon such restrictive regulations.

After this survey, which stated the case for the possibility of restrictive collusion more bluntly and cogently than most similar documents, it was concluded that its chief value lay in furnishing "a factual outline for consideration of the competitive problems which affect an important area of defense supply. . . ." It admitted, however: "No final conclusions as to the competitive status of this industry are now possible. It displays several manifestations that could well indicate the inadequacy or absence of true competition among its individual members. . . . Considering the long record of this industry's readiness to concert of action, coupled with its active unwillingness to supply the information base upon which the reality of these apparent factors could be fully measured, there can be no feeling of assurance that competition regulates this industry's course. . . ."

Upon this incriminatory but uncertain note ends this narrative of twenty-odd years of producer-consumer relations in the field of newsprint. The problem now becomes one of summarizing the evidence here assembled and of drawing such conclusions as seem warranted by the facts.

Printing press at a large city newspaper plant.

CHAPTER VII

Summary and Conclusions

THE STORY just completed has served a double purpose from the author's point of view. First, it has afforded him an opportunity to study two more decades of newsprint history, to pursue the story of publisher-manufacturer relations through the period of post-Depression recovery, World War II, and nearly a decade and a half of postwar ups and downs. Second, it has permitted him to review, as he did earlier in the 1940's, the attitudes and positions of the two protagonists in the perennial struggle to adjust the balance of supply and demand. Such a review, to be useful, should arrive at some conclusions on the last two decades of newsprint history and their relation to the past. The succeeding paragraphs will be devoted to a summary of the narrative and to a statement of the conclusions.

The period 1937 to 1939 was one of shakedown after depression, three rather uneventful years devoted to restoring stability. Newsprint supply was ample, demand was moderate, price not a matter of great controversy, and relationships between producers and consumers were relatively easy. The World War II period opened with good producer-consumer relations, stimulated by Canadian promises to look after their best customer's needs. There ensued a remarkable achievement in industrial logistics in which, during the pressures of a world crisis, the Canadian industry enabled the United States press to operate under surprisingly minor limitations. Domestic regulations set a relatively high level of consumption, protected the small publisher, and left policing of the supply essentially in the hands of the publishers themselves. The domestic industry, too, was allowed to operate at a relatively high level in comparison with that of the Dominion; this, together with the lag which developed between price and costs, caused irritations to the north.

As consumption and production conditions deteriorated in 1943, tensions appeared. Price advanced, but not enough to satisfy the Canadian mills; the machinery of distribution failed to keep an adequate rein on the shortening supply; publishers and Congress applied increasing pressure (which was not relished) on the Canadian mills to increase a supply they were straining hard to maintain. Out of these tensions developed a congressional interest in the newsprint supply question which has continued to the present time. Over-all, both publishers and Canadian mills came through the war reasonably well; United States mills were less successful, and many were taken off newsprint and put on more profitable lines. The years of peace were to test the interaction of booming demand, short supply, and investigative reaction to these problems.

With peace came the problems of transition from strict control to freer operations, and of adjustment of a still short supply to a rapidly increasing demand. The industry itself took a large share in managing the transition from war to peace. The small publishers, no longer protected by guaranteed tonnage, found themselves at an increasing disadvantage as short supply resulted in a near-famine; their larger brethren were also under pressure from advertisers and subscribers. Under these circumstances, the question of supply remained dominant for some time. Canadian mills, made wary by the overbuilding of the twenties, deliberately adopted a policy of relatively slow expansion by speeding up existing facilities rather than constructing new ones; for the time being there was very little increase in the United States' producing capacity. Prices, however, went up repeatedly. The end results were some disturbance in publisher-manufacturer relations, efforts to stimulate Canadian production, and congressional and executive investigation on a considerable scale. Through it all, relations between publishers and manufacturers remained relatively amicable, a situation perhaps aided by the appearance of a buyer's market in 1949.

In the new decade questions of supply were still important, and a good deal of attention was devoted to increasing production. Canada continued to adhere to the expansion-by-speed-up technique, while to the south a new approach was developed through the tax-amortization device; the latter aided the construction of new facilities and started the domestic industry along the slow road toward parity—a road that is still being traveled as this study ends. The watchdog committees set up during the war were continued from Congress to Congress, and their hearings and reports were used to assist the cause of more production on both sides of the border. They were supplemented by the work of the Celler Committee, one of the most active investigations of the monopoly aspects of the newsprint question. The period 1950 to 1955 ends, as did the previous one, with supply and demand in relative balance, and with some indications of weariness over the repeated investigations which had characterized the recent years.

With the mid-fifties came a sudden and unforeseen upsurge in demand which caught all hands unaware and which found United States production beginning, at long last, to make considerable strides ahead. So great was the demand, indeed, that there began to be talk in Canada of new mills, as well as of continuing the postwar speed-up technique of expansion. Optimism continued into 1956 as demand far outpaced supply and as talk of hundreds of millions of dollars devoted to new production for 1958 began to be heard throughout the continent. In the face of these large promises of new tonnage, the A.N.P.A. continued bearish and developed the so-called "cushion" argument to the effect that the mills owed an obligation to provide capacity in excess of normal demand so as to care for an emergency of the kind that had developed in 1955. Pressures on supply kept congressional interest at a high pitch through 1956 and 1957, and in 1958 the Executive branch entered this aspect of the situation once more. By 1957 the optimism of 1955 was resulting in overproduction, and the A.N.P.A. put forth its cushion argument. Matters were thrown into something of a tailspin by the recession toward the end of the year. The story ends in 1958 with the recession apparently at an end, but with hundreds of thousands of tons of capacity idle and with both mills and publishers apparently resigned to a surplus of production for some time to come. An observer might, perhaps, be pardoned for at least raising the question as to whether the overoptimism of the twenties was repeating itself on a somewhat milder scale and without the wholesale bankruptcies which characterized the thirties.

In concluding this, his second book on the newsprint problem, the author believes that it may be useful to compare the conditions of the past twenty years with those of the earlier period covered in *Print Paper Pendulum*. Though such a comparison reveals both similarities and differences, the position of antagonism between opposing interests, despite occasional signs of accommodation, has remained relatively unchanged. The fundamental problems of balancing supply and demand and of reconciling the vigorous and divergent interests of producers and consumers, of course, remain constant; and in this connection it may be well at the outset to repeat the conclusions reached over a decade ago at the time of the original study. These were as follows: ". . . both parties share the responsibility for failure to arrive at a solution. Discounting, however, manufacturers' desire for large dividends on occasionally swollen capital, it is his judgment that over the years the major responsibility for a lack of equilibrium should be laid at the door of the publishers, whose aggressive leadership and unique position for influencing public policy have given them striking advantages over the manufacturers."

The character of the product and its basic ingredients have undergone few changes, but the changes are important ones. Although virtually limited to the introduction of southern pine and of hardwood into the manufacturing process, they have resulted in the building of an entire new industry in a section hitherto served only from a distance and at great cost, and in the provision of new sources of raw material in older producing areas. Economic factors have invariably precluded use of other materials technically suitable for newsprint manufacture.

The functions of the principal parties in the newsprint producer-consumer relationship are not very different from those of an earlier day. A.N.P.A. leadership in the last two decades has been, perhaps, less aggressive than in the days of John Norris and Herman Ridder, but Cranston Williams is hardly less powerful, if somewhat less vocal, than these spokesmen of an earlier day. The power of the press in a democracy is enormous, and any alleged threat to its "freedom," be it failure to maintain an adequate supply of its raw material or an increase in the price of that raw material, brings the congressional representatives of several thousand publishers to instant and respectful attention. This initial advantage of the publishing interest obviously subjects the manufacturer to an initial handicap. To this must be added the repeated suggestions that the manufacturing industry

Typical city newsstand.

has deviated from the path of strict rectitude in connection with national antimonopoly legislation. The minimal factual residue from recent investigations has not prevented repetition of the suggestions—a repetition which has caused the industry to develop an extreme sensitivity to any formal or informal contacts which might aid in reducing existing frictions.

The recent literature contains repeated denials of monopolistic practices. To a student of the problem, as distinguished from one involved in day-to-day industrial operations, the existence or absence of monopoly is less important than the frictions created by repeated assertions and denials of the fact. These repeated assertions have led to repeated inquiries by Congress, the Federal Trade Commission, and the Department of Justice, the effectiveness of which has been minimized by the inaccessibility of essential records, notably outside the United States. The tangible results of the inquiries have in recent years been extremely modest. Although the legal question is an extremely complicated one, the energy devoted to it has in the author's judgment served more to muddy the waters than to contribute to any worthwhile action. There is, of course, no way to measure accurately the extent to which the threat or the fact of investigation may act as a deterrent in the area of collusive action to set prices; even here there seems to be good evidence that uniformity and collusion are not necessarily synonymous.

Mention of investigations calls up another matter which has received considerable attention in the preceding pages. No one can peruse the documents carrying the story of the Brown, Beckworth, Capehart, Celler, Harris, Klein, Humphrey, and Magnuson Committees without acquiring tremendous respect for the pertinacity and general urbanity of those who testify and of those who interrogate and listen. Yet certain critical observations seem justified. The expenditure of energy necessary to bring each successive investigating committee abreast of all preceding investigations and to carry a new one forward is enormous. The drain on the time of legislators and witnesses is not inconsiderable, to say nothing of the cash outlay demanded both of the industries and of the public purse. The actual influence of this costly and cumbersome investigative machinery is difficult to measure accurately. Its effectiveness as an agency of enlightenment is undoubted; its positive effect on price is problematical, since it appears that the most active periods of investigation follow, rather than precede, price increases. It may well be that its negative effect, in preventing a worse thing from happening, is of importance, but it would be difficult to find a yardstick to measure this factor. Scanning some thousands of pages of this manifestation of the democratic process leaves this reader, at least, with a sense of frustration when trying to arrive at accurate conclusions.

Finally, in concluding this study of the newsprint problem, it appears to the author that the situation is less changed for the better than might have been hoped for after two more decades of experience on the part of Congress, manufacturers, and publishers. He can call to mind no piece of useful legislation which has reached the statute book as a result of meticulous and repeated congressional approaches to the problem. The publishers continue to hold the initiative in relations with manufacturers through their easy access to congressional ears and their command of a wide public hearing for any position they may espouse. The manufacturers retain a sensitive attitude born of repeated investigations and oft-denied intimations of price collusion, and they are ever fearful of pressures exerted by publishers. This sensitivity undoubtedly contributes to the continuing difficulty of accommodation. Neither legislation, investigation, nor public pressures will, in the author's judgment, bring these divergent elements into harmonious relationship. If this end is ever to be achieved, it must eventuate from concerted efforts to study mutual problems and prepare some joint approach to their solution. Past history offers more examples of failure than of success in such experiments, but the solution can come only from repeated and well-intentioned efforts by both parties.

Statistical Data, Notes, Bibliography, and Index to *Newsprint: Producers, Publishers, Political Pressures*

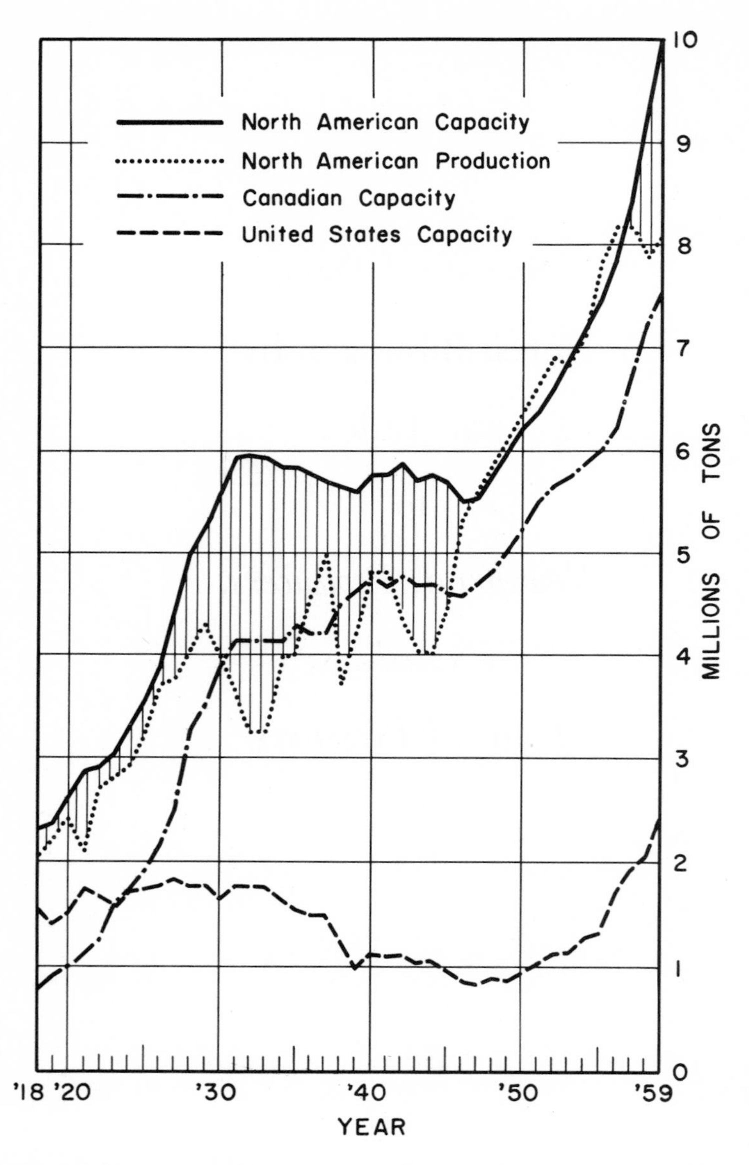

Comparisons Between North American Newsprint Capacity and Production and Between Canadian and United States Newsprint Capacity, by Millions of Tons, 1918–1959.

TABLE I. NEWSPRINT SUPPLY IN THE UNITED STATES
(Millions of Short Tons)

Year	U.S. Production	U.S. Exports	Imports	Indicated New Supply
1918	1,260	110	602	1,752
1919	1,375	111	628	1,892
1920	1,512	46	731	2,197
1921	1,225	17	792	2,000
1922	1,448	26	1,029	2,451
1923	1,485	16	1,308	2,777
1924	1,481	17	1,357	2,821
1925	1,530	23	1,448	2,955
1926	1,684	19	1,851	3,516
1927	1,486	12	1,987	3,461
1928	1,418	11	2,157	3,564
1929	1,392	19	2,423	3,796
1930	1,282	10	2,279	3,551
1931	1,157	10	2,067	3,214
1932	1,009	8	1,792	2,793
1933	946	11	1,793	2,728
1934	961	23	2,210	3,148
1935	912	22	2,383	3,273
1936	921	15	2,751	3,657
1937	946	17	3,317	4,246
1938	820	6	2,274	3,088
1939	939	13	2,612	3,538
1940	1,013	44	2,783	3,752
1941	1,015	70	2,982	3,927
1942	953	42	2,922	3,833
1943	805	35	2,637	3,407
1944	720	31	2,491	3,180
1945	724	44	2,669	3,349
1946	771	28	3,492	4,235
1947	826	28	3,957	4,755
1948	867	28	4,393	5,232
1949	900	39	4,637	5,498
1950	1,015	44	4,864	5,835
1951	1,125	71	4,960	6,014
1952	1,147	105	5,036	6,078
1953	1,084	47	5,006	6,043
1954	1,211	140	4,994	6,065
1955	1,552	207	5,164	6,509
1956	1,717	152	5,570	7,135
1957	1,826	174	5,218	6,870
1958	1,758	127	4,883	6,514

Sources: Production: Newsprint Service Bureau. Exports and Imports: U.S. Department of Commerce.

TABLE II. AVERAGE CONTRACT PRICES FOR NEWSPRINT PAPER: NEW YORK CITY DELIVERY

Year	Price per Ton
1918	$ 64.30
1919	79.40
1920	112.60
1921	111.35
1922	76.80
1923	81.80
1924	80.80
1925	76.80
1926	71.80
1927	71.80
1928	67.50
1929	62.00
1930	62.00
1931	57.00
1932	48.33
1933	41.25
1934	40.00
1935	40.00
1936	41.00
1937	42.50
1938	49.00
1939	49.00
1940	49.47
1941	49.90
1942	50.00
1943	54.66
1944	58.00
1945	60.63
1946	72.57
1947	88.50
1948	97.70
1949	100.00
1950	100.92
1951	110.55
1952	120.45
1953	125.80
1954	126.00
1955	126.00
1956	130.00
1957	133.33
1958	134.00

Source: American Newspaper Publishers Association; Newsprint Service Bureau.

Note: For the years 1918 to 1924, inclusive, the prices shown above were those quoted for the New York City market by a large Canadian company. For all other years an average of published contract prices for this market is given.

TABLE III. NEWSPRINT PAPER CAPACITY AND PRODUCTION: UNITED STATES AND CANADA

(Millions of Short Tons)

Year	Normal Capacity	Actual Production	Per cent of Capacity
1918	2,287	2,030	88.8
1919	2,293	2,224	97.0
1920	2,564	2,450	95.6
1921	2,819	2,077	73.7
1922	2,916	2,591	88.9
1923	3,043	2,815	92.5
1924	3,270	2,899	88.7
1925	3,544	3,149	88.9
1926	3,884	3,752	96.6
1927	4,504	3,775	83.8
1928	4,997	4,030	80.6
1929	5,253	4,376	83.3
1930	5,589	4,073	72.9
1931	5,895	3,673	62.3
1932	5,913	3,195	54.0
1933	5,884	3,228	54.9
1934	5,896	3,872	65.7
1935	5,767	3,995	69.3
1936	5,689	4,456	78.3
1937	5,675	4,944	87.1
1938	5,629	3,713	66.0
1939	5,605	4,114	73.4
1940	5,797	4,783	82.5
1941	5,788	4,786	82.7
1942	5,889	4,408	74.9
1943	5,711	4,024	70.5
1944	5,759	3,985	69.2
1945	5,653	4,316	76.3
1946	5,480	5,277	96.3
1947	5,574	5,646	101.3
1948	5,733	5,850	102.0
1949	5,989	6,076	101.5
1950	6,219	6,294	101.2
1951	6,410	6,641	103.6
1952	6,675	6,834	102.4
1953	6,893	6,805	98.7
1954	7,200	7,195	99.9
1955	7,473	7,743	103.6
1956	7,868	8,186	104.0
1957	8,677	8,222	94.8
1958	9,339	7,853	84.1

Source: Newsprint Association of Canada and Newsprint Service Bureau.

Note: In general, capacity is based on past production records of newsprint machines plus anticipated performance of new equipment coming into operation during the year. Ratios in excess of 100 per cent may reflect above-normal operating time, continuing and accelerating improvements in performance of equipment and temporary use of machines usually devoted to the manufacture of other grades and therefore not included in newsprint capacity. Below-capacity operations may be due to lack of sufficient demand or to shortage of power, major breakdowns of equipment, or other difficulties beyond the producer's control.

NOTES*

CHAPTER I

[1] L. Ethan Ellis, *Print Paper Pendulum: Group Pressures and the Price of Newsprint* (New Brunswick, New Jersey: Rutgers University Press, 1948). Reprinted as an appendix to the present volume.

[2] Still another source of supply in Alaska, based upon woods susceptible of treatment by conventional processes, has been widely discussed but has not yet come into actual production due to economic and political factors to be noted below.

[3] Mills at this time were of two kinds, integrated and converting. The former produced both groundwood and sulphite pulp, completing the entire operation on their own premises. The latter used pulp prepared elsewhere and dried into sheets or "laps" which could be shipped easily and dissolved for use as needed. Both dried pulp and newsprint were dutiable upon entry into the United States.

[4] Dominion law left jurisdiction over Crown lands in the hands of the provinces. In order to insure themselves healthy pulp industries, the principal provincial possessors of Crown-land timber had enacted export restrictions.

[5] L. Ethan Ellis, *Reciprocity, 1911: A Study in Canadian-American Relations* (New Haven: Yale University Press, 1939), deals with this story in detail.

[6] Traditionally, large consumers purchased their newsprint at a predetermined price under contract direct with the mills. At this period these contracts were made annually; later on, as will be indicated below, the tendency was to extend the contract period over five, ten, or even more years. Publishers of small papers, using modest amounts of newsprint and usually not able to establish high credit ratings, bought from jobbers, who in turn contracted with the mills. In times of shortage the large consumers entered the noncontract or spot market where they were willing to pay considerable premiums over contract prices; this threw them into competition with the small fry, who found themselves pinched on both supply and price.

* References have been grouped, normally at the end of a paragraph or more. The reader will thus understand that all text material between two notes ordinarily depends upon the citations in the second one. Most long titles are abbreviated after the first citations. Both full and short titles are listed alphabetically in the bibliography.

[7] The term "rated capacity" as used in the literature is a somewhat artificial one. It is based on past performance, a machine's best sustained production record over any one of the previous ten years being combined with the least "trim" (wastage accruing from trimming full rolls of paper to suit customers' needs) achieved during any one of the previous five years to establish a rating of 100 per cent. Obviously, any improvement which, by speeding up the machine, increasing its running time, or reducing its waste, would increase its output, would make it possible for it to operate at over its maximum rated capacity; in times of shortage the mills generally operated at over 100 per cent.

[8] One continuing side effect of the situation in the later twenties was the development of the zone-pricing system. This was a shift, launched by International on its 1928 sales and later copied throughout the industry, from the f.o.b. mill pricing of the earlier day. Under the f.o.b. system two publishers in the same city might pay different prices for paper from two of International's mills which might be located at differing distances from the consumers. The new system divided the country into zones, in each of which consumers paid an identical base price, except that publishers in certain cities designated, sometimes quite arbitrarily, as "ports" paid a "port price" $1 per ton lower than the base price in the zone. Eventually ten zones were established, prices in each being derived from that charged in Zone 4, which included New York City (publishers in the city itself paid a port price), and being calculated so as to account for differential freight rates. This scheme was of considerable utility in maintaining price uniformity in the industry.

The scheme, at first a confidential one, was used by the ill-fated NIRA and later adopted by the OPA during World War II. A map showing the zones will be found facing p. 98 of Edward Margolin and William P. McLendon, *Transportation Factors in the Marketing of Newsprint*, Transportation Series No. 2, United States Department of Commerce (Washington: Government Printing Office, 1952); cited subsequently as *Transportation Factors*.

CHAPTER II

[1] John A. Guthrie, *The Newsprint Paper Industry: An Economic Analysis* (Cambridge, Mass.: Harvard University Press, 1941), pp. 100–101, 122–26, 223–24. *Newsprint for Tomorrow: Report and Conclusions of the Select Committee on Small Business, United States*

Senate, Including Individual Views of Mr. Thye and Statement of Mr. Schoeppel, Senate Report 1404, 82d Cong., 2d Sess. (Washington: Government Printing Office, 1952), p. 10; cited subsequently as *Humphrey Committee Report.*

[2] *Newsprint Inquiry: Hearings before the Committee on Interstate and Foreign Commerce, United States Senate, Eighty-Fifth Congress, First Session, Pursuant to S. Res. 26, A Resolution Providing for Investigation of Problems Affecting Interstate and Foreign Commerce, February 26, 27, and 28, 1957* (Washington: Government Printing Office, 1957), pp. 67, 134–35; cited subsequently as *Magnuson Committee Hearings. Supplies for a Free Press: A Preliminary Report on Newsprint by the Subcommittee on Newsprint of the Select Committee on Small Business, United States Senate* (Committee Print, Washington: Government Printing Office, 1951), p. 12; cited subsequently as *Humphrey Committee, Preliminary Report. Study of Monopoly Power: Hearings before the Subcommittee on Monopoly Power of the Committee on the Judiciary, House of Representatives, Eighty-First Congress, Second Session, Containing the Proceedings of June 19, 20, 21, 22, 23, 27, 28, 29, 30, and July 10, 11, 13, 18, 19, and 20, 1950, Serial No. 14, Part 6A, Newsprint* (Washington: Government Printing Office, 1950), pp. 218–19; cited subsequently as *Celler Committee Hearings.*

[3] *Celler Committee Hearings,* pp. 395–99. *The Newsprint Service Bureau Bulletin,* No. 283, August 20, 1941, p. 5; cited subsequently as *N.S.B.B.* Beginning with the January, 1951, issue this bulletin bears a monthly date only; after June, 1957, the monthly numbered issues are devoted entirely to statistical material, and the news aspects are taken over by an occasional *News Summary* (cited as *N.S.B., News Summary*) consisting of excerpted quotations from current literature of interest to manufacturers.

Donald C. Cook of the Securities and Exchange Commission told the Celler Committee (June 23, 1950) that as of 1949 the ratio of plant investment to $100 of net sales for five of the large producers averaged over $78; the similar ratio in the steel industry was $42 per $100; in all other manufacturing industries, $27 per $100. The ratio in mills devoted largely or entirely to newsprint was markedly higher than for those whose output consisted of diversified paper products.

[4] Guthrie, pp. 106–07. *Review of the Voluntary Agreements Program under the Defense Production Act: The Newsprint Industry, Re-*

port Dated May 9, 1958, by the Attorney General, Committee on Banking and Currency, United States Senate (Committee Print, Washington: Government Printing Office, 1958), pp. 35–37; cited subsequently as *Attorney General's Review.*

[5] *Celler Committee Hearings,* p. 214.

[6] Robert M. Fowler, *Submission to Royal Commission on Canada's Economic Prospects* (Montreal: Canadian Pulp and Paper Association, 1956), pp. 46–47; cited subsequently as *Fowler Submission.*

[7] Ellis, *Print Paper Pendulum: Group Pressures and the Price of Newsprint* (New Brunswick, 1948), pp. 168–69. Charles W. Boyce, *Newsprint—A Forward Look to 1965* (New York: A.N.P.A., 1957), p. 38; cited subsequently as *Newsprint, Forward. American Newspaper Publishers Association Bulletin, "B" Special: Newsprint* (New York: Published by A.N.P.A. in several series; this particular one, numbered and paged consecutively, will subsequently be cited as *A.N.P.A., B*), No. 261, January 7, 1937, p. 1; No. 263, February 19, p. 11. *Editor & Publisher: The Fourth Estate* (New York: Published weekly, each issue paged separately), Vol. 70, January 16, 1937, p. 6; cited subsequently as *E. & P. Paper Trade Journal* (New York: Published weekly, each issue paged separately), Vol. CIV, February 11, 1937, p. 15; February 25, pp. 51, 53; Vol. CVI, January 6, 1938, p. 16; cited subsequently as *P.T.J.*

[8] *A.N.P.A., B,* No. 265, March 23, 1937, pp. 21–22. *E. & P.*, Vol. 70, March 27, 1937, p. 32; April 3, p. 36. *P.T.J.*, Vol. CIV, April 29, 1937, p. 14. United States Tariff Commission, *Newsprint: War Changes in Industry Series, Report No. 22, Revised* (Washington: Government Printing Office, 1951), pp. 34–35; cited subsequently as U.S. Tariff Commission, *Newsprint.*

[9] The arrangement with the Australian publishers is the "Seven Suppliers' Agreement" on which the Celler Committee was later to expend considerable energy. It is mentioned here in order to point out that it was apparently a matter of common knowledge in the industry when first consummated. *A.N.P.A., B,* No. 278, October 19, 1937, p. 107; No. 279, October 29, pp. 109–10; No. 281, December 1, p. 125. *E. & P.*, Vol. 70, October 23, 1937, p. 10; October 30, pp. 7, 24; December 4, pp. 3, 26; December 25, p. 5. *P.T.J.*, Vol. CV, September 23, 1937, p. 17; October 14, p. 36; October 21, p. 11.

[10] *A.N.P.A., B,* No. 263, February 19, 1937, pp. 9–10; No. 265, March 23, p. 23; No. 282, December 22, p. 133.

[11] *A.N.P.A., B*, No. 282, December 22, 1937, p. 132. *E. & P.*, Vol. 70, July 10, 1937, p. 12; Vol. 71, January 1, 1938, p. 8; January 27, p. 3. *P.T.J.*, Vol. CV, November 11, 1937, p. 13. *The New York Times*, December 19, 30, 1937; cited subsequently as N. Y. *Times*.

Meantime a meeting had been held (October 4, 1937) by representatives of Crown Zellerbach Corporation, Powell River Sales Company, and Inland Empire Paper Company which discussed prices in sufficient detail to render their principals vulnerable to indictment under the antitrust laws. *Celler Committee Hearings*, pp. 1001–06. *The Newsprint Problem: Final Report of the Special Antitrust Committee of the Committee on the Judiciary* (Committee Print, Washington: Government Printing Office, 1953), p. 22; cited subsequently as *Celler Committee, Final Report. Newsprint: Report of the Subcommittee on Monopoly Power of the Committee on the Judiciary, Pursuant to H. Res. 95 (82d Cong., 1st Sess.), Authorizing the Committee on the Judiciary to Conduct Studies and Investigations Relating to Matters within Its Jurisdiction*, House Report 505, 82d Cong., 1st Sess. (Washington: Government Printing Office, 1951), pp. 82–83; cited subsequently as *Celler Committee Report*.

[12] Guthrie, p. 112. *A.N.P.A., B*, No. 287, May 6, 1938, p. 43; No. 298, August 26, p. 91; No. 301, October 14, p. 103; No. 303, November 4, p. 115. *P.T.J.*, Vol. CVIII, January 5, 1939, p. 12.

[13] Guthrie, p. 99. *A.N.P.A., B*, No. 285, March 22, 1938, p. 10; No. 286, April 19, p. 33; No. 304, November 14, pp. 120–21; No. 306, November 30, p. 133. *E. & P.*, Vol. 71, January 15, 1938, pp. 3, 22; April 30, p. 94. *P.T.J.*, Vol. CVI, January 13, 1938, p. 28; January 20, pp. 22, 28; March 10, p. 21; Vol. CVII, November 11, p. 9; Vol. CVIII, February 23, 1939, p. 51.

Royal S. Kellogg of the Newsprint Service Bureau compiled statistics for the entire year which showed that the North American industry operated at an average of 67 per cent capacity throughout the year, approximately 25 per cent below the 1937 level; the Canadian mills averaged 65 per cent, the Newfoundland mills 72 per cent, and those of the United States 84 per cent. Last-quarter operations were only 6 per cent below the previous year's figures. *P.T.J.*, Vol. CVIII, February 23, 1939, p. 37.

[14] *A.N.P.A., B*, No. 293, July 1, 1938, p. 72; No. 312, February 17, 1939, p. 13. *E. & P.*, Vol. 71, April 23, 1938, p. 17; December 3, p. 4; *P.T.J.*, Vol. CVII, August 11, 1938, p. 16. *Celler Committee Report*, p. 120.

Progress toward the goal of southern newsprint production lagged during the year, the private capital necessary to complete financing of the proposed Texas mill being slow in appearing. *A.N.P.A., B*, No. 286, April 19, 1938, p. 33.

Finally, the new mill of the Ontario Paper Company at Baie Comeau, Quebec, came into production, destined to be the last new mill to come into operation in the Dominion until after 1950.

[15] *A.N.P.A., B*, No. 321, June 2, 1939, p. 57; No. 345, December 20, p. 166. *P.T.J.*, Vol. 110, February 22, 1940, pp. 39–40. (With the issue of April 13, 1939, this periodical started using Arabic instead of Roman numerals to designate volume numbers.)

[16] The following references cover the story through the indictments: *A.N.P.A., B*, No. 312, February 17, 1939, p. 13; No. 320, May 26, pp. 55–56; No. 324, July 14, p. 71. *A.N.P.A., Newsprint* (note that a new series of A.N.P.A. bulletins is in effect), No. 12, February 14, 1947, pp. 38–39; cited subsequently as *A.N.P.A., News. E. & P.*, Vol. 72, January 21, 1939, p. 9; May 27, pp. 8, 24. *N.S.B.B.*, No. 257, June 13, 1939, pp. 2–3. *P.T.J.*, Vol. 108, May 25, 1939, pp. 22–24. *Magnuson Committee Hearings*, pp. 215–16. *Celler Committee Hearings*, pp. 206, 1001–06. *Celler Committee Report*, pp. 120–26. *Study of Monopoly Power: Hearings before the Subcommittee on Study of Monopoly Power of the Committee on the Judiciary, House of Representatives, Eighty-First Congress, Second Session, Serial No. 14, Part 6B, Newsprint Exhibits (Including Appendix)* (Washington: Government Printing Office, 1950), pp. 93–102; cited subsequently as *Celler Committee Hearings, Exhibits.*

[17] An attempt to dig into the situation with respect to eastern firms resulted less successfully, thanks in part to International's recent transfer of its base of operations. International's salesmen were instructed to refer all inquiries to Montreal, and further orders were shortly issued to disentangle the files of the International Paper Sales Company from those of the International Paper Company proper, and transfer the former to Three Rivers, Quebec.

[18] *A.N.P.A., News*, No. 362, May 1, 1940, p. 64. *E. & P.*, Vol. 72, September 16, 1939, p. 5. *P.T.J.*, Vol. 109, September 14, 1939, p. 52; October 26, p. 13. Vol. 110, February 22, 1940, p. 59. Vol. 113, August 14, 1941, p. 8.

[19] The Canadian correspondent of the *Paper Trade Journal* remarked complacently in February, 1940, that the year found the industry "in the full tide of one of those swings that alternately have brought

it blessings and curses. This time the blessings are in evidence. Moderate and steady progress in recovery, due to the improvement in general business, was in evidence prior to the outbreak of hostilities, but since the conflict there has been a sharp increase in production and shipments, with every evidence that as long as the European conflict continues shipments will compare favorably with the highest in the history of the industry. Financially, the companies are in better shape than they have been for years. Most of them have already paid off their indebtedness to the banks, which not so very long ago ran into high figures, and although they have not yet begun to give any return on the drastically-reduced capitalization effected during the general reorganization of the industry, the prospect of a return to a dividend-paying basis is not now regarded as remote." *P.T.J.*, Vol. 110, February 22, 1940, p. 59.

CHAPTER III

[1] Ellis, *Print Paper Pendulum: Group Pressures and the Price of Newsprint* (New Brunswick, 1948), p. 169. *American Newspaper Publishers Association: Convention Bulletin* (New York: A.N.P.A., annually, 1941—), No. 1, April 29, 1941, pp. 55–56; cited subsequently as *A.N.P.A., Convention. A.N.P.A., News,* No. 358, March 28, 1940, p. 47; No. 360, April 14, p. 53; No. 364, May 29, p. 81. *E. & P.*, Vol. 73, June 8, 1940, p. 9; Vol. 74, January 25, 1941, p. 24. *P.T.J.*, Vol. 110, February 1, 1940, p. 18; February 8, 1941, p. 10; Vol. 112, January 9, 1941, p. 16; February 6, p. 16; February 20, pp. 40–41. Everest pointed out that the industry was in a position " 'to exert strong measures of control, designed on the one hand to meet the demands of the moment and on the other hand to prevent the accumulation of new excess capacity which may have no market when the war is over. The control, as in most cases, is in price. . . .' "

[2] *A.N.P.A., Convention*, No. 1, April 29, 1941, p. 56. *P.T.J.*, Vol. 111, September 26, 1941, p. 11; November 14, pp. 9, 13; Vol. 112, January 16, 1942, p. 13; January 30, p. 8.

[3] *A.N.P.A., B,* No. 23, March 26, 1942, p. 119. *A.N.P.A., Convention*, No. 1, April 29, 1941, pp. 61–62. *A.N.P.A., News,* No. 362, May 1, 1940, p. 65. *E. & P.*, Vol. 73, May 25, 1940, p. 11; August 17, pp. 3, 20. *P.T.J.*, Vol. 110, February 1, 1940, p. 9.

[4] *A.N.P.A., Convention*, No. 1, April 29, 1941, p. 60. *A.N.P.A., News,* No. 362, May 1, 1940, p. 63. *E. & P.*, Vol. 73, May 25, 1940,

p. 30; Vol. 74, January 25, 1941, pp. 24, 37. *P.T.J.*, Vol. 110, February 1, 1940, p. 9; Vol. 111, July 18, p. 9; Vol. 112, February 20, 1941, p. 44.

[5] *A.N.P.A.*, *News*, No. 350, January 31, 1940, p. 15; No. 8, March 6, 1951, p. 37. *P.T.J.*, Vol. 110, January 25, 1940, p. 31. *Transportation Factors*, pp. 115–16. Charles W. Boyce, *Newsprint Now and in the Next Decade* (New York: A.N.P.A., 1951), p. 36; cited subsequently as *Newsprint Now*. Much of the March 21, 1940, issue of *Paper Trade Journal* (Vol. 110, pp. 116 ff.) is devoted to an account of the Southland project, including considerable historical material.

[6] *A.N.P.A.*, *News*, No. 354, February 28, 1940, pp. 31–32; No. 370, July 25, p. 109.

[7] *P.T.J.*, Vol. 110, February 22, 1940, pp. 74–76.

[8] *A.N.P.A.*, *News*, No. 24, August 13, 1941, pp. 107, 119; No. 2, January 15, 1942, p. 10. *E. & P.*, Vol. 74, August 16, 1941, p. 8; September 6, p. 5; November 22, p. 16; November 29, p. 20; December 13, p. 42. *P.T.J.*, Vol. 112, March 20, 1941, p. 14; May 22, p. 8; July 17, p. 10; August 14, p. 8; August 21, p. 10; August 28, p. 10; September 11, p. 7; October 30, p. 8; Vol. 113, November 27, p. 124; December 11, pp. 7, 10; Vol. 114, February 5, 1942, pp. 40, 42; April 2, p. 7. Canadian losses due to increasing costs were somewhat offset in May when the National Revenue Department gave newsprint producers the status of a "depressed industry," entitling them to an adjustment of from 5 to 10 per cent of their invested capital for purposes of computing excess profits taxation. This of course was in addition to the continuing benefit from the favorable exchange differential.

[9] *Financial Post* comments reprinted in *A.N.P.A.*, *News*, No. 15, May 7, 1941, pp. 68–70. For further evidence of good producer-consumer relations, cf. *P.T.J.*, Vol. 112, May 8, 1941, p. 10; Vol. 113, July 17, p. 10; August 14, p. 8; Vol. 114, February 5, 1942, p. 68. Clarence J. Brown, an Ohio Congressman who was also a newspaper publisher, told the Celler Committee later, apropos the mills' self-restraint on prices, that " 'there wasn't a day they couldn't sell newsprint for twice what they were getting for it.' " *Celler Committee, Final Report*, pp. 6–7.

[10] *P.T.J.*, Vol. 113, July 31, 1941, p. 7; August 21, p. 7; Vol. 118, June 1, 1944, p. 98. McKenna's remarks quoted in *P.T.J.*, Vol. 113, October 16, 1941, p. 9, and *A.N.P.A.*, *News*, No. 30, October 8, 1941, p. 131.

[11] *A.N.P.A., News,* No. 15, May 7, 1941, p. 67. *E. & P.,* Vol. 74, May 10, 1941, p. 35. *Celler Committee Hearings,* pp. 1001–06.

[12] *A.N.P.A., News,* No. 2, January 15, 1942, p. 3; No. 6, February 11, p. 19; No. 12, March 26, p. 41; No. 13, April 1, pp. 43–47; No. 13, March 10, 1943, p. 74; No. 38, April 18, 1945, pp. 228–29. *E. & P.,* Vol. 75, March 28, 1942, p. 6. *P.T.J.,* Vol. 115, July 16, 1942, p. 10. The statement concerning assurances to the manufacturers was made by Royal S. Kellogg to the Boren Committee, October 3, 1946. *Brand Names and Newsprint (Newsprint): Final Hearings before a Subcommittee of the Committee on Interstate and Foreign Commerce, House of Representatives, Seventy-Ninth Congress, Second Session, Pursuant to H. Res. 98, 78th Congress (Extended by H. Res. 93, 79th Congress), A Resolution to Investigate Federal Grade Labeling of Articles or Commodities, and the Discarding of Private Brand Names; Curtailing the Production or Consumption of Newsprint or Papers; and Any Requirements Intending to Bring about Simplification and Standardization of Production, Marketing, and Distribution of Articles or Commodities, as Well as Concentration of Industry or Production, Newsprint, October 2 and 3, 1946* (Washington: Government Printing Office, 1946), p. 80; cited subsequently as *Boren Committee, Final Hearings.*

[13] *A.N.P.A., News,* No. 14, April 8, 1942, pp. 49–50. *P.T.J.,* Vol. 114, April 16, 1942, p. 9. Robert M. Fowler later testified (March 11, 1947) that it was his judgment as a member of the wartime WPTB group that the price received for newsprint in 1942, 1943, and 1944 was "quite inadequate." *Problems of American Small Business: Hearings before the Special Committee to Study Problems of American Small Business, United States Senate, Eightieth Congress, First Session, Pursuant to S. Res. 20, A Resolution Appointing a Special Committee to Study Problems of American Small Business, Part 1, Investigation of Newsprint Shortages and Other Factors Affecting Survival of Smaller Independent Newspapers: I, March 4, 5, 6, and 7, 1947* (3 Parts, paged continuously under somewhat varying titles, Washington: Government Printing Office, 1947), p. 251; cited subsequently as *Capehart Committee Hearings.*

[14] *A.N.P.A., News,* No. 16, April 29, 1942, p. 55. *P.T.J.,* Vol. 114, April 30, 1942, pp. 7, 18; May 7, p. 28; May 14, p. 12; May 28, p. 11; June 1, p. 12; Vol. 115, August 13, p. 9; August 27, p. 9; September 3, p. 13.

[15] *A.N.P.A., News,* No. 29, September 10, 1942, p. 101; No. 34,

October 31, pp. 121–22. *E. & P.*, Vol. 75, September 5, 1942, p. 11. *P.T.J.*, Vol. 115, September 10, 1942, pp. 7, 9; September 24, pp. 7, 16; Vol. 116, February 18, 1943, p. 44.

[16] *A.N.P.A.*, *News*, No. 34, October 31, 1942, p. 117. *E. & P.*, Vol. 75, October 17, 1942, p. 39; October 31, p. 9; November 7, p. 3. *N.S.B.B.*, No. 298, November 14, 1942, pp. 2–3. *P.T.J.*, Vol. 115, October 29, 1942, p. 14; November 5, p. 7; November 19, pp. 9–10. Order M-241 was revised in January, 1943, changing the base period governing production to the last three months of 1941 and the first three of 1942, and reducing the permitted inventory to seventy-five days. *N.S.B.B.*, No. 300, January 22, 1943, p. 2.

[17] *A.N.P.A.*, *News*, No. 39, December 2, 1942, pp. 149–50, 157. *E. & P.*, Vol. 75, December 5, 1942, p. 24. *P.T.J.*, Vol. 115, November 19, 1942, p. 9; December 17, p. 11.

[18] *A.N.P.A.*, *News*, No. 41, December 11, 1942, p. 155; No. 21, May 12, 1943, p. 115; No. 39, August 11, p. 204. *A.N.P.A.*, *Convention*, No. 1, April 26, 1943, p. 13. *E. & P.*, Vol. 75, January 27, 1942, p. 3. *N.S.B.B.*, No. 300, January 22, 1943, p. 7. *P.T.J.*, Vol. 115, December 1, 1942, p. 12; January 7, 1943, p. 7; January 21, p. 7; January 28, p. 7. *Brand Names and Newsprint: Hearings before a Subcommittee of the Committee on Interstate and Foreign Commerce, House of Representatives, Seventy-Eighth Congress, First Session, Pursuant to H. Res. 98, A Resolution to Investigate Federal Grade Labeling of Articles or Commodities, and the Discarding of Private Brand Names; Curtailing the Production or Consumption of Newsprint or Papers; and Any Requirements Intending to Bring about Simplification and Standardization of Production, Marketing, and Distribution of Articles or Commodities, as Well as Concentration of Industry or Production, Part 1, May 10, 24, 25, 26, 27, 28, and June 2, 3, 4, and 8, 1943* (4 Parts, paged continuously under somewhat varying titles, Washington: Government Printing Office, 1943–1944), pp. 2, 6; cited subsequently as *Boren Committee Hearings, 78th Cong. Capehart Committee Hearings*, p. 4. A December, 1942, poll by *Editor & Publisher* showed 447 publishers favoring "reduced consumption by voluntary action," as against 167 favoring a "government order." *E. & P.*, Vol. 78, September 15, 1945, p. 7. In Canada, be it noted, the problem was approached differently, official permits being required for the purchase of paper. *E. & P.*, Vol. 76, January 9, 1943, p. 4.

[19] *A.N.P.A.*, *News*, No. 3, January 12, 1943, p. 15; No. 11, March 3, pp. 65–66; No. 13, March 10, pp. 73–74; No. 21, May 12, p. 116.

E. & P., Vol. 76, January 9, 1943, p. 4; March 6, p. 24; June 12, p. 56; Vol. 80, April 5, 1947, p. 38. *P.T.J.*, Vol. 116, January 25, 1943, p. 7; March 4, p. 7; March 11, pp. 12, 26; March 25, pp. 7, 19. U.S. Tariff Commission, *Newsprint*, p. 35.

Both the A.N.P.A. *Bulletin* and the *Paper Trade Journal* gave prominence to an article by John E. Langdon in the *Toronto Financial Post* which pointed out that " 'Canadian manufacturers are disappointed. They attribute the smallness of the increase to political pressure on Washington by certain American publishers.' "

[20] *A.N.P.A., News*, No. 27, June 9, 1943, p. 141; No. 33, July 12, pp. 171–72; No. 36, July 22, pp. 189–90; No. 56, October 6, pp. 307–08. *P.T.J.*, Vol. 116, June 17, 1943, p. 10; Vol. 117, July 1, p. 8; July 8, p. 9; July 29, pp. 7, 10. It is interesting to note that though a Newspaper Industry Advisory Committee had been counseling the OPA for months, it was only at the end of September that a similar group (the Newsprint Industry Advisory Committee) was set up to represent the manufacturers in their price negotiations with the OPA.

Fred C. Holder of the OPA indicated something of his agency's thinking on the subject of price when he told the Boren Committee (October 2, 1946) that "a major obligation on our part was to see that the American segment of this industry had prices which would permit the fullest possible production, which would return to them their costs plus reasonable profit margins on invested capital, and whenever we found that rising costs threatened their profit position seriously, we granted a price increase on newsprint, extending that same increase to imported newsprint. . . ." Cost figures, however, were for the domestic industry, except for the one instance mentioned above. *Boren Committee, Final Hearings*, p. 15.

[21] *P.T.J.*, Vol. 118, February 17, 1944, pp. 46, 48, summarizes the trade association reports, and points out that the price of newsprint was further than ever below the general commodity level.

[22] *E. & P.*, Vol. 76, January 2, 1943, p. 18; February 6, p. 36. On October 8, 1943, Dr. A. N. Holcombe, Chairman of the WPB Appeals Board, testified that Chandler "wished to pursue a more liberal policy with reference to appeals for additional tonnage than seemed to the Appeals Board to be sound." The board, however reluctantly, permitted him to experiment by accepting his recommendations for extra tonnage, thus contributing to the difficult situation which pres-

ently arose, and making it necessary to tighten operations by amending L-240 in September. *Boren Committee Hearings, 78th Cong.*, p. 907.

[23] *A.N.P.A., News*, No. 7, February 10, 1943, pp. 45–46; No. 9, February 15, pp. 57–58; No. 10, February 25, p. 61; No. 12, March 8, pp. 69–70; No. 21, May 12, pp. 115–16; No. 35, June 14, 1950, p. 1403. *E. & P.*, Vol. 76, February 13, 1943, pp. 3, 22; February 20, pp. 5, 6, 44. *P.T.J.*, Vol. 116, January 28, 1943, p. 7; February 11, p. 7. The A.N.P.A.'s report of its own investigation of the supply situation, published March 8, emphasized a point to become increasingly evident during the remainder of the year, that "the basic problem . . . is the wood supply."

[24] *A.N.P.A., News*, No. 20, May 5, 1943, p. 109; No. 23, May 19, p. 127; No. 24, May 21, pp. 129–31; No. 29, June 18, p. 155; No. 33, July 12, pp. 171–72; No. 34, July 14, pp. 175–77; No. 35, July 16, pp. 183–84; No. 37, pp. 192–93, 195. *A.N.P.A., Convention*, No. 1, April 26, 1943, pp. 11–12. *E. & P.*, Vol. 76, July 10, 1943, pp. 37, 40; July 17, p. 5; August 14, p. 43. *N.S.B.B.*, No. 307, August 13, 1943, p. 4. *P.T.J.*, Vol. 117, July 8, 1943, pp. 7, 9. "Standard newsprint" as defined by the Treasury consisted of 500 sheets, 24 by 36 inches in size and weighing approximately 32 pounds.

[25] *A.N.P.A., News*, No. 39, August 11, 1943, pp. 203–08; No. 43, August 26, pp. 226, 228–29; No. 44, September 3, p. 235. *P.T.J.*, Vol. 117, August 19, 1943, pp. 9, 12. A complicating factor in the Canadian manpower situation was that many French-Canadians in Quebec were not anxious to enter Dominion military service; as farmers, they were exempt; but as woodcutters, they were not. *E. & P.*, Vol. 76, August 21, 1943, p. 42.

[26] The following cover some developments of September and early October, including the analysis mentioned in the last sentence: *A.N.P.A., News*, No. 45, September 9, 1943, p. 239; No. 47, September 10, pp. 251–52; No. 52, September 23, pp. 284–85; No. 54, October 1, pp. 294–96; No. 56, October 6, pp. 309–10. *E. & P.*, Vol. 76, September 11, 1943, pp. 8, 52; September 25, pp. 24, 62; October 2, pp. 6, 24; October 9, p. 14; October 16, pp. 2–7. *N.S.B.B.*, No. 307, September 17, 1943, p. 4. *P.T.J.*, Vol. 117, September 23, 1943, p. 8. *Boren Committee Hearings, 78th Cong.*, pp. 907–20.

[27] *A.N.P.A., News*, No. 57, October 11, 1943, pp. 313–21; No. 64, pp. 357–58; No. 67, October 21, p. 369; No. 69, October 27, pp. 377–79; No. 72, November 4, p. 391; No. 76, November 11,

pp. 415–23. *Boren Committee Hearings, 78th Cong.*, pp. 926–58, 1281–87.

[28] *A.N.P.A., News*, No. 73, November 4, 1943, p. 401; No. 79, November 18, p. 437; No. 89, December 22, pp. 497–98; No. 90, December 24, pp. 501–03. *E. & P.*, Vol. 76, November 20, 1943, p. 7. *N.S.B.B.*, No. 310, November 12, 1943, p. 3. *P.T.J.*, Vol. 117, November 4, 1943, p. 8. *Boren Committee Hearings, 78th Cong.*, pp. 1287–94, 1378–79.

[29] Charles F. Honeywell, *Newsprint Production–Newspaper Consumption: A Cooperative Partnership* (New York: Newsprint Service Bureau [mimeographed], 1958), p. 2; cited subsequently as *Newsprint Production.* Honeywell reported: "Sixteen committees of both houses of Congress have held open meetings on 42 separate occasions on every possible phase of newsprint production and availability . . . from June, 1943, to June, 1957—an average of three meetings per year. . . ."

[30] Its members, in addition to the Chairman, were Lindley Beckworth of Texas, Francis Myers of Pennsylvania, Richard Harless of Arizona, Charles A. Halleck of Indiana, Clarence J. Brown of Ohio, and Charles A. Wolverton of New Jersey, several of whom served on successive committees dealing with the newsprint question and accumulated considerable funds of information and experience in this area. American Newspaper Publishers Association: *Federal Laws Bulletin*, No. 5, January 20, 1945, p. 15; cited subsequently as *A.N.P.A., Federal Laws. E. & P.*, Vol. 78, September 15, p. 56. *Celler Committee Report*, p. 15. *Brand Names and Newsprint: Hearings before a Subcommittee of the Committee on Interstate and Foreign Commerce, House of Representatives, Seventy-Ninth Congress, First Session, Pursuant to H. Res. 98 (78th Congress) (Extended by H. Res. 93, 79th Congress), A Resolution to Investigate Federal Grade Labeling of Articles or Commodities, and the Discarding of Private Brand Names; Curtailing the Production or Consumption of Newsprint or Papers; and Any Requirements Intending to Bring about Simplification and Standardization of Production, Marketing, and Distribution of Articles or Commodities, as Well as Concentration of Industry or Production, Part 1, Newsprint, March 5, 12, April 16, 17, and 23, 1945* (3 Parts, paged continuously under somewhat varying titles; Washington: Government Printing Office, 1945–1946), pp. 97, 203–04; cited subsequently as *Boren Committee Hearings, 79th Cong.*

[31] *E. & P.*, Vol. 76, February 6, 1943, p. 30. N. Y. *Times*, February 4, 1943. *The Congressional Record* (Washington: Government

Printing Office, 1874—), 78th Cong., 1st Sess., pp. 551–52, 554–56, 565; cited subsequently as *Record.*

[32] *E. & P.*, Vol. 76, February 13, 1943, pp. 3, 22. *P.T.J.*, Vol. 116, February 11, 1943, p. 7. N. Y. *Times*, February 9, 1943.

[33] *E. & P.*, Vol. 76, February 15, 1943, p. 6; March 20, p. 30; April 12, p. 13. *Record*, 78th Cong., 1st Sess., pp. 997, 2486, 3245–51.

[34] *A.N.P.A.*, *News*, No. 39, August 11, 1943, p. 205; No. 56, October 6, pp. 308–10; No. 57, October 11, p. 322. *E. & P.*, Vol. 76, August 14, 1943, p. 6; August 21, p. 8; October 9, p. 14. *P.T.J.*, Vol. 117, August 19, 1943, p. 12; September 16, p. 7. *Boren Committee Hearings, 78th Cong.*, pp. 931–32.

[35] *E. & P.*, Vol. 76, October 16, 1943, pp. 2–7. *Boren Committee Hearings, 78th Cong.*, pp. 830–44, 857, 859, 907–20, 940–46, 1155–59, 1241–67, 1281–87, 1298, 1309. Boren reported to his committee in November that nineteen out of twenty-six members of the Newspaper Industry Advisory Committee had been awarded extra tonnage on appeal.

Arthur R. Treanor, in June, 1944, Director of the Printing and Publishing Division of the WPB, explained the difference between an "allocation system" and the "quota system," under which the newsprint situation was being handled: Under allocation, a publisher desiring paper "fills out a form stating how much is desired and its proposed use. All the requests for this material are tabulated and the available supply is apportioned according to relative essentiality." Such a system obviously makes the apportionment dependent upon administrative decision. Under the quota system, publishers were "permitted to consume, automatically and without application to or authorization by the War Production Board, a stipulated percentage of the paper which is used during a base period. . . . Quotas are available to publishers as a matter of right; no administrative discretion whatever is involved." Clearly, any administrative machinery (such as the appeals machinery under L-240) which altered such a system by making special grants would modify the situation in the direction of an allocation system. *P.T.J.*, Vol. 118, June 1, 1944, p. 98.

[36] *A.N.P.A.*, *News*, No. 56, July 13, 1944, p. 295. *P.T.J.*, Vol. 118, March 16, 1944, p. 14; Vol. 119, October 5, p. 8; October 26, p. 32; Vol. 120, January 18, 1945, p. 13; February 22, p. 52.

[37] *A.N.P.A.*, *News*, No. 3, January 12, 1944, p. 13; No. 7, January 17, pp. 39–40. *N.S.B.B.*, No. 312, January 13, 1944, p. 3. *P.T.J.*, Vol. 118, January 13, 1944, p. 17. *Boren Committee Hearings, 78th Cong.*, pp. 1376–78.

[38] *Boren Committee Hearings, 78th Cong.*, pp. 1315–17, 1341–56.

[39] *A.N.P.A., News*, No. 15, February 11, 1944, pp. 87–90; No. 18, February 18, pp. 103–04; No. 20, February 24, p. 121. *E. & P.*, Vol. 77, February 19, 1944, pp. 8, 32.

[40] *A.N.P.A., News*, No. 18, February 18, 1944, p. 121; No. 21, March 1, p. 125; No. 29, April 5, p. 170; No. 33, April 21, pp. 189–90; No. 51, June 26, pp. 269–72; No. 53, June 30, p. 277; No. 57, July 13, p. 299; No. 59, July 19, p. 307. *A.N.P.A., Convention*, No. 2, May 2, 1944, p. 51. *E. & P.*, Vol. 77, March 2, 1944, pp. 7, 40; June 10, p. 56; June 17, p. 12; July 1, pp. 5, 30; July 22, p. 7. The WPB formalized the tonnage-reduction order on September 5; *A.N.P.A., News*, No. 70, September 7, 1944, p. 383.

[41] Years later Fred W. Mears, for forty years an employee of Great Northern Paper Company, testified before a congressional committee that "it was obvious that the demand was just boiling up underneath the controls, many mills began to ask for long-term contracts, . . ." a practice also requested by the consumers in this period. This matter of long-term contracts becomes of considerable importance in the postwar period. *Newsprint Study: Hearing before the Committee on Interstate and Foreign Commerce, House of Representatives, Eighty-Fifth Congress, First Session, on Newsprint Situation, February 18 and June 3, 1957 (Before the Entire Committee), June 17, 1957 (Before the Subcommittee on Commerce and Finance), Printed for the Use of the Committee on Interstate and Foreign Commerce* (Washington: Government Printing Office, 1958), pp. 53, 55; cited subsequently as *Harris Committee Hearings.*

[42] *A.N.P.A., News*, No. 73, September 14, 1944, p. 395; No. 77, September 27, p. 428; No. 79, October 4, p. 439.

[43] *A.N.P.A., News*, No. 91, November 22, 1944, pp. 545–46. *P.T.J.*, Vol. 119, November 2, 1944, p. 7.

[44] *A.N.P.A., News*, No. 85, October 27, 1944, pp. 489–90; No. 87, November 1, pp. 501, 506; No. 88, November 9, p. 509; No. 91, November 22, pp. 535–36, 542; No. 99, December 21, p. 591. *E. & P.*, Vol. 77, October 28, 1944, p. 10; November 4, p. 50. *N.S.B.B.*, No. 323, December 15, 1944, p. 7. *P.T.J.*, December 28, 1944, p. 7.

[45] North American production increased 8 per cent during the year, reversing a downward trend beginning in 1942; United States production was up 1 per cent. *A.N.P.A., News*, No. 5, January 17, 1945, p. 33; No. 14, February 15, p. 80; No. 20, March 2, pp. 123–24; No. 21, March 7, pp. 127–28; No. 27, March 28, p. 153; No.

30, March 30, p. 163; No. 31, April 4, p. 178; No. 32, April 4, p. 184; No. 38, April 18, pp. 228–29; No. 40, April 25, p. 235; No. 49, May 16, p. 289; No. 51, May 23, p. 299; No. 56, June 6, p. 335. *E. & P.*, Vol. 78, April 7, 1945, p. 72. *P.T.J.*, Vol. 120, January 25, 1945, p. 14; Vol. 121, July 19, p. 34; Vol. 122, February 8, 1946, p. 52.

[46] *A.N.P.A., News*, No. 9, January 31, 1945, p. 51; No. 12, February 7, p. 66; No. 17, February 28, p. 107; No. 23, March 14, p. 135; No. 39, April 20, pp. 231–32; No. 58, June 13, pp. 349–52; No. 65, July 6, p. 385; No. 75, August 17, p. 474. *E. & P.*, Vol. 78, February 3, 1945, p. 7; June 16, p. 7. *P.T.J.*, Vol. 120, June 14, 1945, p. 12; June 21, p. 95.

[47] *A.N.P.A., News*, No. 22, March 7, 1945, pp. 131–32; No. 25, March 21, pp. 145–47. *P.T.J.*, Vol. 120, March 8, 1945, p. 32. The Boren Committee, meantime, had been reconstituted to operate through the 79th Congress; its existence was threatened by a general reorganization of the congressional committee system, but, Joseph Martin pointed out: " 'A great many newspaper publishers throughout the country believe that the existence of the so-called Boren committee has been very helpful to them in securing newsprint. . . .' " To this, John W. McCormack agreed, adding that they had been " 'very delicately effective in transmitting their interest in it' " to the members of the House Committee on Rules. *A.N.P.A., News*, No. 22, March 7, 1945, pp. 131–32; No. 25, March 21, pp. 145–47. *A.N.P.A., Federal Laws*, No. 5, January 20, 1945, p. 15; No. 11, February 21, p. 35. *P.T.J.*, Vol. 120, March 8, 1945, p. 32.

[48] *A.N.P.A., News*, No. 75, August 17, 1945, p. 461; No. 77, August 17, pp. 473–74; No. 78, August 22, p. 475; No. 81, August 29, pp. 489–90; No. 84, September 13, pp. 513–15; No. 91, October 10, pp. 556–58. *E. & P.*, Vol. 78, July 7, 1945, p. 8; September 15, pp. 7, 68.

[49] The Boren Committee had also plumped for decontrol by this time. *A.N.P.A., News*, No. 79, August 29, 1945, p. 479; No. 84, September 13, p. 512; No. 87, September 19, pp. 527 ff.; No. 88, September 26, pp. 531–32; No. 91, October 10, pp. 555–56. *E. & P.*, Vol. 78, August 25, 1945, p. 40; September 15, p. 7. *P.T.J.*, Vol. 121, August 23, 1945, p. 13; August 30, p. 11. *Boren Committee Hearings, 79th Cong.*, p. 429.

[50] *A.N.P.A., News*, No. 89, October 2, 1945, pp. 537–38; No. 96, October 24, p. 593. *E. & P.*, Vol. 78, November 1, 1945, p. 11. It

should be noted here that the WPB terminated its activities as of November 3, being succeeded by the Civilian Production Administration (CPA).

[51] *A.N.P.A., News,* No. 105, November 21, 1945, pp. 637–39; No. 106, November 28, pp. 643–44. *E. & P.*, Vol. 78, November 17, 1945, p. 8; November 24, p. 6; December 1, p. 13. *Boren Committee Hearings, 79th Cong.*, pp. 392–435.

[52] *A.N.P.A., News,* No. 107, November 29, 1945, pp. 646–49. A.N.P.A. reported on December 20 that papers using over 59 per cent of the total estimated tonnage had indicated willingness to cooperate with local associations in implementing the New England Plan. *A.N.P.A., News,* No. 114, December 20, 1945, p. 685.

[53] *A.N.P.A., News,* No. 109, December 6, 1945, p. 659; No. 110, December 6, pp. 663–64; No. 115, December 20, p. 689; No. 116, December 27, p. 691; No. 117, December 27, p. 699; No. 119, December 31, p. 703; No. 5, January 16, 1946, p. 25. *E. & P.*, Vol. 78, December 8, 1945, p. 46; December 22, p. 42; December 28, p. 9.

[54] *A.N.P.A., News,* No. 94, October 10, 1945, p. 581; No. 109, December 6, p. 659; No. 111, December 13, p. 667. *E. & P.*, Vol. 78, December 8, 1945, p. 7. *P.T.J.*, Vol. 121, December 13, pp. 11, 28; December 20, p. 16.

CHAPTER IV

[1] *A.N.P.A., News,* No. 38, July 1, 1946, p. 196. *Transportation Factors,* p. 94.

[2] *Newsprint, Forward,* pp. 38–39. There is some indication that for a time at least the Canadian producers hesitated to increase prices for fear of inviting an excess of new capital and a repetition of the oversupply which had characterized the thirties. This reluctance was shortly overcome. Cf. testimony of Clinton D. McKinnon before the Celler Committee, June 21, 1950; *Celler Committee Hearings,* p. 285.

[3] The Canadian production for the entire year topped the 1945 figure by 884,184 tons (27.1 per cent), and 810,528 tons of the increase went to the United States; the mills ran at 96.8 per cent of capacity. United States production reached an all-time low of 837,000 tons. *A.N.P.A., News,* No. 21, March 20, 1946, p. 107; No. 36, June 26, pp. 188–89. *E. & P.*, Vol. 79, April 20, 1946, p. 70. *P.T.J.*, Vol. 124, January 23, 1947, p. 7. *Newsprint Study: Hearings before a Subcommittee of the Committee on Interstate and Foreign Commerce,*

House of Representatives, Eighty-Fourth Congress, on Newsprint Situation, March 15, 1955, January 10 and 25, 1956 (Washington: Government Printing Office, 1956), p. 2; cited subsequently as *Klein Committee Hearings.*

[4] *A.N.P.A., News,* No. 11, January 30, 1946, p. 49; No. 16, February 27, p. 69; No. 24, April 10, p. 119; No. 25, April 16, pp. 123–24.

[5] *A.N.P.A., News,* No. 25, April 16, 1946, pp. 123, 131–32; No. 36, June 26, pp. 188–90.

[6] *A.N.P.A., News,* No. 31, May 22, 1946, p. 165; No. 32, May 29, p. 167; No. 33, June 5, pp. 171–72; No. 34, June 14, p. 176; No. 35, June 19, p. 183; No. 38, July 3, p. 197; No. 43, July 31, p. 217. *E. & P.,* Vol. 79, May 18, 1946, pp. 8, 42; May 25, p. 38; June 8, p. 7. Fowler was now speaking on behalf of the Executive Board of the Canadian Pulp and Paper Association, which had recently replaced the joint CPPA-Newsprint Association of Canada mentioned above; *P.T.J.,* Vol. 122, February 7, 1946, p. 10. He told the Boren Committee in October: "It seemed to me the iron was hot last spring or early summer to get some improvement in production going and started, and the publishers who felt the same way about it also came down in June to make that case. . . . I left my discussion, and the publishers told me they left their discussion" with the OPA, which took no action. *Boren Committee, Final Hearings,* pp. 74–75.

[7] *A.N.P.A., News,* No. 32, May 29, 1946, p. 168; No. 37, June 26, p. 193; No. 38, July 3, p. 195.

[8] *A.N.P.A., News,* No. 39, July 10, 1946, p. 199; No. 40, July 15, pp. 203–04; No. 42, July 24, pp. 215–16; No. 43, July 31, p. 217. *E. & P.,* Vol. 79, July 13, 1946, p. 8. *P.T.J.,* Vol. 129, September 22, 1949, p. 39. *Boren Committee, Final Hearings,* pp. 31, 74, 92.

[9] *A.N.P.A., News,* No. 44, August 7, 1946, p. 221; No. 45, August 9, p. 225; No. 46, August 14, p. 227; No. 48, August 21, p. 237; No. 49, August 23, pp. 241–42; No. 50, August 28, p. 243; No. 51, August 30, pp. 247–48; No. 56, September 25, p. 263. *E. & P.,* Vol. 79, August 3, 1946, p. 8; August 31, p. 13; September 28, pp. 10, 44. *N.S.B.B.,* No. 344, September 16, 1946, pp. 3, 5. *P.T.J.,* Vol. 123, September 26, 1946, p. 23.

[10] *A.N.P.A., News,* No. 57, October 2, 1946, pp. 267–69; No. 59, October 9, pp. 273–74; No. 60, October 14, pp. 277–78; No. 68, November 14, p. 309. *E. & P.,* Vol. 79, October 5, 1946, pp. 7–8; October 12, p. 72; October 19, pp. 16, 40. *N.S.B.B.,* No. 346, November 14, 1946, p. 2; No. 347, December 14, p. 2. *P.T.J.,* Vol. 123,

October 17, 1946, p. 7; November 14, p. 22. *Boren Committee, Final Hearings*, pp. 6–128.

[11] Indications of the spot market operations are found in *A.N.P.A., News*, No. 2, January 8, 1947, p. 5; *Celler Committee Hearings*, pp. 418, 930; and in an interesting article by B. W. von Block, "The Newsprint 'Gray' Market," *E. & P.*, Vol. 82, June 25, 1949, pp. 7, 50. Spot market operations were probably facilitated by enforced British curtailment of purchases, which released large tonnages, contracted to British firms, into the open market.

[12] *A.N.P.A., News*, No. 73, December 11, 1946, p. 331; No. 1, January 3, 1947, pp. 1–2.

[13] *A.N.P.A., News*, No. 7, January 22, 1947, p. 21; No. 9, January 29, p. 25; No. 12, February 14, p. 39; No. 21, March 5, p. 85; No. 24, March 12, p. 96. *E. & P.*, Vol. 80, January 25, 1947, p. 30; February 1, pp. 14, 80; February 8, p. 38. N. Y. *Times*, February 3, 1947. *Record*, 80th Cong., 1st Sess., pp. 1457–65. Senator William Langer of North Dakota had likewise addressed himself to the problem in statements asserting not only that the manufacturing process was subject to monopoly, but that collusion between manufacturers and large publishers endangered the status of the small operator. *A.N.P.A., News*, No. 73, December 11, 1946, p. 331; No. 11, February 5, 1947, pp. 33–34. *N.S.B.B.*, No. 349, February 18, 1947, p. 2.

[14] *A.N.P.A., News*, No. 14, February 19, 1947, p. 47. *P.T.J.*, Vol. 124, February 20, 1947, p. 7.

[15] *A.N.P.A., News*, No. 20, March 5, 1947, pp. 79–80. *E. & P.*, Vol. 80, March 8, 1947, pp. 5, 44. *Capehart Committee Hearings*, pp. 2–13, 21–29, 30–48, 73–112, 161–62, 183–94, 223–75.

[16] The Capehart bill was not acted upon. *A.N.P.A., News*, No. 23, March 12, 1947, p. 91; No. 26, March 14, pp. 105–06; No. 28, March 19, p. 111; No. 34, April 2, pp. 129–30; No. 36, April 9, p. 141; No. 37, April 16, p. 143; No. 45, May 7, p. 191. *E. & P.*, Vol. 80, March 15, 1947, p. 7; March 22, p. 16; April 12, p. 8; May 10, p. 50. *P.T.J.*, Vol. 124, March 13, 1947, p. 43; May 8, p. 33. *N.S.B.B.*, No. 352, May 16, p. 2. N. Y. *Times*, March 9, 14, 27, 1947. *Newsprint Supply and Distribution: Interim Report of the Special Committee to Study Problems of American Small Business, United States Senate, Eightieth Congress, First Session, Pursuant to S. Res. 20, A Resolution Appointing a Special Committee to Study Problems of American Small Business*, Senate Report 150, 80th Cong., 1st Sess.

(Washington: Government Printing Office, 1947), pp. 1–7, 9–11; cited subsequently as *Capehart Committee, Interim Report.*

[17] *A.N.P.A., News,* No. 29, March 24, 1947, p. 113; No. 32, April 2, pp. 121–24; No. 35, April 9, pp. 131–32; No. 38, April 16, p. 147; No. 40, April 16, pp. 157–59; No. 41, April 28, p. 168; No. 68, July 30, p. 280. *E. & P.*, Vol. 80, March 29, 1947, p. 56; April 5, p. 38; April 19, p. 19. Great Northern lagged behind the Canadian firms both in time and amount, announcing a $3.70 increase on July 30.

[18] *A.N.P.A., News,* No. 33, April 2, 1947, p. 126; No. 36, April 9, pp. 139–41; No. 68, July 30, p. 280; No. 70, August 13, p. 286; No. 74, August 29, pp. 303–04; No. 75, September 4, p. 307; No. 84, October 9, pp. 344–45; No. 85, October 16, pp. 347–48. *P.T.J.*, Vol. 125, October 16, 1947, pp. 7, 14–16; Vol. 128, January 13, 1949, pp. 16, 56–60. *Select Committee on Newsprint and Paper Supply: Interim Report of the Select Committee on Newsprint and Paper Supply, Pursuant to H. Res. 58 (80th Congress), A Resolution Creating a Select Committee to Conduct a Study with Respect to Present and Future Supplies of Newsprint, Printing and Wrapping Paper, Paper Products, Paper Pulp and Pulpwood,* House Report 1042, 80th Cong., 1st Sess. (Washington: Government Printing Office, 1947); cited subsequently as *Brown Committee, Interim Report.* The *Final Report,* House Report 2471, 80th Cong., 2d Sess. (Washington: Government Printing Office, 1948), was rendered on December 31, 1948, and is cited as *Brown Committee, Final Report.*

[19] Assistant Attorney General Wendell Berge wrote Senator Lister Hill that the complaints alleged that a " 'conspiracy' " among Canadian concerns supplying about 80 per cent of United States newsprint needs " 'restricts production, fixes prices on exports to the United States and allocates the available supplies to favored newspaper publishers. . . .' " *A.N.P.A., News,* No. 33, April 2, 1947, pp. 125–26. Attorney General Clark's letter of November 20 to Secretary of State George C. Marshall, reprinted in *A.N.P.A., News,* No. 94, November 26, 1947, pp. 384–86, outlines chronologically many of the developments to be recounted below. This, along with *E. & P.*, Vol. 80, June 28, 1947, p. 12, carries important elements of the story, and will not be cited further.

[20] The somewhat complicated corporate organization should perhaps be mentioned at this point. The United States (parent) corporation, International Paper Company, controlled as a wholly owned subsidiary Canadian International Paper Company, domiciled in Quebec; it in

turn controlled as a wholly owned subsidiary International Paper Sales Company, likewise domiciled in Quebec. *Celler Committee Hearings, Exhibits*, pp. 102–09, makes a considerable contribution to the facts which will be woven into the narrative without further citation.

Ralph M. Carson told the Celler Committee (June 28, 1950) that FBI agents had been given complete access to International's records in New York, and had spent months in the files; responding to the subpoena on the Canadian records, he pointed out, would have involved transporting to the States "2,436 separate steel cabinet file drawers embracing all their correspondence and all their files, without which they could not have done business." *Celler Committee Hearings*, pp. 622–24.

After issue of the subpoenas International Paper Sales surrendered the certificate entitling it to do business in New York State, and several officials of International Paper Company divested themselves of connection with International Paper Sales.

[21] *E. & P.*, Vol. 80, July 12, 1947, p. 5.

[22] *A.N.P.A., News*, No. 58, June 25, 1947, p. 243; No. 59, July 2, p. 245. Similar requests to quash subpoenas, made on behalf of Kimberly-Clark Company and Spruce Falls Company, were denied by another United States District Court. *Celler Committee Report*, p. 58.

[23] *A.N.P.A., News*, No. 78, September 17, 1947, pp. 319–20; No. 80, September 24, p. 327. *P.T.J.*, Vol. 125, September 25, 1947, p. 51. Congressman Brown's testimony before the Celler Committee (June 22, 1950) indicates that Clark's assertions of Canadian complacency were perhaps somewhat disingenuous. He pointed out that within a day or so of his own committee's visit to Canada "the then Attorney General of the United States made a special trip to Canada to sit down with some of the high-ranking Canadian officials to discuss the situation . . . and to the best of my information, he was there on the orders of a man holding a very, very high executive position in this country, and he was quite apologetic over the whole situation. . . ." *Celler Committee Hearings*, pp. 327, 343.

[24] *A.N.P.A., News*, No. 94, November 26, 1947, p. 383. *P.T.J.*, Vol. 125, December 27, 1947, p. 7. *Attorney General's Review*, p. 19.

[25] *A.N.P.A., News*, No. 65, July 23, 1945, pp. 269–70; No. 87, October 22, 1947, p. 357; No. 98, December 5, pp. 397–99. *E. & P.*, Vol. 80, October 18, 1947, p. 8. *P.T.J.*, Vol. 125, September 25, 1947, p. 51. Chandler urged that "we must convince the Canadian manufacturers that they are justified in expanding the newsprint production capac-

ity more rapidly and to provide a reasonable margin of rated capacity above the estimated demand." And again, " 'I urge a reasonable approach on the part of publishers. I urge U.S. publishers to discuss frankly with representatives of their suppliers the problems which confront them as newspaper operators. I suggest that the manufacturers consider the problems which are presented by the publishers.' "

Canadians failed to heed this advice, increasing their capacity only 10 per cent between 1946 and 1949, while United States capacity was standing virtually still, though in July, 1947, the owners of the Coosa River Newsprint Company, after leasing an unused ordnance plant from the federal government, had signed with Kimberly-Clark to build and manage a plant at Childersburg, Alabama, which would make a considerable addition to domestic production. *E. & P.*, Vol. 80, June 14, 1947, p. 42. *P.T.J.*, Vol. 125, July 24, 1947, p. 9. *Newsprint, Forward*, pp. 4, 18. In 1958, Charles F. Honeywell was to remind his industry somewhat ruefully: "We failed to sell our customers on the advantages to them of getting increased quantities of newsprint at the earliest possible date to meet the unexpected upsurge in their requirements." *Newsprint Production*, p. 3.

[26] *E. & P.*, Vol. 80, April 19, 1947, p. 62; May 10, p. 13. *P.T.J.*, Vol. 123, December 26, 1946, p. 42; Vol. 124, May 1, 1947, p. 24; Vol. 125, July 10, p. 40; November 20, p. 36. *Capehart Committee Hearings*, pp. 143, 145. *Celler Committee Report*, p. 25.

[27] *A.N.P.A., News*, No. 42, April 30, 1947, p. 174; No. 55, June 18, p. 229; No. 67, July 30, p. 275. *A.N.P.A., Convention*, No. 1, April 27, 1945, p. 41. *E. & P.*, Vol. 79, September 7, 1946, p. 14; Vol. 80, August 16, 1947, p. 10. *N.S.B.B.*, No. 354, July 17, 1947, p. 3; No. 357, October 16, p. 5. *Capehart Committee Hearings*, p. 142. *Celler Committee Hearings*, pp. 782–98.

[28] *A.N.P.A., News*, No. 2, January 7, 1948, pp. 3–4; No. 3, January 12, 1949, p. 8; No. 7, January 21, pp. 21–23; No. 8, January 21, p. 25; No. 18, February 6, p. 79; No. 19, March 3, p. 83; No. 44, August 24, pp. 187–91. *E. & P.*, Vol. 81, January 10, 1948, p. 42; January 24, p. 12. *P.T.J.*, Vol. 126, January 8, 1948, p. 16; February 26, p. 56; March 4, p. 9; April 22, p. 26.

As of January 10, according to *Editor & Publisher*, prices ranged from Great Northern's $87.50, New York port, to $96 charged by most of the large Canadian producers, with at least four other prices between these figures.

At the end of the year Canadian exports to the United States had increased 242,000 tons over the 1947 figures, partly made possible by a drop of 134,000 tons in overseas shipments, and accounting for a net increase of 108,000 tons over 1947.

[29] *A.N.P.A., News,* No. 28, April 28, 1948, pp. 121–22; No. 34, May 19, p. 149. *P.T.J.,* Vol. 126, April 1, 1948, p. 35; April 8, p. 7.

[30] *A.N.P.A., News,* No. 30, May 5, 1948, p. 132. *E. & P.,* Vol. 81, May 1, 1948, p. 7.

[31] *A.N.P.A., News,* No. 50, July 23, 1948, p. 215; No. 51, July 28, p. 217; No. 58, September 9, p. 245. *P.T.J.,* Vol. 127, July 29, 1948, pp. 20, 22, 24; Vol. 128, May 19, 1949, p. 10. *Celler Committee Report,* p. 69. Cranston Williams notified his constituents in early December that spot market prices had dropped below $140 per ton and that overseas mills were offering large tonnage for 1949 at prices which were "subject to negotiation." *E. & P.,* Vol. 81, December 11, 1948, p. 6.

[32] *A.N.P.A., News,* No. 70, November 11, 1948, p. 292; No. 74, November 24, p. 310. *E. & P.,* Vol. 81, September 25, 1948, p. 5; Vol. 83, May 27, 1950, p. 32. *Celler Committee Hearings,* p. 352.

[33] *A.N.P.A., News,* No. 65, October 14, 1948, p. 275; No. 67, October 27, p. 283. *E. & P.,* Vol. 81, September 25, 1948, p. 52. *P.T.J.,* Vol. 127, December 9, 1948, p. 53. A.N.P.A. reported that by October the Trade Commission threat had caused "several major producers" in the steel and other industries to revert to f.o.b. mill-pricing practices.

The "invasion" mentioned above resulted in Trade Commission investigation of fifteen separate trade associations in the paper industry, but produced only two formal complaints, neither of which was directed against the newsprint manufacturers. *Magnuson Committee Hearings,* p. 216.

[34] The following cover the story of events through the end of 1948: *A.N.P.A., News,* No. 78, December 8, 1948, pp. 319–22; No. 80, December 16, p. 332. *E. & P.,* Vol. 81, December 4, 1948, p. 50. *P.T.J.,* Vol. 127, December 23, 1948, pp. 9–11, 53. The author has found no expression of A.N.P.A. sentiment on these developments.

[35] *A.N.P.A., News,* No. 10, January 28, 1948, p. 31; No. 11, February 5, pp. 36–37; No. 18, February 26, p. 82; No. 29, April 28, p. 126; No. 53, August 13, p. 225. *E. & P.,* Vol. 81, January 31, 1948, p. 20. *N.S.B.B.,* No. 367, August 13, 1948, p. 5. *P.T.J.,* Vol. 126, February 12, 1948, p. 7; Vol. 127, August 5, 1948, p. 38. *Survey of Alaskan Newsprint Resources: Interim Report of the Special Committee*

to Study Problems of American Small Business, United States Senate, Eightieth Congress, Second Session, Pursuant to S. Res. 20, A Resolution Appointing a Special Committee to Study Problems of American Small Business, Senate Report 852, 80th Cong., 2d Sess. (Washington: Government Printing Office, 1948), pp. 1–3.

J. D. Zellerbach told the Celler Committee (July 19, 1950) that his company had in early 1948 been involved in an unsuccessful effort, sponsored by west coast publishers, to raise equity capital for a new mill in the continental United States. He estimated the cost of such a mill in 1950 at $130,000 per ton of daily production, reducible by as much as $40,000 if timber were available. With a minimum of 100 daily tons necessary for an efficient operation, the required amount of capital was obviously considerable; Alaskan operations would have involved even greater sums. *Celler Committee Hearings,* pp. 979–80.

[36] *Brown Committee, Final Report,* pp. 1–7.

[37] *A.N.P.A., News,* No. 17, March 16, 1949, p. 83; No. 23, May 4, p. 113. *E. & P.,* Vol. 82, April 23, 1949, pp. 21, 66. *N.S.B.B.,* No. 376, May 17, 1949, p. 3. *P.T.J.,* Vol. 128, January 20, 1949, p. 22; February 3, p. 8; February 24, p. 98; March 24, p. 27; April 14, p. 28; June 2, pp. 7, 9; Vol. 130, February 2, 1950, p. 14. *Magnuson Committee Hearings,* p. 91. Charles E. Moreau informed the Convention of the National Editorial Association toward the end of April: " 'It always comes as a surprise when a period of scarcity in any commodity ends. It seems as though overnight supply has caught up with demand.' " And the Newsprint Committee reported to the A.N.P.A. Convention in the same month: " 'The newsprint emergency is passing. For the first time since 1942, supply and demand are nearing a balance. The spot market for newsprint at high prices has vanished. . . .' "

Only the Powell River Paper Company deviated from the uniform price. *Celler Committee Hearings,* p. 226.

[38] *A.N.P.A., News,* No. 11, February 16, 1949, p. 41. *N.S.B.B.,* No. 374, March 14, 1949, p. 2. *Newsprint Supply and Distribution: A Final Report of the Special Committee to Study Problems of American Small Business, United States Senate, Eightieth Congress, First Session, Pursuant to S. Res. 20, A Resolution Appointing a Special Committee to Study Problems of American Small Business,* Senate Report 47, 81st Cong., 1st Sess. (Washington: Government Printing Office, 1949), pp. 1–2.

[39] *A.N.P.A., News,* No. 19, March 30, 1949, p. 96; No. 24, May 4, p. 115; No. 29, June 8, p. 133; No. 33, June 30, p. 147; No. 35, July 13, p. 153; No. 57, October 19, p. 239. *P.T.J.,* Vol. 128, January 13, 1949, p. 14.

[40] *A.N.P.A., News,* No. 13, February 24, 1949, pp. 67, 70–72; No. 37, July 20, pp. 165–66. *E. & P.,* Vol. 82, January 29, 1949, pp. 11, 32; February 26, pp. 9, 72; March 26, pp. 9, 34.

[41] *E. & P.,* Vol. 82, July 23, 1949, p. 6. *P.T.J.,* Vol. 128, June 2, 1949, pp. 7–9; Vol. 129, July 21, 1949, p. 28.

[42] *A.N.P.A., News,* No. 50, September 21, 1949, p. 209; No. 51, September 28, pp. 211–13; No. 54, October 13, pp. 225–27; No. 56, October 19, pp. 235–37; No. 58, October 26, pp. 241–42; No. 61, November 10, p. 251; No. 68, December 21, p. 278. *E. & P.,* Vol. 82, September 24, 1949, pp. 10, 34; October 15, p. 14; October 22, p. 30; December 3, p. 36. *P.T.J.,* Vol. 129, September 22, 1949, p. 39; September 29, pp. 7, 14; October 6, p. 28; October 13, p. 47; October 27, pp. 7, 12; November 10, p. 7; November 24, p. 16; Vol. 130, February 2, 1950, p. 14.

An interesting and significant development was reported on December 22 when the Coosa River plant started producing. This operation, participated in by over one hundred newspapers, was "the first new source of U.S. newsprint to be developed in the past decade." This was financed by the sale of stocks and bonds to the amount of approximately $18,000,000, and was aided in its inception by the lease of a wartime ordnance plant as the foundation of its operation. *P.T.J.,* Vol. 129, December 22, 1949, p. 10. *Transportation Factors,* p. 117. *Celler Committee Hearings,* pp. 346, 355.

CHAPTER V

[1] *N.S.B.B.,* No. 386, March 17, 1950, p. 7. *Klein Committee Hearings,* p. 111. Charles W. Boyce, *The First Five Years: Report on the Decade 1951–1960 of Newsprint Supply and Demand* (Pamphlet, New York: A.N.P.A., 1956), pp. 19, 20; cited subsequently as *First Five Years. Preliminary Report and Supplements: Newsprint Production and Supply, Committee on Banking and Currency, United States Senate, Prepared by Forest Products Division, Business and Defense Services Administration, U.S. Department of Commerce* (Committee Print, Washington: Government Printing Office, 1956), p. 34; cited subsequently as *Banking and Currency Committee, Preliminary Report.*

Writing in 1957, Charles W. Boyce, in analyzing the period 1945–1955 from the standpoint of the A.N.P.A., listed the following counts on which publishers criticized manufacturers for their "frequent price increases and associated failure to increase productive capacity. . . .":

1. Publishers have been "forced frequently to adjust circulation and advertising rates at a time . . . when population shifts were slowing circulation growth and television had become a strong competitor in advertising."

2. They "saw no serious effort on the part of manufacturers, particularly in Canada, to meet growing newsprint requirements in the United States and especially in overseas markets by commensurate expansion of capacity."

3. They doubted the ability of the Canadian industry to "meet growing requirements upon it by confining expansion almost exclusively to machine speed-ups, the lowest cost form of adding new capacity."

4. They objected to being forced into the spot market, "particularly in 1955 and 1956, partly because some manufacturers unilaterally curtailed deliveries." *Newsprint, Forward*, pp. 37–38.

[2] *P.T.J.*, Vol. 130, February 23, 1950, pp. 56, 71–73; Vol. 131, September 21, 1950, p. 48. *Newsprint Investigation: Hearings before a Subcommittee of the Committee on Interstate and Foreign Commerce, House of Representatives, Eighty-Second Congress, First Session, on Subjects Pursuant to H. Res. 116* (Washington: Government Printing Office, 1951), p. 276; cited subsequently as *Beckworth Committee Hearings.*

It might be noted that minor price adjustments accompanied the real incidence of the Coosa River tonnage in January, when two Canadian concerns eliminated certain charges to customers in the southeastern United States area in deference to the domestic competition. Powell River had taken similar action some weeks earlier in transactions with its west coast and southwestern customers. *E. & P.*, Vol. 83, January 28, 1950, p. 7.

[3] *A.N.P.A.*, *News*, No. 2, January 11, 1950, p. 5; No. 5, January 25, p. 19; No. 7, February 1, pp. 23–24; No. 11, February 16, pp. 37, 39; No. 17, March 8, pp. 73–74. *E. & P.*, Vol. 83, January 28, 1950, p. 46; February 18, p. 12. *P.T.J.*, Vol. 130, February 9, 1950, p. 22; February 16, p. 11. By mid-April, according to the *Montreal Daily Star* (April 19, as quoted in *A.N.P.A.*, *News*, No. 25, April 19, p. 110), he had decided not to visit Canada, boasting: " ' "We don't need to be wined and dined to get first-hand information. . . ." ' "

[4] *A.N.P.A., News*, No. 26, May 4, 1950, p. 107. *E. & P.*, Vol. 83, April 8, 1950, pp. 18, 34; April 22, p. 60; May 13, p. 32.

At the annual convention of the A.N.P.A., Williams was asked: " 'Did the ANPA inspire the Celler Committee to schedule their forthcoming investigation . . . ?' " He replied: "The ANPA did not ask Rep. Celler to start his investigation and it is not asking Rep. Celler to stop his investigation." *A.N.P.A., News*, No. 26, May 4, 1950, pp. 108–09.

[5] *A.N.P.A., News*, No. 33, June 7, 1950, pp. 133–34, and No. 35, June 14, pp. 139–52, carry Inland's queries and Fowler's reply of June 7. Cf. also *E. & P.*, Vol. 83, May 25, 1950, p. 5; June 10, p. 9; June 17, p. 40. *P.T.J.*, Vol. 130, June 1, 1950, p. 6.

[6] *A.N.P.A., News*, No. 37, June 14, 1950, p. 157.

[7] *A.N.P.A., News*, No. 39, June 21, 1950, p. 165. *Celler Committee Hearings*, pp. 87–89. *Celler Committee Report*, pp. 15–16. *Celler Committee, Final Report*, pp. 25–43. N. Y. *Times*, June 17, 1950. The committee's work owed much to the cooperation of the Department of Commerce and to the effectiveness of its Counsel, Professor Edward H. Levi, as this is written, Dean of the Law School of the University of Chicago.

[8] *E. & P.*, Vol. 83, June 24, 1950, pp. 7, 63. *P.T.J.*, Vol. 130, June 29, 1950, pp. 13–14. *Celler Committee Hearings*, pp. 108–61.

Chairman Celler had consulted with the Department of State and had received assurances that there would be no departmental intervention such as had operated to stymie the investigation of 1947. *Celler Committee Hearings*, p. 103.

On the following day he addressed himself to publishers' reluctance to testify, based on their supposed fear of "reprisals," and complained mildly that though the committee did not "like to press them, and we do not want to hurt anybody . . . we have had to develop our preliminary work attendant upon this investigation with a great deal of difficulty because of that fear. That fear may be fancied or it may be actual, I do not know, but we have difficulty in getting publishers to come down here to testify." *Celler Committee Hearings*, p. 280; cf. also p. 596.

[9] *Celler Committee Hearings*, pp. 210–48.

[10] *Celler Committee Hearings*, pp. 300–02. *Celler Committee Hearings, Exhibits*, pp. 135–37.

[11] *Celler Committee Hearings*, pp. 364, 369–70, 407–14, 420–21, 457–501, 823–25.

[12] *Celler Committee Hearings*, pp. 347, 355, 455, 532–33, 547, 678, 773, 931–33.

[13] *Celler Committee Hearings*, pp. 292, 323, 356–57, 564, 583–89, 678.

[14] *Celler Committee Hearings*, pp. 776–77. *A.N.P.A., News*, No. 43, July 6, 1950, p. 183.

[15] *Celler Committee Hearings*, pp. 803–23, 928, 939–41, 982–83, 997–1007, 1132–33.

[16] *A.N.P.A., News*, No. 45, July 14, 1950, p. 189; No. 48, July 26, pp. 199–200; No. 57, September 7, p. 229. *P.T.J.*, Vol. 131, July 27, 1950, p. 41; August 3, p. 15; August 10, p. 14.

[17] *A.N.P.A., News*, No. 63, October 4, 1950, p. 257; No. 70, October 25, p. 284; November 9, pp. 312–13. *E. & P.*, Vol. 83, July 29, 1950, pp. 5, 28; August 12, p. 8; September 23, pp. 13, 60. *N.S.B.B.*, No. 392, September 14, p. 8. *Attorney General's Review*, pp. 26–27. As usual, a complicated and alphabetical hierarchy of administrative agencies blossomed under the Defense Production Act. In descending order, the agencies dealing with newsprint were the Office of Defense Mobilization (ODM), within which was the Defense Production Administration (DPA), which had general responsibility for programs developed under the act. Under it, immediate responsibility lodged in the National Production Authority (NPA), succeeded in 1953 by the Business and Defense Services Administration (BDSA); these last two were agencies of the Department of Commerce.

[18] *A.N.P.A., News*, No. 63, October 4, 1950, p. 255; No. 64, October 11, p. 259; No. 67, October 16, p. 271; No. 68, October 19, p. 275; No. 70, October 25, pp. 281–84; No. 71, November 1, pp. 297–301; No. 73, November 9, pp. 303–06; No. 80, December 6, p. 339. *E. & P.*, Vol. 83, October 21, 1950, pp. 11, 34; October 28, p. 5; November 4, p. 34. *P.T.J.*, Vol. 131, September 28, 1950, p. 9; October 19, p. 12; October 26, pp. 9, 13; November 9, pp. 9, 13–14.

[19] *Newsprint, Forward*, pp. 19–20. *Magnuson Committee Hearings*, p. 147. Average consumption increased by only 55,000 tons during the years 1951–1954, inclusive. Representatives of International told the Magnuson Committee (February 27, 1957): "Manufacturers were led to believe that the upward trend for the future in consumption of newsprint would not be as rapid as it had been in the years immediately following the war. . . ." Reasons commonly assigned for the leveling-off of demand were completion of readjustments from wartime restrictions, expansion of television with consequent inroads

on newspaper advertising, and aggressive campaigns by publishers' associations for economy in use of newsprint; all this was accompanied by demands for narrower roll widths, which, in turn, increased manufacturing costs. For all these reasons this period was one in which some manufacturers were slow to undertake expensive expansion plans.

Whereas both United States and Canadian consumption remained relatively stable during 1951, United States production increased by 11 per cent (110,000 tons) over the 1950 figure. Both United States and Canadian exports increased during the year, under pressure from the International Materials Conference, which urged nations with extensive supplies of scarce materials to share their bounty with the have-not nations. *P.T.J.*, Vol. 134, February 22, 1952, pp. 146–48. *Klein Committee Hearings*, p. 101.

[20] *A.N.P.A.*, *News*, No. 3, January 10, 1951, p. 7; No. 8, January 25, pp. 25–26; No. 48, June 13, p. 219. *P.T.J.*, Vol. 132, January 19, 1951, p. 14; February 2, pp. 9, 12–13. Fowler told the Canadian Pulp and Paper Association (January 26, the day the United States freeze was announced) that one of the "curious phenomena of recent weeks has been the way businessmen, who have for years been extolling the virtues of free enterprise and protesting against interference of governments, have begun to clamour for economic controls. . . . I refuse to believe that we need to get into the whole elaborate paraphernalia of rationing, quotas, advisory committees, administrators, price ceilings, and policing. . . ." In the same address he called attention to a current shortage of sulphur; this was to become a more prominent feature later in the year.

[21] *A.N.P.A.*, *News*, No. 12, February 15, 1951, pp. 38–40. *P.T.J.*, Vol. 132, February 16, 1951, p. 9.

[22] *A.N.P.A.*, *News*, No. 10, February 7, 1951, p. 31; No. 19, March 7, p. 80; No. 20, March 15, p. 90; No. 24, March 28, p. 100. *N.S.B.B.*, No. 397, February, 1951, p. 7; No. 398, March, p. 8. *P.T.J.*, Vol. 132, February 16, 1951, p. 12. *Beckworth Committee Hearings*, pp. 4–5. *Record*, 82d Cong., 1st Sess., pp. 1015, 1749, 1945–46. *Paper Trade Journal* commented, on hearing of the Humphrey Committee: "Thus, we have one more in the continuous round of Brown, Boren, Capeheart [*sic*], the Department of Justice and Celler investigations. All of these during the past five years. What phase this group is going to cover, we cannot imagine. Several things are certain, it will not help to establish a more friendly feeling between the papermaker and the publishers, it will make the Canadians more willing to comply with

the European requests for more paper to help fight Communism and lastly, drive away still further any risk capital which might be attracted to new newsprint mills. . . ."

[23] *A.N.P.A., News*, No. 21, March 15, 1951, p. 89; No. 33, May 2, pp. 131, 134–35; No. 34, May 2, pp. 161–62. *E. & P.*, Vol. 84, April 28, 1951, p. 78. *P.T.J.*, Vol. 132, April 27, 1951, p. 14; May 4, p. 17.

[24] *A.N.P.A., News*, No. 20, March 24, 1951, p. 100; No. 37, May 9, pp. 173–74; No. 75, September 20, p. 327. *N.S.B.B.*, No. 401, June, 1951, p. 3. *Humphrey Committee, Preliminary Report*, pp. 2–20.

[25] *A.N.P.A., News*, No. 37, May 9, 1951, p. 173. *E. & P.*, Vol. 84, May 12, 1951, pp. 11, 84. *N.S.B.B.*, No. 400, May, 1951, p. 3; No. 401, June, p. 2. *P.T.J.*, Vol. 132, June 1, 1951, p. 9. *Celler Committee Report.*

[26] *A.N.P.A., News*, No. 80, October 8, 1951, p. 348. *Beckworth Committee Hearings*, pp. 39–40, 44–45, 49–50, 99, 123, 131–32, 201–02.

[27] *A.N.P.A., News*, No. 45, June 1, 1951, p. 205; No. 47, June 6, pp. 213–15. *P.T.J.*, Vol. 132, June 8, pp. 9, 11. *Beckworth Committee Hearings*, p. 253, pointed to a new Canadian labor scale, effective on May 1, as one reason for the increase.

[28] *A.N.P.A., News*, No. 48, June 13, 1951, pp. 219–20. *Beckworth Committee Hearings*, pp. 288–91.

[29] *Humphrey Committee Report*, pp. 149–50. Canada declined (June 12) to grant the request for suspension of the proposed increase pending discussion, the Canadian Defense Production Minister insisting that it was justified by higher costs and denying that Canadian action violated the January agreement. *A.N.P.A., News*, No. 48, June 13, 1951, p. 220; No. 50, June 15, pp. 228–29.

[30] *A.N.P.A., News*, No. 48, June 13, 1951, pp. 218, 220–22; No. 50, June 15, p. 230. *E. & P.*, Vol. 81, June 16, 1951, p. 40. *Humphrey Committee Report*, p. 149. On the other hand, *Paper Trade Journal* commented (Vol. 132, June 22, 1951, p. 9): "In what may well be the prime blunder of its lifetime, the Office of Defense Mobilization last week scrambled the much-tried patience of the Canadian newsprint industry and breached the long-time harmony between us and our northern friends. The ill-advised blast also placed in jeopardy the price and volume of Canadian market pulps to U.S. mills. . . .

"High-pressured by newspaper publishers who say their existence is threatened by the $10 rise in newsprint price . . . Michael V. Di-

Salle . . . says he is considering naming the price which users can pay for the Canadian product. . . .

"None expects that defense officials can in their lifetime become experts in the ramifications of the North American pulp and paper industry. But when ODM needs the paper we make from the pulp we get from the Canadians, it is well that, in the words of another Canadian, we shake ourselves down into our britches. . . ."

[31] *A.N.P.A., News*, No. 48, June 13, 1951, pp. 217–18; No. 51, June 20, pp. 236–38; No. 59, July 18, pp. 267–71. *Beckworth Committee Hearings*, pp. 265–69. *Humphrey Committee Report*, pp. 149–50. M. C. Walsh, Deputy Chief of the Pulp, Paper and Paperboard Branch of OPS, told the Beckworth Committee of the session with the publishers: "I went into that meeting thinking we were going to be under pressure to go up to Canada and raise a ruckus, but the sense of the meeting really was . . . that the American publishers, much as they hated the price increase from Canada, would hate even more to have any part of their supply cut off. They thought there was a need for negotiation, but they did not want it to be done on an unfriendly basis which would antagonize the supplier. . . ." This statement tends to counter the highly critical point of view taken by *Editor & Publisher*, as quoted in Note 30, just above.

[32] *A.N.P.A., News*, No. 50, June 15, 1951, p. 230; No. 51, June 20, pp. 233–34; No. 52, June 22, p. 239; No. 53, June 27, pp. 243–44; No. 55, July 6, p. 251. *E. & P.*, Vol. 84, June 23, 1951, pp. 12, 15, 36. *Beckworth Committee Hearings*, pp. 237–40, 274. Treanor, formerly a publisher for forty-five years and currently Chief of NPA's Printing and Publishing Division, testified before the Beckworth Committee just after a speech in which he had urged members of the International Circulation Managers Association to go home and push for the development of a newsprint industry in the southern states; his assurance to the committee (June 20) that his agency would do its utmost to expedite the establishment of a domestic industry by granting priorities for new machinery is the first such statement the author has discovered by a responsible government officer. *Beckworth Committee Hearings*, pp. 245, 250, 256.

[33] *A.N.P.A., News*, No. 62, July 25, 1951, pp. 281, 289; No. 67, August 15, p. 299; No. 77, October 5, pp. 338–39. *E. & P.*, Vol. 84, August 11, 1951, p. 10. *N.S.B.B.*, No. 404, September, 1951, p. 2. *P.T.J.*, Vol. 133, August 17, 1951, p. 16. A matter of some peripheral importance to the newsprint story may be mentioned briefly in the

signing of a contract (July 27) between the Forest Service and the Ketchikan Pulp and Paper Company for 1,500,000,000 cubic feet of Alaskan pulp timber. *N.S.B.B.*, No. 403, August, 1951, p. 10.

[34] *A.N.P.A.*, *News*, No. 71, August 29, 1951, pp. 313–14; No. 86, October 25, p. 383; No. 89, November 8, p. 393; No. 94, November 21, p. 411; No. 95, November 28, p. 415; No. 104, December 28, p. 453. *N.S.B.B.*, No. 406, November, 1951, p. 11; No. 407, December, p. 2. *Beckworth Committee Hearings*, pp. 472, 514, 516, 526. One of those interested in new construction was Sir Eric Vansittart Bowater, an English promoter and large-scale producer of newsprint in Newfoundland, who had spent ten weeks in the United States in the interest of establishing a newsprint mill in eastern Tennessee; he announced in November that he was prepared to put $50,000,000 into the project. *A.N.P.A.*, *News*, No. 91, November 15, 1951, p. 402.

[35] *E. & P.*, Vol. 84, October 6, 1951, pp. 7–8; October 13, p. 38; December 8, pp. 7, 36, 61. *N.S.B.B.*, No. 405, October, 1951, p. 3. *Newsprint Now*, pp. 22–23, 39.

[36] *A.N.P.A.*, *News*, No. 63, August 1, 1951, p. 315; No. 79, October 5, p. 345. *N.S.B.B.*, No. 404, September, 1951, p. 5. *Newsprint Investigation: Canadian Supplies, Progress Report of the Special Subcommittee on Investigation of Newsprint and Other Matters of the Committee on Interstate and Foreign Commerce, Pursuant to H. Res. 116 (82d Congress)*, House Report 1093, 82d Cong., 1st Sess. (Washington: Government Printing Office, 1951), pp. 1–7; cited subsequently as *Beckworth Committee Report.*

[37] *A.N.P.A.*, *News*, No. 12, March 4, 1953, p. 60. *E. & P.*, Vol. 85, November 29, 1952, p. 34. *P.T.J.*, Vol. 136, February 20, 1953, pp. 66, 128, 160–66.

[38] *A.N.P.A.*, *News*, No. 4, January 18, 1952, pp. 11–12; No. 10, February 14, pp. 32–35; No. 13, February 20, p. 45; No. 14, February 20, p. 49; No. 17, March 5, p. 77. *E. & P.*, Vol. 85, February 2, 1952, p. 8; February 16, p. 12; February 23, p. 13. *N.S.B.B.*, No. 410, March, 1952, p. 2. *P.T.J.*, Vol. 134, February 1, 1952, pp. 12–13; March 7, p. 9. *Harris Committee Hearings*, pp. 6, 62–63. *Klein Committee Hearings*, pp. 111, 113. The actual new production goal set by the ODM in 1952 was 494,000 tons; additional tonnage to bring the amount up to the 751,000 figure involved an Alaskan project which was to prove abortive as far as newsprint was concerned. It should be emphasized that the road between the granting of a certificate of necessity and newsprint rolling off the machines was a long one, for in 1957

not more than 400,000 of the 494,000 authorized tons were in actual production.

[39] *A.N.P.A., News,* No. 29, April 9, 1952, pp. 123–24; No. 33, April 30, p. 143. *Humphrey Committee Report,* pp. 1–190, which stated the committee's conclusions, based on the evidence submitted, and followed by printing the evidence.

[40] *A.N.P.A., News,* No. 19, March 12, 1952, p. 83; No. 23, March 19, pp. 97–98; No. 38, May 21, pp. 165–71; No. 40, May 29, p. 186. *N.S.B.B.,* No. 410, March, 1952, p. 3. *P.T.J.,* Vol. 134, May 9, 1952, p. 9; May 23, p. 11. *Newsprint Price Rise: Report of Subcommittee No. 5 (Antitrust Subcommittee) of the Committee on the Judiciary, Pursuant to H. Res. 95 (82d Cong., 1st Sess.), Authorizing the Committee on the Judiciary to Conduct Studies and Investigations Relating to Matters within Its Jurisdiction,* House Report No. 505, Part 3, 82d Cong., 2d Sess. (Washington: Government Printing Office, 1952), pp. 1–4; cited subsequently as *Newsprint Price Rise Report.* United States mills followed the Canadian example during the summer and early autumn, being entitled to ask for increases under OPS regulations.

[41] *A.N.P.A., News,* No. 42, May 29, 1952, p. 186; No. 48, June 25, p. 205; No. 50, July 2, p. 213. *E. & P.,* Vol. 85, May 24, 1952, pp. 9–10, 32; May 31, pp. 9–10, 40. *P.T.J.,* Vol. 134, May 23, 1952, p. 9; June 27, p. 35. It may be noted here that the issuance of certificates of necessity for rapid tax amortization of new domestic industries was proceeding with only moderate speed. Great Northern received the eighth such certificate during this period, bringing the total tonnage authorizations up to 375,000 out of a permissible 393,000 tons.

[42] *A.N.P.A., News,* No. 14, February 20, 1952, pp. 49–50; No. 16, February 27, p. 75; No. 30, April 9, p. 127; No. 38, May 21, pp. 169–70; No. 39, May 21, p. 173; No. 41, May 28, p. 180; No. 42, May 29, pp. 185–86. *N.S.B.B.,* No. 411, May, 1952, pp. 2–3; No. 413, June, p. 2. *Record,* 82d Cong., 2d Sess., pp. 6004–05.

[43] *A.N.P.A., News,* No. 50, July 2, 1952, pp. 211–12; No. 56, July 23, pp. 236–38. *Study of Newsprint Expansion: A Progress Report of the Department of Commerce to Subcommittee No. 5 of the Committee on the Judiciary, House of Representatives* (Washington: Government Printing Office, 1952), pp. 22–26; cited subsequently as *McCoy Report.* This report was rendered in response to a request by the Celler Committee's May meeting.

Between the two sessions mentioned above, Representative Harris proposed (June 19) an amendment to the Defense Production Act of

1950 adding the manufacture of newsprint to the list of essential commodities, a device to supplement the tax amortization assistance already in effect by "making it possible for new newsprint manufacturers to secure financial assistance through direct Government loans for this purpose. . . ." *Record*, 82d Cong., 2d Sess., pp. 7659–60.

[44] *McCoy Report*, pp. 2–23. *Hearing before the Antitrust Subcommittee of the Committee on the Judiciary, House of Representatives, Eighty-Second Congress, Second Session, on Newsprint Expansion* (Washington: Government Printing Office, 1952), pp. 2–23; cited subsequently as *Newsprint Price Rise—Hearings*. Officials of W. R. Grace and Company, whose Peruvian plant had been making newsprint from bagasse for twelve years, reported to *Editor & Publisher* as early as June 14 that such paper could not be manufactured in the United States to compete with newsprint selling at $126 per ton. *E. & P.*, Vol. 85, June 14, 1952, p. 12.

[45] *A.N.P.A., News*, No. 74, October 10, 1952, p. 301; No. 88, December 30, pp. 355–56. *E. & P.*, Vol. 85, October 18, 1952, pp. 9, 64. *P.T.J.*, Vol. 135, October 10, 1952, p. 7; December 19, p. 9. Fowler told the Southern Newspaper Publishers Association in November that 1953 would be a " 'comfortable' " year in which publishers could get what paper they wanted from Canada, even to the extent of an extra 150,000 tons over the 1952 consumption. *N.S.B.B.*, No. 419, December, 1952, p. 2.

[46] *A.N.P.A., News*, No. 22, April 27, 1953, pp. 91–93; No. 6, February 3, 1954, p. 15; No. 21, April 21, pp. 85, 92. *P.T.J.*, Vol. 138, January 29, 1953, pp. 52–54; February 5, pp. 18–19. *Klein Committee Hearings*, p. 127.

[47] *A.N.P.A., News*, No. 6, February 4, 1953, pp. 19–20; No. 12, March 4, p. 61; No. 13, March 11, p. 63; No. 15, March 18, p. 69; No. 16, March 25, p. 72; No. 31, June 3, p. 125; No. 50, September 16, p. 179. *N.S.B.B.*, No. 422, March, 1953, p. 7. *Celler Committee, Final Report*, p. iii.

[48] *E. & P.*, Vol. 86, September 19, 1953, p. 11. *Celler Committee, Final Report*, pp. 5–48.

[49] *A.N.P.A., News*, No. 17, March 25, 1953, pp. 75–76. *P.T.J.*, Vol. 136, March 27, 1953, p. 12. Fowler repeated this theme in November in an address to the National Foreign Trade Council, when he asserted that Americans " ' "seem to be clutching at any device, however expensive and uneconomic, that will make you self-sufficient again. . . . If you become, by government promotion or pressure, more

self-sufficient in newsprint, not only will you seriously injure your closest ally in the world, but also your exporters will lose much of their most valuable market." ' " *A.N.P.A., News*, No. 61, November 18, 1953, p. 218.

[50] *A.N.P.A., News*, No. 31, June 3, 1953, p. 125; No. 35, June 24, p. 137; No. 42, August 5, p. 155; No. 53, October 7, p. 185; No. 65, December 9, p. 231. *E. & P.*, Vol. 86, October 24, 1953, p. 34; November 11, p. 44. One significant development in the supply situation during the year was the appearance of newsprint containing upward of 30 per cent of pulp made from hardwood, turned out by the Great Northern Company on the basis of a semichemical process developed at Syracuse University. This product bade fair to ease the pressure on the softwood forests which had hitherto been the foundation of the newsprint industry, and became the foundation of a $32,000,000 expansion program announced by that concern. *A.N.P.A., News*, No. 22, April 27, 1953, p. 91; No. 30, May 27, p. 121. *E. & P.*, Vol. 86, April 25, p. 25. *N.S.B.B.*, No. 425, June, 1953, p. 2. *Magnuson Committee Hearings*, pp. 232–33.

[51] *A.N.P.A., News*, No. 1, January 27, 1954, p. 11; No. 21, April 23, pp. 85–87; No. 1, January 5, 1955, p. 1. *E. & P.*, Vol. 87, January 2, 1954, p. 11; Vol. 89, September 15, 1956, p. 84. *P.T.J.*, Vol. 138, January 1, 1954, p. 7; January 8, p. 7; January 22, p. 7; Vol. 139, January 31, 1955, pp. 60–62. *Magnuson Committee Hearings*, p. 102. *Newsprint Study: Current Newsprint Outlook, Interim Report of the Committee on Interstate and Foreign Commerce, Pursuant to H. Res. 105 (84th Congress)*, House Report 683, 84th Cong., 1st Sess. (Washington: Government Printing Office, 1955), pp. 2–4; cited subsequently as *Klein Committee, Interim Report, 1955*. Apropos the early-1955 bulge in consumption, the A.N.P.A.'s Newsprint Committee reported in April, 1956: " 'No one foresaw this tremendous increase in consumption even as late as November 1954. . . .' " *A.N.P.A., News*, No. 31, April 27, 1956, p. 134. The only evidence of prescience in this matter which has come to the writer's attention is found in the testimony of Fred W. Mears, for many years connected with Great Northern, who told the Harris Committee (February 18, 1957) that manufacturers in 1954 "had the job of selling 100,000 tons of new production. . . . At that time the publishers were so unaware of the future that we were having difficulty in doing it. We even went into the export market to get rid of some of it. Then all of a sudden the avalanche hit and all of the boys were in with a cup. . . . In the

latter part of that year there was some stirring, and I talked to a publisher just after Christmas in 1954 and I said, 'Don't you realize that by Easter you will be in a seller's market?' And he said I was crazy. . . ." *Harris Committee Hearings*, p. 56.

[52] *A.N.P.A., News*, No. 24, May 12, 1954, p. 99. *P.T.J.*, Vol. 138, June 25, 1954, p. 31.

[53] *A.N.P.A., News*, No. 40, August 11, 1954, p. 145. *Study of Newsprint Expansion: Part II, Newsprint Production from Hardwoods, Second Progress Report of the Department of Commerce to the Committee on the Judiciary, House of Representatives* (Committee Print, Washington: Government Printing Office, 1954), pp. 1–368. *Paper Trade Journal* commented sarcastically on this continued interest of the Judiciary Committee and the Department of Commerce, in the light of manufacturers' assurances of ability to cope with possible shortages, alluding to the shifting emphasis of the department on proposed remedies, first bagasse, now hardwoods, and projection of a third via a proposal to study the utilization of waste paper as a source of newsprint supply. Vol. 138, August 13, 1954, p. 30.

[54] *A.N.P.A., News*, No. 18, April 7, 1954, p. 77; No. 37, July 21, pp. 137–38. *E. & P.*, Vol. 87, February 27, 1954, p. 7; July 24, p. 36; October 9, p. 65; November 13, p. 11; December 25, p. 37. A final note may be struck by quoting a statement of R. M. Fowler (read into the Magnuson Committee hearings on February 27, 1957) concerning the annual publisher-manufacturer session at Montreal in December, 1954, where " 'opinions . . . were unanimous in estimating the United States newsprint demand would be virtually at the same level in 1955 as in 1954, perhaps 1 or 2 percentage points higher but no one expected any substantial change in demand levels which had been practically constant for 4 years.' " *Magnuson Committee Hearings*, pp. 137–38.

CHAPTER VI

[1] *A.N.P.A., News*, No. 20, April 15, 1955, p. 81; No. 23, April 29, p. 93; No. 31, April 27, 1956, p. 134. *E. & P.*, Vol. 88, April 23, 1955, p. 90. *P.T.J.*, Vol. 140, January 30, 1956, pp. 43–44. *Newsprint Study: Newsprint Outlook for 1956, Interim Report of the Committee on Interstate and Foreign Commerce Pursuant to H. Res. 105 (84th Congress)*, House Report 1953, 84th Cong., 2d Sess. (Washington: Government Printing Office, 1956), p. 2; cited subse-

quently as *Klein Committee, Interim Report of 1956. Harris Committee Hearings*, pp. 9, 67–68. *Klein Committee Hearings*, p. 179. *Klein Committee, Interim Report, 1955*, pp. 2–3. *Magnuson Committee Hearings*, pp. 91–92.

The reader who searches these and other footnote references will find considerable variety in statistical reports on the newsprint problem. The A.N.P.A.'s figures normally base on current reports by members to the trade association office, and need to be equated to total figures by a shifting factor calculated by the association. The Newsprint Service Bureau's statistician, John J. Zima, publishes, early each year, a review based on completed figures for the previous twelve-month. Occasional statistics appearing in committee hearings and in the reports of governmental agencies derive from various bases. The consumption figures quoted above are from the *Interim Report, 1955*, of the Klein Committee; those on linage and circulation are the A.N.P.A.'s.

[2] *A.N.P.A., News*, No. 4, January 19, 1955, p. 11; No. 5, January 26, p. 15; No. 9, February 16, p. 27; No. 14, March 9, p. 61. *E. & P.*, Vol. 88, January 22, 1955, pp. 42, 54; January 29, pp. 8, 38; May 21, p. 73. *Magnuson Committee Hearings*, pp. 23–24, 137 ff., 147. Figures on production increases noted above come from the Newsprint Service Bureau; statistics given the Klein Committee were more modest, putting the United States increase at 22 per cent. In either case the increase was phenomenal.

One untoward consequence of the boom, apparent in 1955 and more aggravating to consumers in 1956, was the fact that publishers normally contracted for more paper than they expected to use, expecting the mills to reduce deliveries if customers needed less than contract figures. This caused the mills little pain in normal times, as they could sell the surplus over contract figures to non-contract buyers. With the boom, however, publishers began to demand full contract deliveries. This found the mills in the position of having contracted for more tonnage than they could produce, and they were forced to cut back deliveries, a situation hardly conducive to harmonious relations with newsprint-hungry purchasers. *Banking and Currency Committee, Preliminary Report*, pp. 2–3.

[3] *A.N.P.A., News*, No. 13, March 2, 1955, p. 57; No. 16, March 16, p. 69; No. 29, June 2, p. 118. *Activity of the Committee on Interstate and Foreign Commerce, 84th Congress, 1st Session, Report of the Committee on Interstate and Foreign Commerce Pursuant to Section 136 of the Legislative Reorganization Act of 1946, Public Law*

601, 79th Congress, and House Resolution 105, 84th Congress, House Report 1681, 84th Cong., 2d Sess. (Washington: Government Printing Office, 1956), pp. 8–9, cited subsequently as *Klein Committee Report, 1956*. *Newsprint Study: Newsprint Outlook for 1957, Interim Report of the Committee on Interstate and Foreign Commerce Pursuant to H. Res. 105 (84th Congress)*, House Report 2973, 84th Cong., 2d Sess. (Washington: Government Printing Office, 1957), pp. 1–2; cited subsequently as *Klein Committee, Newsprint Outlook, 1957*.

[4] *A.N.P.A., News*, No. 23, April 29, 1955, pp. 93–97; No. 31, April 27, 1956, p. 134. *E. & P.*, Vol. 88, April 30, 1955, p. 16; May 28, p. 30. *P.T.J.*, Vol. 139, May 9, 1955, pp. 31, 60. One method of newsprint conservation in common use at this period was narrowing the column width, in turn making it possible to order narrower rolls from the mills; this device enabled publishers to save from 2 to 3 per cent on tonnage.

[5] *P.T.J.*, Vol. 139, July 4, 1955, pp. 8, 17; July 25, pp. 32–33.

[6] *E. & P.*, Vol. 88, July 2, 1955, pp. 9, 40; August 6, p. 34; October 8, pp. 7, 70; October 15, pp. 6, 9.

[7] *A.N.P.A., News*, No. 59, October 19, 1955, pp. 223, 225; No. 61, October 26, pp. 229–31, 233–37; No. 63, October 28, pp. 243–44; No. 64, November 2, pp. 247–49; No. 65, November 10, pp. 251–53; No. 70, November 23, pp. 269–71; No. 72, December 7, pp. 277–78; No. 76, December 21, p. 289; No. 1, January 4, 1956, p. 3. *E. & P.*, Vol. 88, October 22, 1955, pp. 6, 9–10; October 29, pp. 6, 9; November 12, p. 15; November 26, p. 15. *P.T.J.*, Vol. 139, October 24, 1955, p. 7. The A.N.P.A. promptly reprinted (October 19) a report from the *Toronto Star* showing that Canadian paper mill profits were running 20 per cent ahead of 1954 figures during the first half-year.

[8] *A.N.P.A., News*, No. 64, November 2, 1955, p. 249; No. 73, December 7, pp. 279–80; No. 76, December 21, pp. 289–90. *E. & P.*, Vol. 88, December 10, 1955, pp. 10, 54. *N.S.B.B.*, No. 455, December, 1955, p. 3.

[9] *A.N.P.A., News*, No. 61, September 18, 1957, p. 244. *E. & P.*, Vol. 89, March 24, 1956, p. 12. *P.T.J.*, Vol. 140, January 30, 1956, pp. 51–53. *Harris Committee Hearings*, pp. 9, 67–68. *Klein Committee, Newsprint Outlook, 1957*, p. 2. *Magnuson Committee Hearings*, pp. 91–92. At the January hearings, to be mentioned directly, both the A.N.P.A. and the Forest Products Division of the Department of Commerce assured the Klein Committee that small publishers would

receive assistance in securing supplies of newsprint; this promise was faithfully performed.

An indication of the continued optimism of the early year is found in an article stating that the North American industry expected to spend $350,000,000 to increase capacity by 25 per cent by 1958, and in an A.N.P.A. compilation indicating that continental capacity would reach 9,427,730 tons by the end of that year. Despite this optimistic attitude, Cranston Williams refused to take a bright view of the long-run prospects, being quoted as saying: " 'I don't expect an unending month-by-month shortage of newsprint, but the long-term outlook is not encouraging. After completion of the present North American expansion program in 1958, I think another half-million to a million tons of new capacity must be added by 1960 to prevent a shortage due to ever-rising U.S. and world consumption. . . .' " *A.N.P.A., News,* No. 30, April 26, 1956, p. 130.

[10] *A.N.P.A., News,* No. 4, January 11, 1956, p. 13; No. 6, January 18, pp. 21–22; No. 9, January 25, pp. 31–33; No. 10, February 1, p. 35. *E. & P.*, Vol. 89, January 14, 1956, pp. 9–10; January 21, p. 15. *N.S.B.B.*, No. 456, January, 1956, pp. 7, 12. *Klein Committee Hearings.* It will be remembered that these *Hearings,* pp. 100–43, carried a *Preliminary Report: Newsprint Production and Supply and Newspaper Circulation, Advertising and Newsprint Requirements,* a very useful study compiled by the Forest Products Division, BDSA, United States Department of Commerce.

[11] *A.N.P.A., News,* No. 23, March 14, 1956, p. 106; No. 25, March 28, p. 109; No. 26, April 4, p. 113; No. 27, April 11, p. 117; No. 29, April 18, p. 125; No. 30, April 26, p. 129. *E. & P.*, Vol. 89, April 21, 1956, p. 22. *N.S.B.B.*, No. 459, April, 1956, p. 2. *P.T.J.*, Vol. 140, March 26, 1956, p. 13. *Klein Committee Hearings,* p. 3. R. C. Doane, President of International, told his stockholders in May, apropos the company's two new southern mills, that " 'The reborn confidence on the part of the newsprint manufacturing industry is being demonstrated every month as the industry continues to increase its capacity. . . . Several big postwar questions have been resolved. The press has met the challenge of television. . . . Confidence has also been restored in the ability of the market to pay prices for newsprint that will justify the high investment required for new productive capacity that must be built. . . .' " *E. & P.*, Vol. 89, May 26, 1956, p. 54.

[12] *A.N.P.A., News,* No. 31, April 27, 1956, pp. 133–40. *First Five*

Years, pp. 19–22. That the immediate plight of the small publisher was perhaps less dark than the A.N.P.A. and the Klein Committee painted it was indicated by replies of over thirty paper dealers in twenty states to a questionnaire sent out by the Research Department of the Weekly Newspaper Bureau; the majority returned affirmative answers to two questions: " 'Are you assured of getting as much newsprint in 1956 as you had in 1955?' " and " 'Will your 1956 supply be adequate to take care of the demand from your regular customers?' " The majority, too, replied negatively to the final query: " 'Are any of your customers suffering from lack of newsprint supply?' " *N.S.B.B.*, May, 1956, p. 3.

[13] *A.N.P.A.*, *News*, No. 52, August 8, 1956, p. 217. *E. & P.*, Vol. 89, August 4, 1956, p. 65. *P.T.J.*, Vol. 140, May 21, 1956, pp. 33, 37; June 11, p. 23; June 18, pp. 45, 51; July 2, p. 30; August 6, p. 15; August 13, p. 23; September 24, p. 34. *N.S.B.*, *News Summary*, November 15, 1956, pp. 3–4. *Harris Committee Hearings*, p. 10.

[14] *A.N.P.A.*, *News*, No. 31, April 27, 1956, pp. 133–34; No. 36, May 16, p. 155; No. 62, October 4, p. 253; No. 66, October 24, p. 267; No. 73, December 6, p. 292; No. 77, December 28, p. 305; No. 1, January 4, 1957, p. 1. *E. & P.*, Vol. 89, September 15, 1956, p. 84; October 6, p. 15; October 27, p. 10; December 8, p. 75. *P.T.J.*, Vol. 140, November 5, 1956, p. 25. Abitibi's action, as usual, started a procession of similar increases.

[15] *A.N.P.A.*, *News*, No. 6, January 23, 1957, pp. 19–21; No. 10, February 19, 1958, pp. 33–36; No. 24, April 24, pp. 103–04. *E. & P.*, Vol. 91, April 5, 1957, p. 38. *N.S.B.*, *News Summary*, April 11, 1957, p. 5; May 2, p. 4. *P.T.J.*, Vol. 142, February 10, 1958, p. 25; February 17, pp. 27–28; March 17, pp. 46–48. *Klein Committee*, *Newsprint Outlook, 1957*, pp. 4–5. *Pulp, Paper, and Board: Supply-Demand, Report of the Committee on Interstate and Foreign Commerce Pursuant to Section 136 of the Legislative Reorganization Act of 1946, Public Law 601, 79th Congress, and House Resolution 99, 85th Congress*, House Report 573, 85th Cong., 1st Sess. (Washington: Government Printing Office, 1957), pp. 17–19, 25, 126, 198–99; cited subsequently as *Harris Committee Report*. *Pulp, Paper, and Board Supply-Demand: Newsprint Outlook, Report of the Committee on Interstate and Foreign Commerce Pursuant to Section 136 of the Legislative Reorganization Act of 1946, Public Law 601, 79th Congress, and House Resolution 99, 85th Congress*, House Report 1868, 85th Cong., 2d Sess. (Washington: Government Printing Office, 1958), pp. 12–13, 18, 36–37; cited

subsequently as *Harris Committee, Supplementary Report.* In a survey article on January 6 the A.N.P.A. announced that publishers were entitled to expect of the newsprint industry: "Nothing less than a stable uninterrupted flow of sufficient supply to satisfy requirements and provide a cushion for emergencies. Nothing more than a price which is sufficient to support this capacity, and provide an adequate profit margin—over the long range—for newsprint producers.

"This is not the case at present. ANPA believes it will not be the case in the foreseeable future unless newsprint producers are willing to revise their thinking in a spirit of fair play and cooperation with the market they supply."

[16] *A.N.P.A., News,* No. 1, January 4, 1957, pp. 1–2; No. 3, January 9, p. 7; No. 5, January 16, pp. 15–16; No. 7, January 23, p. 21; No. 10, February 6, p. 33; No. 11, February 14, p. 35. *E. & P.,* Vol. 90, January 5, 1957, p. 6; January 19, p. 9.

[17] *A.N.P.A., News,* No. 3, January 9, 1957, p. 8; No. 5, January 16, pp. 16–17; No. 7, January 23, pp. 21–22; No. 8, January 30, p. 25; No. 10, February 6, p. 34; No. 11, February 14, p. 35. *E. & P.,* Vol. 90, January 26, 1957, p. 75. *Magnuson Committee Hearings,* pp. 226–27. *Record,* 85th Cong., 1st Sess., pp. 590, 1268–71, 1555. The full Committee on Interstate and Foreign Commerce, chaired by Harris, held hearings on February 18 and June 3, and a subcommittee, chaired by Peter F. Mack, Jr., of Illinois, sat on June 17. For convenience in the narrative, the work of both will be referred to under the name of Congressman Harris.

[18] *A.N.P.A., News,* No. 13, February 20, 1957, p. 43; No. 14, February 27, pp. 51–52. *Harris Committee Hearings,* pp. 2–57. These cover the proceedings of February 18.

[19] *A.N.P.A., News,* No. 41, June 12, 1957, p. 167. *Harris Committee Hearings,* pp. 67–85.

[20] *A.N.P.A., News,* No. 41, June 12, 1957, p. 167; No. 44, June 19, pp. 179–81. *Harris Committee Hearings,* pp. 102–05. *Harris Committee Report,* pp. 1–15.

[21] The story of the Magnuson Committee Hearings, which occupied February 26, 27, and 28, 1957, is found in the following: *A.N.P.A., News,* No. 12, February 27, 1957, pp. 47 ff.; No. 18, March 6, p. 82; No. 19, March 13, pp. 87–88; No. 22, March 20, p. 96. *E. & P.,* Vol. 90, March 2, 1957, p. 9. *P.T.J.,* Vol. 141, March 25, 1957, pp. 9, 45. *Magnuson Committee Hearings,* pp. 1–236. They evoked a retrospective

outburst by F. M. Fox, President of St. Lawrence Corporation, addressing his stockholders on April 10 after the price increases had become effective, in which he referred to the " 'current disturbance' " as " 'a routine performance that . . . occurs automatically, at any price level and at any increase.

" 'The current rash of investigations and fulminations is, for producers, merely one more in a long and now tedious series. . . .' " *A.N.P.A., News*, No. 32, May 1, 1957, p. 129. *E. & P.*, Vol. 90, April 20, 1957, pp. 19, 142.

[22] *E. & P.*, Vol. 90, March 9, 1957, p. 10; September 7, p. 63. *Record*, 85th Cong., 1st Sess., pp. 3376, 4257–58, 16685.

[23] *A.N.P.A., News*, No. 19, March 13, 1957, p. 85; No. 29, April 24, p. 117; No. 30, April 26, pp. 119–24; No. 36, May 22, p. 145; No. 41, June 12, p. 167; No. 46, June 26, pp. 185–86; No. 50, July 31, pp. 209–10; No. 53, August 7, p. 214; No. 56, August 21, pp. 225–26; No. 61, September 18, p. 245. *E. & P.*, Vol. 90, April 27, 1957, p. 18; May 18, p. 62; July 20, pp. 13, 46. *N.S.B., News Summary*, June 26, 1957, p. 1. *P.T.J.*, Vol. 141, March 4, 1957, pp. 19, 35, 46–48; May 6, pp. 27, 30; June 24, p. 23; July 8, p. 11; October 14, p. 37. *Newsprint, Forward.* The testimony of a Deputy Postmaster General to the House Committee on Post Office and Civil Service (in March) to the effect that publishers were in proper position to stand a 15 per cent increase in postal rates may indicate that the $4 price increase would have few permanently deleterious effects. *E. & P.*, Vol. 90, March 23, 1957, p. 10.

[24] *A.N.P.A., News*, No. 66, October 16, 1957, p. 259; November 11, p. 269; No. 78, December 27, p. 295; No. 1, January 3, 1958, p. 3. *N.S.B., News Summary*, undated, but probably around mid-September, 1957, pp. 1–2; October 23, 1957, p. 2; November 15, p. 2. *P.T.J.*, Vol. 141, September 23, 1957, p. 25; October 21, p. 13; Vol. 142, February 4, 1958, p. 38; March 3, p. 26.

[25] *A.N.P.A., News*, No. 1, January 3, 1958, p. 3; No. 6, January 29, p. 17; No. 7, February 5, pp. 22–23; No. 8, February 14, p. 26; No. 14, March 5, p. 69; No. 22, April 16, p. 100; No. 24, April 24, p. 103; No. 37, July 2, pp. 145–46; No. 38, July 9, p. 147; No. 41, July 23, p. 157; No. 57, October 22, p. 197; No. 1, January 7, 1959, p. 1; No. 8, February 18, pp. 25–27. *E. & P.*, Vol. 91, April 19, 1958, p. 30; April 26, p. 108. *N.S.B., News Summary*, January 8, 1958, pp. 1–2; January 28, p. 1; February 28, p. 3; May 23, p. 2;

July 18, p. 2; July 25, p. 2; August 19, p. 2; October 7, p. 1; January 2, 1959, p. 3. *P.T.J.*, Vol. 142, February 3, 1958, p. 13; March 17, p. 13; August 11, p. 15; October 20, pp. 56–57; November 17, p. 27. *Harris Committee, Supplementary Report*, pp. 1, 9, 20. Apropos manufacturers' long-range optimism, M. J. Foley of Powell River told the Montreal Institute of Investment Analysts (October 10): " 'We expect another period of rapid growth to begin in the early sixties. We find no reason for pessimism about any of our present wood products.' " *A.N.P.A., News*, No. 56, October 16, 1958, p. 195.

[26] *A.N.P.A., News*, No. 1, January 3, 1958, p. 1; No. 30, May 21, p. 123. *E. & P.*, Vol. 91, February 1, 1958, p. 12; May 24, p. 9; May 17, p. 16. *N.S.B., News Summary*, October 23, 1957, p. 1; February 28, 1958, p. 2. The *Attorney General's Review*, which will be analyzed herewith, has already been cited.

BIBLIOGRAPHY*

Activity of the Committee on Interstate and Foreign Commerce, 84th Congress, 1st Session, Report of the Committee on Interstate and Foreign Commerce Pursuant to Section 136 of the Legislative Reorganization Act of 1946, Public Law 601, 79th Congress, and House Resolution 109, 84th Congress, House Report 1681, 84th Cong., 2d Sess. (Washington: Government Printing Office, 1956). (*Klein Committee Report, 1956.*)

A.N.P.A., general. See *Bulletins of the American Newspaper Publishers Association.*

Attorney General's Review. See *Review of the Voluntary Agreements Program. . . .*

Banking and Currency Committee, Preliminary Report. See *Preliminary Report. . . .*

Beckworth Committee Hearings. See *Newsprint Investigation: Hearings. . . .*

Beckworth Committee Report. See *Newsprint Investigation: Canadian Supplies. . . .*

Boren Committee, Final Hearings. See *Brand Names and Newsprint (Newsprint). . . .*

Boren Committee Hearings, 78th Congress. See *Brand Names and Newsprint . . . Seventy-Eighth Congress. . . .* These hearings were issued in four parts, paged continuously, under somewhat varying titles.

Boren Committee Hearings, 79th Congress. See *Brand Names and Newsprint . . . Seventy-Ninth Congress. . . .* These hearings were issued in three parts, paged continuously, under somewhat varying titles.

Boyce, Charles W. *The First Five Years: Report on the Decade 1951–1960 of Newsprint Supply and Demand* (Pamphlet, New York: American Newspaper Publishers Association, 1956). (*First Five Years.*)

Boyce, Charles W. *Newsprint—A Forward Look to 1965* (Pamphlet,

* Abbreviated titles used in the notes following the first citations are listed alphabetically, with cross references to the full titles.

New York: American Newspaper Publishers Association, 1957). (*Newsprint, Forward.*)

Boyce, Charles W. *Newsprint Now and in the Next Decade* (Pamphlet, New York: American Newspaper Publishers Association, 1951). (*Newsprint Now.*)

Brand Names and Newsprint: Hearings before a Subcommittee of the Committee on Interstate and Foreign Commerce, House of Representatives, Seventy-Eighth Congress, First Session, Pursuant to H. Res. 98, A Resolution to Investigate Federal Grade Labeling of Articles or Commodities, and the Discarding of Private Brand Names; Curtailing the Production or Consumption of Newsprint or Papers; and Any Requirements Intending to Bring about Simplification and Standardization of Production, Marketing, and Distribution of Articles or Commodities, as Well as Concentration of Industry or Production, Part 1, May 10, 24, 25, 26, 27, 28, and June 2, 3, 4, and 8, 1943 (Washington: Government Printing Office, 1943). (*Boren Committee Hearings, 78th Congress.*)

Brand Names and Newsprint: Hearings before a Subcommittee of the Interstate and Foreign Commerce Committee, House of Representatives, Seventy-Eighth Congress, First Session, Pursuant to H. Res. 98, A Resolution to Investigate Federal Grade Labeling of Articles or Commodities, and the Discarding of Private Brand Names; Curtailing the Production or Consumption of Newsprint or Papers; and Any Requirements Intending to Bring about Simplification and Standardization of Production, Marketing, and Distribution of Articles or Commodities, as Well as Concentration of Industry or Production, Part 3, Newsprint, October 7 to 25 and November 22, 1943 (Committee Print, Washington: Government Printing Office, 1943). (*Boren Committee Hearings, 78th Congress.*)

Brand Names and Newsprint: Hearings before a Subcommittee of the Committee on Interstate and Foreign Commerce, House of Representatives, Seventy-Eighth Congress, Second Session, Pursuant to H. Res. 98, A Resolution to Investigate Federal Grade Labeling of Articles or Commodities, and the Discarding of Private Barnd Names; Curtailing the Production or Consumption of Newsprint or Papers; and Any Requirements Intending to Bring about Simplification and

Standardization of Production, Marketing, and Distribution of Articles or Commodities, as Well as Concentration of Industry or Production, Part 4, Newsprint, January 25, 27, and 28, 1944 (Washington: Government Printing Office, 1944). (*Boren Committee Hearings, 78th Congress.*)

Brand Names and Newsprint: Hearings before a Subcommittee of the Committee on Interstate and Foreign Commerce, House of Representatives, Seventy-Ninth Congress, First Session, Pursuant to H. Res. 98 (78th Congress) (Extended by H. Res. 93, 79th Congress), A Resolution to Investigate Federal Grade Labeling of Articles or Commodities, and the Discarding of Private Brand Names; Curtailing the Production or Consumption of Newsprint or Papers; and Any Requirements Intending to Bring about Simplification and Standardization of Production, Marketing, and Distribution of Articles or Commodities, as Well as Concentration of Industry or Production, Part 1, Newsprint, March 5, 12, April 16, 17, and 23, 1945 (Washington: Government Printing Office, 1945). (*Boren Committee Hearings, 79th Congress.*)

Brand Names and Newsprint: Hearings before a Subcommittee of the Committee on Interstate and Foreign Commerce, House of Representatives, Seventy-Ninth Congress, First Session, Pursuant to H. Res. 98 (78th Congress) (Extended by H. Res. 93, 79th Congress), A Resolution to Investigate Federal Grade Labeling of Articles or Commodities, and the Discarding of Private Brand Names; Curtailing the Production or Consumption of Newsprint or Papers; and Any Requirements Intending to Bring about Simplification and Standardization of Production, Marketing, and Distribution of Articles or Commodities, as Well as Concentration of Industry or Production, Part 2, Newsprint, July 23 (Seattle), July 26 (San Francisco), July 31, 1945 (Los Angeles), September 17, 1945 (Washington, D. C., on Nylon Hosiery) (Washington: Government Printing Office, 1945). (*Boren Committee Hearings, 79th Congress.*)

Brand Names and Newsprint (Newsprint and Nylon Hosiery): Hearings before a Subcommittee of the Committee on Interstate and Foreign Commerce, House of Representatives, Seventy-Ninth Congress, First Session, Pursuant to H. Res. 98 (78th Congress) (Extended by H.

Res. 93, 79th Congress), A Resolution to Investigate Federal Grade Labeling of Articles or Commodities, and the Discarding of Private Brand Names; Curtailing the Production or Consumption of Newsprint or Papers; and Any Requirements Intending to Bring about Simplification and Standardization of Production, Marketing, and Distribution of Articles or Commodities, as Well as Concentration of Industry or Production, Part 3, Newsprint and Nylons, November 14, 16, and 20, 1945 (Washington: Government Printing Office, 1946). (*Boren Committee Hearings, 79th Congress.*)

Brand Names and Newsprint (Newsprint): Final Hearings before a Subcommittee of the Committee on Interstate and Foreign Commerce, House of Representatives, Seventy-Ninth Congress, Second Session, Pursuant to H. Res. 98 (78th Congress) (Extended by H. Res. 93, 79th Congress), A Resolution to Investigate Federal Grade Labeling of Articles or Commodities, and the Discarding of Private Brand Names; Curtailing the Production or Consumption of Newsprint or Papers; and Any Requirements Intending to Bring about Simplification and Standardization of Production, Marketing, and Distribution of Articles or Commodities, as Well as Concentration of Industry or Production, Newsprint, October 2 and 3, 1946 (Washington: Government Printing Office, 1946). (*Boren Committee, Final Hearings.*)

Brown Committee, Final Report. See *Select Committee . . . Final Report. . . .*

Brown Committee, Interim Report. See *Select Committee . . . Interim Report. . . .*

Bulletins of the American Newspaper Publishers Association.

The association issues *Bulletins* on a variety of subjects connected with its activities. The following have been used in the present study; all are published in New York by the association:

"B" Special; Newsprint: A.N.P.A., B.

Convention Bulletin: A.N.P.A., Convention.

Federal Laws Bulletin: A.N.P.A., Federal Laws.

Newsprint Bulletin: A.N.P.A., News.

Capehart Committee Hearings. See *Problems of American Small Business. . . .*

Capehart Committee, Interim Report. See *Newsprint Supply and Distribution: Interim Report. . . .*

Celler Committee, Final Report. See *The Newsprint Problem: Final Report. . . .*

Celler Committee Hearings. See *Study of Monopoly Power . . . Part 6A, Newsprint. . . .*

Celler Committee Hearings, Exhibits. See *Study of Monopoly Power . . . Part 6B, Newsprint Exhibits. . . .*

Celler Committee, Report. See *Newsprint: Report of the Subcommittee. . . . .*

The Congressional Record (Washington: Government Printing Office, 1874—). (*Record.*)

E. & P. See *Editor & Publisher.*

Editor & Publisher: The Fourth Estate (New York: Editor & Publisher, 1894—; weekly). (*E. & P.*)

Ellis, L. Ethan. *Print Paper Pendulum: Group Pressures and the Price of Newsprint* (New Brunswick: Rutgers University Press, 1948).

Ellis, L. Ethan. *Reciprocity, 1911: A Study in Canadian-American Relations* (New Haven: Yale University Press, 1939).

First Five Years. See Boyce, Charles W.

Fowler, Robert M. *Canadian Pulp and Paper Association: Submission to Royal Commission on Canada's Economic Prospects* (Montreal: Canadian Pulp and Paper Association, 1956). (*Fowler Submission.*)

Fowler Submission. See Fowler, Robert M.

Guthrie, John A. *The Newsprint Paper Industry: An Economic Analysis* (Cambridge: Harvard University Press, 1941).

Harris Committee Hearings. See *Newsprint Study: Hearings before the Committee. . . .*

Harris Committee Report. See *Pulp, Paper, and Board: Supply-Demand, Report. . . .*

Harris Committee, Supplementary Report. See *Pulp, Paper and Board Supply-Demand: Newsprint Outlook. . . .*

Hearing before the Antitrust Subcommittee of the Committee on the Judiciary, House of Representatives, Eighty-Second Congress, Second Session, on Newsprint Expansion (Washington: Government Printing Office, 1952). (*Newsprint Price Rise—Hearings.*)

Honeywell, Charles F. *Newsprint Production—Newspaper Consumption: A Cooperative Partnership* (mimeographed pamphlet, 1958). (*Newsprint Production.*)

Humphrey Committee, Preliminary Report. See *Supplies for a Free Press. . . .*

Humphrey Committee Report. See *Newsprint for Tomorrow. . . .*

Klein Committee Hearings. See *Newsprint Study: Hearings before a Subcommittee. . . .*

Klein Committee, Interim Report, 1955. See *Newsprint Study: Current. . . .*

Klein Committee, Interim Report of 1956. See *Newsprint Study: Newsprint Outlook for 1956. . . .*

Klein Committee, Newsprint Outlook for 1957. See *Newsprint Study: Newsprint Outlook, 1957. . . .*

Klein Committee Report, 1956. See *Activity of. . . .*

McCoy Report. See *Study of Newsprint Expansion: A Progress Report. . . .*

Magnuson Committee Hearings. See *Newsprint Inquiry. . . .*

Margolin, Edward, and William P. McLendon. *Transportation Factors in the Marketing of Newsprint,* Transportation Series No. 2, United States Department of Commerce (Washington: Government Printing Office, 1952). (*Transportation Factors.*)

N.S.B., News Summary. See *Newsprint Service Bureau, News Summary.*

N.S.B.B. See *The Newsprint Service Bureau Bulletin.*

The New York Times (New York, 1851—). (N. Y. *Times.*)

Newsprint for Tomorrow: Report and Conclusions of the Select Committee on Small Business, United States Senate, Including Individual Views of Mr. Thye and Statement of Mr. Schoeppel, Senate Report 1404, 82d Cong., 2d Sess. (Washington: Government Printing Office, 1952). (*Humphrey Committee Report.*)

Newsprint, Forward. See Boyce, Charles W.

Newsprint Inquiry: Hearings before the Committee on Interstate and Foreign Commerce, United States Senate, Eighty-Fifth Congress, First Session, Pursuant to S. Res. 26, A Resolution Providing for Investigation of Problems Affecting Interstate and Foreign Commerce,

February 26, 27, and 28, 1957 (Washington: Government Printing Office, 1957). (*Magnuson Committee Hearings.*)

Newsprint Investigation: Canadian Supplies, Progress Report of the Special Subcommittee on Investigation of Newsprint and Other Matters of the Committee on Interstate and Foreign Commerce, Pursuant to H. Res. 116 (82d Congress), House Report 1093, 82d Cong., 1st Sess. (Washington: Government Printing Office, 1951). (*Beckworth Committee Report.*)

Newsprint Investigation: Hearings before a Subcommittee of the Committee on Interstate and Foreign Commerce, House of Representatives, Eighty-Second Congress, First Session, on Subjects Pursuant to H. Res. 116, Part 1 (Washington: Government Printing Office, 1951). (*Beckworth Committee Hearings.*)

Newsprint Now. See Boyce, Charles W.

Newsprint Price Rise—Hearings. See *Hearing before the Antitrust Subcommittee. . . .*

Newsprint Price Rise: Report of Subcommittee No. 5 (Antitrust Subcommittee) of the Committee on the Judiciary, Pursuant to H. Res. 95 (82d Cong., 1st Sess.), Authorizing the Committee on the Judiciary to Conduct Studies and Investigations Relating to Matters within Its Jurisdiction, House Report 505, Part 3, 82d Cong., 2d Sess. (Washington: Government Printing Office, 1952). (*Newsprint Price Rise Report.*)

The Newsprint Problem: Final Report of the Special Antitrust Subcommittee of the Committee on the Judiciary (Committee Print, Washington: Government Printing Office, 1953). (*Celler Committee, Final Report.*)

Newsprint Production. See Honeywell, Charles F.

Newsprint: Report of the Subcommittee on Monopoly Power of the Committee on the Judiciary, Pursuant to H. Res. 95 (82d Cong., 1st Sess.), Authorizing the Committee on the Judiciary to Conduct Studies and Investigations Relating to Matters within Its Jurisdiction, House Report 505, Part 1, 82d Cong., 1st Sess. (Washington: Government Printing Office, 1951). (*Celler Committee Report.*)

The Newsprint Service Bureau Bulletin (New York: Newsprint Service Bureau, monthly numbered issues, cited by number, month, and page; beginning with the January, 1951, issue, an exact date is omitted). (*N.S.B.B.*)

Newsprint Service Bureau, News Summary (New York: Newsprint Service Bureau, June, 1957 ff.; an occasional mimeographed issue). (*N.S.B., News Summary.*)

Newsprint Study: Current Newsprint Outlook, Interim Report of the Committee on Interstate and Foreign Commerce, Pursuant to H. Res. 105 (84th Congress), House Report 683, 84th Cong., 1st Sess. (Washington: Government Printing Office, 1955). (*Klein Committee, Interim Report, 1955.*)

Newsprint Study: Hearing before the Committee on Interstate and Foreign Commerce, House of Representatives, Eighty-Fifth Congress, First Session, on Newsprint Situation, February 18 and June 3, 1957 (before Entire Committee), June 17, 1957 (before Subcommittee on Commerce and Finance). Printed for the Use of the Committee on Interstate and Foreign Commerce (Washington: Government Printing Office, 1958). (*Harris Committee Hearings.*)

Newsprint Study: Hearings before a Subcommittee of the Committee on Interstate and Foreign Commerce, House of Representatives, Eighty-Fourth Congress, on Newsprint Situation, March 15, 1955, January 10 and 25, 1956 (Washington: Government Printing Office, 1956). (*Klein Committee Hearings.*)

Newsprint Study: Newsprint Outlook for 1956, Interim Report of the Committee on Interstate and Foreign Commerce Pursuant to H. Res. 105 (84th Congress), House Report 1953, 84th Cong., 2d Sess. (Washington: Government Printing Office, 1956). (*Klein Committee, Interim Report of 1956.*)

Newsprint Study: Newsprint Outlook for 1957, Interim Report of the Committee on Interstate and Foreign Commerce Pursuant to H. Res. 105 (84th Congress), House Report 2973, 84th Cong., 2d Sess. (Washington: Government Printing Office, 1957). (*Klein Committee, Newsprint Outlook, 1957.*)

Newsprint Supply and Distribution: A Final Report of the Special Committee to Study Problems of American Small Business, United States Senate, Eightieth Congress, First Session, Pursuant to S. Res. 20, A Resolution Appointing a Special Committee to Study Problems of American Small Business, Senate Report 47, 81st Cong., 1st Sess. (Washington: Government Printing Office, 1949).

Newsprint Supply and Distribution: Interim Report of the Special Committee to Study Problems of American Small Business, United States Senate, Eightieth Congress, First Session, Pursuant to S. Res. 20, A Resolution Appointing a Special Committee to Study Problems of American Small Business, Senate Report 150, 80th Cong., 1st Sess. (Washington: Government Printing Office, 1947). (*Capehart Committee, Interim Report.*)

P.T.J. See *Paper Trade Journal.*

The Paper Trade Journal (New York: Lockwood Publishing Company, 1872—; weekly). (*P.T.J.*)

Preliminary Report and Supplements: Newsprint Production and Supply, Committee on Banking and Currency, United States Senate, Prepared by Forest Products Division, Business and Defense Services Administration, U.S. Department of Commerce (Committee Print, Washington: Government Printing Office, 1956). (*Banking and Currency Committee, Preliminary Report.*)

Problems of American Small Business: Hearings before the Special Committee to Study Problems of American Small Business, United States Senate, Eightieth Congress, First Session, Pursuant to S. Res. 20, A Resolution Appointing a Special Committee to Study Problems of American Small Business, Part 1, Investigation of Newsprint Shortages and Other Factors Affecting Survival of Smaller Independent Newspapers: I, March 4, 5, 6, and 7, 1947 (Committee Print, three parts, with slightly varying titles, paged continuously; Washington: Government Printing Office, 1947). (*Capehart Committee Hearings.*)

Pulp, Paper, and Board Supply-Demand: Newsprint Outlook, Report of the Committee on Interstate and Foreign Commerce Pursuant to Section 136 of the Legislative Reorganization Act of 1946, Public Law 601, 79th Congress, and House Resolution 99, 85th Congress, House Report 1868, 85th Cong., 2d Sess. (Washington: Government Printing Office, 1958). (*Harris Committee, Supplementary Report.*)

Pulp, Paper, and Board: Supply-Demand, Report of the Committee on Interstate and Foreign Commerce Pursuant to Section 136 of the Legislative Reorganization Act of 1946, Public Law 601, 79th Congress, and House Resolution 99, 85th Congress, House Report 573, 85th Cong., 1st Sess. (Washington: Government Printing Office, 1957). (*Harris Committee Report.*)

Record. See *The Congressional Record.*

Review of the Voluntary Agreements Program under the Defense Production Act: The Newsprint Industry, Report Dated May 9, 1958, by the Attorney General, Committee on Banking and Currency, United States Senate (Committee Print, Washington: Government Printing Office, 1958). (*Attorney General's Review.*)

Select Committee on Newsprint and Paper Supply: Final Report of the Select Committee on Newsprint and Paper Supply, Pursuant to H. Res. 58 (80th Congress), A Resolution Creating a Select Committee to Conduct a Study and Investigation with Respect to Present and Future Supplies of Newsprint, Printing and Wrapping Paper, Paper Products, Paper Pulp and Pulpwood, House Report 2471, 80th Cong., 2d Sess. (Washington: Government Printing Office, 1948). (*Brown Committee, Final Report.*)

Select Committee on Newsprint and Paper Supply: Interim Report of the Select Committee on Newsprint and Paper Supply, Pursuant to H. Res. 58 (80th Congress), A Resolution Creating a Select Committee to Conduct a Study with Respect to Present and Future Supplies of Newsprint, Printing and Wrapping Paper, Paper Products, Paper Pulp and Pulpwood, House Report 1042, 80th Cong., 1st Sess. (Washington: Government Printing Office, 1947). (*Brown Committee, Interim Report.*)

Study of Monopoly Power: Hearings before the Subcommittee on Study of Monopoly Power of the Committee on the Judiciary, House of Representatives, Eighty-First Congress, Second Session, Containing the Proceedings of June 19, 20, 21, 22, 23, 27, 28, 29, 30, and July 10, 11, 13, 18, 19, and 20, 1950, Serial No. 14, Part 6A, Newsprint (Washington: Government Printing Office, 1950). (*Celler Committee Hearings.*)

Study of Monopoly Power: Hearings before the Subcommittee on Study of Monopoly Power of the Committee on the Judiciary, House of Representatives, Eighty-First Congress, Second Session, Serial No. 14, Part 6B, Newsprint Exhibits (Including Appendix) (Washington: Government Printing Office, 1950). (*Celler Committee Hearings, Exhibits.*)

Study of Newsprint Expansion: A Progress Report of the Department of Commerce to Subcommittee No. 5 of the Committee on the Judiciary, House of Representatives (Washington: Government Printing Office, 1952). (*McCoy Report.*)

Study of Newsprint Expansion: Part II, Newsprint Production from Hardwoods, Second Progress Report of the Department of Commerce to the Committee on the Judiciary, House of Representatives (Committee Print, Washington: Government Printing Office, 1954).

Supplies for a Free Press: A Preliminary Report on Newsprint by the Subcommittee on Newsprint of the Select Committee on Small Business, United States Senate (Committee Print, Washington: Government Printing Office, 1951). (*Humphrey Committee, Preliminary Report.*)

Survey of Alaskan Newsprint Resources: Interim Report of the Special Committee to Study Problems of American Small Business, United States Senate, Eightieth Congress, Second Session, Pursuant to S. Res. 20, Eightieth Congress, Second Session, A Resolution Appointing a Special Committee to Study Problems of American Small Business, Senate Report 852, 80th Cong., 2d Sess. (Washington: Government Printing Office, 1948).

Transportation Factors. See Margolin, Edward.

United States Tariff Commission. *Newsprint: War Changes in Industry Series, Report No. 22, Revised* (Washington: Government Printing Office, 1951). (U.S. Tariff Commission, *Newsprint.*)

Index

All government agencies are listed alphabetically by name of agency. Unless otherwise indicated, they are U.S. agencies.

Abitibi Power and Paper Co., 98, 109, 117, 130, 151, 160–62, 177, 196, 201, 206, 208
Agriculture, Department of, 118
Alaska, 105, 109, 111, 117–19, 124–25, 127, 129, 132, 156, 179–80, 193, 215, 244
American Newspaper Guild, 128–29, 134
American Newspaper Publishers' Association (A.N.P.A.), 6–11, 18, 28–40 *passim*, 44–74 *passim*, 83–90 *passim*, 96–110 *passim*, 117, 121, 128–29, 135–42 *passim*, 149, 155, 164–71 *passim*, 177–85 *passim*, 192–220 *passim*, 232–33
American Press Association, 32
American Pulp and Paper Association, 43, 47, 66, 85, 106, 124, 219
Antitrust action. *See* Monopolistic practices
Antitrust and Antimonopoly Committee, Senate, 210
Arnall, Ellis, 176–77

Bagasse, 4, 181, 187, 212
Banking and Currency, Senate Committee on, 199, 210, 224
Beckworth, Lindley, 154, 188
Beckworth Committee, 154, 160–61, 164–69, 176–77
Boeschenstein, Harold D., 67, 74, 80, 82
Boren, Lyle E., 64–84 *passim*, 100
Boren Committee, 57–93 *passim*, 100–03, 135, 154, 259
Bowater, Sir Eric, 195
Bowater Paper Co., 22, 145–46, 195, 216
Bowater's Paper Mills, Newfoundland, 188
Bowaters Southern Paper Corp., 170, 187, 209
Boyce, Charles W., 44, 167–68, 171, 202, 220
Brown, Clarence J., 90, 103, 145
Brown Committee, 109–11, 125–26, 135, 154
Business and Defense Services Administration (BDSA), 186–87, 193, 200, 211, 271
Business Records Protection Act (Ontario), 159, 225

Canadian International Paper Co., 17, 109, 112–17, 148–49, 263
Canadian newsprint industry, 5–6,

17–18, 27, 53–54, 75, 92, 117, 133, 139–41, 146–47, 152, 169–71, 188, 195, 201
Canadian Paper Sales, Ltd., 112–16
Canadian Pulp and Paper Association, 75, 106, 170, 221, 225
Canfield, William F., 142–43
Capacity, mill, 17, 29, 43–44, 59, 119, 134, 139–40, 152, 170, 172, 182, 202, 207, 212–13, 220–22, 243, 245
Capehart, Homer, 104, 106–08, 123, 127, 188
Capehart Small Business Committee, 104, 107–10, 118, 124–25, 127
Capehart Trade Policies Subcommittee, 122–24, 127
Case, Francis, 84–85, 179
Caspar, Albin R., 148, 216
Celler, Emmanuel, 134, 142, 144, 147–51, 178–79, 188, 196, 209
Celler Committee, 51, 122, 134–60 *passim*, 172–84 *passim*, 189, 226, 231
Cement Institute decision, 120, 122, 127
Chandler, W. G., 60, 63, 81, 117
Civilian Production Administration (CPA), 90–91, 96–98
Clark, Tom C., 111–16, 264
Clayton Antitrust Act, 225
Collusion, price. *See* Monopolistic practices
Commerce, Department of, 105–06, 150, 177–78, 183, 186, 198–99, 205, 211, 213, 271
Competition. *See* Monopolistic practices
Consolidated Paper Co., 117
Consolidated Paper Sales, Ltd., 120
Consumption, 47, 53–56, 58–64, 68–69, 71–73, 83–84, 86, 96, 102, 122, 134, 152, 168, 170, 185–86, 191–92, 194, 198, 207–08, 222. *See also* Order L-240; Rationing
Controls. *See* Government controls
Cooperation, manufacturer-publisher, 45, 51, 101–02, 173, 181–82
Coosa River Paper Co., 27, 126, 134, 141, 187, 222
Cost, of newsprint production, 23, 47, 53, 121, 166–67, 169, 176, 180–81, 216–18, 246
Crown Zellerbach Corp., 27, 39, 50–51, 90, 121, 145, 148, 165, 172–74, 187, 216, 225, 248
Currency, Canadian, fluctuations in, 40, 98, 126, 130–32, 151, 177–78, 196
Cushion argument, 202, 207–08, 212–13, 215–16, 218–20

Defense Production Act of 1950, 151, 223, 271
Defense Production Administration, 180, 271
DiSalle, Michael V., 153–54, 161–65
Distribution problems, 49, 89–91, 97, 102–09
Dollar, Canadian. *See* Currency, Canadian

Duplessis, Maurice, 29, 135
Dwight, William, 205, 208

Editor & Publisher, 30, 38, 58, 59, 68, 109, 119–20, 135, 139–41, 164, 168, 177, 194–96, 198, 206
Eisenhower, Dwight D., 223
Exchange, rate of. *See* Currency, Canadian
External Affairs, Department of (Canadian), 73, 163, 170

F.o.b. mill pricing, 122–24, 127, 245
Federal Trade Commission, 14–15, 28, 32–38, 50, 108, 111, 120, 122–23, 127, 147, 159, 206, 209–10, 218, 223, 225, 235
Finnish newsprint, 32
Flambeau Paper Co., 24
Forest Service, 118–19, 125
Fowler, Robert M., 97, 100, 106, 109–11, 117, 122, 135–42, 150, 153, 155, 161–63, 165, 170, 176, 181, 184, 197, 199, 217, 221–22, 225
Fulbright, J. William, 199, 223–24

Gary Paper Mills, 24
Goddard, Henry W., 112–15, 144
Government controls, 15, 44, 49–50, 52–71, 76, 80–84, 86–91, 96–102, 106, 150, 153–54, 161, 165–66, 176–77, 200, 229–30, 257. *See also* Rationing
Government investigations, 11–12, 14–15, 28, 36–40, 50–51, 71–75, 77, 93, 100–01, 103–16, 123–28, 131–32, 134–35, 142–50, 154–60, 166–69, 171–74, 177–79, 181–84, 186–89, 193, 196–97, 199–201, 209–19, 222–27, 235–36. *See also* Beckworth Committee; Boren Committee; Brown Committee; Capehart Small Business Committee; Capehart Trade Policies Subcommittee; Celler Committee; Federal Trade Commission; Harris Committee; Humphrey Committee; Klein Committee; Justice, Department of; Magnuson Committee
Graustein, Archibald R., 146–47
Great Lakes Paper Co., 24, 222
Great Northern Paper Co., 5, 7, 27, 30–31, 35, 43, 48, 117, 126, 148, 164, 187, 195, 197, 201, 216
Groundwood. *See* Wood pulp
Guthrie, John A., 21, 22, 143, 174–76

Hardwoods, 187, 212, 233, 278
Harris, Oren, 210–11, 213
Harris Committee, 210–15
Hawley Pulp and Paper Co., 27, 39, 50–51
Hawley-Smoot Act of 1930, 144
Hearst press, 17, 24, 89
Herty, Charles H., 5, 32, 46
Hinman, John H., 121, 146–47
Howe, C. D., 81, 155, 163, 176

Humphrey, Hubert, 154, 163, 188
Humphrey Committee, 155–58, 163, 171–76

Inland Daily Press Association, 60, 136, 139, 142–43, 181
Inland Empire Paper Co., 24, 39–40, 51, 248
Interior, Department of, 118
International Brotherhood of Papermakers, 36
International Paper Co., 7, 16–18, 22, 30–31, 35, 43, 48, 51, 53, 112–15, 121, 145–46, 151, 172–74, 188, 192, 195–97, 201, 216, 222, 224–25, 249, 263–64
International Paper Sales Co., 37, 249, 264
International Typographical Union, 163
Interstate and Foreign Commerce, House Committee on, 71–72, 154, 182–83, 193, 210–15
Interstate and Foreign Commerce, Senate Committee on, 122, 197, 199, 209. *See also* Magnuson Committee

Japanese wood pulp, 193
Jobbers, 103–06, 108, 110, 154, 244
Johnson, Edwin C., 127, 179
Judiciary, House Committee on the, 183, 187. *See also* Celler Committee
Judiciary, Senate Committee on the, 127–28
Justice, Department of, 14, 28, 35, 37–39, 50, 103–16 *passim*, 131, 147, 159, 177–78, 196, 209, 218, 223–27, 235

Kellogg, Royal S., 37, 69, 101, 248
Ketchikan Pulp and Paper Co., 125
Klein, Arthur G., 193, 196, 199–200
Klein Committee, 193, 196, 199–201
Korean War, 133–34, 149–53, 188

L-240. *See* Order L-240
Lightweight newsprint, 64, 69, 77–80, 83–84

McCoy, H. B., 178, 181, 211–13
Magnuson, Warren, 197, 199, 209–10, 218
Magnuson Committee, 22, 197, 209–10, 213–19
Mann Committee, 11–12
Manpower, 40, 53, 55, 65–66, 69–70, 73, 77, 255
Manufacturing process. *See* Bagasse; Hardwoods; Softwoods; Sulphite pulp; Technological developments
Mead, George H., Co., 36
Meyer, August B., 22–23, 216
Michigan Paper Co., 24
Monopolistic practices, 6–11, 14–15, 22–23, 38–40, 50–51, 88–89, 103–08, 111–16, 120, 122, 128–29, 131, 134–35, 142–49, 151–52, 156, 159–60, 166, 172, 174, 178–79,

183–84, 209–10, 218, 223–27, 235, 248
Moreau, Charles E., 105, 122–24, 145–46

National Defense Advisory Commission, 44
National Editorial Association (NEA), 90, 104–05
National Industrial Recovery Act (NIRA), 51, 160, 245
National Production Authority (NPA), 166, 177, 179, 181, 271
Nelson, Donald M., 54, 60, 67–68, 74, 76
New England Daily Newspaper Association, 89–90
New England Plan, 92, 102
New York State Publishers' Association, 153
New York Times, 7, 11, 17, 24, 165
Newark Evening News, 22, 217
Newspaper Industry Advisory Committee, 54–71 *passim*, 76–91 *passim*, 97, 163
Newsprint. *See* Canadian newsprint industry; Consumption; Cost; Lightweight newsprint; Price; Production; U.S. newsprint industry
Newsprint Association of Canada, 29, 36, 40, 45, 70, 75, 82–83, 106, 155, 161, 168, 171, 182, 217
Newsprint Consumers' Emergency Committee, 103
Newsprint Industry Advisory Committee, 88, 96, 163, 165–66
Newsprint Information Committee, 219
Newsprint Price Outlook, 129–30
Newsprint Service Bureau, 37, 59, 69, 101, 123, 248
Norris, John, 6–11, 14, 233
Noyes, Linwood I., 64, 70

Office of Defense Mobilization (ODM), 176, 211, 271
Office of Price Administration (OPA), 52–58 *passim*, 79, 83, 86, 91, 96–102, 121, 160, 245, 254
Office of Price Stabilization (OPS), 153, 161, 165–66, 176–77
Office of Production Management (OPM), 49–50, 54
Olympic Peninsula, 180
Ontario Paper Co., 24
Order L-240, 55–90 *passim*, 102, 105, 131, 154, 257. *See also* War Production Board
Overconsumption, 63
Overproduction, 6, 16–17, 202–05, 207

Pacific Mills, 39
Paper, other grades, 5–6, 14, 86, 128, 164, 181
Paper Trade Journal, 149, 152, 176, 194–96, 202
Peavey Paper Mills, 24
Pejepscot Paper Co., 24
Perry, John H., 32, 35, 38, 142
Potter, Charles E., 206, 209–10
Powell River Co., 40, 151

Powell River Sales Co., 40, 50, 205, 206, 208, 248
Price, fluctuations in, 15–16, 18, 29–31, 35, 43, 48, 52–53, 57–58, 83, 91, 98–102, 109, 117, 121, 151, 154–55, 160–66, 176–78, 188, 193–97, 205–09, 242. *See also* Currency, Canadian; Spot market
Price leadership, 22–23, 225
Price tie-in contracts, 24, 147
Pricing policies, 21–24, 52, 120–24, 127–28, 145–46, 225. *See also* F.o.b. mill pricing; Monopolistic practices; Zone-pricing
Production, 5, 16, 35–36, 47–48, 54–56, 59, 71, 75, 82–83, 85–86, 96–98, 101–02, 111, 117, 126, 133–34, 139–41, 167–68, 180, 183, 185–88, 192, 201–05, 207–09, 215–16, 219–21, 241, 243. *See also* Capacity; Overproduction
Publishers. *See* American Newspaper Publishers' Association; Publishers, small
Publishers, small, 16, 39, 55–56, 60, 89–92, 102–09, 124–25, 131–32, 152–53, 157–58, 172–73, 178–79, 183, 198–201, 215, 217, 244
Publishers' Paper Co. *See* Hawley Pulp and Paper Co.

Rationing, newsprint, 54–56, 65, 74, 103, 106, 150, 154
Reconstruction Finance Corporation, 32, 46, 177, 179
Restrictive Trade Practices Commission (Canadian), 206, 209
Ridder, Herman, 8–11, 233
Rogers, J. and J., Co., 201
Roosevelt, Franklin D., 69–70, 75

St. Croix Paper Co., 48, 57
St. Lawrence Corp., 196–97
St. Maurice Valley Paper Co., 120
Scudder, Richard, 22, 217
Sherman Antitrust Act, 7–8, 15, 47, 51
Shortages. *See* Manpower; Production
Slocum, R. W., 193–95, 201, 205
Small Business Committee, Senate. *See* Capehart Small Business Committee; Humphrey Committee
Softwoods, 5, 31–32, 45, 181, 187, 233
Southern Newspaper Publishers Association, 110
Southern newsprint production, 31–32, 37, 45–46, 111, 127, 156, 233, 249
Southland Paper Mills, 27, 37, 43, 45, 126, 145, 187
Speed-ups, production. *See* capacity
Spot market, 103, 105, 110, 126, 129, 131, 141, 154, 158, 186, 193, 195, 201, 244, 262
Spruce Falls Power and Paper Co., 17, 24
State, Department of, 76, 112–16, 170–71, 177, 197, 210, 215
Steinman, J. Hale, 87–88, 97

Stevenson, Louis T., 194–95
Sulphite pulp, 3–4, 69, 79, 125, 160
Supply and demand. *See* Consumption; Production
Supreme Court, 120

Tariff Commission, 144
Tariffs, 5, 7–14, 27, 79
Tax concessions, 166–67, 169–70, 180, 184, 188, 211
Technological developments, 5, 181
30-pound paper. *See* Lightweight newsprint
Thomason, S. E., 68, 75
Ticoulat, G. J., 165, 216, 219
Tongass National Forest, 119, 125, 180
Toronto Financial Post, 48, 52, 139, 194
Trade Commission. *See* Federal Trade Commission
Trade Policies, Senate Subcommittee on. *See* Capehart Trade Policies Subcommittee
Treanor, Arthur R., 77, 165–66
Treasury, Department of, 64, 69, 77
Truman, Harry S., 96, 101

U.S. newsprint industry, 5–6, 37, 46, 86–87, 92, 99, 106, 123, 133, 135, 146–47, 150, 166–70, 179–80, 183, 186–88, 192, 194–95, 201, 211. *See also* Southern newsprint production

Vining, Charles, 29, 45, 49, 83, 85

War Manpower Commission, 66, 69, 74
War Production Board (WPB), 53–90 *passim,* 257
Wartime Prices and Trade Board (WPTB) (Canadian), 48, 52–54, 63, 73, 81–82, 87
West Tacoma Newsprint Co., 27
Western Newspaper Union, 142
Williams, Cranston, 37, 74, 88–89, 99, 101, 105, 107, 130, 135, 142, 149, 178–79, 198, 200–01, 208, 211, 213–17, 221, 233
Wilson, Charles E., 163, 176
Wood pulp, 3–4, 100–01, 125, 129, 160, 169
World War I, 14–15, 95
World War II, 40, 43–93 *passim,* 150, 229–30

Zellerbach, James D., 146, 148, 202
Zellerbach Paper Co., 39
Zone-pricing, 39, 46, 120–24, 126–28, 143, 147, 159–60, 225, 245

Appendix

Print Paper Pendulum

Group Pressures and the Price of Newsprint

CONTENTS

I	The Product and the Problem	3
II	The Woodpulp Era, 1878–1897	10
III	The Issue Joined, 1897–1907	18
IV	The Tariff Battle Opens, 1908–1909	39
V	Tariff Battle: Conclusion, 1910–1913	69
VI	World War and Aftermath, 1914–1921	90
VII	Overproduction and Depression, 1922–1929	125
VIII	Efforts to Combat Depression, 1929–1936	142
	Notes	172
	Bibliography	203

To Lewis M. *and*
Catherine H. Ellis

PREFACE

THE FOLLOWING narrative is a case study in business pressures. The newspaper publisher has naturally sought cheap raw material. The newsprint manufacturer has naturally tried to pay dividends to his investors. The inevitable frictions have arrayed the two interests on opposite sides of a long series of controversies. The story takes the form of successive swings of the pendulum. Short periods of high-priced newsprint, made possible by national emergency, tariff favors, or manipulation among manufacturers, have had double consequences: on the one hand, heavy profits have brought large increments of new investment capital into the business, with consequent periods of overproduction and low prices; on the other, high prices have organized publishers into vocal pressure-groups to correct alleged abuses to the end of securing cheaper paper, usually with satisfactory results. These pendulum swings have occurred against a background of shifting areas of supply, of changing tariff policy, and of a revolution in the scale and organization of production. It is this story, against this background, which the author has tried to tell.

Any success he may have achieved is, as always, shared with others. The Rutgers University Research Council provided him with a semester of that uninterrupted time so essential to research, and has likewise supported the publication of the study. The American Newspaper Publishers' Association made available otherwise inaccessible material in its files. Mr. Royal S. Kellogg, of the News Print Service Bureau, long a generous purveyor of assistance to anyone manifesting an academic interest in the newsprint industry, has read and criticized the entire manuscript. Mrs. Dale A. Harris spent a fair share of a warm summer struggling with the typing of the manuscript. Why wives should be appended, as a sort of afterthought, to lists of acknowledgments, escapes this author. Bowing to this custom he puts last, but by no means least, Elizabeth Breckenridge Ellis, who patiently observed the evolution of this study.

L. Ethan Ellis

Rutgers University
September, 1947.

Print Paper Pendulum

Group Pressures and the Price of Newsprint

CHAPTER I

The Product and the Problem

NEWSPRINT, as the term will be used in the following narrative, is a wood pulp paper which came into general use in the United States in the 1870's. It combines mechanical pulp, made by a process developed in Germany in the 1840's and used first in this country in the late 1860's, with chemical pulp, made here in the 1880's, in the ratio of approximately 80 per cent wood pulp to 20 per cent chemical pulp. Both processes were originally patented, but this protection expired before large-scale production became a fact. Inertia and prejudice slowed the adoption of the new article. Once it gained a foothold, however, it rapidly displaced paper made from rags and straw in supplying newspaper publishers, who were forced to seek a cheaper medium for their hungry readers.[1]

A brief description of manufacture will introduce the reader to many of the terms which appear in the story to follow. The process, while subjected to many refinements and repeatedly speeded up, has remained basically unchanged. Spruce has proved the most adaptable of several usable varieties of wood. This has profoundly influenced the geographical, economic, and political aspects of the industry. The location of large stands of spruce in proximity to abundant water power first led to the establishment of newsprint mills in the northeastern United States. When overcutting reduced the timber available, the domestic industry moved westward as far as Wisconsin. With further decrease in the supply, Canada's enormous resources were tapped. However artificial the boundary in an economic sense, utilization of Canadian wood has introduced questions of import and export restrictions, of conservation, and of business organization which have greatly affected the delicate balance between supply and demand which it is the purpose of this study to examine.

In the making of mechanical or groundwood pulp the logs, cut into bolts and barked or "rossed," are forced hydraulically against grindstones revolved rapidly by water or electric power. The resultant fibers are short and stiff and in addition to the useful cellulose retain the original components of the wood. The fibers, suspended in the water played over the stones during the grinding process, are screened to remove large particles; and if the fiber is to be used in a converting mill (one which does not manufacture its own pulp, but converts into paper pulp produced elsewhere), it is dried into sheets or "laps" and stored pending shipment. In the so-called integrated mill, manufacturing both pulp and paper, the screened pulp, still mixed with water, is stored in tanks until needed. Economical operation of this process depends upon the close juxtaposition of large amounts of wood with cheap and abundant water power, since at normal paper prices steam grinding has been prohibitively expensive.

A chemical process provides the long-fibered sulphite pulp which combines with the mechanical variety into a paper strong enough to survive the high-speed operation of modern newspaper presses. The wood, reduced to small chips, is placed in a brick-lined steel "digester" where it is cooked under pressure for several hours with a liquor made by sending sulphur dioxide gas through a tower packed with wet limestone. This cooking removes the lignin and other soluble constituents of the wood and leaves a practically pure cellulose fiber ready for screening and drying, or for wet storage if the fiber is for immediate use.

In the actual making of newsprint the two types of pulp are combined in the proper proportions. If the paper is being made in a converting mill, the dried laps must first be mixed with water. In the integrated mill both groundwood and sulphite pulps are stored in tanks until needed, then blended and pumped to the paper machines in a mixture containing only one-half of one per cent solids. This machine, usually of the Fourdrinier type, begins with an endless belt of finely woven bronze wire, from 70 to 100 feet in length and from 164 to 304 inches in width, carried over rollers at speeds from 800 to 1600 feet per minute. From this point the paper making process consists of removing the water from the pulp. This is accomplished by gravity, suction, pressure, and heat. A considerable amount of water escapes through the wire mesh; more is drawn out by a series of suction boxes beneath the screen. By the time it leaves the screen, the mixture is strong enough to be carried to blankets running between rollers which reduce the water content to 70 per cent. Other rollers, heated by steam, remove more water; still others called calendars impart a smooth surface. Within a few seconds the watery mixture has traveled 300 feet through the machine and emerges as newsprint to be wound on reels preparatory to being slit to proper width and rewound on the cores which will carry it to the presses.[2]

In the early stages of the story the newsprint consumed in this country was made from home-grown wood and home-made pulp. Presently, with demand increasing and local supplies declining, imported pulpwood, on which there has never been an import duty, began to supplement the domestic article. These trends persisting, foreign pulp began to come in over gradually lowered tariff barriers. This shift was stimulated by shrewdly designed export restrictions by the principal Canadian producing Provinces upon pulpwood cut from the Crown lands, which Dominion law left under provincial jurisdiction. The next result of the increasing demand, the lowered domestic tariffs, and the provincial export restrictions was to move an ever-larger proportion of pulp manufacture across the northern border. Next sustained consumer pressure first reduced and then removed the tariff on newsprint. This and other factors, induced a rapid expansion of the Canadian paper industry, which overtook and passed that of the United States in 1925–1926. In the later stages of the story the problem has become one of dividing the market (at times a shrinking one) between the relatively declining domestic production and the growing Canadian manufacture, often produced and marketed at a low margin of profit, which constituted a danger to the domestic producer.

The circumstances briefly outlined above may have suggested that questions of supply and demand were likely to play an important role in the story of newsprint paper. It is the repercussions of these factors which this study proposes to examine from the time when wood pulp paper became a factor in the 1870's until the depression of 1929 disappeared into the war clouds of the later 1930's. The protagonists are two: on one hand the manufacturers of pulp and paper, operators of extensive and expensive properties whose stockholders expected dividends and who therefore desired a maximum price for their output; on the other, the consumers of this output, the newspaper publishers of the United States who looked to secure the cheapest possible supply of their raw material, newsprint. This statement of objectives will indicate the antithetical position of the two groups: if the publisher gets cheap paper the manufacturer's profits are less. In the light of the antithesis, the question of supply and demand looms large. An abundant supply puts the consumer in the enviable position of being able to bargain with competing suppliers; a short supply, especially when combined with a sudden or excessive demand, enables the producer to reap the profits of a panic market.

The solution of the problem, if there be one, must be found in terms of price. Ideally, this would be one which provided the publisher with cheap paper at a profit to the manufacturer.[8] In practice such a happy medium is extremely difficult of attainment. Human nature being what it is, the publisher's idea of cheap paper tends, in the producer's view, to be priced below all reason; conversely, the producer's idea of a proper margin of profit tends to savor of extortion to the publisher. The result has been a series of pressures exerted by both groups to attain their ends. When feasible the producer has sought tariff favors at the hands of government. When placed on the defensive in this respect, he has tried to avert the withdrawal of such favors already received. From time to time he has resorted to collusive action to raise or to maintain the price level to his own advantage. The same objective has on other occasions been sought by combinations among producers. When opportunity offered, rigid contract terms have been imposed upon purchasers. From time to time efforts, not too successful, have been made to raise prices by controlling output. It has been the producer's misfortune that many of his protective devices have run counter to currents of popular thinking, rendering him vulnerable to attack by a canny adversary. Thus, efforts at combination coincided with popular sensitiveness to violations of the anti-trust laws. Again, general hostility to protectionism in the early years of the present century helped to strip away this bulwark of the industry. The producer, therefore, may claim to have been waging a defensive battle against those who would make it difficult for him to make a living, as well as against those natural forces which have rendered his business a difficult one through the diminution of his raw materials.

Per contra, the consumer has pointed to aggressive actions by grasping capitalists, intent upon paying dividends on swollen stock issues. He has charged producers with trying to shelter an adult industry behind a tariff wall constructed to protect an infant. He has asserted that there were deliberate violations of the country's anti-trust laws as a means of extracting further tribute. In this series of controversies the consumer has,. by and large, found himself in a favorable position. He is among the most vocal of his countrymen. His publications offer a sounding board from which to air his views much more effectively than any available to an opponent. His organization, the American Newspaper Publishers' Association, is one of the most effective of pressure groups, to whose desires official Washington gives careful if sometimes unwilling heed. Its leadership in the crucial stages of the story about to be unfolded was active and energetic to a point bordering at times on fanaticism.

The resultant interaction of the factors sketched above has been a series of episodes, extending over many years, in which publishers and manufacturers have generally been arrayed in opposition. The publishers, intent upon securing cheap newsprint, have taken advantage of every opportunity to bear the market. Circumstances have frequently assisted them. Every national crisis or swing of the business cycle which brought a temporary shortage of paper and consequent high profits has enticed large new aggregates of capital into the newsprint field. This in turn has brought overproduction, competition, and low prices. Consumers have been alert to manufacturers' efforts to overcome these disadvantages. When short supply or sudden demand created high prices, publishers have typically struck with whatever weapon was convenient. Not infrequently they have anticipated a rise and have sought to discount it in advance by aggressive measures of their own. Drives for tariff removal and prosecutions under the antitrust laws aided in lowering prices over a period of years, in part by opening the way to imports from Canada. Having achieved free trade in paper and its materials, publishers directed their attention around 1920 to removing Canadian export restrictions likely to contribute to shortage and high prices. The NIRA was attacked as an instrument of monopoly in the 1930's, largely because of its price-raising potentialities. In the intervals, when overproduction forced prices down, publishers' activity was less noticeable

Whether because of natural factors or the policies of publishers, periods of declining prices have occupied by far the greater share of the years since 1875. A brief flurry in 1879–1880 was succeeded by a long decline until 1897–1898. Formation of the International Paper Company and other factors then raised prices briefly until about 1900, followed by a drop until late in 1903. Another drop followed until the year beginning in October, 1906, when a rise began which was terminated by the Panic of 1907. This ushered in a period of decline lasting until a war-induced boom in 1916–1917 and a postwar boom from 1919 to 1921. The market then remained in the buyer's hands from 1922 until the mid-1930's. Each of these periods of rising prices finds publishers actively trying to reverse the trend. It is to the examination of the repercussions of publisher-manufacturer relations upon the problem of supply and demand that the narrative now turns.

CHAPTER II

The Wood-Pulp Era, 1878–1897

THESE YEARS introduce a number of elements important in the newsprint story but bring few of them to a conclusion. Changing production processes, greatly increased demand, overproduction, falling prices, tariff legislation, and efforts at combination as a defense against low prices all enter the picture. The 1880's witnessed the completion of the shift to wood pulp newsprint, and the end of the decade found the country ready for a phenomenal boom in newspaper publication and circulation.[1] The turn of the new decade also brought the first of the series of swings to high prices which, with increased demand and the advantages of the new paper, brought new money into the industry and contributed to overproduction and a long price decline lasting well into the 1890's. This continued price depression finally brought the manufacturers to consider combination as a remedy, and toward the end of the period moves to this end were fairly well advanced. This sets the stage for a more active policy by the publishers, which developed in 1897. Tariff legislation and the emergence of Canadian interest in the pulp and paper problem make 1897 a focal point in the story. Meantime, several minor chapters of tariff history, devoted mainly to wood pulp, must be noted in order to provide a setting for the tariff battle which develops after 1900.

While wood-pulp paper was taking possession of the newsprint market in the 1870's, paper makers found themselves in increasingly difficult straits because of overproduction. Effects of the Panic of 1873 persisted until well toward the end of the decade, and on August 28, 1878, the desperate manufacturers gathered at Saratoga Springs, New York, and formed the American Paper Makers' Association.[2] Co-operative effort to tailor production to demand seemed the logical suggestion, and the convention adopted a proposal to reduce it by one-sixth for a six-month period. This was brought to naught by the unwillingness of some mills to carry out the scheme.[3] Gloomy forebodings were temporarily dispelled, however, by the appearance late in 1879 of a short but definite boom. Prosperity seems to have returned with a vengeance and found manufacturers so lacking in raw materials as to cause a short supply and give the producer control of the market. Prices went up from five or six cents to ten cents per pound by March, 1880.[4] It would probably be incorrect to attribute the next decade and a half of overproduction and declining prices to this boom alone; an expanding market, wider use of wood-pulping machinery (the patents on which expired in 1884), and the improvement of the national economy after the Panic of 1873 each played a part. Overproduction and declining prices did develop, however, and the prompt and vigorous reaction of publishers to the brief spell of high prices clearly indicates their sensitiveness to any change unfavorable to them in the balance of supply and demand.

This sensitiveness was first reflected in a rash of bills introduced into the second session of the Forty-Sixth Congress (December, 1879–June, 1880) proposing to lower or remove the duties on pulp, newsprint, and their constituents.[5] By February, 1880, the matter had reached a stage of maneuvering which, while terminating without specific legislative action, ties in with the general contemporary concern over the tariff and brings out some interesting sidelights on the newsprint situation. The initiative came from metropolitan publishers in New York and Chicago, some of whom seem to have held free-trade sentiments and others to have been interested merely in cutting prices. The drive was spear-headed by George Jones of *The New York Times* and Erastus Brooks of *The New York Express*, the latter claiming to speak on behalf of eight thousand newspapers.[6] The most promising approach was an attack on the duty on wood pulp, the process being still under patent and hence vulnerable as a monopoly. "Dried pulp" had been protected by a duty of 20 per cent ad valorem under legislation going back to the Act of July 30, 1846, and continued by subsequent enactments.[7] This provision, inserted in a general list of items, obviously could not apply to wood pulp, since that product had not been in existence in 1846. On March 13, 1872, however, Secretary of the Treasury George S. Boutwell of Massachusetts (in which state the paper industry then centered) had ruled that wood pulp was dutiable under the "dried pulp" provision of the Act of March 2, 1861. The obvious inference was that Boutwell had interpreted the law broadly in favor of his compatriots. The injustice, it was urged, could be rectified by a proper interpretation of the Act of July 14, 1870. This being unlikely of attainment, it was proposed to amend the tariff by a bill introduced by Fernando Wood on March 8, specifically declaring wood pulp free of duty.[8]

This proposal launched the Committee on Ways and Means on a series of hearings during which the wood-pulp question became involved in the problem of general tariff revision, which Congress was not yet willing to undertake. The net result, therefore, was the rather thorough airing of the matter, and the retention of the duty on pulp, a manufacturers' victory, credit for which was for many years modestly arrogated to himself by Warner Miller, of Herkimer, New York. Miller, a colorful character who with William E. Russell of

Massachusetts had played an important part in the development of wood-pulp manufacture, was then a member of Congress, as was Russell. Both appeared before the committee in opposition to Jones and Brooks, denying the charges of monopoly and urging that removal of the duty would ruin the industry.[9] So cogently did Miller argue, and so obvious was his own interest in his argument, that he was known as "Wood-pulp Miller" to the end of his days.

Henceforward wood pulp becomes increasingly entangled in the larger tariff story. It was a period of considerable public concern with the question, and this particular session became a battleground between two points of view as to the best approach to tariff revision, one group favoring piecemeal change and another a full-dress revision. The publishers evidently preferred the piecemeal technique, feeling that their scheme would thus be more likely to succeed. Representative Richard W. Townshend of Illinois introduced by subterfuge a general revision bill, and in the wrangle which followed, any opportunity for action on the Wood bill was lost, though at one stage seven of the thirteen members of the Ways and Means Committee were said to favor it. Presently the end of the session approached, a presidential election was in the offing, and the tariff question was shunted off into discussion of a commission to investigate the whole matter. From the evidence available it would appear that credit for saving the manufacturers' protection at this point should be divided between Miller and the general political situation.[10]

The brief flurry of prosperity of 1879–1880 gave way to an unbroken era of overproduction and increasingly unrestricted competition. Sporadic efforts to balance production and consumption received short shrift from the producers, and by 1887 the manufacturers' association went on record as being opposed to control of wages, hours, or prices.[11] As the *Paper Trade Journal's* annual resumés of the years succeeded one another, the refrain became a monotonous one: too much paper for the market to consume; too many mills in production; too much new money going into paper manufacture; new lows in price from year to year. A typical statement must suffice. Loren Allen, reporting to the News Division of the Paper Makers' Association in August, 1889, voiced this dirge: "we find things in an unsatisfactory condition, no unanimity of opinion and little or no disposition to work in concert to better the outlook. Each manufacturer seems to think he is as wise as his neighbor and proposes to seek his fortune in his own way, regardless of consequences to others. Ruinously low prices and overproduction are the reports from all quarters . . ."[12]

Things being as they were, it was not at all unnatural that thoughts turned again to combination and consequent curtailment of production. The rather sketchy evidence points to two separate efforts in this direction prior to 1897. The first developed over several months during 1893–1895, and seems to have taken the direction of a trust arrangement, the Knight case having demonstrated the weakness of the Sherman Act.[13] By December, 1896, a second scheme, in the form of an agency to control the sales of mills turning out 1300 tons of paper daily, was reported on the point of consummation, but it failed to materialize.[14] Thus as 1897 opened the groundwork had been laid, in excessive output, low prices, and unsuccessful efforts to combat these evils, for a third try which brought the International Paper Company into being early in 1898.

Meantime, some tariff changes had been registered since the flurry of 1880. These are minor in themselves and mainly important as regards wood pulp, since little or no newsprint was being imported prior to 1897. They must, however, receive some attention as background, since the question was to become a principal battleground of the conflicting interests of publishers and manufacturers. It is perhaps worthy of note that pulp and paper received such slight attention in view of the importance of the tariff in national politics in the 1880's and 1890's. This is perhaps to be explained by the fact that cheap paper made it unnecessary for the publishers to force the issue, while the manufacturers, placed on the defensive in 1880, were not in a position to do anything aggressive and in fact agreed to reductions in order to avoid antagonizing the publishers. The manufacturers' next warning of impending danger appeared in the report of the Tariff Commission, rendered to Congress in December, 1882, which precipitated the debate resulting in the so-called Mongrel Tariff of March 3, 1883.

This report recommended the free-listing of pulpwood and wood pulp,[15] but the Act was less severe, free-listing wood, levying 10 per cent ad valorem (a reduction from 20 per cent) on pulp and 15 per cent (down from 20 per cent) on unsized newsprint. The debates throw no light on this action, but Miller (now a Senator) in later years asserted that he counselled congressional committees in favor of both reductions.[16] Grover Cleveland's forthright tariff stand forced the issue upon Congress, and the debate on the Mills Bill of 1888 furnished the most thorough airing of the question in many years, though failing to eventuate in legislation. There is no evidence of publishers' activity before committees of either House. The manufacturers were more active, rather trying to hold the line against reductions than to raise the rates, as if fearful of antagonizing the press. As introduced in the House the bill proposed to free-list wood pulp and to cut the 15 per cent ad valorem rate on unsized newsprint to 12 per cent, a 20 per cent reduction. The House sustained the committee on newsprint, but the Senate substitute, introduced as a political weapon in the 1888 campaign, restored the rate to 15 per cent. Although Mills proposed to free-list pulp, sufficient pressure was exerted to induce retention of the 10 per cent rate of 1883 in the House bill, and the only change was an amendment adopted in the Senate changing the duty to a specific one of $2.50 per ton, a slight reduction. Neither House nor Senate proposal was enacted, and there was relatively slight interest in the matter.[17]

The McKinley Tariff of October 1, 1890, continued newsprint at the 15 per cent ad valorem level established in the Act of 1893, but changed the 10 per cent rate on mechanical pulp to a specific one of $2.50 per ton. This increased the actual levy somewhat and brought out a difference of opinion between the importers of wood pulp and the domestic producers. The importers, who had been bringing chemical pulp from Europe and evidently profiting by undervaluing it at the customs, desired the product free-listed, or kept on an ad valorem basis. The domestic producers, subjected to what they considered unfair competition by virtue of the undervaluation, preferred the specific duty, which went into the bill. The McKinley Act also for the first time made a distinction between mechanical and chemical pulp, levying $6.00 per ton on the unbleached sulphite which entered somewhat into the production of newsprint. These differences were brought out in the hearings before the Ways and Means Committee, and there was little debate on the matter in either House.[18]

Before the next tariff legislation, the Wilson-Gorman Act of August 27, 1894, the paper trade had momentarily reflected the prosperity of the early 1890's and more permanently the panic of 1893.[19] The Wilson Bill passed the House without mention of pulp or paper in the debate, carrying newsprint at 12 per cent ad valorem (down 3 per cent from the McKinley level) and returning both mechanical and chemical pulps to 10 per cent. The Finance Committee reduced the news rate to 10 per cent at one stage, but by the time the section was adopted it was back to the McKinley level of 15 per cent, at which it went into the law without debate. The pulp question again aroused some interest. A number of domestic manufacturers urged retention of a duty specific in type, and Senator William P. Frye of Maine put this request in the form of an amendment to the bill which would have left the rates as they were in the McKinley Act. He was joined by Jacob H. Gallinger, of New Hampshire, who asserted that the change to ad valorem would lower the duty, because of the depressed price of the product, and so work a hardship on the producers. Their arguments were unavailing, however, and the 10 per cent rate prevailed.[20]

CHAPTER III

The Issue Joined, 1897–1907

Several important developments characterized the decade opening in 1897. An initial tariff skirmish gave the manufacturers an advantage, as did the formation of the International Paper Company early in 1898. These events, together with the higher prices accompanying a boom in 1897–1898, warned the publishers that they must guard their interests. The year 1897 also saw the appearance of one of the most colorful figures in the newsprint controversy, that of John Norris, who was to become the nemesis of the manufacturers, teaming with the Publishers' Association in a partnership which eventually sealed the doom of protection on newsprint. A brief period of high prices after the formation of the International was followed by another decline until late in 1903. The policies of the manufacturers then determined the publishers on an active campaign. The next year, 1904, they spent in sparring for an opening, there seeming to be some doubt as to whether it would be best to proceed under the anti-trust acts or by revision of the tariff. Eventually both plans were followed, and by 1907 a full-scale assault was launched, with overtures being made to all branches of the government in an effort to secure the publishers' desires. Against these domestic developments must be considered an increasing Canadian interest in the problem.

The initial round was fought at a hearing of the Ways and Means Committee on December 31, 1896. Prior to this the manufacturers at a New York session had formulated their wishes, including maintenance of the existing rate on newsprint and a return to specific duties of $2.00 on groundwood and $4.00 on unbleached sulphite. These were lower than the McKinley duties, but somewhat above the existing level.[1] At the hearing John Norris projected himself into the proceedings, which took on "a character not entirely looked for." Norris was at the time business manager of the *The New York World,* which used, according to his assertion, one-thirteenth of the total newsprint tonnage consumed in the United States. He asserted at this point that he appeared neither for the *World* nor for publishers generally, but as an individual who felt the need to inform the committee "of the fact that the newspaper manufacturers of the United States have perfected their arrangements for a combination by which every newspaper shall be at the mercy of a central selling agency and by which the price of newspaper shall be raised, and by which these gentlemen shall derive an additional profit of from five to six million dollars a year out of their investment, and thereby tax knowledge and diminish the educational possibilities of the newspaper press . . ."[2]

Norris' statement to the committee was his first lengthy public exposition of a point of view which was to be reiterated many times, and of a technique compounded of fact, half-truth, and innuendo which he developed by constant use over many years into a theme with variations—the ill-intent of the manufacturers of newsprint toward the consumers of their product. He raised the bogey of combination, alleging that even as he spoke arrangements were all but completed for a union of Eastern mills through a selling agency to raise the price of news to two and one-half cents per pound (it was then, he said, about two cents). He suggested the complete removal of the duty on newsprint. This, he argued, would prevent the fruition of the combination by subjecting its members to the competition of the exhaustless forests and water power of Canada, while at the same time contributing to the conservation of our own natural resources. When pressed on particular points he took refuge in the statement that he was merely furnishing information, which could be used by the committee as it saw fit. He denied that removing the tariff would also remove the industry to Canada, asserting that it would merely check the possibility of higher prices through monopolistic control. He doubted the efficacy of the combination, if formed, giving it as his opinion that high prices would drive publishers into manufacturing, with a restoration of low prices through competition.

Miller and Russell replied on behalf of the manufacturers. Russell with some asperity denied the fact of combination or the intent of any possible combination to raise prices. Under questioning, he and Miller sketched the two plans of co-operation already mentioned, indicating that the first failed because of inability to reach agreement upon the valuation of property involved and asserting that the second, or sales-agency plan, while the subject of prolonged negotiation, had accomplished nothing and was not expected to do so. Miller claimed that the manufacturers had practically dared the publishers, if these feared higher prices, to make contracts "at the present rates for five years or for all time to come."

Before the introduction of the Dingley Bill on March 18, 1897, Norris had carried his fight before the American Newspaper Publishers' Association and enlisted its influence in behalf of his project, albeit not without misgivings on the part of some members.[3] Rehearsing his appearance before the Dingley committee, he asserted that this group had decided to recommend a duty of $1.65 per ton on mechanical pulp, which would increase the cost of paper by five cents per hundredweight. He then moved "That a committee of three be appointed to secure the abolition of the duty on pulp and paper." This evoked conflicting sentiments among those present, some feeling that papers which had just gone through the McKinley campaign advocating the protective principle might balk at asking favors for their particular interest. His motion carried, however, and he was chosen chairman of the committe constituted under it.

The scene now changes to Washington, where the Dingley Bill progressed to passage against a background of overproduction, low prices, and anxious Canadian interest in the development of American tariff policy.[4] Debate opened on March 22, 1897. The committee proposed 15 per cent ad valorem on newsprint (the Wilson-Gorman rate) and a return to a specific levy on mechanical pulp, placed at one-twelfth of a cent per pound or $1.67 per ton, as had been forecast by Norris. The House debate produced no discussion of these proposals, and the bill passed as introduced.[5]

At this juncture some brief notice should be paid to the development of Canadian policy. By this time, of course, much United States paper was being produced from Canadian pulpwood, which had so far been subjected to no limitations in its movement across the border. The interest of American pulp manufacturers in continuing this situation is fairly obvious. The inroads of the mills on the forests were already causing suggestions, rather precocious, it is true, that perhaps our supplies of spruce might not be inexhaustible.[6] Free access to Canadian spruce would postpone, if not avert, the evil day. On the other hand, some Canadians were already thinking that part of the profits of pulp-making would look well on Canadian bank balances. At least as early as 1893 they were urging their government to place an export duty on pulp and logs with the object of forcing American capital into Canadian pulp manufacture. The issue arose again in 1896 and became a bone of contention in the political campaign which brought Sir Wilfrid Laurier to power as head of a Liberal Government in June.[7] While the Dingley Bill was before the House, Laurier's group was also formulating a tariff under the influence of conflicting points of view on the matter of an export duty on pulpwood. The early tendency seems to have been to resist pressure to impose the duty, perhaps because the Government was still hopeful of inducing the United States to enter reciprocity negotiations.[8] The bill introduced in April indicated that the Government had apparently abandoned the idea of reciprocity, but sensitiveness to American reactions, or possibly a desire to bargain, produced a bill without restrictions on pulpwood exportation. As the Dingley Bill progressed through the Senate and it became increasingly likely that it might contain provisions inimical to Canadian interests, the pressure increased and early in June Finance Minister William S. Fielding gave notice that the Government would ask for power to impose an export levy on logs, pulpwood, and some ores, though at the same time he insisted that there was no intention of applying the duties immediately if permission were accorded.[9] Parliament granted the Government permission to impose the export duty in the tariff act, which passed about the same time that the Senate was adopting the paper section of the Dingley Bill, with new provisions to be noted below which contained a threat to Canada. There is little doubt that both arrangements contained an element of potential threat.[10]

As introduced in the Senate May 4, the pulp section was amended. In Paragraph 390 mechanical pulp was subjected to a duty of seven and one-half cents a hundredweight or $1.50 per ton as against the $1.67 of the House bill. A retaliatory proviso was attached: "That if any country or dependency shall impose an export duty on pulp wood, the amount of such export duty shall be added, as an additional duty, to the duties herein imposed upon wood pulp, when imported from such country or dependency." The newsprint section continued the House rate of 15 per cent ad valorem. The pulp proposal passed the Senate with but a single voice raised in dissent, George G. Vest of Missouri objecting to loading the consumer with a double burden. Before passage the newsprint section also received a proviso, on motion of William B. Allison of Iowa, "That no such paper shall pay a less rate of duty than three-tenths of 1 cent per pound." This, said Allison, was the equivalent of 15 per cent ad valorem. It changed the duty from ad valorem to specific and placed it at a minimum of $6.00 per ton. It was this action which threw the paper section into conference and may be taken as the forerunner of what happened to it in the Conference Committee.[11]

On July 21 the Senate considered the Conference Committee report. The pulp section came in essentially as it had originally passed the House, with the duty increased to $1.67 per ton. The paper section was altered in such fashion as to bring charges, at the time and later, that there had been manipulation in the committee to raise the paper duty for the benefit of the manufacturers. As reported, and as it eventually went into the Act, Paragraph 396 carried a sliding scale of specific duties beginning with three-tenths of a cent per pound on newsprint, valued at not over two cents per pound, five-tenths of a cent on that valued above two cents and not above two and one-half cents, and so on. A retaliatory proviso also appeared for the first time at this point: "That if any country or dependency shall impose an export duty upon pulp wood exported to the United States, there shall be imposed upon printing paper when imported from such country or dependency, an additional duty of one-tenth of 1 cent per pound for each dollar of export duty per cord so imposed, and proportionately for fractions of a dollar of such export duty." In reporting to the House, Dingley asserted that the new specific duty was set "at the same equivalent ad valorem rate that passed the House, and the same rate as in previous tariffs . . ."

The committee was attacked in the Senate because of the

addition of the provisos, unique in the pulp and paper paragraphs of the bill, on the ground that it had inserted new legislation (the retaliatory proviso regarding paper), and because it was alleged that the change to a specific levy, plus the proviso, would work an increase in the paper tariff. This last charge was based upon the current price of paper. The $6.00 per ton minimum would be equivalent to 15 per cent ad valorem on paper selling at $2.00 per hundredweight. It was alleged later, however, that the average price of paper was $1.75 in the East and that the New York papers were getting their paper for $1.65 delivered. On this basis the $6.00 specific rate would conceal a substantial increase favorable to the mill men.[12] Allison insisted, however, that careful cost analyses, based on customs valuations, indicated that the sliding scale proposed by the committee was equivalent to slightly less than 15 per cent ad valorem, and the conference report was accepted.[13] Thus the tariff warned Canada against interfering with the free passage of pulpwood across the border, raised the rate on wood pulp and newsprint, and put the publishers on notice of a change in the situation. Rising prices in the autumn of 1897, the formation of the International Paper Co. early in 1898, and its temporary influence in maintaining these prices further warned them that an issue was appearing.[14]

While Congress busied itself with the tariff, the newsprint market was the prey of "the most intense competition and lowest prices for newspaper ever seen . . ." during the first half of 1897. Prices stiffened during the autumn, and by mid-April of 1898 a swing to a seller's market had taken place, a swing which preceded the abnormal conditions produced by the Spanish-American War.[15] The swing was very welcome to a newcomer in the paper field, the International Paper Company, incorporated January 31, 1898, under the leadership of practical paper makers rather than promoters, guided principally by Russell. Originally composed of mills formerly owned by seventeen concerns, it soon absorbed most of the mills east of the Mississippi and controlled from two-thirds to three-fourths of the total newsprint output of the country. It was, in the words of a trade journal, "born of the fear of bankruptcy and ruin, as competition among the manufacturers had gone beyond all reasonable bounds . . ."; another exulted that "the war of price is over . . ." Per contra, the *World*, in caustic vein, charged the formation of a trust "to monopolize the business, raise the price of paper $8 a ton and levy a tax of not less than $4,000,000 a year . . . This is a conspiracy to tax knowledge, to levy tribute on education, to blackmail intelligence itself. Unfortunately the tariff duties aid the conspiracy. They not only prevent Canadian and other foreign competition in the sale of paper, but they exclude Canadian wood pulp. The free admission of wood pulp and paper would go far to crush the conspiracy. What is to be done about the matter? Will any attorney general enforce the laws, State or national, against such conspiracies in restraint of trade? Will Congress, seeing clearly that the paper and pulp duties thus aid and abet robbery, repeal those duties?" [16]

This development was of course a challenge to the publishers. At the Association's annual meeting, February 18, John Norris took the floor to discuss Question 35 on the agenda: "The White Paper Combine. Is it a sure go, and will it necessarily be hostile to the interests of the newspaper publisher?" He answered the first part with an affirmative, and went into the story of the formation of the "trust," giving statistics to show that the new organization was badly overcapitalized, the member plants having been absorbed at a figure per ton of daily production out of all relation of the facts.[17] He suggested, not too hopefully, that if the newspapers could be induced to unite, Congress might be persuaded to repeal the duty on unsized newsprint.

At this point William Cullen Bryant, a member of the

Board of Directors, interjected to report on an informal semi-social meeting between the board and representatives of the combine a few days earlier, at which mutual problems were discussed. The meeting was held at the instance of Hugh J. Chisholm, vice-president of the International, and the result, to Bryant's way of thinking, indicated that the prospects for co-operation between the two groups were not too dark; this would constitute a negative answer to the second half of the rhetorical question above. In fact, he asserted, the mill men had promised that "if any of you gentlemen wish to take any shares of stock in the company you will be taken in on the ground floor." Norris was considerably nettled, since he had not been invited or informed. As on an earlier occasion, discussion disclosed differences of opinion among the membership, but again produced a motion for a committee, this time of five members, "for the purpose of guarding the interests of the A.N.P.A. in connection with the movement of the paper trust . . ."[18]

Newsprint prices rose rapidly under the double impetus of the war and the manufacturers' combination, and whereas paper had been selling in 1897 for $1.60, by May, 1898, it was bringing from $2.25 to $2.40. The demand dropped sharply by mid-June, but by that time another forum was being prepared for rehearsal of the conflicting claims of publishers and manufacturers.[19] This was the meeting in July of the Joint High Commission, charged with ironing out a tangled series of Canadian-American problems, among them commercial reciprocity. This brought up the question of export restrictions, permission to levy which had been granted to the Laurier Government, but not exercised. This failure to act raised the alternative of independent provincial limitations; it also produced a division of domestic opinion, the pulp makers favoring restrictions and the frontier settlers, who supported themselves for a time by cutting pulpwood for export, being opposed. The Dominion authorities, naturally, did nothing about imposing restrictions, in the hope of using this abstention as a bargaining instrument in possible reciprocity negotiations. As the time for the meeting approached, the pulp makers seemed to experience a change of heart, and in August the Canadian Lumbermen's Association adopted resolutions urging free importation in return for free exportation, i.e., that the United States should freely admit pulp and manufactured lumber if Canada allowed logs to leave the Dominion without restrictions.[20] This produced immediate complications by allying the American lumbermen, opposed to the entry of manufactured lumber, and the American paper makers, opposed to the free entry of Canadian pulp. The Canadian pulp manufacturers seconded the lumbermen in mid-September in resolutions demanding an immediate export duty on pulpwood equal to the American import duty on pulp unless the United States remove her levies on both mechanical and chemical pulp.[21] As the Joint High Commission's meetings approached futility, the Canadian position completed the circle and returned to support of export restrictions on the theory that the United States was dependent upon Canada for her supply and would have to buy anyway, regardless of the tariff on wood pulp.[22]

Against this background the domestic interests waged another round of their battle, the story of which must be pieced together, since the Commission held its sessions in secret. Warner Miller addressed a session on September 1, seconding the American lumbermen, who had argued against removal or reduction of protective duties. In December John Norris presented a brief, which went also to the press and all members of Congress, urging removal of pulp and paper duties as a means of combatting the paper trust. He rehearsed the charges of overcapitalization made earlier, adding that many high-cost and inefficient mills had been taken into the combine at inflated values. January 7, 1899, Miller again appeared, amplifying his earlier statement and replying to Norris in particular. Since his first approach had proved unpalatable to some staunch Republican papers, Norris prepared another, based on the theory that tariffs should be removed to conserve American forests. This abandoned the tax-on-knowledge approach and made no mention of the ultimate objective of the publishers—removal of the tariff. It went to the Commission in January and was followed by a direct approach on January 30, when a deputation from the publishers met the President and the members of the Commission and presented a third brief compounded of the two earlier ones. There the matter rested, as the Commission presently broke up in disagreement.[23]

The next year, 1899, brought few developments in the domestic scene until a last-quarter price boom alerted publishers once more.[24] Canadians further canvassed the problem of policy, with three possible courses of action receiving attention. Advocates of Dominion-imposed export duties on wood reminded themselves of the retaliatory provisions of the Dingley Act. A possible way of securing the same end without this involvement was suggested in a proposed sharp increase of the Dominion stumpage dues (levies on wood actually cut), with a rebate of most of these in the case of wood pulped in Canada. And, as before, the wood-producing Provinces toyed with the idea of local restrictions. Through it all there appears a growing concern with the problem, perhaps not entirely unconnected with an American drive to secure timber limits in Canada, and a rising feeling that Canada had come to command the situation through control of the raw material now becoming increasingly essential to the American paper mills.[25]

The price boom of late 1899 stimulated the normal reaction: numerous legislative proposals, which slumbered in committee pigeonholes because of desire to avoid the general tariff discussion which their presentation would precipitate, and an investigative proposal suggested by the publishers at their annual convention in February. W. S. Hutchins, of the Washington (D. C.) *Times*, asserting that the best quotation he had been able to secure from the mills was between $2.75 and $3.00, added that he did not wish to invite a fight with the trust, but desired to know what could be done to better the situation. Responding, H. E. Baldwin of the Joliet (Ill.) *News*, introduced a resolution recording the Association's desire for removal of the tariff on wood pulp. The following discussion clearly indicated a continued difference of opinion. Finally the convention demanded an inquiry into the paper situation by a special congressional committee, particularly into the increase in price, commonly believed due to action of the trust. This, as Thurlow Weed once told William H. Seward, broke no eggs, but showed an anxious interest.[26] The only other domestic development was the incorporation of the General Paper Company, a combination of twenty-six mills in Wisconsin, Michigan, and Minnesota, into a selling agency whose function was to eliminate competition in order to put the Western mills on a par with the International.[27] In Canada the first-fruits of restrictive sentiment were found in Ontario's regulation forbidding the exportation of pulpwood cut from the Crown lands, under Dominion practice left under provincial jurisdiction. This was the first of a series of similar restrictions enacted over a period of years by the forest Provinces and is to be properly considered as a move brought about by the failure of the central government to take action. It was dictated by a sense of grievance against the retaliatory provisions of the Dingley Act and by a desire to stimulate the growth of a Canadian wood-pulp industry.[28]

A relatively quiet period followed until 1904. Prices started down under the impetus of new production, particularly that of the Great Northern Paper Co. which entered the market in November, 1901. The buyer soon regained control of the situation and with supply and demand more or less in equilibrium there was little incentive for the publishers to wage an aggressive campaign. John Norris kept in training for his marathon attack against the International Paper Co. by an appearance before the Industrial Commission in April, 1901, in which he added nothing to his previous arguments. In a refutation of Norris, President Chisholm freely admitted that a combination had been formed and that prices had gone up thereafter under pressure of rising costs. He denied Norris' charges of monopoly, insisting that there were twelve hundred pulp and paper mills outside the combine. Nothing of moment occurred until the International raised prices following a four-day shutdown in November, 1903, allegedly carried out to shorten the supply and so pave the way for the increase, but actually motivated, in part at least, by fear of strikes among the workers.[29] These factors, aggravated early in 1904 by heavy snows, transportation troubles, and an extra demand for paper created by the outbreak of the Russo Japanese War, gave impetus to another campaign during which the publishers favored the manufacturers with their attentions.

Their convention in February was again the scene of vigorous discussion initiated by Don C. Seitz of the *World*, who urged the Association to "assail Congress in the interest of free pulp and free paper . . ." and announced that he had been authorized to subscribe ten thousand dollars to a fund for this purpose. Herman Ridder of the *Staats-Zeitung*, who was presently to play a major role in developments, seconded this with a promise of a thousand dollars. Condé Hamlin of *The St. Paul Pioneer Press* suggested another approach when he proposed a suit against the General Paper Co. under the anti-trust act. These diverse but not necessarily antagonistic proposals provide a keynote for the year's developments: the publishers were anxious for action but not quite sure of the best method; as a result they sparred for an opening, finally adopting the anti-trust idea as most promising after tentative feelers toward both legislative and executive branches had met with discouragement. Opportunity to follow this lead was furnished by the introduction of a resolution into the House on March 7 by George L. Lilley of Connecticut asking that the newly created Department of Commerce and Labor "investigate the causes of the present high prices of the white paper used for the printing of newspapers in the United States and the great scarcity of the same, and whether the said conditions have resulted, in whole or in part, from any contract, combination in the form of trust or otherwise, or conspiracy in restraint of commerce among the several States . . ."[30]

The publishers seized avidly upon this fortuitous opportunity to focus public attention.[31] Seitz and Norris occupied the first day's hearings. The former, after advocating tariff reduction to the publishers in February, easily adapted himself to the approach through anti-trust laws which at the moment seemed more promising. In addition to repeating the old charges against the International he attacked the sales-agency scheme of the General Paper Co. and added charges of collusion between the two trusts to divide the territory at the Indiana line, with the eastern combine agreeing not to invade the western area except to serve old customers. He alleged further that the International had arranged with the eastern independents, except the Great Northern, to buy all surplus production, thus keeping it off the competitive market. Norris, now business manager of the New York *Times*, repeated Seitz' accusations against the two combines and added a proposal for removing the tariff from wood pulp, which he asserted would make possible the establishment of converting mills, operating on a comparative shoestring, which could furnish sufficient white paper to break the combines' hold. In response to committee queries as to why the publishers did not openly press Congress and the administration to reduce duties, they admitted that not all the press agreed on such a course and hinted darkly that the International had inserted clauses in its contracts prohibiting its customers from making statements inimical to the trust. They preferred, therefore, to move by indirection, securing Congressional support for a "voyage of discovery" via the Department of Commerce and Labor as a preliminary to application to the Attorney General for prosecution under the Sherman Act.

A week later the Committee reconvened to hear the manufacturers' rebuttal. Chester W. Lyman presented the case, consisting of personal comment plus a sworn statement by President Chisholm and Tom T. Waller, a Vice President, in the form of a parallel-column refutation of the publishers' claims which, it was carefully noted, were not made on oath. The combined statements brought out that the publishers' drive was not unanimous, but was spearheaded by two papers only, customers of the Great Northern rather than the International. It was then asserted that the animus of Seitz and Norris derived from two factors: first, that during the recent drought they had tried unsuccessfully to buy from the International when their own contractor could not supply their needs; and second, because the International had refused to sell them paper under contract at a lower figure than its regular customers received.

With an air of considerable confidence the statement continued: "There is not now and never has been any combination, agreement, or arrangement of any kind or description between the International Paper Company and the General Paper Company; nor has there been any such combination, agreement, or arrangement between the International Paper Company and any other paper manufacturer, excepting only three companies, part of whose product is sold on a commission basis." As to the charge of apportionment of territory, "Such statement is absolutely false." Further: "The International Paper Company to-day and at all times has been willing to offer its product at the market price to all and any purchasers of paper, irrespective of territory or former source of supply, providing always that freight rates made the delivery permissible and the purchaser was willing to pay the value that the International Paper Company placed upon its product to its own customers at such time as the International Paper Company had surplus product . . ." Relative to the charge of buying surplus from the independents: "Such is not the fact. We have at various times purchased from three other manufacturers of paper before referred to a limited amount, approximately 10 per cent of our own production, these purchases having been made to meet the unforeseen growth and extraordinary demands of parties with whom we had contracts . . ." As to the charge of prohibiting purchasers to print hostile comment: "The International Paper Company has not now, and never did have, any such agreement, or any similar agreement, or any agreement to that effect with any paper whatsoever . . ." In a confident conclusion it was asserted that "If the International Paper Company has done or is doing anything in violation of established law, it is amenable to the action of the courts, and the Department of Justice has been established for the purpose and charged with the duty of prosecuting any such violations . . ."

This forthright statement may have given the publishers pause; at any rate the next move was directed not against the International but the General Paper Co. The paper committee, consisting of Seitz, Norris, and Hamlin, conferred with the Department of Justice on April 26. They submitted evidence in their possession which seemed similar to the facts which in the Addystone Pipe Case had resulted in the dissolution of a trust. The investigation then promised was conducted in collaboration with the publishers. These circularized the A.N.P.A., the Associated Press, and the Publishers' Press with requests for evidence of combination. The Department of Justice sent a representative to the Associated Press convention in September to gather information, supposedly either James M. Beck (who had prepared the Government's case against the Northern Securities Co.) or Frank B. Kellogg, both of whom had already been engaged to prepare evidence. As a result of these activities suit was entered in St. Paul, Minnesota, on December 27, to have the alleged combination declared unlawful and to enjoin its members from further actions in pursuance of such a combination. Thus was launched a long and complicated prosecution which in 1906 resulted in a decree ordering the dissolution of the company, the first outstanding publishers' victory.[32]

There followed an unhappy period for the manufacturers. With the General Paper Co. under fire in the West, competition in the East broke the International's control of price in the summer of 1904, and overproduction and unrestricted competition forced prices down through 1905 and into 1906 while production costs were mounting. These developments drove the mill men to desperation and set the stage for the happenings of 1907 which oriented the publishers' attack toward the tariff. Late in 1906 demand caught up with supply, and by October a boom was on which lasted until the Panic of October, 1907.[33] This boom, gathering momentum through the winter, brought increased purchases which led to a shortage by April, 1907. Shortages begat price considerations and by summer manufacturers had begun to think of ways to offset the recent lean years. This in turn put publishers on the *qui vive* and in the autumn a situation developed which made the tariff a focal point for some years to come. By the time the boom collapsed with the Panic in October, contracts had been made at increased prices and forces had been set in motion which carried through the ultimate removal of all tariff restrictions on pulp and newsprint.[34]

The rising cost of raw materials, particularly wood, brought forebodings of price increases as early as February. By July John Norris was predicting that the big users would have trouble renewing their contracts at the old figures. A buyer for Wisconsin mills, short of wood, traveled fifteen hundred miles to Quebec to buy fifty thousand cords in the summer. A speculator in New York allegedly tied up twenty thousand tons of paper. And as a background to all these happenings, Canadian sentiment began to focus upon a determined drive to prohibit the exportation of pulpwood as a means of annexing a larger share of the pulp-and-paper business of the continent. Never far from the surface since 1900, this policy emerged in February, and by June a full-dress campaign was underway. Sentiment was divided between advocacy of Dominion and Provincial action, and between export duties and absolute prohibition of exportation, but the main point was increasingly clear—Canadians were becoming conscious of the power of possession, and were debating only the best means of wielding their weapon. They were aided in their propaganda by a gloomy government report that Americans were consuming between three and four times the annual growth of domestic pulpwood.[35]

Under all these circumstances the management of the International Paper Co. decided upon two drastic changes in policy. Like others in the field, it had been accustomed to making long-term contracts to large purchasers with prices set either for the duration of the contract or reviewable periodically during its life. In practice the consumers held the mills to their contracts during periods of rising prices, but refused themselves to be bound if prices dropped. In the early summer the executive committee decided to limit new contracts to a single year and to raise the price to $2.50 in a desperate effort to retrieve the financial situation.[36] In early September a number of mill representatives met in New York and according to the trade press decided upon another increase of fifteen cents, making the carload price $2.65 on quantities under two thousand tons. Thus the so-called "independents" followed the earlier example of the International, and the die was cast.[37]

This challenge had to be met. Ridder's story of subsequent events tells how he was threatened with a price increase by his supplier, made his contract under this duress, and proceeded to call a special meeting of the A.N.P.A., of which he was then President, for September 18 to discuss the situation.[38] This gathering, held in conjunction with the annual convention of the Associated Press, may be taken as the opening gun of the publishers' all-out campaign. It is worthy of note, however, that a vocal minority still felt that the manufacturers were justified in price increases, which the publishers ought to put up with, and doubted the efficacy of tariff removal as a panacea. Norris' resolutions, which were adopted, offered alternative procedures through the tariff and the Sherman Act, though he seems to have been apprehensive that the latter might not be successful, legal advice having indicated that although the manufacturers were sailing close to the wind, their organization might not be in violation.[39]

Publishers' policy during the remainder of the autumn followed the double line just indicated, with a tendency to push the tariff aspect upon the attention of President Theodore Roosevelt. In mid-November Attorney General Charles J. Bonaparte indicated his willingness to proceed against the paper combine upon receipt of proper evidence.[40] A committee headed by Medill McCormick of *The Chicago Tribune* waited upon Roosevelt on November 7 and presented the publishers' account of their sufferings at the hands of the manufacturers.

Some contemporaries were so unkind as to suggest that the President's agile mind saw an opportunity to enlist press support in diverting attention from the Panic, responsibility for which was being laid on his shoulders, by calling attention to the exactions of a trust. At any rate, he was quoted as promising "that he will recommend to Congress the abolition of the duty on press paper, wood pulp and the wood that goes into the manufacture of paper; also, that he will make a recommendation to the Department of Justice that it take immediate steps to ascertain whether the anti-trust laws are being disobeyed by the manufacturers of paper . . ." [41]

Although the sequence of events is not entirely clear at this point, Rooseveltian ardor, if actually aroused, was quickly replaced by political caution. The possibility that such a recommendation might open the whole tariff question was not lost upon the President, who wanted no such result. He soon began to temper his proposal and to justify it as a conservation measure rather than as tariff revision. By the time his message went to Congress on December 3 his recommendation was confined to wood pulp and qualified by suggesting that as a *quid pro quo* Canada agree not to levy upon the exportation of wood. It was removed by five printed pages from his more famous pronouncement in favor of general tariff revision, to take place after his successor had assumed office. The fact, however, that he could be induced to make even such a left-handed gesture as this is a commentary at once upon the power of the press and upon the flexibility of his supposedly adamantine stand on the question of tariff revision. The message itself reads: "There should be no tariff on any forest product grown in this country; and, in especial, there should be no tariff on wood pulp; due notice of the change being of course given to those engaged in the business so as to enable them to adjust themselves to the new conditions. The repeal of the duty on wood pulp should if possible be accompanied by an agreement with Canada that there shall be no export duty on Canadian pulp wood . . ."[42]

The decade 1897–1907 produced significant aspects of the story under survey. Publishers' interests were challenged successively by tariff discriminations in favor of the manufacturers, by successive swings to high prices, and by a double movement toward combination among the mills. Responding somewhat reluctantly to these challenges under the leadership of John Norris and others representing the metropolitan press, their Association proceeded to defend its interests. Choice between the two avenues of approach, the tariff and the anti-trust laws, was rendered difficult by circumstances and the long-time convictions of many publishers, but eventually the latter was pressed as more promising, while the former was not forgotten. As a sort of specter in the background emerged the increasing likelihood of shortages of raw material which counselled adoption of conservation measures. This possibility in turn whetted Canadian appetites for a chance to devote their tremendous resources to supplying the American market, with the conviction growing that the initial step in manufacture should be transferred to northern pulp mills. For the moment the tariff emerges as the villain of the piece.

CHAPTER IV

The Tariff Battle Opens, 1908–1909

PAPER PRICES, set before the Panic, remained high despite the slack consumption and retrenchment which followed. The publishers' drive therefore must needs be continued in 1908. The technique paralleled that of 1907: a double push directed toward both combination and the tariff. This push gathered hitherto unprecedented momentum, elicited a further presidential blessing, became involved in partisan congressional maneuvers, and was sidetracked only at the last moment by taking traditional refuge in investigation by a special committee—wise tactics in an election year when any tariff discussion might be the fuse which would lead to the dynamiting of Republican hopes. The investigation, one of the most thorough of its kind in our history, postponed the evil day for the manufacturers, who had faced it with equanimity; it found the publishers still not unanimous in following the lead of the metropolitan papers which increasingly assumed the direction of the fight; and it uncovered a mine of fact and opinion worked by all subsequent students of the newsprint problem.[1]

The earliest move was Ridder's letter to Attorney General Bonaparte under date of February 10, 1908, replying to Bonaparte's request of November 13, 1907. This contained information on efforts to stifle competition in various lines of paper manufacture, particularly the fiber and manila pool, members of which were subsequently indicted and fined.[2] On the 19th he directed a letter to members of the Association charging that paper mills were being closed and production was being curtailed in order to maintain the price level. On March 16 he circularized "every publication in the United States" in a bulletin which brought the tariff aspect to the foreground, where it was to remain until 1913. This bulletin reprinted documents already mentioned and warned publishers that the "situation is acute. Time is the essence of success just now. A letter written within the next forty-eight hours should be extremely helpful in accumulating a sentiment in Congress for the protection of printers and publishers." This resulted in a flood of letters during the rest of March and early April and was doubtless influential in evoking Roosevelt's second request for action.[3]

The President sent a special message on March 25 urging passage of a select list of measures before Congress adjourned. While urging adequate preparation prior to general revision, he asserted that "one change in the tariff could with advantage be made forthwith . . ." Repeating his earlier suggestion that wood pulp be free-listed as a conservation measure, he went further and advocated "a corresponding reduction upon paper made from wood pulp . . ." when coming from areas which did not impose export restrictions. The same day John Sharp Williams, minority leader, announced that he would obstruct the legislative process until several proposals, one of which dealt with the paper question, were assured of passage. This precipitated a filibuster which was an intermittent element in succeeding developments. Meantime, on March 3, Congressman Frederick C. Stevens of Minnesota introduced a bill to remove the paper and pulp duties with retaliatory levies in case export duties were imposed. This became the main objective of the publishers until Congress adjourned.[4]

Events crowded upon each other and moved to a climax in April. With publishers demanding congressional action and with gleeful Democrats making sport of their Republican brethren for not permitting it, Speaker Joseph G. Cannon introduced on April 2 two resolutions directed to the aspects of the problem relating to the anti-trust laws. These resolutions called upon the Attorney General and the Secretary of Commerce and Labor for information about any prospective prosecutions of the International Paper Co. The resolutions were adopted on April 8 after a partisan debate. The reply from the Department of Commerce and Labor was negative. Bonaparte informed Congress on April 13 that he had several weeks earlier turned over all the evidence in his possession to the United States Attorney in the appropriate district, with instructions to conduct further investigations and, if these disclosed sufficient evidence, to proceed with indictments under the Sherman Act. He continued: "Up to the present time no evidence has been obtained by the officers of this Department sufficient to justify the institution of legal proceedings, either civil or criminal, against any alleged combinations of wood-pulp or print-paper manufacturers. The information obtained, however, justifies further investigation of the facts, and such investigation is in progress." He indicated his belief that a thorough inquiry might give proof of dereliction.[5] On April 17, the day before Herbert Knox Smith, of the Bureau of Corporations, submitted his report to Congress, President A. N. Burbank of the International Paper Co. visited the Department of Commerce and confidently invited "a searching investigation" of the company's books as a means of demonstrating the "absolute inaccuracy" of Ridder's statements about its operations.[6]

Pressure on the tariff aspects had meantime been developing. After an interview on April 7 Ridder reported: "I am satisfied with the attitude of Speaker Cannon on this question." He later told the Publishers' Association that Cannon had "practically agreed . . ." to let tariff removal go through. When faced with a specific demand to recognize a motion to suspend the rules and permit passage of a particular measure, however, he bethought himself of the possible political consequences and refused, as he put it later, to be "bulldozed." He took refuge in the introduction of a resolution (April 20; passed with commendable celerity on April 21) proposing a select committee of six to investigate a long series of allegations contained in fourteen "whereases" designed to place the publishers' contentions in an unfavorable light. Republican supporters of the proposed research urged the necessity of knowledge prior to action, there being no consensus about whether the high price of paper was due to the tariff, to combination, or to legitimate increases in production costs. One question raised, pertinent here as through all the discussion, was how a tariff, essentially stable since 1890 and through three successive enactments, could suddenly raise paper prices. Democratic opponents combined ridicule of Republican tariff timidity in a presidential year with accusations of trying to circumvent the "old German devil," head of the publishers, in his desire to put through any one of several proposals slumbering in pigeonholes of the Ways and Means Committee. Thrown in for good measure were bitter attacks on Cannonism, part of the filibustering maneuvers which had characterized most of the month. Thus the "Mann Committee," composed of four Republicans and two Democrats, was launched upon a strenuous career of investigation which lasted until February, 1909, occupied weeks of its members' time, took them upon thousands of miles of travel, and piled up hundreds of thousands of words of testimony upon all phases of the problem.[7]

The story of the events of 1908 should be concluded prior to an attempt to evaluate the committee's work, though this involves consideration of some of its activities. The Publishers' Association, in session April 22–24, viewed the Cannon Resolution as a subterfuge which must be combatted by force. Their tactics were compounded of compliance with the demands of the Mann Committee for testimony, which must be furnished, and continued pressure to secure passage of the Stevens Bill, their main objective as long as any hope remained. A formulation presented by Norris on April 22 condemned the Mann Committee and demanded a vote on this measure; it was accompanied by telegrams to all members of Congress seconding this idea. The Committee opened its sessions almost immediately, possibly with the idea of calming the publishers' indignation, and a press delegation consisting largely of Illinoisans (a gentle gesture in Cannon's direction) was appointed to wait upon both Congress and the committee on the 25th. The Association preceded its committee by a telegram to Mann urging action on the Stevens Bill. Norris, spokesman for the publishers, arrogantly rehearsed the papermakers' misdeeds and demanded of the committee a statement of its scope and method of procedure. He stated that the Stevens Bill comprehended the entire range of the publishers' desires, since its passage would break the hold of the combination by restoring competition. His testimony occupied most of the committee's attention for two weeks, when the manufacturers took over.[8]

If Norris was arrogant, the manufacturers were confident. On their behalf David S. Cowles thanked all members of Congress for "declining to unjustly discriminate against our industry, in spite of the coercive attitude of the press . . ." He foreshadowed the industry's defense by declaring that an increase in the costs of pulpwood and labor far outweighed higher paper prices, which incidentally, he asserted, were much less than the publishers had implied. Monopoly was denied. This confidence was matched by the publishers' reluctance to appear in their own behalf; as the hearings moved along it was necessary for both Mann and Ridder to urge them to appear before the committee. On May 3 Ridder privately urged publishers to persuade their Congressmen to support the Stevens Bill, and on the 11th a deputation visited the Speaker on the same errand. The Mann Committee's preliminary report, rendered May 28, was a disappointment to the publishers, for the majority, while not yet ready to commit itself on a permanent tariff policy, attacked the Stevens measure as an insufficient safeguard against Canadian export restrictions. A minority report signed by the Democratic members vigorously supported it. Following the report Mann introduced, by request, a bill said to have had the approval of the State and Treasury Departments and to have been based on a provision in the Dingley Tariff permitting the President to negotiate reciprocal agreements under proper safeguards. This was designed to open the way for removal of the duties if Canada could be persuaded to abandon her restrictions.[9] Congress adjourned two days later; this marked the end of activities for the session.

The poor prospects of the Stevens Bill and the evident intention of the Mann Committee to continue its investigation beyond the adjournment of Congress, together with the none-too-enthusiastic support which the publishers gave their cause, warned the advocates of tariff removal that they were in for a long fight. Before Congress disbanded, Ridder had approached a selected list of publishers with a proposal to hire the willing John Norris for a two-year period to press their cause. It was invidiously suggested that this was done as an individual and not as President of the A.N.P.A., with the implication (which will be supported by evidence below) that the Association's drive was not unanimously supported. Be that as it may, Norris resigned as business manager of the *Times* on June 11 to accept, at a salary of fifteen thousand dollars a year for a two-year period, a task which he had been vigorously prosecuting for years without pay. The A.N.P.A. directors ratified his appointment in a resolution preceded by a formidable series of "whereases" which recited that publishers were "surprised and startled . . ." by recent revelations to the point where it was incumbent upon them to continue the work already begun upon a sounder financial basis than before. Thus began a formal connection which was to continue through the publishers' final triumph in the Underwood Tariff of 1913.[10]

The summer witnessed a few developments. Ridder kept his memory green by a letter to Roosevelt demanding more active steps against combination in various branches of the industry. He also succeeded in getting William Jennings Bryan and the party which nominated him for the Presidency to endorse free pulp and paper in a platform plank which asserted that "Existing duties have given to the manufacturers of paper a shelter behind which they have organized combinations to raise the price of pulp and of paper, thus imposing a tax upon the spread of knowledge. We demand the immediate repeal of the tariff on pulp, print paper, lumber timber, and logs, and that these articles be placed upon the free list."[11] The American Paper and Pulp Association indicated awareness of the coming battle and tightened its belt. President Cowles warned the executive committee of the serious threat to the already too slight tariff protection and counseled "drastic steps" to have the duty retained. As a result the presidency became a full-time position with the function of gathering statistics for the use of the trade. A committee of twenty-five was chosen to assist in providing material for presentation to the proper authorities. Arthur C. Hastings, who soon succeeded to the presidency, announced in his initial communication that "the matter of prices will not be touched upon by this bureau, but we hope in the course of a few months to be able to furnish any member of the association full information regarding the output of his particular grade of paper, the demand for same and the stocks on hand at some particular period . . ." He later admitted that his function was "to educate the manufacturers of paper to the frame of mind whereby they get for their product all the market will warrant." The A.P.P.A. thus followed a trend common during the period, away from outright combination toward formation of trade associations as a means of lessening competition.[12] The next area of conflict was the passage of the Payne-Aldrich Tariff, to which attention will be given after a brief survey of the Mann Committee's activities.

As has been noted, the publishers' delegation arrived for the Mann Committee hearings bearing a chip on its collective shoulder and warning of its "mistrust [of] any inquiry which does not carry with it an assurance of substantially immediate action by both Houses . . ."[13] Norris' opening address charged that all proceedings were intended to delay relief long overdue, promised to furnish proof of manufacturers' misdeeds sufficient to justify piecemeal tariff revision in the publishers' favor, and truculently demanded the range of the committee's inquiry. Mann mildly replied that what the committee wanted was information, and proceeded to extract six volumes of it from both parties and all available sources. The committee busied itself in Washington until May 23 and during the autumn months spent considerable time in the Middle West and in Canada adding to its store. Entering upon his task, as far as could be ascertained, without preconceptions, Mr. Mann presided over a meticulously careful investigation, marshaling the protagonists along with considerable urbanity until an occasionally recalcitrant or evasive witness called forth the acerbity of which he was a master.

Norris occupied the floor the major part of the time for thirteen days, other publishers testifying two full days and parts of three others, with Norris filling in when no publishers were available. The manufacturers filed briefs on May 14, followed by testimony by Cowles, Lyman, Hastings, and other leaders of the industry covering six days, with one day allocated to representatives of labor in the mills. During the Washington hearings Mann took the committee to Hudson Falls, New York, to see the mill of the International Paper Co. and familiarize its members with actual operations. The committee visited several mills and forests in Wisconsin and Minnesota during September and October, held a hearing in Chicago in November, and traveled to Canada in the same month. Two days' testimony at Washington in December completed the formal sessions, and a final report was rendered in February, 1909.

From the first Norris manifested greater facility in assertion, invective, and implication than in hard facts, often permitting his hearers to believe that statements and statistics covering the whole paper industry were confined to newsprint. Mann frequently became impatient with these tactics and from time to time took Norris sharply to task, but was never able to halt them completely. Norris' animus toward the manufacturers was indicated early in the story by a statement which became notorious in the days to come. Though somewhat divorced from its context as later quoted, his statement relative to the International Paper Co.: "I have a theory that I can break these people . . ." is not overdrawn.[14] His main argument was first directed to the removal of the duty on pulp, on the supposition that with this product entering freely, along with free wood, paper manufacture could be divorced from its existing confinement to the areas where water power was abundant and manufacturing was susceptible to concentrated control. The Stevens Bill would of course attain this objective and so break the trust and restore competition. He further asserted that the so-called "independents" in the East were organized into a community of interest to raise prices through a selling agency, while the western mills, despite the dissolution decree of 1908, were still operating in collusion through a "traffic manager." He accused the International of artificial curtailment of output to raise prices and reiterated his standard charges of overcapitalization, overcutting, abuse of tariff benefits, taxation of intelligence, and arbitrary apportionment of customers among the mills. On April 30 Mann pinned him down to admission that the charges of the publishers concerning the exactions of the mills had been exaggerated and had been accompanied by inaccurate statistics from which incorrect inferences could easily be drawn. Presently Norris let it be known that his group would rest its whole case on the fact of combination, with consequent unjustifiable price increases; he desired at this point, he said, to avoid the tariff question until the fact of combination had been demonstrated, and spent a considerable amount of time in trying to establish his thesis.

It soon became increasingly apparent that the publishers were not responding with great alacrity to their opportunity to bedevil the manufacturers. Mann had written to all members of Congress asking them to secure the presence of their constituents who might have interest on either side. On May 1 McCormick asked Mann to order the publishers to appear, since Ridder's strongest request had not availed to bring them in. On the same date Ridder was pleading by telegraph with twelve hundred members of the Associated and United Press groups: "Will you go to Washington next week, if necessary, to testify? Don't hesitate to appear in your own interest . . ." McCormick furnished Mann with a list of forty publishers to whom the chairman sent a special exhortation: "The committee begs to ask whether you will appear before the committee within the next few days and furnish the committee information as to the present and previous prices paid by you for paper, and under what terms of contract . . ." On May 4 McCormick himself sent out telegrams, and on May 6 the committee sent out nearly seven thousand letters to all papers listed as having a circulation of upwards of fifteen hundred, enclosing a questionnaire asking for sworn statements of the prices paid for newsprint over a period extending back to 1890.[15] A leading query was for a judgment whether publishers would be benefited by an immediate removal of the tariff on pulp and paper. When this, together with a follow-up request, elicited only 1,822 replies by mid-June, the committee abandoned further efforts to pursue the matter.[16] About the same time the publishers, perhaps under the impetus of embarrassing questions by the committee, took up the cudgels and on May 12–13 telegraphed thirteen hundred newspapers and sent letters to eighteen thousand publications urging prompt and full replies to the committee's questionnaire. Norris asserted that this was done to assure all publishers that the inquiry was not, as had been the general opinion, an unfriendly one. It was not until May 6 that publishers testified in appreciable numbers, and even here Norris was compelled to step into the breach from time to time.[17]

Their story was a repetitious one of higher prices and increased trouble in securing paper. Repeated inquiry by Thetus W. Sims, a minority member of the committee, to learn whether one set of duties could be removed without disturbing the whole tariff structure led Norris to specify again that the sum of the A.N.P.A. tariff program was removal of duty from groundwood and cheap newsprint, and did not include chemical pulps or fine papers. Sims was also insistent upon drawing out the publishers to determine whether removal of duties would break the combination and reduce prices; here opinion was not unanimous, not all publishers being willing to follow Norris in this particular. On May 13–14 Mann interrogated Norris sharply on the accuracy of A.N.P.A.

charges and forced him again and again to admit that assertion was a larger ingredient of his testimony than real evidence; Norris finally admitted that he expected the committee to gather the evidence on his charges by questioning the International people. On the whole the publishers failed to come off too well before the committee and hardly proved their claims of combination. Their chief spokesman was rudely handled. They did not agree among themselves on the probable effectiveness of removing the duties in lowering prices. The hearings contain many excerpts from contemporary editorial comment, gathered in part by Mann and in part by the manufacturers, which show this divergence. Some opposed tariff reduction on principle. Others maintained that a minority composed of metropolitan papers had secured control of the A.N.P.A. and were using it to their own ends. There was a considerable amount of self-righteous comment by publishers of higher-priced papers that the "penny press," unable to make ends meet, was using this device to get its chestnuts pulled out of the fire.[18]

The manufacturers' case was opened by Cowles of the A.P.P.A., who paid his respects to Norris, denied the charge of combination on behalf of his organization, and denied knowledge of such practices in the industry. He asserted that removal of the tariff would have a tendency to depress the price of paper and would furthermore open the door to foreign competition, both Canadian and Scandinavian, to the detriment of the already impoverished paper industry. He gave it as his considered opinion that most of the large papers were covered by contracts at figures so low as to leave them untouched by any increases which had been imposed. He declared that the whole move was as much a bear raid as any staged on Wall Street and referred to a conversation between himself and Ridder "within forty-eight hours" in which the latter had admitted willingness to do anything within his power to reduce paper prices. Others followed him in denying combination and insisted that there was nothing sinister in a simultaneous price increase by virtually all companies. Lyman entered a general bill of exceptions to Norris' charges in an official statement signed by President Burbank: "The International Paper Company has not now and has not had any agreement or understanding for fixing or maintaining prices or curtailing output of any kind or description with any other paper manufacturer or sales agency whatever.

"It is not a party to any combination. It is not a party to any gentlemen's agreement, or any other agreement affecting prices or output. It has stood and proposes to continue to stand absolutely alone in the sale of paper and in the conduct of its business in every respect . . ." Removal of the duties, the statement continued, would probably have little immediate effect, "but if what the publishers claim is true it would probably eventually transfer the industry to Canada . . ." This would eventuate through stimulating erection of Canadian mills which could undersell those in the States.

Several spokesmen went into details on various phases of the problem, admitting that the International set the price for the industry, repeating denials of any intent to raise the price to $3.00, and asserting that in their opinion the publishers' hullabaloo had been raised by Norris, Seitz, and Ridder, with one eye on their personal pocketbooks. They were inclined to be evasive when queried by Mann about collusion in raising prices in the autumn of 1907, admitting that meetings were held, but denying that prices were set. Sims made the pertinent point that it was most peculiar that they were so careful not to discuss the very thing they would be most likely to discuss. One or two were frank enough to admit that the reason they raised prices was because they needed the money and thought they could get it. A number agreed that tariff removal would be likely to move the industry north of the border unless Canada could be bound to allow free exportation of pulpwood. Mann's questioning of the manufacturers in several instances indicated his interest in a reciprocal agreement with Canada involving removal of the duty on pulp in return for the foregoing concession on Canada's part, which coincides with his bill, mentioned above.

The preliminary report of the majority reflects the trend of the evidence, and without stating it in so many words, justified, with some reservations, the *Paper Trade Journal's* exultant headline: "PAPER MEN WIN." Summarizing the publishers' contentions that prices were up because of a combination of trust and tariff factors, it admitted the increase on new contracts but declared that circumstances justified some increase, without specifying how much. While noting that such manufacturers as had appeared had denied under oath the existence of combination to raise prices, and while admitting that the committee had not found such evidence, the conclusion was that "considerable evidence was presented which might excite suspicion that such a combination had been made and was in existence." Thus the verdict on the publishers' charges was for the moment a Scotch one, but the manufacturers could not rest very easily. Although the committee was not ready to commit itself on a permanent tariff policy, its unwillingness to assent to the removal of existing import taxes without assurances from Canada that it would not impose export duties on paper, pulp, or wood gave more comfort to manufacturers than to publishers. Continuing, the report stated: "It would seem that for the American publisher to be assured of low prices for his paper, it is essential to maintain paper mills in the United States. Any policy that would give the Canadian mills a preferential advantage over American mills in obtaining the raw material at a lower price must inevitably result in the dismantling of American paper machines and the ultimate dependence of American publishers on Canadian mills . . ." The retaliatory duties of the Stevens Bill (on pulp, equal to the export duty imposed; on paper, one-tenth of a cent per pound for each dollar of export duty levied on a cord of pulpwood) were insufficient to justify the risk taken in passing that measure removing all import duties on pulp and newsprint. Still left in abeyance were the charges of combination and the question of a proper tariff rate. The last of these was to be fought again in the Payne-Aldrich Tariff debate, to which the Mann Committee's final report was to furnish an important footnote.[19]

The Ways and Means Committee held a hearing on November 21, 1908, preparatory to the framing of the bill which eventually became the Payne-Aldrich Tariff of 1909. Norris appeared with a fifteen-thousand-word brief which became the subject of acrimonious discussion. The paper-makers' team of Hastings, Cowles, and Lyman took up the rebuttal in a session which lasted from mid-morning until nearly midnight. Most of the standard arguments were rehearsed, some adapted by new emphases to changing circumstances.[20] In response to an early inquiry about his program Norris sounded a new note, perhaps suggested by recent developments connected with the Mann Committee: "Free pulp, free paper, *and reciprocity with Canada for free pulp wood, free paper, and free pulp*" (author's italics). This, probably the most important new feature of the hearings, proposed to remove American duties on pulp and newsprint from Canada in return for Canadian assurances of no restrictions on exports of wood, pulp, or paper. In addition to repeating at length his usual arguments about tariffs and manufacturers' combinations, Norris emphasized particularly the aspects of labor and conservation in the problem. American mills, it was charged, paid their labor less than Canadian, thus robbing the workers of their share of the benefits of protection. He capitalized on the current interest in conservation by emphasizing the inroads the manufacturers were making upon American forests, which were totally unable to provide for the industry's needs. At the same time he charged them with buying rights to huge Canadian tracts as speculations against an American shortage, using money for this which should have gone into improving their American properties. He gave fantastic figures on Canadian spruce resources, asserting that with American cutting stopped altogether, Canada possessed sufficient timber to supply the American market for two hundred years without any attempt at replacement.[21]

Opening for the manufacturers, Hastings paid his respects to Norris' recital: "I never did like that paper, and this is the third or fourth time I have heard the most of it." So frequently had Norris charged combination among manufacturers that their unanimous denial was almost an automatic response. Their main attention was devoted to urging retention of existing tariff rates. Removal, they asserted, would open the domestic market to European as well as Canadian competition, which would be disastrous because of European investors' willingness to take a lower income on their investments. The tariff, low in comparison with that on other commodities, was mainly useful as an insurance policy. As Hastings put it: "We believe that when business is normal and the demand equal to the supply the tariff has little or no direct influence on prices. During times of depression it is a protection to the home manufacturer, but with the present tariff, under any conditions, the rate is not so high but what foreign paper or pulp can be imported into this country to supply the demand without particular hardship to the consumer." Remove the tariff, however, and the inevitable, though possibly not immediate, result would be the closing of American mills and the gradual transfer of the industry to Canada within ten years. This aspect of the situation received much greater attention than in any previous period. Furthermore, reduction of the duties would be the reverse of a conservation measure, as Norris had argued, for it would force the domestic producers to cut their timber indiscriminately as a means of meeting the new Canadian competition which would result; as much as five million acres would be devastated, according to one statement.

The Mann Committee rendered its unanimous final report on February 19, 1909, prior to the introduction of the Payne Bill.[22] It gave cold comfort to the mill men. It admitted frankly the inadequacy of domestic spruce to supply prospective needs and by the same token confessed dependence upon the Canadian product. It proposed retention of the existing duty of one-twelfth of a cent per pound ($1.67 per ton) on mechanical pulp, with the proviso that this be remitted in the case of pulp coming from any area which imposed no export restrictions.[23] To induce the removal of existing Canadian restrictions, a *quid pro quo* must be offered. This was to take the form of reducing from $6.00 to $2.00 per ton the duty on newsprint valued at not over two and one-fourth cents per pound, again on condition that no interference should be given to the exportation of wood, pulp, or paper; any such levy would restore the full $6.00 rate. The retention of the $2.00 rate was justified on both revenue and protective grounds, and was asserted to be about equal to the difference in cost of production in the two areas. It was, in the words of one of the committee, an effort "to perpetuate the American newsprint paper industry in this country. We want to continue the newsprint manufacture and have newsprint paper sold at as low a price as is consistent with a fair profit. The only way that can be secured is by opening our ports under proper reciprocal arrangements by granting Canada some concessions for the admission of its pulp and paper in return for their free pulp wood, and at the same time adequately protecting the American paper manufacturer." This was obviously intended as an olive branch extended to Canada to insure continued supplies of raw materials by the reciprocity of giving the Canadian finished product free access to our market. The report, however, was vulnerable in at least one respect: What was intended as an olive branch south of the border could be interpreted north of it as a club waved under Canadian noses to force abandonment of perfectly legitimate provincial restrictions of long standing under which contractual obligations had been incurred. The subsequent story will show that this antithesis between the olive branch and the club was to be one of the crucial problems of the coming months. Moreover, it took no great discernment to discover in the committee's recognition of Americans' dependence upon Canadian wood a potent weapon which might if necessary be brandished in retaliation.[24]

The report left the leading journal of the paper industry completely speechless for over two weeks, after which it commented caustically on the "incomprehensible" recommendations of the committee. The change of front involved in the proposal to cut duties was interpreted in the light of a desire to conserve domestic forest resources. After taking some time to formulate a defense, Hastings spoke for the manufacturers. He charged that the committee's tariff-reduction proposals had never been supported by more than a small minority of the publishers, one that was composed mainly of Democrats "whose principles and beliefs coincide with their desires in this matter . . ." The suggested scheme left the manufacturers "aghast at the danger of ruin which confronts them." He pointed to the fact that the final report made no mention of the charges of monopoly and conspiracy in restraint of trade which had formed the original basis of the investigation. He denied the prediction of ultimate failure of the domestic supply of raw material, alleging that vegetable fiber and other woods could be used in the event of exhaustion of the spruce forests. He asserted that repeal of the duties would defeat the object of conservation by forcing domestic producers to strip their timber lands in order to recoup their investments against the competition of cheap Canadian paper. The reason why the Government "should surrender an industry to another country by legislation . . . is, in our opinion left altogether obscure . . ." The organized publishers left no record of their attitude toward the report; doubtless they occupied themselves with trying to decide whether this half-loaf was, or was not, an improvement upon no bread.[25]

It now becomes necessary to examine the tortuous legislative history of the pulp and paper sections of the Payne-Aldrich Tariff Act. This is essentially a narrative of the way in which the controversy over print paper became involved in the larger tariff problem, its subjection to conflicting pressures, and its emergence in a practical victory for the manufacturers, in hope deferred for the publishers, in the creation of an embarrassing international situation, and, in the long run, in a heavy contribution to the downfall of the Republicans in 1912. It furnishes an excellent commentary on the involved and sometimes devious processes by which tariff rates are arrived at in general revisions, and perhaps even points a moral in the direction of a more scientific approach, if such there be.

Payne's introductory remarks threw light on the process by which these sections of the act were framed. He announced that he had already satisfied himself, before the Mann Report came in, that mechanical pulp might be free-listed without injury to any domestic interest. The report, therefore, merely reinforced his own judgment. He had not, he said, come to any decision regarding newsprint, and adopted the recommendation of the committee in this respect. Thus the bill embodied the exact terms of the Mann Report; adopted them, Payne asserted, under the impression that both publishers and manufacturers were satisfied with its solution of the question. It will be recalled that the manufacturers had waited some time before deciding what line their dissatisfaction with the Report should take; it was during this period that the schedules were set, and Payne adhered to them despite the manufacturers' protests later received.[26]

It was soon apparent that it was useless to appeal to Payne for rate changes in either direction. Both sides turned to the Senate where, before the Finance Committee, on the floor, and before the Conference Committee, pulp and paper, along with lumber, hides, and gloves, became the storm center of complicated maneuvers which finally resulted in a considerable increase in the paper rates, to the corresponding discomfiture of the publishers. The House debate covered many of the routine arguments previously adduced and was notable mainly for pronouncements by Stafford (already noted) and Mann. The latter took the floor on March 31 to insist that he and his committee had refused to be bulldozed by either party to the controversy. He had, he said, resisted newspaper pressure to make a stand for a tariff reduction in the preliminary report, published on the eve of a hot political campaign when the tariff was an issue. He had on the other hand recommended tariff reductions in the final report, despite manufacturers' desires to the contrary. He asserted that Government intervention was the only possible means of securing an adequate domestic supply of spruce; otherwise eventual dependence upon Canada was inevitable. He once more extended the olive branch of reciprocity to Canada by means of his Report and the provisions of the Payne Bill: "we offer to exchange with Canada a freer market for her pulp and paper products for a freer and fuller opportunity of securing from her the raw material with which to maintain our own pulp and paper mills." [27]

The Senate Finance Committee engaged in its usual anticipatory explorations prior to House action on the Payne Bill on April 9. Norris reported to the annual convention of the Publishers' Association (April 22) that he had been summoned to Washington about five weeks earlier and told that the Senate "had been fixed up against us, and that there was trouble for us unless we could bring pressure from the newspapers of the country." He finally visited Nelson W. Aldrich, chairman of the committee, in company with Ridder and Seitz, on April 6. Aldrich's attitude was not very friendly at first; he opened by asking how far his callers considered themselves representative of the nation's press, since he had been informed that their program was the work of interested agitators. At another session Norris met in Aldrich's office in a two-and-a-half hour discussion with Senator Reed Smoot and representatives of the A.P.P.A. and the International Paper Company. Aldrich stated frankly that he was a protectionist and would be governed in the matter at hand by the comparative cost of manufacture in the United States and in Canada. Norris pointed out that cost figures were available in the Mann Committee Report; Aldrich refused to accept these, but accepted from Lyman others purporting to show a Canadian cost of $8.00 per ton less than that in the United States. On the basis of these figures the manufacturers opposed any change in the duties. Norris championed the Mann-Payne proposal, the publishers evidently having decided to take this half-loaf rather than strive for complete removal of the paper duties. Neither side would compromise its position, and the conference dispersed. Norris gave the devil his due, however, and commented on Aldrich's willingness to listen—an attitude to which Aldrich was probably not unaccustomed, since he was being subjected to pressure from fifty thousand manufacturers while trying to adjust the rates on four thousand items. The committee evidently reached an impasse similar to that of the conference, for the Aldrich substitute was reported without a clause concerning pulp and paper.[28]

There ensued a period of relative quiet while the Senate busied itself with other affairs. The Publishers' Association circularized the upper House urging adoption of the House proposals, and adopted resolutions commending Cannon (!) for instigating the Mann Committee and the Committee for its valuable work. In June Norris sought a committee hearing in order to rebut some of the evidence on Canadian costs already in the record. Early in the same month Sir Lomer Gouin, Prime Minister of Quebec, threatened further restrictions on the exportation of pulpwood.[29]

The lull was broken on the seventeenth when Aldrich reported the proposals governing pulp and paper. Wood pulp was left untouched for the moment, but the Finance Committee recommended doubling the House proposal on newsprint, raising the rate to $4.00. The issue was sharply drawn by an amendment offered by Norris Brown of Nebraska, the effect of which would be to put newsprint on the free list. He called attention to Gouin's recent threats and asserted that it was our duty to make the first move toward conciliating Canada rather than one which would antagonize her. Eugene Hale of Maine, a paper State, objected on the other hand to even this modest concession, asserting that had the committee considered the difference in the cost of labor, as well as in the cost of wood, it would have recommended a rate of five or six dollars; actually he claimed, American wood cost $6.00 per ton, and American labor $2.00 per ton more than Canadian. A hot discussion followed, with sharp differences on the question of labor costs, with Hale charging that the Mann Committee investigation had been superficial in this regard. Aldrich seconded this charge, admitting his refusal to accept the Mann Committee figures on costs, and maintaining that neither the publishers nor the manufacturers had furnished him with adequate evidence on relative production costs with the single exception of figures on the Belgo-Canadian Company, on the accuracy of which both sides agreed. Hale's colleague William P. Frye, Jacob H. Gallinger of New Hampshire, and others participated in the debate, which lasted for most of two days before the Brown amendment was defeated.[30]

After some further discussion Robert M. LaFollette of Wisconsin proposed an amendment making the Aldrich proposals effective until July 1, 1912, when the rate would revert to $2.00 per ton; this, he said, would give the Western mills time to change to other grades of paper not requiring spruce. Aldrich presently took the floor and delivered a strong indictment of Canada, which country, he said, had recently "officially announced" its purpose to transfer the pulp-and-paper industry north of the border. He asked rhetorically whether we should help this effort to destroy our economy. Asserting that the Mann Committee had not given sufficient consideration to the difference in wood costs, confining its figures to the differential in labor and materials (ascertained to be $2.00 on the ton), he maintained that the Finance Committee's investigations had disclosed a differential of $4.00 per ton of paper in the cost of wood. It was this differential, disregarding the Mann Committee's figure, which the Finance Committee suggested as the duty, despite the fact that it did not account for all the difference in cost of production.

Referring to provincial export restrictions as "the methods of the middle ages," he announced that "if all they have to do is to make a threat of this kind and the American Senate prostrates itself before them, then we will reduce this duty or repeal it. If we intend to protect this great industry in the United States, then we ought to strengthen the duty. We ought to put upon the importation of pulp and pulp wood and paper in the United States such restrictions as will notify the Dominion of Canada that this is not entirely a one-sided proposition, that we have some interests to serve, and that we have some rights to maintain on this side of the line . . ." He also indicated that the committee proposed to apply the new maximum and minimum provisions specifically to pulp, paper, and wood from Canada. These stated that in case of undue discrimination by any country or province against American products, an added levy of 25 per cent ad valorem might be charged as a maximum duty after March 31, 1910. This could be used as a club to prevent such actions as the threatened Canadian export restrictions. Aldrich, however, was fearful that such general regulations might not suffice to ward off the Canadian danger, and so it was proposed to add amendments "safeguarding the interests of the United States with reference to these discriminations, and not to leave it to maximum and minimum provisions" alone. After some further debate the LaFollette amendment was rejected and the Aldrich proposal of $4.00 per ton adopted in Committee of the Whole.[31]

The following day Aldrich offered his substitute for the wood-pulp provision. It continued the rate of one-twelfth of a cent per pound, or $1.67 per ton, as of the House Bill, but in addition to the Mann Committee's conciliatory proviso remitting this in return for Canada's abandonment of export restrictions, it imposed a countervailing duty equal in amount to any possible export levies, plus a retaliatory proviso doubling the duty on pulp in case the exportation of pulp, logs, or wood for use in the manufacture of pulp should be prohibited. Thus the net result of the Finance Committee proposals was to withdraw half of the Mann Committee's $4.00 *quid pro quo* on newsprint, and on pulp to add a double club of countervailing duties to forestall export taxes and of doubled duties to forestall export prohibition—these to be invoked *unless* provincial restrictions were removed, as an alternative to the

Mann offer to remove all duties *if* restrictions were removed. He admitted that his proposals would impose a penalty on the American people if it were necessary to import these articles, but held, contrary to the Mann Report, that domestic spruce would last indefinitely, and insisted that he was "simply asking them, in a persuasive way, to remove unreasonable restrictions which they are placing upon the export of articles to the United States." His scheme, in a nutshell, was that unless Canada was willing to let her pulp and paper come to us without export restrictions, she must expect to push them into the United States over a slightly higher tariff wall.

Somewhat later he proposed the addition of a countervailing duty to the print-paper section (which, it will be noted, had already been adopted) adding to the proposed $4.00 duty the amount of any export charge on wood, pulp, or paper exported to this country, and a further retaliatory proviso that if the President proclaimed any export prohibition or restriction to be unduly discriminatory against the United States, the duty should be doubled. The retaliatory duty on pulp was at the same time changed to depend upon presidential proclamation. After conference with Brown, the latter introduced two proposals, the first admitting pulp free until the President proclaimed undue discrimination, whereupon $1.67 per ton would be levied. The newsprint rate was left at $4.00 until a presidential proclamation of undue discrimination, whereupon it would be doubled. The effect of these would be to make retaliation dependent upon presidential proclamation rather than automatically operative. Brown also pointed out that his amendments opened the way to exploration of the whole question by the President in conjunction with other interested governments. The Brown substitutes were agreed to without debate, and went into the bill as it passed the Senate.[32]

In the Conference Committee report (which became the

Payne-Aldrich Act of August 5, 1909) the section on pulp resembled the final Aldrich version except for the retaliatory provision: mechanical pulp was to be taxed $1.67 per ton, but to enter freely from any area not limiting the exportation of printing paper (paper had not been included in the original Aldrich version), pulp, or wood; the countervailing provision was retained, but the retaliatory clause doubling the duties upon presidential proclamation of undue discrimination was omitted. The paper rate was changed from $4.00 as originally passed by the Senate to $3.75, with a surtax of $2.00 additional, plus the amount of any export levy, in case of export restrictions. The larger retaliatory aspects of the matter were taken care of by the general maximum and minimum provisions, allowing the imposition, after March 31, 1910, of maximum duties of 25 per cent ad valorem, above the regular duties, against any area which unduly discriminated against the United States. More immediately, the countervailing and surtax provisions might involve complications with the Canadian Provinces, Ontario (which had forbidden exportation of Crown-land wood) and Quebec (which had not yet done so, but was considering it, and which already taxed wood exports). Ontario stood to lose by the countervailing duty, and Quebec might well be induced by the same levy to follow Ontario into complete prohibition. It was against this possibility that the maximum and minimum provisions were designed to operate as a club, since further restrictions might, if interpreted as undue discrimination, operate to invoke the maximum rates against Canadian exports to the United States.[33] Most immediate of all, however, was the peril to the publishers involved in the $3.75 newsprint rate, which to them constituted an altogether unpalatable alternative to the $2.00 Mann-Payne arrangements. The emergence of this grievance must now receive attention.

There is no evidence available to indicate that the publishers were actively represented before the Conference Committee; the manufacturers' interest was supported vigorously by Frye and evidently by Hale. The trade press gives him fulsome praise for his work in maintaining a high rate on newsprint, though the evidence is not so clear from other sources. Payne seems to have offered to split the difference between the House and Senate rates and settle on $3.00, but, as he reported to the House, the Senate conferees refused because of the alleged higher cost of wood in the United States. It was at this point that Frye's influence was apparently exerted. Taft's letters contain a number of references to his desire to hold the rate at $3.00; he seems to have been impressed with the need for a fairly high figure by LaFollette. As the Conference Committee wrangle wore on, other items such as lumber and hides bulked larger, and the print-paper matter tended to recede into the background in his correspondence; indeed, he must have agreed to the $3.75 rate some days before the report was completed. Mann also appeared before the committee, but his testimony was evidently not given much weight; Payne considered that the Mann proposal of $2.00 per ton was more a diplomatic move to induce Canada to relax her restrictions (as indeed it was) than a reflection of actual cost differentials. On the whole, the higher Senate rate would appear to be the result of the predisposition of its leaders toward the protective principle combined with the aggressive activities of certain Senators and the indifference of the publishers, this last perhaps due to their not knowing much of what was going on in the Conference Committee.[34]

The feature of the debate on the Conference Committee's report was Mann's attack on its paper provisions and his vote against it because of them. He expressed satisfaction with the pulp provisions, which he had drafted for the committee and which allowed free importation from those Provinces which removed or did not impose restrictions on the exportation of wood, pulp, or paper. The paper clause and the maximum provision, however, destroyed any possible good effect of this. The maximum tariff, he pointed out, would make the duty on pulp $1.67 plus 25 per cent ad valorem on pulp worth currently $20 per ton, or $6.67. He compared favorably the conciliatory aspects of his own proposal of $4.00 reduction on newsprint with the Senate scheme, which would have raised the duty from $6.00 to $8.00, and with the conference measure, which would leave it, if the Canadian restrictions were not removed, at $5.75, or at $3.75 if these were removed. He gave his "deliberate judgment . . . that under the provisions of the House bill no new restrictions upon the exportation of pulp wood would have been imposed by the Canadian Provinces and the existing restrictions would have been removed and that our print-paper industries would have obtained a plentiful supply of pulp wood from Canada at reasonable cost for all time . . ." He repeated on another occasion his belief that Canada would have accepted his proposal and the Provinces would have removed their restrictions had the $2.00 rate on print-paper been enacted into law.[35] He believed that the scheme as it stood would cause prohibition or further restriction of pulpwood exports and thus raise the cost of newsprint in the United States by creating a scarcity of raw material. He also pointed out a joker in the maximum tariff clause, in a statement that our minimum rates should apply only so long as the President was satisfied that another country "imposes no export duty or prohibition" upon exportation of goods to this country. This, he said, was inserted into the bill in the conference, and was aimed at imposing the maximum tariff on pulp and paper coming from Quebec. He dubbed the whole scheme a big stick waved at Canada, in contrast with his own olive branch, and warned his hearers of the wrath to come when the publishers began paying the higher paper prices inevitably in store. The conference report presently passed the House, with Mann one of twenty Republicans who failed in a parliamentary maneuver to send it back to conference.[36]

The immediate results of the tariff legislation were as follows: The Canadian Provinces refused to submit to the Payne-Aldrich club and relax their export restrictions. This meant that print paper coming from Crown-land wood cut in Ontario and Quebec paid $5.75 after August 26, 1909, when a Treasury Department ruling imposed the $2.00 surtax. Ontario wood pulp continued to pay $1.67 on entry into the States; that from Quebec paid $1.92, thanks to the countervailing provision which added her twenty-five cent export levy. On September 6 Premier Gouin announced prospective prohibition of exportation of Crown-land wood. Fundamentally the relations between the United States and Canada had been endangered by the possibility of imposition of the maximum rates against the Dominion on March 31, 1910, which in the case of paper would make the duty approximately $14.50 per ton. All in all, the manufacturers had won a considerable victory. Paper duties had been cut only slightly, pulp duties not at all. Canada, the essential source of raw material, had been antagonized and an international problem had been created. Publishers' first reaction to all this was, in effect, "it might have been worse," and a search for a scapegoat. The luckless Taft bulked too large to miss, and as time passed he became increasingly the object of their attention in an effort to persuade him to further action. It is not uninteresting to note that the publishers appropriated the Mann Committee proposals unto themselves and by September were talking as if these had all along represented their desires, whereas previous pages have indicated that the Mann proposals marked only a way station on the road to the free pulp and paper which had been the publishers' original goal.[37]

The reader who has not lost himself in the details of hearings and debates will discern in the recent story a tug-of-war which, while see-sawing back and forth, has not yet resulted in victory for either contestant group. Publishers' pressure activated the Mann Committee, originally designed as a piece of Fabian tactics by the harassed Republicans wary of tariff legislation in a presidential year. Its initial report put the manufacturers ahead. Its final report, issued on the eve of a general revision, caused a mild surge toward the publishers by conditionally recommending downward revision. Alarmed, the manufacturers nerved themselves and, with the aid of friends in the Senate, virtually eliminated downward revision on their items. As the chapter closes, the issue is still in doubt with manufacturers resting in their places and publishers digging in for another pull, hoping to catch their adversaries off balance.

CHAPTER V

Tariff Battle: Conclusion, 1910–1913

RECENT PAGES, concerned primarily with the tariff, have been developing international overtones. These overtones tend, until the end of 1911, to usurp the main theme. The newsprint question, indeed, becomes so enmeshed in the tangles of Canadian-American relations that its role, though important, becomes secondary. This is due partly to the facts of the case and partly to the not-unadroit tactics of the publishers, who found in reciprocity a means of achieving their personal ends while appearing to be contending unselfishly for the American farmer and a great public principle of international comity. With free newsprint a happy incident of the reciprocity legislation, the publishers had only to press their temporary victory to a more permanent one in the Underwood Tariff of 1913.

Against this background other decisive events have come to pass. The American producers, seeing the handwriting traced dimly on the wall in the Payne-Aldrich Act and limned more definitely by reciprocity and depletion of the domestic spruce supply, began to transfer their pulp plants and later their paper mills to Canada, avidly abetted by their Canadian compatriots. There began thus an infiltration of American capital into the Canadian paper industry which has been one of the most significant developments of the present century and which, while not simplifying the problem of Canadian-American relations regarding paper, rendered the tariff decreasingly apt as an instrument toward its solution. The first and obvious result was a stimulus to the Canadian industry and a corresponding check to that below the border. Whereas in 1909 the United States had produced its entire newsprint supply, imports then being negligible, a decade later two-thirds of the newsprint consumption came either directly or in the raw state from foreign sources, mainly Canadian, and by 1926 Canadian newsprint production outstripped the record output of United States mills.[1] This shift to Canada ushered in a period of overproduction comparable to that in the States in the eighties and nineties, which helped to hold prices stationary or to force them down. Publishers were therefore reasonably complacent for a time, having won their tariff fight and being saved from high prices by the Canadian production. It is worthy of note, however, that less price reduction than expected resulted from these developments. The period of quietude thus induced lasted until the crisis of war sent prices rocketing and again arrayed the protagonists in line of battle.

Two attempts were made toward the end of 1909 to break the impasse with Canada. One attempt was made by two bills introduced by Mann early in December in line with the publishers' desires. The first was a standard free-paper-and-pulp offer in return for removal of Canadian restrictions and prohibitions. This, it will be noted, went beyond Mann's committee proposals. The other would postpone the effective date of the maximum rates from April 1, 1910, until January 1, 1911, giving the President time to explore the question of undue discrimination at greater leisure. This would minimize the danger of a trade war with Canada. It fell by the wayside in the face of Cannon's hostility and Taft's desire to postpone tariff legislation pending a report of the newly created Tariff Commission.[2] The second attempt proposed to implement the threat contained in the maximum provisions of the Payne-Aldrich Act. Gouin had meantime (September 6) announced formally Quebec's plan to follow Ontario in prohibiting exportation of Crown-land wood, though it was presently reported that action would probably be postponed until September 1, 1910. This moved Lyman, of the International, to comment on certain compensating features which might render such action of little value to the Provinces. There was first the fact that American forests would supply the market's needs for some years to come; second, many American concerns owned large Canadian tracts in fee, whence wood could be exported free from provincial interference. Again, much wood was already cut and so beyond local control. Finally, he unsheathed the club of maximum duties: "It would be an unfortunate thing to have to invoke the application of this provision against any of the provinces of Canada on account of their attitude in this matter of pulp wood exportation, but this provision was incorporated into the law for just such a purpose and was so drawn as to exactly cover this particular situation." [3]

The period following the Payne-Aldrich legislation must have remained one of the least pleasant memories of William Howard Taft. It witnessed the focussing of several acutely embarrassing factors. His Winona speech defending this limping revision did not soothe those honestly aggrieved at the party's failure to keep its promise. The revolt against Cannonism and Insurgent recalcitrance destroyed effective control of the House. A mid-term Congressional election impended, with all its latent dangers. The newspaper press cloaked its peculiar disappointment at the Payne-Aldrich rates in a general attack on the administration's tariff failure. Added to these factors was the possibility of complications with Canada over the maximum rates. This, however, was also an opportunity, for it afforded a chance to initiate a wider activity in reciprocity negotiations. Continued newspaper pressure on the President by the disappointed publishers doubtless contributed to his willingness to enter this wider field.[4]

Manifold pressure was applied during the pendency of the maximum-rate question directed simultaneously at the Administration and at the manufacturers. Ridder's letter of October 18, 1909, sounded a warning note apropos of Taft's ill-advised sanction of the $3.75 rate on newsprint. This rate, Ridder alleged, had prompted Quebec to forbid pulpwood exports, with the result that "The country is now in a fair way for a trade war with Canada because of your apparent failure to read carefully the Mann Committee's recommendations . . . We trust that you can find some method of rectifying the mistake into which you were led . . ." Norris, now referred to in the trade press as "Microbe" Norris, placed alleged evidence of manufacturers' misdeeds under the anti-trust acts in the hands of a United States District Attorney late in December. These concerned the insertion by the mill men of so-called "trade customs" in the annual contracts; the publishers declared that these were instruments of price regulation and suggested a contract form of their own as a remedy, but nothing further developed. While the maximum tariff was still a threat, a proposal was launched to rush through Congress the Mann Bill postponing the effective date of this potential disturber of the Canadian-American peace. At the same time, and later, steps were taken to urge the passage of Mann's other bill providing for free pulp and paper in return for free wood.[5]

Meantime the President undertook to remove the threat of the maximum tariff. France and the Dominion had negotiated a trade treaty whereby, in return for concessions granted, French goods paid the intermediate scale of the Canadian three-level tariff upon importation into Canada. Study convinced United States tariff experts that unless Canada extended to this country concessions in the Canadian market similar to those accorded French products, Canada would be "discriminating" within the terms of the Payne-Aldrich Act, and her goods entering the United States would be subject to the maximum rates after March 31. After complicated negotiations in which Taft took a personal hand, Canada extended to the United States a largely formal concession of intermediate rates which made it possible for the President to announce that there was no discrimination. During the discussion Taft proposed and the Canadians accepted an offer to pursue the question of trade relations on a broader scale, looking toward reciprocity.

This episode, while it averted a danger, solved no problems for either publishers or manufacturers. The former still had to contend with the Payne-Aldrich rates (though in fairness it should be noted that the Treasury Department restricted the retaliatory aspects of that Act to Crown-land pulp and paper and admitted the products of privately held land at the regular rates); the manufacturers were disappointed at Fielding's statement that he had refused to urge the Provinces to modify their export policies. The results of this abstention were quickly apparent. The Quebec Parliament had been in session since March 15, waiting for the cat to jump. On April 1 Gouin announced a ban on exportation of unmanufactured pulpwood from the Crown lands, the effective date being presently set for May 1. This meant that thousands of square miles of timber limits, acquired by United States interests with the intention of exporting the wood, were immobilized unless the situation changed radically. It ranged Quebec export policy squarely alongside Ontario's, and evidenced anew provincial determination to transfer pulp manufacture to the Dominion. From the standpoint of the present narrative, it meant that further action was called for.[6]

While Taft and his advisers were looking hopefully to continued reciprocity discussions within a short time, the publishers returned to the charge. Their immediate objective was the Mann Bill removing duties from pulp and paper in return for removal of restrictions, though in the face of Quebec's action it is difficult to see how this could have been more than a makeweight in the reciprocity negotiations. The Publishers' Association adopted resolutions urging its passage, and Ridder wrote Taft a strong letter in the same vein late in April.[7] Their attitude changed within a few days, for on May 5 Charles M. Pepper of the Bureau of Trade Relations of the Department of State, a principal adviser of the Administration through the reciprocity period, told Taft that they were urging immediate negotiation of a special treaty limited to pulp and paper, with a view to seeking ratification before Congress adjourned. This shift seems to have been based on the feeling that a special arrangement in treaty form might be less likely to precipitate a general tariff discussion and in all probability was an attempt to stampede the Administration into action. The only apparent explanation of this *volte-face* is Ridder's contention that a paper famine was imminent. A strike in the International mills had increased the price of paper on the "spot" or noncontract market by $9.00 per ton within a few weeks, and on March 31 the Commissioner of Corporations reported that the stock on hand in the mills was only 19,907 tons, or less than a six-day supply. Back of this was doubtless the fear that the manufacturers might take advantage of the Quebec embargo to raise the price, though Pepper pointed out that the International had already cut enough wood on its Crown-land limits to maintain production at current levels for a year and a half, and official reports repeatedly indicated that the major proportion of wood imports came from private lands. In advising against this method of procedure, Pepper indicated his belief that the most feasible plan would be to include pulp and paper in a general trade discussion, which he hoped might be inaugurated shortly.[8]

The Canadians were unwilling to open negotiations, as Pepper had hoped, and the summer saw relatively few developments. In June, Norris advised the publishers to bear the market in view of increasing production, and in July the paper mills were advised to curtail output, which was done. Prices declined, and stocks accumulated. Pepper explored the possibilities of securing wood from Newfoundland, by means of reciprocity negotiations, in order to build a backfire against Quebec's intransigence.[9] This intransigence, however, was manifested again in a second step in the provincial campaign to move the pulp industry northward. In midsummer (effective as of September 1) the provincial authorities announced an export embargo on pulpwood cut from land held on so-called "location tickets." These were documents issued to prospective settlers permitting them to clear one hundred acres prior to actual occupation, and they were susceptible to abuse by those who secured the tickets merely as a means of getting the wood.[10] The impression gained ground in some American governmental circles that the Canadian prohibitions were not, after all, likely to be of great immediate influence, since it was estimated that only about 15 per cent of the Quebec pulpwood cut came from Crown lands. This, added to the enormous supplies stacked up prior to May 1, led Pepper in September to repeat his earlier judgment that the government should not yield to publishers' pressure for a separate and special treaty, but should persuade them to wait on a general reciprocity negotiation. This did not prevent Ridder from circularizing his constituents in the same month with an appeal to obtain from their Congressional candidates assurance that they would favor "the immediate adoption of a reciprocity agreement with Canada and Newfoundland . . ."

upon the same terms as the Mann Bill, still gathering dust in a committee's pigeonhole.[11]

The Taft Administration, with one eye on the November election, sought to launch its reciprocity program in October, and the pulp-and-paper question took its place along with other considerations in the larger program. Pepper was still convinced that provincial restrictions would not affect the supply for an indefinite period; he nevertheless counseled that in the general negotiations the United States should offer to remove the countervailing levies of $1.67 on pulp and $2.00 on paper, and should further reduce the Payne-Aldrich rate on the latter from $3.75 to $2.00. The American delegation to a conference held at Ottawa early in November carried instructions calling for a $2.00 rate on newsprint coming from Provinces laying no export restrictions. This offer was coupled with others relative to manufactures which gave the Canadian negotiators pause and precipitated a contest of maneuver in which the paper question, as far as the record shows, received only incidental consideration. The meeting terminated without decisive action on the main issues, though the $2.00 rate on newsprint was tentatively agreed upon and the Canadian delegates left the way open for later discussion of pulpwood.

Conferences were resumed in Washington on January 7, 1911, and continued through the twenty-first. The agreement was announced on the twenty-sixth in the form of proposals for concurrent legislative action rather than a treaty. The American delegation proposed the $2.00 rate on newsprint, with removal of countervailing levies, but a loophole was left whereby this might be modified "if in view of the unwillingness of the Canadian Provinces to remove their pulp-wood restrictions except in return for outright free paper the President thinks the American publishers are entitled to this concession." The Canadians evidently made no concessions, for the scanty records available show that early in the negotiations the

Americans were thinking in terms of free paper in return for removal of export restrictions. Thus the matter finally stood, Fielding being unwilling to commit his Government to the application of pressure to the Provinces; the whole episode testifies to the fact that "State Rights" is not a peculiarly American tradition. The summarizing memorandum of agreement stated: "We stand on free print paper, on condition of the removal of restrictions on the exportation of pulp wood by the Canadian provinces. The Canadian negotiators assent to our putting this condition precedent in our legislation, while at the same time not including it in the proposition which they will lay before Parliament . . ." Fielding's letter to Philander C. Knox indicating the Canadian concept of the agreement repeated this idea: "With respect to the discussions that have taken place concerning the duties upon the several grades of pulp, printing-paper, etc. . . . we note that you desire to provide that such articles from Canada shall be made free of duty in the United States only upon certain conditions respecting the shipment of pulp-wood from Canada. It is necessary that we should point out that this is a matter in which we are not in a position to make any agreement. The restrictions at present existing in Canada are of a Provincial character. They have been adopted by several of the Provinces with regard to what are believed to be Provincial interests. We have neither the right nor the desire to interfere with the Provincial authorities in the free exercise of their constitutional powers in the administration of their public lands. The provisions you are proposing to make respecting the conditions upon which these classes of pulp and paper may be imported into the United States free of duty must necessarily be for the present inoperative. Whether the Provincial Governments will desire to in any way modify their regulations with a view of securing the free admissions of pulp and paper from their Provinces into the markets of the United States must be a question for the Provincial authorities to decide. In the meantime the present duties on pulp and paper imported from the United States into Canada will remain. Whenever pulp and paper of the classes already mentioned are admitted into the United States free of duty from all parts of Canada, then similar articles, imported from the United States, shall be admitted into Canada free of duty." [12]

The publishers were interested observers of the November negotiations but continued to press for passage of the Mann Bill as a means of softening the price of paper without the risks of a reciprocity treaty.[13] They were evidently won over to support of the Administration technique, as they were given advance notice of the terms of the agreement, which Ridder communicated to his constituents two days before they were publicly announced. He made the point, implicit but not included in any official pronouncement to date, that the agreement provided "for the admission of print paper and wood pulp free of duty when made from wood cut on private lands or free from restrictions of exportation.

"If ratified by Congress, this arrangement will immediately and automatically insure a full supply of print paper free of duty, and will exert a pressure upon the provincial authorities which will ultimately force them to remove their restrictions on exportations of pulp wood . . ." Complacent approbation followed on publication of the agreement: "This draft is entirely satisfactory to publishers. It will provide for the immediate entry of print paper and wood pulp from Canada. The snarl with the provinces of Canada has been completely avoided by an entirely new turn to the stipulations, which now follow the wood—not the province. If wood is free from restriction, such as wood from private lands, the products of that wood will come into the United States free of duty . . ." [14] The agreement thus adroitly avoided disturbing Canadian provincial autonomy and won over the American publishers by giving them access to raw materials free of duty, a cheap price for such powerful support. It remained to convey this gently to legislative ears. On February 4 Secretary Knox wrote Sereno E. Payne, of the Ways and Means Committee, a judiciously worded hint which was eventually translated into legislation: "Inasmuch as this proposed conditional arrangement has not been accepted by Canada as a part of the agreement, except in the sense that, when, and if, it is made operative by American legislation to secure free admission of these articles into the United States from all parts of Canada, Congress may, without impairing the agreement arrived at by the negotiators, work out this result in its own way. As, for instance, by maintaining the present status until the Provincial restrictions are removed, *or, by presently admitting free paper and pulp manufactured in Canada unaffected by the restrictions, should Congress believe this latter method of dealing with the subject would expedite the removal of the restrictions.*"[15] (Author's italics.)

If publishers were complacent, manufacturers were indignant. While evidently not consulted during the negotiations, their obvious goal would be an arrangement insuring reciprocal concession for loss of protection upon their own product. Instead, they found that any hope they might have of exporting their paper to the Canadian market was deferred by the terms of the agreement to the day when all provincial restrictions were eliminated—an extremely problematical point of time. Hastings promptly advanced to the defense of his interest, arguing in a letter broadcast to the industry that free land wood was ample to supply its needs for years to come. There was no need, therefore, to seek safety in forcing removal of provincial export restrictions, since a sufficient supply was in sight even if these remained unimpaired. The weapon proposed to secure this removal—abolition of protection on paper—would meantime destroy the American industry. Effectuation of the agreement would, he asserted, be "the most disastrous blow ever handed to the paper industry of the United States . . ." He exposed the political motive of the Administration, asserting that "for the purpose of getting the influence of newspapers they are subsidizing them through the print paper section of the treaty, for all the rest of the schedule . . ."[16]

A presidential message of January 26 published the agreement and stoutly defended it, but made no mention of paper. Two days later a bill was introduced to effectuate its terms. As published, and as the bill was originally introduced, the agreement proposed to admit Canadian pulp and paper (the latter valued at not over four cents per pound) free of duty when no export tax or prohibition was levied upon export, as part of the general agreement, and dependent upon its adoption by both parties. This was referred to the Ways and Means Committee, where Chairman Payne refused to sponsor it and the duty devolved upon Samuel W. McCall of Massachusetts. The Committee heeded Knox's hint to Payne, however, and when the bill was reported back to Congress on February 11, the original provisions had been excised and a new Section 2 had been added carrying the pulp and paper provisions into operation immediately the American Congress acted, and regardless of Canadian acceptance or rejection of the agreement as a whole.[17]

Meantime a storm was gathering about the agreement which the present narrative, being devoted to newsprint, must endeavor to avoid while listening to its rumblings. High among the particulars of reciprocity was the mutual free admission of many agricultural products. Likewise some rates on manufactures were reduced. These proposals frightened the American farmer and manufacturer alike: the farmer because he foresaw an influx of Canadian wheat, pork, and barley, and the manufacturer because he saw in the reduced rates a break in the protective dike behind which his infant industries had approached robust adulthood. A remarkable phenomenon ensued. The protected interests developed a previously unparalleled solicitude for the farmer, about to be submerged under an avalanche of foreign foodstuffs. The farm press responded to the stimulus so thoughtfully provided, and a hue and cry was raised against the agreement, a hue and cry which the American Protective Tariff League regarded with benevolent complacency. Less complacent, however, were the mid-western Insurgents, who had led the van in opposing the Payne-Aldrich Tariff as an inadequate measure of reform, now unhappily forced to oppose tariff reform *á la* Taft since it was objectionable to their constituents.

The McCall Bill moved to passage against this background. The Ways and Means Committee hearings, February 2–9, were devoted mainly to opponents of the proposal, though Norris and Seitz appeared to express the publishers' approval. They served mainly as a sounding board for assertion and counterassertion, with little new material on either side. Norris referred to the agreement optimistically as "the greatest economic advance that has been made by the United States in the present generation . . ." but was vigorously heckled by both Democrats and Republicans. The bill passed the House and went to the Senate, where it fell between the stools of Republican hostility and a press of end-of-session business and failed to pass, despite stout publishers' propaganda on its behalf. On February 9 Norris called publishers' attention to the benefits the bill would confer through "providing for free print paper when made from free wood." Enclosures were broadcast to publications in several agricultural states, which were intended to enlist farm support but which failed to mention the advantages which would accrue to publishers through the agreement. Norris seemed mildly surprised later when this oversight was called to his attention. On the seventeenth Ridder sent out a communiqué which was to plague him later: "By request, private to editors. It is of vital importance to the newspapers that their Washington correspondents be instructed to treat favorably the Canadian reciprocity agreement, because print paper and wood pulp are made free of duty by this arrangement." [18]

The President called the new Congress in special session on April 4 to made amends for the failure of the preceding Congress. Its House was Democratic, thanks to the 1910 elections, and the Democrats would support tariff reform even at Republican hands; the difficulty was that they wished to go beyond reciprocity and enact further reforms, which the President insisted should await a report from the new Tariff Commission. However, he could count upon staunch support of reciprocity, and the bill was introduced again, this time under the sponsorship of Oscar Underwood, and passed the House promptly on April 21. The debates barely mentioned newsprint. It was the Senate again which became the crucial battleground, and through the long weeks of a hot Washington summer weary hearings and sultry debate moved reciprocity slowly forward. Taft marshaled all his resources for the fray, appealing, as did his opponents, to the farm interest to support his scheme. Senate Hearings, opening in May and lasting into June, offered all hands another opportunity to rehearse oft-repeated lines, the main difference between these and previous performances being a somewhat greater emphasis by the manufacturers upon the inevitable destruction of the domestic industry if reciprocity were enacted. The curious discrepancy between publishers' interests and publishers' propaganda was again brought out. Ridder's "By request, private to editors . . ." dispatch was called to his attention by Senator F. M. Simmons of North Carolina, who noted its frank avowal of self-interest. The Senator then asked, ". . . do you think the newspapers of your association have stated to the people with equal frankness the reason why they are favorable to it?" After some squirming, Ridder admitted that he could not name a single paper which had editorialized so frankly.[19]

Two developments occurring during the Senate Hearings merit brief mention. On May 17 the Tariff Commission presented a report of its investigation into the pulp-and-paper situation indicating that newsprint cost $32.88 to produce in the United States as against $27.53 in Canada, a differential of $5.35 (of which the cost of wood accounted for $4.71) in favor of the Dominion. Although this would normally have been considered a good Republican argument for protection against a cheaper foreign commodity, the exigencies of the situation transformed it into a plea for reciprocity as a means of cheapening cost to the American consumer.[20] The other was the presentation to the committee of the so-called "Root Amendment," which had been before the Senate in the regular session, but which received more attention at this time. Elihu Root represented New York, whose many papermakers would be adversely affected by reciprocity. In their interest, if not, as charged, at their direct instigation, he proposed to amend the bill to make it conform to the agreement as originally drafted, so that no pulp or paper should enter from Canada until all provincial restrictions had been removed. This of course was a threat to all the publishers' plans and as such constituted a grave danger. Taft admitted privately that it was in accord with the agreement, and evidently agreed tacitly to its introduction. When its full potentialities became apparent, however, he worked on Root to abandon it, to no avail. Root appeared before the Finance Committee to urge it, and it came to a vote on the floor, only to be defeated (June 22) after occupying the Senate's attention for parts of three days and receiving Root's somewhat apologetic support. At about this stage of the debate reciprocity became entangled with Democratic efforts at piecemeal tariff revision, and passage was delayed until July 22, with final signing on the twenty-sixth. Taft had won the battle which would do much to defeat his party in 1912, as the whole episode had pounded deeper the Insurgent wedge driven into Republican solidarity during the Payne-Aldrich debate. The publishers' fight was also victorious, as Section 2 allowed immediate entry to the products of wood from privately held forests.[21]

The manufacturing interest was more or less resigned to passage of the Act, but not pleased with the prospects. *The Paper Trade Journal* commented: "A gift of the news print industry has been made to Canada, to please the newspaper publishers of this country . . ." Though this doubtless reflects the exaggeration of immediate dejection, it is a fact that reciprocity marked a step in what was doubtless an inevitable northward procession. For at least two decades American papermakers had been discounting this prospect by investment in Canadian timber limits. Even the slight reductions of the Payne-Aldrich Act, combined with Quebec's new policy, accelerated the process. Reciprocity stimulated it still further by calling general attention to newsprint, and Canadian and American capital rushed into the paper-and-pulp business in unprecedented volume. In mid-December, 1911, it was reported that within the past seven months since the passage of the Reciprocity Act eighty-one new concerns capitalized at over eighty-three millions had been incorporated, forty-nine of them (twenty-seven in Canada and twenty-two in the States) with over forty-one millions of capital. This optimism was eventually to be reflected in the overproduction of the 1920's, but at the moment prospective profits outweighed caution. One immediate hope of the publishers was not realized: reciprocity did not reduce the price of paper, since Canada was not at once equipped to produce on a scale sufficient to compete in the United States market. Supply and demand were in close balance during 1911, and prices held fairly even throughout the year. This in turn meant hope again deferred for the publishers, despite their victory in reciprocity, and made necessary the waging of one last round in the battle for free newsprint in the Underwood Tariff of 1913.[22]

Little occurred in 1912. The papermakers appointed a committee to secure repeal of reciprocity, but the matter was not pushed vigorously, and although nine bills to this effect had been introduced by April 24, only one reached the discussion stage, and it specifically excepted Section 2 from its operation. A considerable number of efforts were made to induce Taft to recommend repeal as a means of regaining farm support in the election of 1912, but he refused to be moved by this consideration, and the offer remained on the books. After the election one trade journal remarked that he had probably done his worst to the industry, which might, however, expect worse from his successor.[23] One aftermath was that several European nations claimed the right to send goods to this country duty free on the strength of the gratuitous concession to Canada contained in Section 2 and the most-favored-nation clause of their treaties with the United States. The State Department recognized the obligation, but the Treasury Department wanted the income. The matter was finally referred to the courts, which in 1913 upheld the claimant nations, and small amounts of pulp and paper from six of them claimed free entry until the Underwood Act of 1913 went into effect.[24] The effect of reciprocity on prices became apparent during the year, which saw largely increased Canadian production. A drop of about three dollars per ton was registered, and prices remained low into 1916.[25] Canadian imagination was equal to the task of evading the Payne-Aldrich restrictions on Crown-land products by the end of the year. Quebec producers, emulating an earlier example in British Columbia, prevailed upon the Government to remove its restrictions upon exportation of logs cut from the tracts of the four leading paper producers. These producers had no intention of exporting logs, but removal of the restrictions permitted them to claim free entry for their paper, which was accorded by the United States.[26] Faced by the increasing influx of Canadian paper produced at cheaper prices, American high-cost mills began shifting to other grades of paper on which the margin of profit was greater.[27]

Woodrow Wilson's victory in 1912 made tariff revision inevitable. Chairman Underwood of the Ways and Means Committee inaugurated hearings before the new Administration took office, and the paper sections of the tariff came under review on January 17, 1913. By this time the manufacturers were in a well-nigh hopeless position. Reciprocity allowed free pulp and paper from private Canadian holdings; Quebec was on the way to short-circuiting the Payne-Aldrich barrier against Crown-land products; the favored nations were clamoring at the gates. Small wonder that one witness referred to the paper industry as "the poor relation at the tariff table, its place being very far below the salt . . ." The fact that it was likely to be joined by a host of other poor relations under Democratic ministrations failed to mitigate the circumstances, and the hearings opened with the manufacturers distinctly on the defensive.[28] Hastings tempered his argument to the wind of congressional opinion and asserted that papermakers wanted no change unless the committee should find that increased duties would bring increased revenue. He proposed that if any area should forbid or restrict the importation of paper, pulpwood, or mechanical pulp, similar restrictions should be imposed upon like importation into the United States plus a countervailing levy to the amount of any export charges. Elon R. Brown, another manufacturers' spokesman, would repeal Section 2 of the Reciprocity Act and leave the Payne-Aldrich regulations intact. The perennial Norris sailed a new tack, charging the domestic manufacturers with exporting low-priced newsprint to almost the amount of increasing Canadian importations, with the object of starving the local market and so offsetting these importations. He urged removal of all duties and restrictions upon entry of newsprint and its constituent pulps. Norris and the International exchanged the usual courtesies. When the bill was reported on April 22 the manufacturers' worst fears were realized: its practical effect was to remove all bars from the free entry of newsprint and mechanical pulp from any part of the world; although countervailing duties were proposed to apply to any areas levying export taxes, these were meaningless, since none were then in effect.[29] Publishers must have been supremely confident of the outcome, for the next day the Paper Committee asked the annual convention of the A.N.P.A. to bring its functions to an end with the signing of the new tariff.[30] The House debate dealt mainly with the retaliatory aspects and with the question whether passage of the bill carried with it repeal of Section 2 of the Reciprocity Act, and, if so, whether the rest of the reciprocity offer was thereby withdrawn. As passed by the House, no provision was made for a retaliatory levy in case Canada imposed an export duty on paper, newsprint being on the free list; retaliatory provisions were applied to paper valued above two and one-fourth cents per pound, of which no great amount was imported at the time. The Reciprocity Act had admitted newsprint freely up to a value of four cents per pound. Adoption of the Underwood top limit of two and one-half cents left paper valued between these levels subject to duty and so rendered Section 2 nugatory. W. S. Hammond, in charge of this schedule in the House debate, gave his personal opinion that repeal of Section 2 carried the whole legislation with it, but declined to speak except for himself. When the pulp section came up it was proposed to put both chemical and mechanical pulp on the free list, but in case Canada put an export levy on newsprint or mechanical pulp, retaliation would go into effect upon *chemical* pulp, of which Canada at that time produced little. Mann attacked this failure to provide retaliatory measures as leaving no means of preventing Canada from monopolizing the pulp-and-paper business by taxing or prohibiting exports of newsprint and mechanical pulp.

The House passed the measure as just outlined and the same questions were raised in the Senate about the failure of the bill to protect the supply of raw material for American mills against possible provincial interference. Henry Cabot Lodge of Massachusetts charged that it was a scheme "to enable Canada to force the erection of paper mills by American capital on Canadian ground . . ." on the part of "certain great newspapers . . ." seeking to secure cheap paper even at the cost of destroying an American industry. An amendment presently eliminated even the retaliatory provision relative to chemical pulp, and the bill passed to the echo of Smoot's apostrophe to John Norris: "I think perhaps it would be perfectly proper now for me to extend congratulations to Mr. John Norris upon the successful conclusion of this long fight; and the Newspaper Publishers' Association ought to increase his wage from now on . . . my friend Norris is safe in leaving the Senate gallery, in abandoning the corridors of the Capitol, and going back to New York to-night and reporting the successful termination of the fight he has been waging for so many years . . ."[31] The A.N.P.A. commented comfortably on the Act, signed October 3, 1913, that it "admits free of duty news print paper and wood pulps from all parts of the world and without qualification of any sort. The purpose of the creation of the Paper Committee has been accomplished. The market for paper buyers has been broadened to the utmost. Retaliation against foreign countries in pulps and paper supplies has been stopped. The days for a tax upon knowledge are gone . . . Publishers are to be congratulated upon the end of the contest. Uncertainty is over . . ." [32] The same *Bulletin* carried notice of Norris' resignation from the Committee on Paper which he had served so long and so successfully.

Thus ends the story of the fight for free newsprint so closely identified with the name of John Norris since the 1890's. No student of his career would deny the singleness of purpose with which he pursued his goal, though one may well share the impatience which his enemies, and those who heard him through long hours of propaganda, developed at his long and sometimes disingenuous harangues against the evils of the "trust" and the benefits of free trade. The story itself, drawn out though it has been in deference to the importance of the tariff fight, must still be viewed in the perspective of the larger study; it marked an episode in a series of swings of the pendulum, prepared by Norris's groundwork, initiated by Herman Ridder as a result of fear of high prices in 1907, and carried through fundamentally as a means of lowering prices. That it contributed largely to the transfer of the industry to Canada (an eventuality doubtless inevitable anyway) was probably incidental to its prime movers. That it did not immediately contribute to their prime goal, reduction of paper prices, was undoubtedly a source of unhappiness to them; prices remained virtually stationary through 1913, 1914, 1915, and well into 1916, though the signs of a new boom were on the horizon by the close of 1915. It was finally the crisis of war and its economic accompaniments which raised prices once more and so ushered in the next round in the long contest between publishers and manufacturers, to which we now turn.

CHAPTER VI

World War and Aftermath, 1914–1921

THE YEARS from 1914 through 1921 opened with a period of low prices and high Canadian production which constituted a logical accompaniment of the industry's northward march following removal of the tariff. The outbreak of war in 1914 found the United States at a low ebb economically, and after a momentary spurt all hands adopted a wait-and-see attitude. War-born prosperity was disturbed by two price crises, each invoking publisher-instigated attacks on the manufacturers. Involved also were government efforts to improve the situation, including arbitration between the parties, investigation of conditions, and a prosecution of the manufacturers for violation of the anti-trust laws. The period also discloses a widening breach between the large and small press and at least some tentative efforts to compose differences between the former and the manufacturers. At the end a renewed gesture of pressure on Canada to remove export restrictions ends in failure.

The period between the revolution in the newsprint tariff and the outbreak of war in 1914, while too short to establish trends, reflected changing conditions. The threat of Canadian competition discouraged the building of additional news mills in the States. Both Canadian and American capital went into Canadian enterprises on a considerable scale until early in 1914, when it was reported that Canadian banks were declining to make further advances on new properties. The Canadian industry was expanded more rapidly than American market conditions warranted. In February, 1914, the International reported to its stockholders: "That the future growth of your company must be largely in the development of its Canadian properties is more a cause for concern to labor and the public generally than to you." Some mills turned to other grades of paper where the margin of profit was greater than on news, and some water power was diverted to production of electricity. Imports of Canadian paper increased enormously, multiplying fivefold between 1912 and 1914. Such a striking increase, while doubtless in part a reflection of reciprocity and its aftermath, would hardly have developed entirely from the products of the free forests opened by the Act of 1911; tariff removal played no inconsiderable role. Withal, the price of newsprint sold on contract (about 90 per cent of the American consumption was thus sold at this time, leaving only a small remainder to be disposed of on the open or spot market) remained remarkably steady to June, 1916, at slightly under two cents per pound. This steadiness tended to belie the claims of those who had urged removal as a means of lowering prices. Thus it would appear that the outbreak of hostilities in the summer of 1914 found the newsprint industry seeking an even keel after recent disturbances.[1]

The American economy was not in a flourishing condition when Europe went to war. Papermakers, however, found themselves fairly well situated, with demand good and stocks of materials high. President Philip T. Dodge of the International could therefore cable from London directing his subordinates "to protect at all hazards the interests of our contract customers, and having done this to assist to as great an extent as conditions will permit such of our competitors' customers as may ask for assistance, but under no circumstances to take any unfair advantage of the situation." One of these subordinates assured the Publishers' Association that manufacturers were "never better prepared to take care of a situation such as the present one . . . there is not the slightest indication of a desire on the part of the paper manufacturers to take any unfair advantage of existing conditions. The producer and consumer of Print Paper should work hand in hand and in the closest harmony." A momentary rush of business lasted through August, 1914, and was followed by precautionary measures which, with some minor fluctuations, held the market steady until late in 1915. By this time the paper market began to reflect business improvements, shortages of various materials entering into manufacture, and the increased demands of world-shaking events upon the supply of newsprint. Before these signs became apparent, however, most of the supply had been placed under contract for 1916 at prevailing prices, so that the boom which developed midyear, and whose signs had been preparing late in 1915, applied mainly to the spot market. It was this boom which brought the first great price crisis of the period covered in this chapter and so brought publishers and manufacturers again face to face.[2]

Against this shifting background the manufacturers had already taken steps which would have aroused the publishers and created a crisis in any case and which eventually ran the mill men foul of the anti-trust laws. It was probably inevitable that a cheaper Canadian product would drive American mills to curtail production or divert machines to other grades of paper. It was probably just as inevitable that the publishers would attack these actions as collusive efforts to rig the market. As early as January, 1914, publishers were accused of launching reports in Washington pointing to a "comprehensive agreement both as to prices and markets between the United States and Canadian paper mills." About a year later the *Paper Trade Journal* carried a condemnatory editorial campaign urging that the Sherman Act be enforced or repealed. In March, 1915, the Publishers' Association charged that manufacturers were trying to establish uniform prices but had not yet succeeded completely. And on April 1, 1915, the News Print Manufacturers' Association was established, including most of the producers on both sides of the Canadian border. This was a deliberate effort to rectify the conditions of oversupply which had characterized the market for the past several years by reducing competition among the members. The organization operated through a secretary, Mr. George F. Steele, whose office provided the statistics necessary to the operation of the scheme, and an executive committee of five representing 82 per cent of the Association's production. In September, 1915, arrangements were completed whereby three American concerns took over sale of the products of a number of Canadian mills in an effort to stabilize prices by preventing consumers from playing one supplier against another. Later in the autumn the Publishers' Association began asking its members for information which would support charges of collusion among the mills.[8]

The year 1916 saw a trend toward manufacturers' control of the market. Profits had been considerable while costs of production were fairly stable until the second half of the year. Demand and supply had been approximately in balance as 1915 closed. The new year saw considerable prosperity, accompanied by an advertising boom which caused the large newspapers to make heavy demands upon their suppliers. Previous competitive conditions had made it possible for publishers to exact favorable contract terms from the mills, both in price and volume of deliveries. This favorable position had fostered careless use of paper, and soon the larger publishers found themselves unable to meet their needs under contract terms. They then competed in the spot market for the small proportion of the supply there was available. They could well afford to pay high prices for small lots, as cheap contract deliveries still left a low average cost. Smaller papers, however, dependent upon the spot market, found their costs rising to unheard-of heights. Jobbers increased their prices, and a panic market shortly developed, with manufacturers and middlemen reaping a golden harvest. Paralleling these developments, the mills inaugurated new sales policies which added to publishers' costs by setting selling prices f.o.b. mill rather than delivered to railroad siding or pressroom. By the end of the year, when large contracts were up for renewal, the manufacturers found themselves favorably situated, with high prices, tighter contract terms, and a large demand. By the same token, both large and small publishers felt the pinch of manufacturers' exactions.[4]

Under these circumstances there developed for a time a divergence of interest between the large publishers and their smaller compatriots. The large users of newsprint, protected by contracts until the end of the year, felt the pressure of price increases less quickly than the smaller papers which bought on the open market.[5] Secretary Steele of the News Print Manufacturers' Association began early in 1916 to harp on the fact that the situation was becoming critical. The Publishers' Association took note of the matter by running a strong campaign urging economy of consumption on the part of all papers, but its official publications for months studiously avoided the question of combination among the mills.[6] On April 5 Steele promoted a meeting between his association and the publishers to discuss matters, but it accomplished nothing. Presently the small publishers began to make their influence felt in Congress. The impetus seems to have come largely from Oklahoma, whose Senator Robert L. Owen introduced a resolution which the Senate adopted on April 24 in the following terms: "*Resolved,* That the [Federal] Trade Commission is hereby requested to inquire into the increase of the price of print paper during the last year, and ascertain whether or not the newspapers of the United States are being subjected to unfair practices in the sale of print paper." [7]

Thus was launched a far-reaching investigation, freighted with heavy consequences of ill-will between the manufacturers and government, which was to eventuate in prosecution of the N.P.M.A. under the Sherman Act. The inquiry started with the manufacturers indicating their good-will toward the publishers, and expressing their anxiety to co-operate with government. Steele's weekly letter to his constituents expressed the feeling that recent attacks had been made by irresponsible publishers, "and certainly not by the American Newspaper Publishers' Association, with which body we are on the most amicable terms. We are particularly pleased with the fairness and squareness displayed by Mr. L. B. Palmer, the efficient manager . . . in his relations with us." The Executive Committee petitioned the Commission for a hearing, alleging that their Association had been "grossly misrepresented . . ." in recent days, and Steele tendered "all the facilities of our organization, and [we] hope that our assistance may facilitate the investigation both in point of time and expense." [8]

The Trade Commission started its investigation forthwith, and at first received the cordial co-operation of the Manufacturers' Association, while the market rapidly passed into a runaway stage in the summer. (In mid-July Steele reported that "there is no open tonnage of which we have knowledge anywhere on this continent today.") The inquiry was made by questionnaire to publishers and manufacturers, and by examination of the industry's books as far as staff limitations permitted. Publishers were asked to submit details of all contracts entered into since the beginning of 1913 and of all spot market purchases, together with any information which might support allegations of irregular procedures among the manufacturers.[9] The inquiry gathered momentum during July, and on August 1 a public hearing was held at Washington. President Dodge presented the point of view of the International, and the Publishers' Association was represented by Col. F. P.

Glass, Chairman of a re-constituted Paper Committee, though none of the great dailies sent a spokesman. By this time the publishers, if Glass represented them, were suspicious of the manufacturers. He reported "many evidences of a concert of action . . ." but admitted lack of "legal proof of a combination or a conspiracy . . ." affecting output or prices. Publishers, he said, were doing their utmost to secure proof of collusion.[10]

The Publishers' Association's first open suggestion that all was not well within the industry came on August 17, when a telegram to members announced that "Monopolistic prices now prevail . . ." Shortly after this (August 29) the Trade Commission pointed out to the manufacturers that evidence indicated that small publishers were paying exorbitant prices, and asked what their Association could do to assure such papers of adequate supplies and to protect them against excessive prices. On September 6 the manufacturers submitted their new contract form, with its added burdens on publishers; the following day Senator Duncan U. Fletcher of Florida secured passage of a Senate Resolution calling for a broader investigation of the paper industry than that under which the Trade Commission had been operating since April. Following an amicable meeting in New York on September 14 between Trade Commission, publishers, and manufacturers, the latter drafted a reply to the Trade Commission's earlier suggestions. From this point forward the tempo of events speeds up, with pressure on the manufacturers becoming more and more severe, and with publishers becoming increasingly alarmed at continued high prices as the time for contract renewal approached.[11]

In mid-October Steele reported that he had received within the past two weeks over fifteen hundred "radical and abusive" articles regarding the oppressive tactics of the manufacturers. About the same time the Publishers' Association engaged the services of A. G. McIntyre, a Canadian and former trade journal editor, to take charge of its paper interests. Late in the month a letter from the Philadelphia *North American* to Chairman E. N. Hurley of the Trade Commission sharply criticized that body for failing to secure and publish the facts of the paper situation prior to the time for making contracts. Responding to this pressure the Commission on November 3 announced a hearing for December 12, and, without drawing any conclusions, retailed some current facts. These indicated that most contracts had been made at somewhat under $40 per ton, f.o.b. mill, prior to the 1916 boom. The first half of the current year had seen contracts made at $60, the second half at $65, while the spot market ranged as high as $140. The average cost of producing a ton of paper during the first half of the year was set at $33. In the face of these threatening signs the International announced a 1917 price of $65, subject to certain adjustments which reduced the figure somewhat. Meantime, behind the scenes, the Trade Commission seized the confidential files of the President of the International, and in December those of the Executive Committee of the N.P.M.A. And, also behind the scenes, the Publishers' Association was sending its members samples of propaganda to be directed to newspaper advertisers, variants upon the following theme:

"Mr. Advertiser:

Mr. Paper Manufacturer is after you. He asks us to collect from you thirty to seventy dollars a ton profit for him instead of the ten to fifteen you have paid him. He has been making fifteen to twenty-five per cent on his investment, but now insists that you buy his mill during 1917, and let him keep it, too.

We're kicking. What are you doing?" [12]

As the hearing approached it appeared that the manufacturers' tactics (the partial responsibility of the jobbers for conditions should not be entirely forgotten) had aroused both small and large publishers to a pitch of hostility equal to that of the mill men. The hearing itself, however, developed a further divergence among the publishers. The Trade Commission launched a bombshell at the outset by issuing a set of figures compiled by its investigators showing prices, costs, and profits in the paper trade. Criticism was invited, and the Commission evidently intended to cross-examine the manufacturers, who had had no previous intimation as to what was in store for them, and no advance knowledge of the figures, which, however, they did not challenge. Manufacturers' counsel T. T. Ansberry objected to cross-examination of his clients and accused the Commission of having pre-judged the matter, rendering further discussion useless. Later proceedings made it apparent that the metropolitan publishers were resigned to paying over $60 for their paper, had made contracts satisfactory to themselves, and so were not as completely out of sympathy with the manufacturers as were the small fry of the publishing business, whose representatives made a loud outcry. Their main complaint was the widening of the margin between the price paid by themselves and by the large buyers on contract.

After an intermission the Commission asked manufacturers to justify their prices, but again counsel refused to reply, making a counter-request for suggestions as to methods of distribution which would aid the small consumers whose interest was presently most at stake. After a rather hot session in which publishers' disagreement was again apparent, arrangements were made for a further meeting, on December 16, of committees representing small publishers, large publishers, manufacturers, and the Trade Commission. In the interim the A.N.P.A. Paper Committee, its Board of Directors, and some invited publishers met in New York on the fifteenth and adopted a report to the Trade Commission expressing their belief that there had been established "some manner of control of paper prices and distribution." Many feared, however, that complaint on their part would endanger their paper supply, and it was therefore hoped that the Commission's inquiry would speedily fix responsibility for conditions. At the December 16 session the manufacturers' representatives, frankly admitting that it was a seller's market, proposed a scheme whereby the large consumers should release 5 per cent of their contracted supply, which the Trade Commission would then distribute to the small publishers at the contract rate. This of course pinched the large consumers by threatening to cut their lucrative advertising space, and the A.N.P.A. representatives entered several technical objections and asked the manufacturers to secure the 5 per cent not from themselves, but from other consumers whose quotas, it was alleged, had not been reduced during the emergency. This session and another held on the eighteenth adjourned without decisive action to give the manufacturers time to study the figures presented by the Commission.[13]

Meantime, on the fifteenth, H. E. Varner, President of the North Carolina Publishers' Association, took the initiative in turning over to Attorney General T. W. Gregory evidence of combination among manufacturers to raise prices. The record is not crystal-clear at this point, but it is reasonable to infer that this was a counsel of desperation, as large consumers' dissatisfaction with the 5-per cent scheme left the small publishers in an isolated position. Gregory promptly announced that he had turned the matter over to an assistant. On the twenty-first this assistant, G. Carroll Todd, was invited into conference by the Trade Commission "regarding the feasibility of the Department of Justice proceeding prior to the completion of the investigation on the part of the commission." The following day the Commission agreed to prepare a statement and brief of its inquiry so far as it pertained to violations of the

Sherman Act, and have these ready for submission to the Department of Justice not later than January 5, 1917. The hearings were resumed on December 29, but terminated abruptly when the manufacturers declined to go further into the Commission's cost figures. Matters had thus moved forward some distance since the April date when the manufacturers confidently requested a thorough investigation of their affairs by the Commission. This had evidently proved more searching than they had anticipated and, together with the pressure of the publishers, even though the latter were not entirely united among themselves, had created a distinctly unpleasant situation. Developments in 1917 were to be still less pleasant.[14]

This year was characterized by parallel efforts to aid the small publishers, whose plight was the most important element of the situation. The Trade Commission, on suggestion of the publishers, proposed to arbitrate the price question. As has been indicated above, the Department of Justice had evinced an interest, and favored procedure via indictment of the manufacturers under the Sherman Act. This alternative, which would undoubtedly jeopardize the arbitration, might also embroil the large consumers in a tangle with the manufacturers. The Department persisted in its course, however, and a federal grand jury prepared evidence resulting in indictments, even while the Trade Commission was working out its arbitration scheme. In light of the indictments the arbitration proposal faced difficult sledding, and the Commission shortly decided to join in the attack on the manufacturers. The United States presently entered the World War, and the Commission in a final report admitted failure to solve the problem and recommended governmental control of the paper industry, including power to fix prices. This was evidently too strong a potion for the large publishers, and a split developed within the A.N.P.A. with the smaller publishers favoring the Trade Commission proposal and the larger consumers, safely ensconced behind reasonably good contract arrangements, fearful for freedom of the press under government control of distribution. Presently a scheme was arranged by the large publishers whereby the plight of their smaller brethren was eased somewhat. Paper prices dropped under the double influence of unfavorable publicity and a waiting period characterizing American entry into the war, and the manufacturers found a way out of their uncomfortable predicament. The end of the year found contracts being made on a basis somewhat more favorable to publishers. The problem was not solved, however, as 1918 witnessed a war-born prosperity which again increased demands for paper, made further efforts at regulation necessary, and started another price inflation which rose to unprecedented heights in 1920–1921 and was in no small measure responsible for developments of the ensuing decade.[15]

The year opened with the Trade Commission, which had no legal authority to enforce any proposals which it might make, appealing to the Department of Justice for co-operation in securing relief from the papermakers' combination tactics. The manufacturers were warned by a friendly member of the Commission that they were skirting the line of unfair competition, and shortly thereafter a group of them sponsored a meeting in Chicago (January 26) with publishers and members of the Trade Commission, at which unsuccessful efforts were made to compose differences. Manufacturers insisted that increased costs justified higher prices, but failed to produce figures to back their contention. The publishers proposed that the Trade Commission arbitrate the opposing claims and establish a fair price for paper, but President Dodge of the International opposed such governmental interference with private business. For the publishers, Glass accused the mill men of seeking to delay action.[16]

On February 10 it became known that the Department of

Justice would seek indictment of papermakers on the basis of evidence to be taken by a federal grand jury in session in New York. Mark Hyman and Bainbridge Colby were retained as special assistants to conduct the investigation. Thus warned of their peril, the mill men hastened to Washington for conferences with Francis J. Heney, retained as special counsel by the Commission, and after some negotiation, manufacturers representing one-third the production of the United States and Canada proposed a scheme similar to that brought up at the Chicago meeting. The Commissioners, after securing acquiescence of publishers and jobbers, agreed on February 15 to accept the arbitration task as of March 1, 1917. Both large and small publishers apparently acquiesced in this arrangement. An effort was made to secure immunity for the manufacturers who were under fire in New York, but at the insistence of the Justice Department and of some publishers, the inquiry was continued. Again a difference of opinion arose among the publishers; one group, represented by Glass and the Paper Committee, believing that the velvet glove surpassed the iron hand as a means of solving the immediate problem, opposed further pressing of charges. Other publishers were irked at that part of the scheme which involved giving up 5 per cent of their 1916 consumption, but finally agreed when the Commission insisted upon this prior to assuming responsibility for the arbitration.[17]

Pursuant of this mandate the Trade Commission issued a statement on March 3, its first full-fledged pronouncement since the original resolution of April 24, 1916, a sweeping condemnation of the practices of jobbers and manufacturers during recent months. It characterized as unreasonable the increased prices under 1917 contracts, asserting that "There is not now, and has not been, a serious shortage of news-print paper . . ." though the close balance between supply and demand made economy of consumption urgently necessary.

Higher prices had "been due in part to the fact that free competition has been seriously restricted in the news-print paper industry." Paper was manufactured to within twenty-seven thousand tons of consumption, and the difference was taken from reserves, so that, though hard to get, it was always available if buyers would pay enough for it. In view of these circumstances the Commission announced that a price of $50 per ton, f.o.b. mill in carload lots, was sufficient to enable the seven manufacturers who had signed the arbitration agreement, and eleven others who had not, to make adequate profits during the period from March 1 to September 1, 1917. To secure this price publishers must agree to restrict their use of paper to their necessary minimum, with an additional cut of 5 per cent if this proved necessary to keep the smaller papers supplied. Most of the publishers involved signed the agreement promptly. While disclaiming any pressure, the Commission believed it to be in the public interest to suspend criminal proceedings then under way against signers of the agreement as long as they observed the terms.[18]

The plan faced two fatal obstacles: the manufacturers felt that the price proposed was too low, and publishers were slow to agree to the 5 per cent reduction in consumption quotas. It was asserted in the trade that those who negotiated with Heney had been given to understand that the Commission would find that increasing production costs would justify a selling price of close to $60 per ton. Some manufacturers were accused of trying to intimidate their customers by threats of cutting off supplies after September 1 in case the latter accepted the Commission's scheme. On the other hand enough publishers did sign to threaten the profits of some manufacturers. At any rate, the scheme limped along through March, as the United States prepared to enter the war against Germany, a step taken early in April. With this crisis in the offing it appeared that demand might exceed productive capacity.

Under these circumstances the Trade Commission on April 5 moved more vigorously against the N.P.M.A. by ordering its legal department to prepare a complaint under which proceedings might be taken to improve conditions in the industry. Before this could be completed the New York grand jury handed up indictments (April 12) against seven men identified with the industry, four of whom had signed the arbitration agreement, and whose organizations controlled nearly half of the daily output of newsprint. This of course was fatal to the Commission's plan, and late in May two large manufacturers (G. H. P. Gould and Edward W. Backus) withdrew from the scheme, which presently collapsed.[19]

The Department of Justice, engaged in a number of antitrust litigations, was in no hurry to press the prosecution of the indicted manufacturers. In fact, setting of a trial date in October was taken to mean that two other important cases relating to the Steel and Harvester Trusts would be decided before proceeding with the newsprint matter.[20] On June 13 the Trade Commission presented its final report on the newsprint affair, lugubriously reporting that its efforts "to restore competitive conditions in the newsprint industry . . . have failed." It made public for the first time in some detail the methods by which the N.P.M.A. operated on behalf of over 80 per cent of continental production of newsprint. Since price-fixing was not the prime object at the moment, the Association operated through other channels, such as allotment of customers, prorating tonnage of new mills among publishers so as to prevent the new production from operating as a competitive factor, curtailment of production, and prevention of plant expansion. By these devices the market was controlled effectively and each member was left to collect as much as possible from his customers, particularly the small publishers so unfortunate as to be without contract protection. Finally, it set forth proposals for the future, suggesting "That all mills producing and all agencies distributing print paper and mechanical and chemical pulp in the United States be operated on Government account; that these products be pooled in the hands of a Government agency and equitably distributed at a price based upon cost of production and distribution plus a fair profit per ton." This was not a proposal to have the Government operate the mills; management and distribution were to remain under existing machinery, but operated under public supervision. Canadian co-operation in the establishment of a similar governmental control was to be sought; failure to secure it would be followed by importation only on Government account.[21]

This immediately posed the problem of governmental policy and set in motion the wheels of propaganda and of legislation. The Paper Committee of the Publishers' Association expressed wholehearted endorsement of the Commission proposals, characterizing them as "workable, practical and scientific . . ." The New York *Times*, however, voiced the hope that this dangerous experiment in governmental control over private industry might be avoided. A few days later Senator Owen introduced a resolution authorizing the President "to appoint an agency under the jurisdiction of the Department of Commerce to take over and to operate on Government account for the term of the war . . . all mills producing print paper . . . in the United States . . ." On June 20 Senator Marcus J. Smith of Arizona presented another measure drafted after conference with members of the Trade Commission and more suitable to them than the Owen Resolution. These raised the issue of press censorship and of government interference with business and brought the publishers post haste to Washington. Chairman Glass of the Paper Committee on June 21 pressed for adoption of a resolution sustaining Trade Commission control of paper, a proposition designed, as Trade Commission policy consistently had been, to protect the small publishers. The majority of those present, mainly large publishers, opposed it. The Paper Committee took this as a vote of "no confidence" and threatened to resign; presently, however, it was decided to try to reverse this decision by a referendum among the smaller publishers who had not attended the meeting. By July 10 it was reported that the vote was two to one in favor of the Trade Commission's ideas. Prices softened in July and the drive for government regulation slackened correspondingly. Early August saw completion of an arrangement made through Roy Howard of the United Press and the Federal Trade Commission whereby the Paper Committee secured paper and pulp from Lord Northcliffe's Newfoundland mills for the relief of the smaller publishers. This eased the immediate situation, and by early September it was being predicted that 1918 contract prices would be around $60 per ton, a reduction from the 1917 level.[22]

Meantime the Government had experienced difficulties in securing bids for its paper supply and had been forced to order the International Paper Co. to supply newsprint needed for an official publication.[23] This was a warning that the problem was still short of a solution, and on September 22, just before Congress adjourned, Smith introduced a more drastic proposal authorizing the Trade Commission to "supervise, control, and regulate . . ." the production and distribution of paper and pulp. This went beyond the price-fixing applied to wheat, coal, and steel, and called for actual government operation. It was characterized as "a plain and final warning . . ." to the manufacturers, delivered with particular force by virtue of the fact that the resolution was reported to the Senate on October 5, immediately before adjournment but in plenty of time for Smith's vigorous denunciation of the manufacturers to be broadcast during the period when 1918 contracts were to be made. The resolution was left hanging like a Damoclean sword over the manufacturers and the larger publishers while Congress went home for a short recess.[24]

The indicted manufacturers were still to be dealt with. Successive postponements removed the trial from its original date of October 8 to November 12 and then to November 26. During the interval it became apparent that backstage efforts were being made to settle the criminal proceedings on some basis which might render the severity of the Smith Resolution unnecessary by trading price reductions for lenient treatment of the delinquents. The pressure of combined events improved the contract situation, and on November 10 the Publishers' Association *Bulletin* announced contentedly that consumers "are finding little difficulty . . . in protecting themselves for next year under much more reasonable terms than they had anticipated." The Great Northern proposed a contract price of $50, f.o.b. mill, plus increased production costs, which evidently influenced the situation somewhat. Under these circumstances no one was particularly surprised at the announcement on November 26 that agreements had been concluded obviating further trial procedures.[25]

These provided a compromise whereby the manufacturers escaped by payment of nominal fines, the large publishers received some immediate relief and a guarantee against future ruinous increases, their smaller brethren secured large immediate reductions, and the Trade Commission's control over prices was extended somewhat. The court disposed of the indictments by accepting pleas of *nolo contendere* from all the defendants except Gould, against whom the Government's case was less convincing. By pleading *nolo contendere* the manufacturers technically withdrew their former pleas of not guilty and agreed not to contest the issue. Practically they admitted that the activities of the N.P.M.A. violated the Sherman Act. Fines totaling eleven thousand dollars, another practical admission of guilt, were assessed against the individual defendants. They consented to the dissolution of the Association as an unlawful restraint of trade. A petition in equity enjoined against further violations of the Sherman Act. Thus the pressing emergency was disposed of. An agreement between Attorney General Gregory and the manufacturers, executed on the same date, sought to provide against future trouble. It fixed the price of roll news in car lots, f.o.b. mill, at $60 per ton from January 1 to April 1, 1918; the sheet news used by small publishers was to sell at $70, with somewhat higher prices in both instances for smaller lots. After April 1 the Commission was to set maximum prices and to stipulate contract terms, subject to appeal to the judges of the Second Circuit, whose decision was to be final. This presumably strengthened the position of the Trade Commission by giving it some control over maximum prices, a constitutional development considered important by contemporaries.[26]

It presently appeared that the settlement might have troublesome loopholes, and the small publishers were soon reported to be circulating a petition urging passage of the Smith Resolution, fearful that the manufacturers might not abide by their agreement, as had been the case with the February 15 arrangement. The Trade Commission itself appeared to share these fears, as it wrote to Senator Frank B. Kellogg of Minnesota (December 6) and to Smith (December 13) duplicating the publishers' request. It was stated that a number of producers had not signed the agreement with the Attorney General, and hence were not amenable to Trade Commission price control. Furthermore, the agreement did not include control of paper distribution and of pulp prices and distribution. Under these circumstances, the Commission felt, the Smith Resolution would act as a useful club in case severe shortages made its regulatory task a difficult one.[27]

The year 1918 was marked by two main developments,

against a background of minor price shifts.[28] In January an unsuccessful effort was made to implement Trade Commission control of the paper business by enacting the Smith Resolution as a safeguard to the smaller publishers. Most of the year was marked by a contest of maneuver between makers and consumers, each trying to use the machinery of the November 26, 1917, agreement to its own advantage. This contest demonstrated quite thoroughly the weakness of the machinery and the ineffectiveness of the Trade Commission without controls stronger than those provided.

It will be recalled that the Smith Resolution, still before Congress for action, called for government operation, under the Trade Commission, of the manufacture and distribution of pulp and paper at a fair margin of profit to be determined by that body. Producers dissatisfied with prices so fixed might accept 75 per cent of the established price and sue in the United States District Courts for such further sums as they deemed justifiable.[29] It represented the Trade Commission's conception of desirable regulatory machinery and had received the support of small publishers. It was bitterly debated on four legislative days in January and defeated despite desperate efforts of its sponsor to salvage some part of its effectiveness by accepting amendments designed to placate its opponents. In opening the debate (January 8) Smith proposed amendments conforming the resolution to other wartime legislation and making government operation of the industry dependent upon Presidential discretion rather than automatic. He read into the record a letter from Trade Commissioner William B. Colver stating that the Smith scheme "embodies essentially the recommendations made in our final report." Much recent history was rehearsed in the early discussion and Smoot, a Republican, criticized the scheme on the ground that it conferred too much power upon the President, a Democrat. This opposition to centralization was not confined to one side of the Senate, for Thomas W. Hardwick of Georgia joined in objecting to government entry into business, particularly condemning the danger of establishing what might amount to political control over the press.

This danger to freedom of the press was hammered home vigorously and the ugly word "socialism," always calculated to arouse a flutter of fear, was injected into the debate. Smoot returned to the charge and openly claimed that the Smith Resolution was advocated by publishers because they thought that under its operation they could obtain paper more cheaply than under the agreement proposal. The debate presently became the vehicle of an attack upon the Administration, and nothing new was added to the points already made. Smith's amendment giving the President power to initiate government operation was defeated and after some further discussion the resolution itself followed into limbo. A similar resolution was presented to the House, where it was hoped the atmosphere might be more favorable, but nothing came of it. The debate and contemporary comment made it abundantly clear that the Smith Resolution movement was in the interest of the small publishers and also that the large press was indifferent or actively opposed, ostensibly on the ground of censorship, practically on the ground of governmental interference with private business—an interference which they were quite willing to condone in the case of the manufacturers.

The conflict between publishers and manufacturers was continued through 1918 within the framework set up in November, 1917. It shows the Publishers' Association, with no discoverable division between large and small members, working unitedly to keep prices down but failing to do so because of rulings of both the Federal Trade Commission and the courts. Since these developments have but little to do with the main thread of the present story, a mere outline must suffice. The Trade Commission hearings, called to establish the price as of April 1, 1918, opened in February and dragged on into June, partly through failure of manufacturers to present their cost figures promptly. These figures, it was argued when they were finally presented, necessitated a selling price of at least $80 per ton if operations were to be profitable. On the other hand, the publishers presented arguments to show that $50 was the outside limit of proper price. On June 18 the Trade Commission set a price of $62. The disappointed manufacturers appealed to the courts, as the agreement specified they might, and on September 28 the judges set the price at $70. The manufacturers had meantime applied to the Trade Commission for an adjustment on the April 1 price to allow for increased costs of labor, freight, and wood, and October 19 the first two of these were added to the $70 price, bringing the total to $75; the wood allowance was not granted. The many ramifications of these proceedings indicate that publishers were alert to protect their interests; they also show the cumbersomeness of the machinery provided for settlement of the price problem during the war. The end of the war emergency late in 1918 reduced the pressing importance of these problems and left the way open for the development of others. Perhaps the real significance of the events of 1917 was the restoration of a competitive market, against which the detailed story of price maneuvering tends to sink into relative insignificance.[30]

The year 1919 marks the opening of the postwar era the manifestations of which became more apparent in 1920 and the results of which carried over into the 1930's. Wartime controls on the use of paper (not discussed in the present study) were removed. The publishers failed in their efforts to lower the $75 price set in 1918, and contracts for 1919, covering the major part of newsprint consumption, were let at approximately that figure. The lapsing of effective Trade Commission power to influence prices left the market subject to the normal influence of supply and demand. Here the 1916–1917 situation repeated itself with variations: unprecedented demand put an unexpected strain upon a hitherto unequalled supply, and shortages, real or fancied, created a panic market in 1920, the seeds of which were sown in 1919. High prices again begat pressures in various directions. At home occurred the usual investigations, designed to uncover any possible irregularities, and once more efforts were made to induce removal of restrictions on the export of Crown-land pulpwood. Two periods of extremely high prices in four years produced their inevitable result in stimulating entry of new capital into the paper business, causing an unhealthy expansion in the Canadian industry. Thus the period 1919 to 1920 marks a transition between the aftermath of war and a mushrooming production creating long-standing problems in its own right.

It should first be noted that whatever troubles developed were not the result of reduced supplies. The total continental production increased every year from 1913 through 1920 with the exception of 1918. The mills produced in 1919 thirty-two per cent more paper than in 1913, and in 1920 forty-five per cent more.[31] There was nearly two months' supply at the beginning of 1919, according to current consumption, either on hand or in transit—an ample margin. The spot market was sufficiently below the contract level so that paper was being exported at $66 per ton for want of domestic purchasers. Under these easy circumstances there developed a boom which carried the spot market to $140 in November and set the stage for 1920 contract prices on a level considerably above that of 1919. The causes of this phenomenon were outside the control of either publishers or manufacturers of newsprint, but the boom affected both profoundly. Increasing business activity and the success of wartime advertising campaigns operated by the Red Cross and Liberty Loans were reflected in larger advertising budgets; these in turn brought revenue to the publishers but demanded ever-larger supplies of paper; to insure these, manufacturers were put under pressure to increase the output of their already overstrained mills.[32] These, though producing at full speed, were unable to keep up with the demand, and by early August it was reported that they had only four days' stock on hand.

If the foregoing analysis is correct it should indicate that publishers' lack of foresight in allowing cheap paper to be exported was partly to blame for what occurred, though a crisis would probably have developed had all exports been retained. Be that as it may, consumption presently outstripped production, and by July the spot price exceeded the contract average. This found the publishers, as in 1916, bidding against each other in the spot market and driving the price to new heights. Even yet, however, the manufacturers did not anticipate the developments of 1920, and most contracts were let at less than $90 per ton.[33]

Such price increases inevitably stimulated discussion, and several Congressional proposals called for investigations. The evidence available connects the publishers only indirectly with the initiation of any of these proposals, though all were in line with their oft-expressed policies. In August Senator James E. Watson of Indiana proposed to have the Department of Agriculture investigate the pulpwood resources of the country, including Alaska, and recommend measures of conservation and utilization. Senator James A. Reed's (Missouri) Resolution of August 20, adopted with little debate, was more pointed in its application: "*Resolved*: That the Committee on Manufactures or any subcommittee thereof is hereby authorized and directed to investigate the newsprint paper industry and to ascertain whether it is now or has been engaged in discriminatory, unjust, or illegal practice, and whether the prices now being charged for newsprint paper, or similar products, are excessive and the causes for existing prices . . ." Edwin D. Ricketts of Ohio introduced the most elaborate proposal (December 3) calling for a select committee to investigate, among other matters, the question of monopoly control.[34] None of these was acted upon, and 1919 passed into 1920 under a quickening demand which boded ill for the future.

Conditions approached panic in the spring and summer, and prices rose steadily throughout the year. Contracts were let at $90 for the first quarter, $100 for the second, $115 for the third, and $130 for the fourth, the last figure carrying over into the first quarter of 1921. By mid-April spot prices ranged up to $300. Again the small press, unprotected by contracts, was the principal sufferer, and the large publishers could afford to be relatively complacent, though still heavily burdened. Again the situation was complicated by large purchasers competing with small purchasers in the spot market and hoarding their purchases. Harried buyers complained of a shortage of newsprint amounting to famine, though careful observers pointed out shortly after mid-year that there was enough to go around if properly distributed. Small publishers, however, were too busy making desperate moves to stave off imminent ruin to listen to any reassurances. Their larger brethren too, while not in such dire straits, faced the future with misgivings.[35]

Proposed remedies were numerous, but none was immediately effective. The Publishers' Association's principal theme was economy in the use of newsprint. This was urged first through a special Committee on Print Paper Conservation, which failed to accomplish the desired results. The Directors and the Paper Committee in March asked all publishers to cut consumption 10 per cent and to request all advertisers to reduce their space by the same figure. The Annual Convention urged the membership to stay within its 1919 consumption figures, and many followed this suggestion. This action was credited by the Paper Committee with reducing the spot price from $320 to $220 within a short time.[36] The Association also took steps to procure European newsprint, previously imported in negligible amounts, and, acting on the presumption that a hundred thousand tons of imports would break the spot market, had by September secured quotations of $150 per ton, c.i.f. New York; it was estimated that contracts for 1921 delivery exceeded the hundred-thousand-ton mark. The Publishers' Buying Corporation, representing over two hundred smaller papers, took the same trail across the sea, and 582 tons entered from Europe on August 16. Finally, several large consumers of newsprint such as the Hearst papers in New York and Chicago, the Hartford *Courant*, and the Baltimore *American*, found themselves in short supply and pursued a similar course.[37] In April the Newsprint Service Bureau held a meeting of manufacturers at which two of these, International and George H. Mead Co., agreed to ask their customers to release from 1 to 2 per cent of their contract tonnage during April, May, and June for relief of those dependent upon the spot market. Presently a group of the smaller publishers organized the Publishers' Buying Corporation as a co-operative purchasing agency. This was based on the theory that there was no paper famine and that the problem was one of careful distribution of a supply which would be adequate if properly managed.[38]

As often happens in time of stress, attempts were made to use the machinery of government to redress economic imbalance. Of a score or so of proposals introduced in Congress, three reached the point of discussion on the floor of one or both Houses. None produced affirmative results, but from the composite discussion the outlines of a picture began to emerge. This showed the small publishers, fearful for their lives, grasping at the traditional methods of prosecution of the manufacturers and threats toward Canada. It showed the larger publishers less bitterly antagonistic toward the mill men than in 1917, and both manufacturers and large publishers more fearful of oppressive government regulation than of each other. Brief mention may be made of a resolution passed by the House on March 15 calling on the Secretary of Commerce for such information as he could furnish relative to shortage in the supply of newsprint, whether contract or other devices had given advantage to one class of newspaper over another, "and such information as he may have in regard to the issuance of any regulations governing the distribution and consumption of said print paper." The debate indicated Congressional belief in a real shortage of paper, but elicited no information on the queries addressed to the Secretary, as he replied that he had no data and had received no authority to issue any regulations governing distribution of newsprint.[39]

April, May, and June witnessed discussions of two more important proposals. The Reed Resolution of August 20, 1919, directing an inquiry under the Committee on Manufactures into possible "discriminatory, unjust, or illegal practice . . ." on the part of the newsprint industry had been left in abeyance during the fight over the Versailles Treaty. Hearings opened on April 28 before a subcommittee of which Reed himself was head. Glass represented the Publishers' Association. He reported that Senator Robert M. LaFollette of Wisconsin had been in touch with the Association the previous autumn requesting co-operation in preparing a case. The matter had been submitted to the Board of Directors, which had "indicated an unwillingness to take any official part in the procedure." The reasons given were first, that the Association was still in debt on expenses incurred during the Trade Commission investigation; second, "a growing skepticism as to the efficiency of the Government in curing the cause which was regarded as fundamentally economic . . . I am very doubtful whether the Government could do very much to relieve the situation that exists throughout the whole world . . ." A representative of the New York *Times* doubted the efficacy of governmental action, asserting that the remedy for present ills lay rather in decreased consumption and increased production. Paul Patterson, representing the Baltimore *Sun*, declared that the manufacturers were in part discouraged from making the plant expansions which might have cared for the existing emergency by fear of governmental regulation of the market to their detriment, as well as by the possibility of prosecutions such as that of 1917. The publishers, he asserted, should share the blame because of their bullying attitude toward the manufacturers at that time: "I think it is pretty well recognized that it was a mistake at that time to have ridden the manufacturers so hard . . ." a mistake which publishers should not be led into repeating.[40]

Frank Munsey advocated government regulation of the sources of both paper and pulp. His testimony was countered by a letter from William Randolph Hearst asserting that the day of government regulation of the paper business was past. Thus the attitude of the larger papers was mainly on the side of laissez faire in the interests of better publisher-manufacturer relations. On the other hand, the spokesmen of the smaller publications continued, as in 1917, to blame the mills and the jobbers for their troubles. Courtland Smith, representative of the American Press Association, asserted on May 7 that half the country papers would fail unless immediate relief was afforded them, and charged the manufacturers with conspiring "to regulate production so that prices might continue to mount." This idea of combination among the mills was repeated by other small-publisher representatives to the point where it may be taken as representative of their attitude. Chester W. Lyman seconded the large publishers' dislike of government action to lower the spot market price, blamed federal interference for the existing shortages, and joined

Arthur Hastings, another paper man, in recommending decreased consumption as a remedy. The hearings closed on a minatory note with Chairman Reed announcing his unwillingness to see a few large papers wax fat while their smaller brethren went out of business.[41]

The subcommittee report was rendered on June 5, 1920, a few minutes before Congress adjourned. It came in over the name of David I. Walsh of Massachusetts, Reed withholding his signature. It asserted the belief that manufacturers had persisted in the practices outlawed in the 1917 agreement by acting in collusion to charge "excessive, unreasonable, and wholly unfair prices" on the basis of "practically identical" contracts. It condemned a loophole clause in the 1917 agreement through which, by mutual agreement, a price might be charged higher than the maximum fixed by the Trade Commission. This joker, it was insisted, had rendered all the other provisions of the agreement nugatory. To remedy these evils it recommended immediate prosecution of manufacturers guilty of violating the anti-trust laws or the agreement of 1917, a tax on excessively large Sunday editions, amendment of the Lever Food Control Act to include newsprint, and "if the Government's efforts to fix and maintain a reasonable price appear to be futile because of a virtual monopoly in the print-paper industry or because of continued protests from the manufacturers that the supply is running dangerously low, we recommend that the Government by law establish a newspaper print board to supervise the manufacture and distribution of newsprint paper; and to enter into a co-operative organization with the country newspapers which would eliminate the jobber or middleman and enable the country press to buy newsprint at the lowest mill rate." It closed on a note criticizing the Senate for adjournment without taking action on this and other pressing matters. It thus reflected essentially the point of view which had produced the developments of 1917.[42]

Whereas the Reed Resolution proposed to solve the problem of supply by attacking domestic monopoly, the Underwood Resolution offered an international approach to the same question by providing increased amounts of wood for American mills through removal of provincial export restrictions. This was of course aimed at the immediate emergency; it may well be viewed, moreover, as the last tentative move toward creating a situation where the domestic industry could expand. With its failure there was left no alternative to the increasing removal of the manufacture of paper, as well as pulp, north of the Canadian border. To clarify this generalization, a brief review of the Canadian situation may be in order. It will be remembered (cf. pp. 29, 64) that the forest Provinces had forbidden the exportation of unmanufactured wood cut on the Crown lands. This had, under American legislation, subjected them to retaliatory levies on Canadian paper made from Crown-land wood and exported to the States. To circumvent this the export restrictions had been removed from Crown lands held by Canadian companies, with the tacit understanding that no wood should be exported. Thus Canadian-made paper from Crown-land wood could enter the United States without penalty. This satisfied everyone except the American holders of Crown-land limits who had no mills in Canada, and thus found their extensive holdings immobilized by Canadian ingenuity.

The unfortunate aspects of this situation soon presented themselves to American interests, and as early as April, 1919, reports emanated from Canada of renewed agitation for removal of provincial export restrictions.[43] Shortly thereafter "important news print producing companies" issued a pamphlet, "International Fair Play," urging that American holdings of Quebec Crown-land wood be freed for export. This, it was argued, "would afford an indefinite supply of raw material at moderate cost to our paper mills, would reduce and hold stable the selling price of news print and would insure the permanent price-regulating competition of our mills with the Canadian mills which are not subject to our laws or regulations . . ." Consumer support was solicited, and it was argued that publishers' influence, "unitedly and energetically exercised, will be sufficient to move Congress to negotiate with Canada, and particularly the Provincial Government of Quebec, the restoration of the property rights in the pulp wood on the Crown land limits acquired by United States interests prior to 1910 . . ." Another paragraph carried a potential threat to restrict Canadian access to the American coal and sulphur needed by Dominion manufacturers.[44]

As a measure of relief Senator Oscar Underwood of Alabama introduced a resolution (February 2, 1920), calling for presidential appointment of a five-man commission to negotiate with Dominion or provincial governments for cancellation of restrictions on the exportation of pulpwood and newsprint. Though the evidence available gives no indication of pressure from the publishers, Underwood was soon quoted as thinking that all publishers should back the resolution. When it came up for debate on February 25, its language had been toned down in deference to Canadian feelings, but Section 2 contained what its sponsor denominated "a big stick" to deal with possible Canadian recalcitrance. This provided that in case of inability to secure the removal of restrictions, the commission "shall investigate, consider, and report to the Congress what action should be taken by the Congress that will aid in securing the cancellation of said restrictive orders in council . . ." This to Underwood implied retaliatory embargoes in case of failure. In urging passage of the resolution he maintained that its introduction was "in response to an almost unanimous request of the newspapers of the United States . . ." because of their desire to have newsprint included (this in spite of the fact that at the time there were no restrictions on the exportation of newsprint); the real point at issue, he admitted, was pulpwood. The technique of appointing a presidential commission was adopted in order to establish direct contact with Canada, thus short-circuiting the State Department, which had to deal with Canada through the Court of St. James, and which had hitherto demonstrated its inability to do anything more than "throw rocks." It was the only possible method, he insisted just prior to passage of the resolution on February 27, to provide sufficient newsprint to save the small newspapers, in addition to its efficacy in saving the domestic newsprint industry.[45]

The Resolution slumbered in the House Committee on Foreign Affairs for some time, lacking pressure from either publishers or manufacturers, but hearings were finally scheduled for April 26. Underwood appeared in support of his resolution. He complained of the ineffectiveness of the Department of State in dealing with the matter in hand, and charged the Department with obstructing the resolution. He suggested as an explanation that some newspapers having contracts with Canadian mills had persuaded the Department to this point of view. He was followed by W. E. Haskell, Vice President of the International, who asserted that the resolution was "the only measure yet presented to Congress which contains assurance of a sufficient quantity of pulp wood to perpetuate the present production of our paper mills, to justify the installation of new machines, and to save the great pulp and paper industry of the United States." He generously pointed out that it also provided "the only practical means of providing sufficient production of newsprint in the United States to secure the lives of the smaller newspapers." He was seconded by H. C. Hotaling, representing the National Editorial Association, made up of five thousand small newspapers, and by other manufacturers and spokesmen for smaller publishers. The A.N.P.A., however, was absent. In fact, at almost the same time its Paper Committee was presenting to the Annual Convention a resolution opposing congressional interference with the newsprint situation.[46]

The House passed the measure on June 3, amending it to have the commission report to the President instead of to Congress, and President Woodrow Wilson pocket-vetoed it, in all probability because of strongly hostile representations made by the Dominion Department of External Affairs. The Canadian authorities considered it as an attempt to dictate the manner of regulating the Crown lands, and as such, a derogation of Canadian sovereignty. The very appointment of the commission would be "regrettable." As for Section 2, its language was found to be "unusual in public measures relating to dealings with a friendly country; but the suggestion of a threat which it is impossible to avoid, would in the circumstances of the present case be quite out of place and would offer a serious affront without cause."[47] This episode, and particularly its overtones, make it reasonably apparent that though the hand may have been that of Esau (the small publishers), the real voice of Jacob, speaking through both Underwood and his resolution, was that of the American manufacturer, anxious to release his supplies of restricted wood. Together with the Reed Resolution debates, the events of 1920 indicate clearly enough that the small publishers were willing to grasp at any means, domestic or international, to secure relief and that the large press was mitigating its hostile attitude toward the manufacturers, and had joined the latter in objecting to governmental action as a means of improving conditions. It was the small publishers who made it possible to keep alive the pressure for government regulation of the industry.[48]

The newsprint market reflected somewhat tardily the recession of 1921. From the first-quarter peak of $130 per ton, f.o.b. mill, four successive reductions drove the price down to $70 for the first quarter of 1922, where it held steady for a year. The January, 1923, level of $75 held until July, 1924, when prices began a long toboggan slide which lasted the rest of the decade. The drop of 1921 reflected not only the general recession, but also expansion of production beyond the normal capacity to consume, and moved so rapidly that by April spot prices were below the contract level.[49] The drop in price relieved the pressure on consumers, and little was heard of government investigations. The Fordney-McCumber Tariff legislation of 1921–1922 evoked the last-gasp efforts of the manufacturers to secure protection of newsprint against European competition, but Canadian-American financial relations in the industry were too closely intertwined by this time to warrant proposing protection on the continental product, and the only important immediate development was a new definition of "standard newsprint" in terms of the use to which it was to be put, rather than the valuation per pound. By this definition standard newsprint "is the commercial name for paper used in printing newspapers . . ."

The Underwood Resolution was repassed by both Houses with minor modifications, little debate, and retention of the obnoxious Section 2. In November the British Ambassador reported that the Canadian views of May 27, 1920, were still adhered to; that the Government would not consent to a foreign mission dealing with the Provinces; and that, while the commission method of dealing with the Dominion Government was considered "inappropriate," a direct communication from the Government of the United States would receive the usual "most careful consideration." President Warren G. Harding passed the matter off in December by announcing that no commission would be appointed for general discussions, since the Dominion Government had expressed its willingness to consider individual cases of alleged discrimination as these came up. Quebec had meantime acquired a new Premier, Mr. L. A. Taschereau, who stoutly affirmed that as long as his tenure lasted, so long should the embargo endure —a reflection of Canadian interest in conservation which had been growing rapidly with the new decade. And in 1923 this was reflected further by passage of a Parliamentary resolution authorizing the Dominion Government to prohibit at any time the exportation of any or all kinds of pulpwood.[50]

The period just discussed has involved essentially the attitude of our principal reagents—publishers and manufacturers —to two crises. The most significant phase has been the appearance of a divergent point of view between the large and the small publishers, with consequent results on the policy of the Publishers' Association. During the first crisis of 1916–1917 the large publishers were first complacent toward the manufacturers and then opposed to too drastic prosecution because of fear of governmental interference with private enterprise; Paper Committee and Association policy, as far as it can be determined, reflected the pressure of the small publishers for action against monopoly. During the second crisis Association policy reflected large consumers' fears of government controls not dissimilar to those of the manufacturers themselves; the small fry were left to fight their own battle.

CHAPTER VII

Overproduction and Depression, 1922–1929

THE NEWSPRINT story now enters a period of expanding production, particularly in Canada, brought about by a number of factors. The enormous prices of 1916–1917 and 1919–1920, coupled with the ever-increasing appetite of the American public for news, attracted investment capital to the Canadian industry. This movement was stimulated by provincial authorities in Quebec and Ontario, anxious to exploit domestic resources of wood and water power and rivals in Dominion industrial development. Hovering on the fringes were the stock promoters so characteristic of the 1920's, not unwilling to inject a modicum of their peculiar brand of "water" into a situation ripe for speculative development. Under these stimuli Canadian output increased from eight hundred thousand tons in 1920 to four million tons in 1930, while the American production, although increasing up to 1926, failed to keep pace.[1] Supply soon exceeded demand, with consequent falling prices which pleased the publishers and for some years minimized their activities. Promoters and politicians at first discounted the growing discrepancy between supply and demand, and money continued to pour into the industry. By 1927 Canadian producers were looking to consolidation as a remedy for overproduction and dropping prices. This was unsuccessful, and in 1928 a deal between Hearst and the Canadian International Paper Co. destroyed what was left of the price structure, threw the industry into a slump, and brought the Premiers of Quebec and Ontario to an effort at stabilization through political pressure. Stabilization meant not only controlled production but a higher price level, and forced the publishers to canvass the question of wherein lay their own best interests. Thus by the time the United States entered its time of trial in 1929, the paper industry had for months been struggling with a private problem wherein the larger depression only compounded confusion.

Economic recovery in 1922 speeded consumption to a point where it momentarily outpaced production, the new Canadian increment not being able to keep up with the demand.[2] This resulted in a full-dress economy campaign by the Publishers' Association, including formation of a national News-Print Conservation Committee with subcommittees in each State, with the object of reducing consumption by 10 per cent in the hope of influencing the autumn contract price. The move succeeded only in moderating the increase, as $75 was fixed as the figure for the first half of 1923. This was the last increase for many years; in fact, there followed a procession of reductions which carried the price to $65 prior to the debacle of 1928. Between 1922 and 1929 the decline amounted to 16 per cent, while consumption mounted from two million tons (1921) to three million, eight hundred thousand tons; the general commodity price level meantime remained relatively stationary.[3]

Against this background of falling prices was enacted a series of events which brought Canadian-American paper relations to the fore. The threat to Canada contained in Section 2 of the Underwood Resolution has already been mentioned. Congress presently reversed the Wilson tariff policies in the Emergency Tariff Act of 1921 and the companion Fordney-McCumber Act of 1922. These contained two added threats, one actual and one potential. Many agricultural commodities, prominent among Canadian exports and free-listed by the

Democrats, were again subjected to duties. Again, the so-called flexible provisions permitted the President, acting on information furnished by the Tariff Commission, to alter rates to a maximum of 50 per cent to equalize American production costs with those in competing areas. While these irritations were arising, Canada was following an evolution through which the United States had previously passed in the conservation of her natural resources, including her forests. Earlier optimistic estimates of pulpwood reserves were being revised downward following investigation and, as the Department of External Affairs had put it in 1920, "the more the position is analysed by experts the less encouraging it becomes." Finally, Canadian financial interests were again, as earlier in the century, alert to investment possibilities in the paper industry. In a previous era provincial restrictions had aided in the northward movement of the pulp industry. Could not further restrictions complete this movement and eventually do as much for paper manufacture? Any attempt to assess relative importance among these factors savors of the ancient hen-or-egg dilemma; the net result was obvious: a movement for complete prohibition of the export of unmanufactured wood from both fee and Crown lands at the hands of either Dominion or provincial authorities. This was in vigorous life in 1922 and flowered into action in 1923.[4]

The spearhead of this drive was one Frank J. D. Barnjum, a large timber owner, variously described as an ardent conservationist and as a front for Canadian manufacturing interests. Whatever his motivation, his methods were spectacular. Early in 1923, for example, he offered two thousand dollars in prizes for the essays arguing most convincingly in favor of an export embargo. His techniques struck a popular chord, and pressure was applied to the Government. This created an embarrassing political situation, since pioneer settlers in Quebec and Northern Ontario made their first "crop" by cutting pulpwood; the income thus derived maintained them until their land was brought under cultivation. An embargo would destroy the competition between American and Canadian buyers which maintained the price at a satisfactory level. Furthermore, though it might be good in the long run, the fact remained that in the immediate event of an embargo Canadian facilities were insufficient to absorb the cut. Caution was therefore desirable, and when a measure was finally adopted (June 20, 1923), it merely provided that the Government might in its discretion make prohibitory regulations. This was hedged by Prime Minister W. L. Mackenzie King in an oral statement that pulpwood grown by farmers on their own land would be exempt from any future restrictions, and by a secret Order in Council excepting from such regulations all wood exported under contracts dated earlier than June 1, 1923. Furthermore, a Royal Commission of investigation was appointed, with the promise that no action would be taken prior to its report.[5]

This proposal constituted a threat to American owners of timber limits held in fee and to American mills dependent upon Canadian pulpwood. The manufacturers promptly met in New York and organized a Committee for the Perpetuation of the Paper Industry in the United States, headed by Henry W. Stokes, President of the American Paper and Pulp Association. This group interrogated Charles E. Hughes, Secretary of State, and was assured that the Department was on watch and that the Dominion Government would investigate before taking action. The American Consul General at Ottawa was advised of the seriousness with which the Department regarded the question and the adverse effect of an embargo upon the organs of public opinion in the States as well as upon good relations between the two governments. He was permitted to indicate that the United States would not submit to an embargo "without retaliation of a far-reaching character." Hughes told the British representative in Washington that "the Canadian Government must realize that in this matter if they proceeded along the lines suggested that [*sic*] they would be taking the American newspapers and our publishers by the throat, and that one could hardly imagine a case in which there would be a more serious and immediate reaction on the part of the American public." [6]

The hearings of the Royal Commission lasted for five months, and, together with other discussions, brought out divergent Canadian viewpoints. The argument for conservation which had served as the fuse to touch off the question received less stress as time went on, being more or less relegated to the background in favor of the profit motive. As this emerged, its inconsistency with conservationism was pointed out; forcing American capital to build paper and pulp mills in the Dominion would hardly husband domestic resources. Furthermore, the forest Provinces, particularly Quebec, were sensitive on the point of local autonomy, and Taschereau made several pronouncements that the matter should be left in provincial hands. Back of this was undoubtedly the hostility of small landowners and of the settlers who made the initial pulpwood harvest on their new holdings. Finally, as the discussion continued through 1924, 1925, and into 1926, it seemed difficult for the paper interests to reach unanimity as to policy. The result was that the Government hesitated to take a step which would expose it to domestic complications and inevitable difficulties with the United States.[7]

The Royal Commission filed its report in July, 1924. It left the question of an embargo to the discretion of the Government, without making any formal recommendation, the burden of its argument being directed to conservation, with some attention to an export tax as a possible alternative to the embargo. Agitation was revived early in 1925 with this alternative to the fore as a possible means of securing some action while avoiding the multiple antagonisms promised by an embargo. Again in 1926 the Canadian Pulp and Paper Association demanded an embargo, but by this time a tremendous expansion had taken hold of the Dominion newsprint industry and embargo, export tax and other considerations faded into the rosy dawn of a great boom. Only an occasional Cassandra was found as yet to decry the dangers of overproduction which came in its train.[8]

This expansion, to which the embargo agitation no doubt contributed by stimulating the already rapid movement of American capital into the Canadian industry, was accelerated still further by developments of 1924–1925 which deserve more detailed attention than the limits of this study can give them. It was during these years that the great International Paper Company definitely turned its face toward the forests and water power of Canada as the prime base of its enormous operations. The move was preceded by the retirement in June, 1924, of President Philip T. Dodge, who had guided the company for ten years, and the choice of his successor, A. R. Graustein, member of a Boston law firm, a financier rather than a paper man, though recently concerned with the management of Canadian paper mills. The Dodge regime had launched the International in the Canadian paper-making field through a mill at Three Rivers, Quebec. Shortly after Graustein's accession rumors sprang up that the International was about to acquire the Riordon Paper Co., in whose reorganization he had recently been involved, as the beginning of a shift of its operations to Canada. This was denied at the time, but early in 1925 the rumors took form through acquisition by the International Paper Company of Canada, Ltd., of mills, water power, and timber, adding the Riordon and Gatineau properties to its original holdings. The deal was said to involve an outlay of twenty-seven million dollars for ninety-five hundred square miles of territory, an area equal to that of Massachusetts, Connecticut, and Rhode Island combined, which would within a few years enable the company to produce a thousand tons of paper per day. Graustein was quoted as modestly asserting that the transaction "means nothing less than the transfer of a large part of the American newsprint industry to Canada." [9]

The International's move furnished at once an answer to the embargo question and a further impetus to the feverish activity characterizing the Dominion newsprint business. New capital was reported to have entered the industry at the rate of three and one-half million dollars a month in 1924, and the trade journals resounded in 1925 with accounts of new enterprises about to be launched, of mergers and consolidations among established firms, and of the tremendous growth of hydroelectric power which was a natural concomitant as well as a fine field for the speculatively inclined. By this time, too, the Cassandras were beginning to appear in numbers. Warnings of prospective overproduction began to be heard early in 1925 when it was learned that Canadian mills had not been running full in 1924 and that capacity exceeded current demand. The same year, 1925, Dominion production exceeded that in the States during seven of the twelve months, and was only eight thousand tons behind on the year's total. Well might Taschereau, who had told a group of touring American industrialists in June, 1924, that Quebec had some American capital but would like more, warn the Canadian Pulp and Paper Association on January 29, 1926: "I believe we are very close to over-production . . . I believe that new firms should not be encouraged too much, and established firms, which have built up this Province should be protected to the fullest extent." The piper was about to collect his fee.[10]

During 1926 the International became the bellwether of continued plant expansion, proposing expenditures of thirty million dollars in Quebec and twenty-five million dollars in

New Brunswick during 1926–1928 in the related paper and public utility fields. Nearly a thousand daily tons of new Canadian production were readied for the market in 1925, and by May, 1926, predictions were that over eighteen hundred more would come in during the current year. The figures when compiled showed an increased continental production of 24 per cent over 1925, with Canada outstripping the United States for the first time by one hundred ninety-five thousand tons. Fears that the market might not absorb this great amount were temporarily allayed by the failure of the usual summer slump in consumption to materialize, and in August the mills were reported running at 99 per cent of capacity. The turn of the year, however, brought renewed warnings from financial quarters of the dangers inherent in the situation. Two particularly dangerous portents also appeared. For one, a small but noisy minority in the Quebec legislature attacked the firmly entrenched Liberal Government for bartering provincial resources to American capitalists for an inadequate return. For another, the Publishers' Association, reporting overproduction in the spring of 1927, announced that spot market sales were well below the contract price of $65, in effect since January 1, 1926, and that "it is generally reported that much of the product, through freight or other adjustments, has sold at a mill price of less than $65 per ton." This cautious suggestion that the price structure was not entirely intact indicated that the piper was coming still closer.[11]

He knocked and demanded payment in 1927, but was put off until 1928. Overproduction and price cutting were admitted facts in this year. In March it was estimated that, by August, mill capacity would exceed demand by fifteen hundred tons daily, and earlier predictions had called for twelve hundred tons of new production daily by the end of the year. Both Ontario and Quebec authorities let it be known that new mills would be discouraged as dangerous to production already in the market or under construction. And by mid-May the Eastern mills were running at 80 to 85 per cent capacity. Under these circumstances protective measures were in order.[12]

These took two forms: continuation of the mergers which had characterized the industry since 1925 and which looked to greater facility in controlling output and price, and adjustment of sales machinery to the same end. This is not the place to set the process of consolidation in its proper persepctive in the hectic pyramiding of securities which marked the later 'twenties; suffice it to say that by the end of the year three major groups had been created: the Abitibi Power and Paper Company, Ltd., with 1,814 tons' capacity per day, the International with 1,694 tons, and the St. Maurice Valley Company with 909 tons. A few independents, such as Price Brothers, Laurentide, Wayagamack, Brompton, and St. Regis supposedly were unattached. The sales reorganization occurred in May, 1927, with the formation of the Canadian Newsprint Company to co-ordinate the functions of the St. Maurice Valley Sales Corporation, Ltd., the George H. Mead Company, Ltd., and the Canadian Export Paper Company, Ltd. It was in turn closely affiliated with the Canadian Paper Sales Company, Ltd., William N. Hurlbut serving as President of both concerns until March, 1928. The Canadian Newsprint Co. bought paper from the mills and through its subsidiaries sold it to the consumers. The latter thus lost direct contact with the manufacturers. The scheme made it possible for the Canadian Newsprint Co. to control production, prorate orders among the mills on the basis of rated capacity, allocate sales, and, it was hoped, determine prices to the advantage of its constituents. In an effort to keep its mills at maximum operation the Canadian Newsprint Co. negotiated in the summer a tentative contract with the Newspaper & Magazine Paper Corporation, purchasing agent for the Hearst newspaper empire. This called for annual purchase, over a ten-year period, of two hundred fifty thousand tons of newsprint at a figure considerably below the $65 level of contract prices. Deliveries were to begin with 1928. It was seemingly the ramifications of this arrangement which set in motion the events of that year to which attention must now turn.[13]

This year the piper collected his fee for the dance of overproduction to which he had piped his tune through the 'twenties. Hearst and the International Paper Co. emerge as joint antagonists in the opening of a price war which was to result in disaster to the Canadian mills, to produce political efforts at price stabilization, and in turn to arouse the A.N.P.A. from its comfortable satisfaction with lowering prices. This was waged against a background of continued overproduction, with 1928 capacity rated up to 25 per cent above any possible consumption. The year also witnessed an innovation in sales practice, a reflection of unsettled market conditions. Since 1917 sales had been f.o.b. mill; beginning with 1928 the manufacturers absorbed a percentage of the freight depending upon the distance of the consumer from the mill. The area east of the Mississippi was divided into zones, and the net result of the new scheme was some reduction of the mill price as compared with 1927. The arrangement between the Canadian Newsprint Co. and the Newspaper & Magazine Paper Corporation (hereafter referred to as "Hearst" in the interest of brevity) was in effect during the early part of the year. In March control of the Newsprint Co. changed hands, and on April 21 its new management served notice that the contract would no longer be honored. Two members of the Newsprint Co., the Anglo-Canadian Pulp and Paper Company, Ltd., and the Brompton Pulp and Paper Company, Ltd., found it to their advantage to withdraw and offer their tonnage to Hearst at approximately the same rates as those of the original contract. This resulted in the dissolution of the Newsprint Company in September.

Following the Hearst–Brompton–Anglo-Canadian agreement, the International on May 29 announced what amounted to a $62 price for the remainder of the year. This brought Premier Taschereau into the picture with a statement that the paper companies "must not cut prices." August saw the provincial Premiers, Taschereau and G. Howard Ferguson of Ontario, warning the manufacturers that "the natural resources of the country shall not be depleted at a financial loss to the country. Sales of an enormous tonnage of news print at low prices would represent a national loss." By September it appeared that not all of the large producers looked with favor at governmental interference; some of them were said to face with equanimity a finish fight among the mills with the prize of control going to the survivors. In view of the huge operations of the International and its obvious ambitions, it came to be considered one of those most likely to prove recalcitrant.

Hearst injected the next disturbing factor. On October 10 his subsidiary asked for written bids for one hundred forty thousand tons of newsprint per year for a five-year period. The International Co. was the successful bidder, at a price of approximately $57 per ton, freight allowed, in the New York zone. This amounted to $50, f.o.b. mill, and marked a complete break in the price of paper. The International Co. had for years made uniform prices to all its customers. Therefore on October 30 it announced the extension of the Hearst price to all of them. The danger to other Canadian producers was immediately apparent, and appeals were made to the provincial Governments; responding to these, Ferguson pointed a warning finger at the Nipigon Corporation, Ltd., an International subsidiary. Calling attention to the fact that the company was a beneficiary under contracts with the Province, the terms of which were in default or arrears, he continued: "unless the people interested in the operation of this industry take some immediate steps to put the industry on a more satisfactory basis and improve the present situation, the Government will be compelled to give serious and immediate consideration to what action it should take under existing contracts to protect the interests of this Province, its industries, its settlers, its wage earners and its people generally."

This was accompanied in November by the formation, under the aegis of the Premiers, of the Newsprint Institute of Canada, Ltd., including the major producers except the International, the West Coast mills, and the Spruce Falls Power and Paper Company, Ltd., the last affiliated with the New York *Times*. This body was to control and limit production and to allocate orders on the basis of rated productive capacity. The ultimate success of any such scheme depended, of course, upon the ability of the Premiers to induce the International and Hearst to co-operate with its proposals, which obviously involved setting a price higher than the Hearst-International figure. There followed weeks of extremely tangled negotiations in Montreal and New York, during which President Graustein was called on the carpet by Taschereau, stood his ground for a time, and eventually, along with Hearst, agreed to a compromise settlement on February 26, 1929. By this compromise a price of approximately $55 per ton, f.o.b. mill, was established under contracts drawn to run for five years, which most of International's customers, in addition to Hearst, hastened to sign. This was accomplished by pooling and averaging the Hearst contracts, reducing the price he paid to Brompton and Anglo-Canadian, and increasing that paid to International. For the moment the Premiers had won their fight against fifty-dollar paper and had established the principle of political interference in the paper industry. This had been done, however, at the cost of considerable bitterness and without permanently relieving a bad situation, as new production was still being readied to enter the market and the inflated values of recent years still characterized the financial structure of the industry. Furthermore, the fundamental problem of security for the industry had not been faced or solved.[14]

It remains to trace briefly the relation of the Publishers' Association to the events just chronicled. A family quarrel concerning the propriety of the Paper Committee's conduct of its affairs produced an unusually complete record of the development of policy into the spring of 1929.[15] For six years during the nineteen-twenties the Association's Paper Committee had been headed by E. P. Adler of the Davenport (Iowa) *Times*. According to his own testimony he had deliberately attempted to reverse the Norris policy of bludgeoning the manufacturers into submission. Though a buyer's market characterized his tenure, he had held numerous meetings with the manufacturers, through which he had co-operated in the orderly conduct of the successive price reductions in such fashion that the market was not disrupted. This policy he believed to be to the advantage of the publishers as well as of the mills.

In August, 1928, he advised S. E. Thomason of the Chicago *Journal*, at the time Paper Committee Chairman, that the Association should take steps to prevent the price of paper from dropping too rapidly and sending the market into a disastrous slump. Thomason advised against this procedure, and the Paper Committee confined its activities to reporting the facts of the rapidly deteriorating situation as rapidly as these could be obtained. A special convention of the Association was held in New York on November 12–14, 1928, after the announcement of the Hearst-International fifty-dollar contract. It should be noted parenthetically that this competition was open, that the International figure was not the lowest bid received by Hearst, and that conditions were such that contracts could probably have been let at lower prices—in other words, the operation of free competition would have forced prices down still further. Thomason informed the convention of his belief that setting the price level too low would drive many mills out of business so that, when demand quickened, the inevitably short supply would cost publishers more than would be temporarily gained by low prices.

Meantime the conferences between the mills and the Premiers continued, and on December 14 the Paper Committee and the Board of Directors met successively with Graustein and with representatives of the Canadian mills.[16] From these discussions it developed that the International had been informed during the week of December 2 that, although its Hearst contract might be allowed to stand at $50, it must charge all its other customers the $55 price which by this time had been agreed upon for 1929. In addition to governmental interference, this directive would have caused the International to violate its promise of October 30 and its long-standing practice of one price to all customers (a policy to which the Publishers' Association had also subscribed for years). At this point the publishers informed both sets of manufacturers that the Association "stood firmly for a freely competitive newsprint market, free of governmental or co-operative control . . ." and viewed with "alarm and distrust any efforts to control the price of newsprint which interfered with free competition." At the same time, responding to Canadian pleas that the Hearst price would be disastrous, the publishers agreed that too low a figure benefited neither themselves nor the mills, but still insisted "that the suggestion of price control by manufacturers' agreement or by Government intervention could not leave the newspaper industry complacent." The statement concluded with a promise to watch developments and inform the membership if free competition were being endangered. This shows the Association, as represented by Paper

Committee and Directors, demanding uniform prices and opposing governmental attempts to amend the law of supply and demand, but hinting that prices ought not to be cut too sharply. It indicates, too, that the policy of the publishers in considerable measure paralleled that of the International Paper Co.

Developments at the spring Convention revealed a split in the membership, reminiscent of earlier days, on the part of a group whose spokesman was E. K. Gaylord, an Oklahoma City publisher. This element objected to the Paper Committee's actions as truckling to the manufacturers, particularly the International. It accused Thomason and the Committee of telling the manufacturers, in effect, that the Association was not insistent upon a low price for its newsprint, and of urging the mills to get together and charge a price higher than that then prevalent. This was equivalent to charging the Committee with willingness to see the law of supply and demand amended by the manufacturers, if not by governmental action. This policy, it was asserted, encouraged Graustein not to hold out to the bitter end against the Premiers' efforts to make him raise his price to Hearst, and resulted ultimately in publishers paying from $5 to $7 more than would have been the case had free competition prevailed.

Glass, a predecessor of Thomason on the Paper Committee and former President of the Association, expressed himself as opposed to the current point of view "that big combinations of capital are for the wholesome benefit of the entire people and of any one industry in this country." The Sherman Act, he insisted, was still on the books, and he recalled how in former years the Association had stood for its enforcement. This of course raised the question whether the Adler-Thomason policy or that of John Norris was most in the publishers' interest, and Glass feelingly declared: "If the association is going to turn itself over to the combination of print paper manufacturers in this country and say it is to our interest to do everything in their interest, well and good. I don't believe in that policy. I think it is a reversal of the policy of ten years ago, when this association spent so much money in trying to bring about a different result." The decision on policy had already been made when Thomason had returned an evasive answer in January to an inquiry from Assistant Attorney General William J. Donovan asking for evidence of manufacturers' violations of the Sherman Act. At the end of the discussion the Association voted confidence in the Paper Committee's actions, and Thomason resigned as its Chairman. The whole episode indicates the desire of the management to see prices stabilized, even if stabilization involved payment of a higher price than might have been secured by completely free competition. The smaller publishers may perhaps be pardoned for indulging in a few qualms at this point.[17]

The waning 1920's thus found the paper industry contending with its own problems when it was swallowed in the depths of international depression in 1929. As with other branches of the economy, its ills were in considerable measure of its own making, born of failure, under the impetus of profit-greedy promoters, to limit expansion to likely demand. The plight of the mills was plain enough: their need was for some method of stabilization whereby supply and demand might be balanced, unemployment and ruthless destruction of the forests be averted, and danger to the economic structure be minimized. As has been indicated, the issue soon became a political one in the Dominion, with provincial authorities alert to prevent cutthroat competition from taking toll of weaker companies and exhausting natural resorces on unprofitable levels. This sense of public responsibility developed more slowly below the border, and it was not until the landslide of 1932 brought in the Democrats with their more socially minded program that the NIRA experiment faced some of the same problems with which Canadians had been struggling for years. The concluding chapter will endeavor to trace the development of publishers' policy, foreshadowed in the events of 1928–1929, in the light of political efforts to speed economic recovery on both sides of the border.

CHAPTER VIII

Efforts to Combat Depression, 1929–1936

IT WILL BE recalled that as part of the February 26 arrangements the International Paper Co. offered its customers five-year contracts. These provided that for 1930 and each succeeding year the company would indicate, before November 30 preceding, what the coming contract price would be. This meant that any steps to induce price changes for 1930 must be initiated prior to this date in 1929. Many Canadian manufacturers had done badly during the year. Mills ran generally at about eighty-five per cent capacity, turning out four hundred thousand tons above the four million tons consumed. The impetus of previous years carried sixty-five millions of new capital into the Canadian industry.[1] Under these circumstances it was inevitable that Canadian members of the Newsprint Institute, who watched the International's mills running at over one hundred per cent capacity while their own were held down by agreement, should urge improvement in the basic price so that Canadian investors might receive dividends. The Premiers were also interested in better prices; they were interested, too, in distributing the tonnage equitably so as to keep a maximum number employed during a difficult period. Neither were they very happy at seeing the International's mills eat up Quebec spruce in defiance of the Newsprint Institute plan of controlled production. They faced, however, a difficult dilemma: if the price were raised, production would go down, and fewer people would be employed. These facts furnish the setting for the price maneuvers of late 1929.[2]

These maneuvers resulted in Canadian failure to raise prices, a failure brought about by policies of the Publishers' Association and the International Paper Co., working toward a common end though probably not in concert. Publishers' policy crystallized in opposition to higher prices; the International preferred continued large production at current figures to controlled production at higher rates; their combined pressure was too much for Premiers and Newsprint Institute together, and the 1930 price remained at the 1929 level after efforts of Institute members to raise it had proved abortive. By early October the manufacturers were in session discussing 1930 prices, and by the middle of the month it was an open secret that the Hearst-International contract was the dreaded obstacle to increases. Taschereau soon announced his desire for these, and promised that the Provinces would again intervene if a price war threatened. He followed this by stating that Americans were welcome in Canada, but must "live . . . a Canadian life and not injure our basic industries by unwise competition . . . public opinion will not agree to be dictated to nor have our national resources imperiled for the benefit of a most lovable neighbor."

The Publishers' Association met on November 11–13, with the Paper Committee still without a Chairman, the Board of Directors having been unable to persuade anyone to succeed Thomason. The Board refused to commit the Association on the newsprint question, but invited discussion. A cautiously worded resolution was adopted, showing that the members "viewed with deepest concern the continued effort being made to negative the operation of the law of supply and demand and to substitute in its stead an artificial control of the price of newsprint and reaffirms its approval of the uniform contract price basis." While the publishers were in session Graustein was in Montreal (November 12), on summons by Taschereau, who, said Graustein, insisted that the International charge $60 for its 1930 paper; this demand was repeated by long-distance telephone on November 25. Developments warranted the calling of a special Publishers' Association convention for December 9. By this time both Premiers had threatened the International with reprisals if it did not increase prices to $60, and two Canadian concerns, St. Maurice Valley and Abitibi, had announced such a step.

The Paper Committee by this time had a Chairman (W. G. Chandler of the Scripps-Howard chain), and the A.N.P.A. a policy, though still not too vigorously expressed, of opposition to price increases. Resolutions proposed to seek redress at Federal hands, asserted the present to be an inopportune time to advance prices, and committed the newsprint question to the Directors and Paper Committee with power. Upon adjournment of the Convention the interim body met and directed messages to the Newsprint Institute and the mills (including Price Bros.) which had announced price increases: "your proposal as to price and terms was unanimously disapproved. . . ." A subcommittee met three days later with Institute representatives. Here the publishers' proposal was unveiled: President E. H. Butler "stated that if the manufacturers should maintain the present price for newsprint for 1930, and should meet with the members of the publishers' committee to discuss the situation of future prices from every angle, publishers would then be in a more receptive mind for consideration of a three-year contract on the basis of prices and conditions which might be determined at such meetings; but that if the present program as to price and conditions is maintained, the natural reaction on the part of publishers would be that such a stand is arbitrary, and would result in causing customers to seek other sources of supply, including encouragement of importation of foreign newsprint." On December 20 the committee summoned Graustein and expressed itself as opposed to any rise in price. The following day the International announced "through the American Newspaper Publishers' Association that the present price of $55.20 a ton for newsprint would remain unchanged for the first six months of 1930." Thirty days' notice would precede any increase after July 1, 1930. By the end of the year the Institute companies had given in and followed the International's price, despite Taschereau's threat to appeal to the Dominion Government for assistance in the provincial fight against that company. Publishers' threats, including that of European competition, plus International's recalcitrance had thwarted plans for controlled production.[8]

As depression deepened in 1930 the publishers were moved toward a less intransigent attitude on prices by fears lest a worse fate befall them through industrial mergers which over a period of time might produce even more evil results. Premier Taschereau found himself increasingly crowded between the entrenched position of the International Paper Co. and the desire of Institute mills for greater income—a cross-fire which shortly stimulated political opposition in the Province and induced in the Premier the peevishness which sometimes accompanies ineffective effort. Publishers, Premier, and Institute all conducted their operations with a weather eye on the International, its co-operation being the condition precedent to the success of any scheme for stabilization. Merger talk continued, Institute control broke down, and a free market was in sight as the year ended; in sight, too, was insolvency for a large share of the Canadian industry.

Pursuant to President Butler's suggestion of December 9, 1929, the Paper Committee held long discussions with Col. John H. Price, of Price Bros., Chairman of the Newsprint Institute. These resulted in a proposition, presented in a letter of April 10, 1930, the subject of considerable debate at the

Publishers' annual meeting of April 23–25. This agreement between Institute and Committee suggested a solution in terms of gradually increasing price over a three-year period, predicated of course on the co-operation of the International, whose five-year contracts at the moment dominated the picture. It represented a degree of co-operation between publishers and Canadian manufacturers which reflected a much more realistic attitude toward the plight of the mills than had previously characterized A.N.P.A. policy.

As presented to the convention by Chairman Chandler of the Paper Committee, the Association's choice lay between two alternatives: (a) to let matters take their course in the hope that conditions would hold prices level, or even reduce them during 1931; or (b) assume that stabilization in the industry, accompanied over a period of years by some rise in paper prices, would best serve the interests of both publishers and manufacturers. Price's letter reflected the latter, suggesting that the existing rate be continued through 1930, with increases of $2.00 per ton in 1931, a like figure in 1932, and of $1.00 in 1933, these arrangements to be written into three and one-half year contracts effective July 1, 1930, and with the understanding that the Association would encourage its members to patronize Institute mills. The Committee, while expressing its belief that stabilization was essential, passed the report to the convention without endorsing Price's rates. It suggested further its belief that continuance of present prices would lead to consolidations which, by concentrating control in fewer hands, would in the long run "place newsprint prices on a much higher level than if the present competitive situation continues on a price stabilization program." Chandler's comments made it abundantly clear that the whole scheme was predicated on International's willingness to adjust prices upward on the five-year contracts negotiated in 1928, which still had three years to run. He gave his personal opinion that unless some such scheme were adopted, there would be an era of cutthroat competition and runaway prices, followed by consolidations which would leave the publishers worse off than ever.

Adler suggested an alternative five-year program, to take effect January 1, 1931, but was informed that the Institute felt unable to commit itself beyond the limit proposed by Price. It was pointed out again that Price had secured agreement to his scheme only over spirited opposition among his own group, indicating the desperate nature of the situation. F. I. Ker of the Hamilton (Ontario) *Spectator*, a member of the Committee, pointed this up sharply: "If the matter drifts on one ultimate thing is going to happen that can happen in two ways: Either by natural means or by unnatural means, the supply of newsprint paper from Canada is going to be restricted. The natural means are the failures of the high cost mills. The unnatural means are the merger of mills and the cutting off of manufacture in the high priced mills. I assure you that one of those alternatives is very much closer than many of you believe . . . I have a feeling that some of the large manufacturers would not be at all sorry to see the Institute's latest proposal turned down . . ." Glass and Gregory expressed themselves in opposition to stabilization, on the theory that the whole scheme was a hold-up by the mills, after which resolutions were adopted approving "the principle of a broad economic stabilization of production and distribution of newsprint paper over a period of years . . ." but studiously avoiding the price question by asserting that "the price to be paid for newsprint at any time is a matter to be determined by each publisher in the exercise of his own independent judgment." [4]

Meanwhile Canadian production dropped to sixty per cent of capacity, and Premier Taschereau tried with decreasing effectiveness to press the International into acquiescing in higher prices. This ineffectiveness was caustically referred to by Mayor Camillien Houde of Montreal, leader of the Opposition: "Here is a company whose object is patent, notorious, to wipe out other industries of the same nature in this province, and the Prime Minister, and the Cabinet and the Government are unable to prevent that attitude." The political implications of the newsprint slump were obvious enough in Canada, where much government revenue was derived from stumpage dues; inadequate prices would endanger payment of the dues and, in turn, imperil any Government caught by such a default. It is thus understandable why Taschereau, goaded by Houde, and by the specter of default, threatened the International with increased dues (in a speech to Parliament, January 14) asserting: "we owe nothing to the International, that it owes us nothing, we are therefore very free in our relations with the company."

A deputation of workers visited him early in February to complain that while their mills were forced under the Institute agreement to run at seventy per cent capacity, the International mills were running one hundred per cent or more. He could only reply that this permission had been granted in return for International's promise to take its United States mills off production of newsprint; he further hinted broadly that if the Canadian concerns were alive to the possibilities, they would combine among themselves and force the International to agree to higher prices, but admitted that his own efforts had not yet succeeded. A few days later he delivered a pin-prick by refusing International permission to cut trees under the legally-prescribed size, with resultant disemployment of several hundred woodchoppers. This seems to have been the extent of governmental accomplishment during 1930.[5]

The Canadian situation deteriorated steadily throughout the year, and by the time the Price proposal was submitted to the Publishers' Association, rumors of mergers were in circulation, giving support to statements made before the Publishers' convention. These continued through the summer, and though none had been completed, by November the prospect appeared imminent. Meantime the Newsprint Institute encountered increasing difficulties. Newfoundland mills, International mills, and some Canadian mills which entered production after the scheme was elaborated were able to run to capacity, to the dissatisfaction of members; some nominal subscribers seem to have taken their tonnage-limitation agreements lightly. In September an arrangement was consummated whereby Hearst bought into the Canada Power and Paper Corporation, Ltd. This concern was the largest producer of newsprint in the world, having absorbed the St. Maurice, Wayagamack, Laurentide, and Belgo-Canadian companies to amass an annual capacity of three-quarters of a million tons. Since Canada Power had been one of the influential members of the Newsprint Institute and presently became one of the most active proponents of consolidation, it was apparent that the Institute's days were numbered. Col. Price shortly resigned as head of the Institute.

The end of the year found matters in a state of flux. By December the Newsprint Institute had abandoned its efforts to restrict competition for business, and the Paper Committee was advising the Publishers' Association to deal with such firms as seemed likely to stand aloof from the proposed mergers. An open market was in prospect for 1931. This, however, did not promise a complete solution of the problem. Many Canadians began to feel that the best method was to abandon efforts to sustain prices by such agencies as the Newsprint Institute and let things find their own level through competition which would eliminate the weaker mills, particularly in the States, and permit the stronger Canadian mills to take over the market and raise prices. The other alternative, through consolidation, carried its own problems, involving closing down high-cost Canadian mills and absorbing their valuation into a capital structure already swollen beyond reason; there was serious doubt whether the low-cost mills could carry these frozen assets at profitable levels. At all events, the future was not bright.[6]

International and Canada Power announced early in the year that there would be no change in price, but buyers who took the trouble to do so could find lower prices and competitive bidding. Canadian firms were now in such dire straits that many of them went into receivership. One of these was the Minnesota and Ontario Company, which, after being shut down for some months for reorganization, went back into production and by late March was offering paper below the contract rate in order to secure business. This seems to have precipitated the action which followed, in which Institute mills cut prices without consulting the International and forced the latter to follow suit—the first time for some years that the International had failed to call the tune. In mid-April reductions of $3.00, retroactive to January 1, were announced, as well as a further cut of $2.00 effective May 1, reducing the f.o.b. price to $50 ($57 New York). Canadian mills with a total production of 6,774 tons daily followed this lead, as did International somewhat more tardily on May 16. It also proposed a price schedule to carry through six years on a gradually ascending scale in an effort at stabilization. The original reductions came out about the time of the Publishers' annual convention, and the Paper Committee gave its opinion "that existing conditions do not call for any action by your Committee at this time." On December 2 the International was quoted as asserting that prices would hold steady through 1932, but five days later a Canadian announcement dropped another $4.00, making the New York price $53 for the coming year, and the International promptly followed.

These events reflected a hectic year in Canadian newsprint history, the details of which lie outside the sphere of this study, but whose broad outlines must be kept in mind. Bankruptcy and reorganization formed the keynotes of the story and indicate why it was impossible longer to maintain an agreed price. Merger talk continued, but action was again deferred. The problem was by this time in the hands of a committee representing banking interests which was surveying the industry with a view to recommending a solution in terms of mergers. Meantime, nature had begun to take its course in the reappearance of competitive prices. To the publishers, this offered an opportunity to exert further pressure for still greater reductions, but Chandler's report to their fall convention exhibited greater sympathy toward the hard-pressed mills than consumers had been wont to manifest. While insisting that newsprint price reductions had failed to offset the decline in advertising revenue, he nevertheless asserted that "with rare exceptions, publishers do not welcome conditions that result in loss to investors and inadequate pay to workers in the newsprint industry. Demoralization of our source of supply predicates trouble for us." He went on to point cautiously to the dangers of a runaway market and to suggest the desirability of an orderly rather than pell-mell reduction of prices. A signpost was here erected pointing to better relations between old-time enemies.[7]

It will be noted from the foregoing account of 1931 that events were preparing the way for two possible solutions of the price question: one, through removal of the weaklings by competitive prices; the other, consolidation to save as many mills as possible. Neither had run its course to completion. The next year, 1932, repeated this story, with the addition of revived suggestions of pooling (reverting to the principle of the Institute plan) as a remedy, all this against a background of reduced consumption and advancing insolvency in the

Canadian industry. In fact, by September all the leading Canadian concerns except International and some newspaper-affiliates were either in bankruptcy or knocking at its portals. The bankers' committee continued its inconclusive measures. These were based upon a statistical study of the industry as a basis for consolidations which would save a maximum number of mills. Unfortunately, each time a mill went into reorganization, the whole question of its relation to the proposed consolidation must be canvassed with the new management in the light of new conditions. By the time the committee had completed its studies in the early autumn, a price war had broken out and reached such proportions as to make immediate stop-gap measures more essential than the committee's long-run proposal.

In June, Price Bros. underwent a reorganization which brought Lord Beaverbrook into control. He announced that Price Bros. would not participate in the proposed merger being worked out by the bankers' committee. In mid-September this concern announced a drastic price reduction, from $53 to $47.50, New York. This evidently reflected cutthroat competition on the part of smaller producers, offering low prices in order to keep running at full speed, combined with competition from Finnish and Scandinavian paper which could be deposited at New York on favorable terms because these countries had followed Britain off the gold standard. International shortly met Price Bros. and cut still further to $46, New York, thus again taking the lead in setting prices. Freight and other allowances reduced the practical price level to $45, where it remained until the beginning of 1933. Thus was inaugurated a bitter price war, attended by much switching of contracts, which drove the spot market to $38 and which by late October made a world-wide crisis imminent. In the scramble International took contracts away from its Canadian rivals to a point where the situation became desperate. Under these circumstances Premier Taschereau entered the picture with a repetition of his earlier warnings of governmental intervention unless the mills succeeded in getting together. The evidence at hand does not indicate the origin of the next proposal, probably a counsel of desperation, in the form of a renewal of the pooling device formerly embodied in the Newsprint Institute. This evidently gained headway as a temporary expedient, though the bankers' committee still clung to the idea of consolidation as a permanent solution of the problem. The year thus ends with the immediate emphasis upon cutthroat competition, with the International seemingly ahead, with pooling and prorated distribution suggested as a proximate solution of the problem, and with consolidation still hopefully considered by the financial interests.[8]

With 1933 the focus of attention moves temporarily south of the border, where shifting tides of politics brought a new Administration into power at Washington. The expedients of the Rooseveltian New Deal included the National Industrial Recovery Act (NIRA), designed to aid the American economy to lift itself by its bootstraps. While primarily directed toward domestic affairs, it was viewed hopefully to the north as a possible stabilizing factor in the Canadian situation through its potential influence on prices. While the Canadian industry in a sense marked time waiting for developments, the price competition continued. On April 18 the International announced a further reduction of $5.00, bringing the level down to $40, New York. This reduction, like others before it, seems to have resulted from competitive prices made by small independent producers and mills in receivership. The summer saw a ray of hope in the signing of the NIRA (June 16), succeeded by a further threat of price warfare when the Powell River Company contracted with Scripps-Howard for paper at $30, delivered in Philadelphia.

Events of the autumn, to be noted presently, furnished a temporary stay to more price-cutting. Nothing was accomplished on the consolidation scheme.[9]

The National Industrial Recovery Act and its effectuating agency, the National Recovery Administration (NRA), proposed to attack the problem of depression from the rear, by arbitrarily raising wages and shortening hours of employment in an attempt to create buying power which in turn would stimulate business into activity. To facilitate the necessary industrial agreements, any limitations under the antitrust laws were repealed. Each industry was to be organized under a Code Authority composed of its own members for the management of its own affairs through the agency of a Code of Fair Competition. One main objective of the whole proposal was, of course, raising prices. It should not be too difficult to fit these basic principles into the newsprint picture. American manufacturers, depressed like their Canadian counterparts, would be likely to welcome any machinery by which prices could be increased, particularly if such machinery could be adjusted to lessen Canadian competition. Canadian producers, though not directly involved, would be willing to co-operate in the hope of halting the ruinous price competition under which the industry had labored for years. Only the consumer of newsprint might be in a mood to object to increased raw material prices while his finished product was still subject to depression conditions. The result of these factors was another period of hostility between publishers and manufacturers which lasted as long as did the Blue Eagle of the NRA.[10]

The newsprint industry was presently organized under the name of the Newsprint Manufacturers of the United States and prepared a code for presentation to the NRA. As filed in mid-July it boldly tackled the price problem. After commenting on the unprofitable prices ($40–41, New York) in effect in the industry, it proposed: "Until a price having proper relation to cost can be determined for the industry, and approved by the President, the minimum base price of newsprint in the industry shall continue to be $46 a ton . . ." A month later a modified and shortened code was filed, covering hours and wages, but leaving price for later determination. Evidently still a third code was completed just prior to the first public hearing on September 6. Most of the testimony was devoted to a snarl over the code's attempted definition of standard newsprint and over wages and hours, but Elisha Hanson, counsel for the Publishers' Association, fired the first gun of a bitter battle over prices. Hanson voiced the Association's objection to a code provision for the establishment of a "standard method for determining current cost of any product of the industry, and for a requirement that no member shall sell any such product below cost." He argued that "application of this provision is susceptible of manipulation to bring about any price increase which the industry figures it can get away with." And finally, "no more striking monopolistic effort could be cited than this attempt of a small group of manufacturers, who admittedly cannot supply half of the country's requirements, to set up a control, through this code, of the price structure of newsprint paper." Canadians, watching hopefully, were disappointed at the failure to provide restrictions which would prevent northern manufacturers from underselling domestic producers.[11]

The next move was a meeting, held on the invitation of General Hugh S. Johnson, general administrator of N.R.A., on October 24. It gathered representatives of United States, Canadian and European manufacturers for the purpose of establishing a minimum price for newsprint. Those present agreed to a three-week armistice in the current price war (which was continued from time to time into the spring of 1934) and to recommendations made by C. R. McMillen of the St. Regis Paper Company, recently appointed industrial adviser to the NRA on paper codes. All hands agreed to adhere to three price stipulations: (a) no price to be established for any delivery after 1934; (b) no price for 1933 or 1934 deliveries to be below present prices, set at $41; (c) no price to be set for 1934 without provision for quarterly revisions to bring it into line with current figures. General Johnson pointed out the complexities of the newsprint problem and warned the Canadians of the desirability of co-operation by indicating that under the law tariffs might be revised upward if necessary in the interest of domestic producers. It would seem that this was a gratuitous threat, as Graustein, who was present, suggested a Canadian organization to parallel the News Print Manufacturers' Association, and Taschereau, when the proposals were published, promptly promised that Quebec's producers would comply with any minimum price set in Washington. The Newsprint Export Manufacturers' Association of Canada was formed in early November to implement Taschereau's promise. President Franklin D. Roosevelt signed the Newsprint Code on November 17, and it went into operation ten days later, without any price-fixing provisions.[12]

On January 6, 1934, the Code Authority, again approaching the price-fixing problem, proposed what came to be referred to as the Supplemental Code. This recommended an agreement between Canadian and American producers not to exceed the $41 minimum, to file information on price schedules and their revision, and to establish a joint committee of four from each association with power to confer "with respect to the stabilization of the industry and the elimination of unfair practices and destructive competitive prices and to report the results of such conferences with their recommendations to the Associations." The agreement was to be terminable November 10, 1934, upon notice given one month earlier. It also proposed that the Code Authority be given the power to adjust or modify prices on the basis of changes "in the cost of manufacturing or in the value of the dollar and by conditions in the newspaper publishing industry." This was submitted to the Paper Committee of the Publishers' Association, was disapproved in its entirety by that body, and became the subject of a public hearing on February 1 at which it was vigorously opposed by the publishers.[13]

This proposed Supplemental Code called forth, in addition to the A.N.P.A.'s unqualified hostility, a considerable expression of individual and Association opinion on the part of the smaller press. These appeared either spontaneously or in response to a request by W. W. Pickard, Deputy Administrator of NRA in charge of newsprint.[14] They indicate clearly the previously-evident division between the large and small press, and show the latter more favorably inclined toward the manufacturers, whose recent treatment of them was the subject of frequent praise. The small-fry looked to the Code to maintain the equality of treatment and the level prices as between large and small consumers which had recently characterized the policy of the manufacturers, particularly of the International Paper Co. They expressed themselves as willing to pay a bit more for their paper in order to perpetuate this stability in their relationships with their suppliers, and accused the metropolitan press of being willing to destroy the domestic industry in order to secure a favorable price differential from foreign manufacturers. They also manifested a desire to preserve the domestic industry as a check on foreign competition. On the whole they tend to clarify the position of the A.N.P.A. in relation to the problem at hand.

In presenting the Supplemental Code at the hearing of February 1, Edgar Rickard, Chairman of the Code Authority, stated that the original Code signed November 17, 1933, provided no protection for domestic mills against foreign imports. He reported that under existing conditions of over-supply in relation to demand there had been "an irresistible pressure on the part of individual companies to secure as large a volume of sales as possible." He showed that newsprint had been offered and sold as low as $30 per ton, and also offered on a guaranteed differential of $8.00 lower than any price quoted by domestic producers. He presented figures showing that paper cost twenty-four American producers $43.28 per ton during the first half of 1933, without allowance for fixed charges or dividends. He noted an exchange of letters between the Code Authority and the Publishers' Association in which the latter served notice of its intention to "take every proper step to prevent . . . approval . . ." of the Supplemental Code. A representative of the Michigan League of Home Dailies, a manufacturer, R. S. Kellogg, Secretary of the Newsprint Code Authority, and the Chairman of the Paper Industry Code Authority seconded Rickard's position.

Hanson opened the publishers' attack on the Supplemental Code. His initial statement indicates clearly the Association's approach:

"The purpose of this Supplemental Code is twofold:

"First, to set up a monopoly in the manufacture and sale of newsprint paper for use in the United States; and

"Second, to obtain for the monopoly absolute power over the price to be extracted from consumers of newsprint paper.

"The parties to the proposed monopoly are the Canadian and United States manufacturers of newsprint paper. Their God-parent, they hope, will be the NRA.

"Their proposal in its entirety is repugnant not only to the anti-trust laws of this country but to the expressed prohibition against monopolies in the National Industrial Recovery Act. It is violative of sound business economics. And it is contrary to the public interest . . ."

He directed his plea further toward the inability of the

domestic industry to meet American needs, showing how, since 1926, it had been unable to supply as much as half the total requirements of the market. And he noted particularly that the proposed arrangement involved concerted action by both Canadian and American producers under an agreement whereby no price changes could become effective without acceptance by both. These provisions, he insisted, placed the Supplemental Code in violation of the NIRA, the Sherman Act, the Clayton Act, and the Federal Trade Commission Act. He pointed out, too, that for every dollar of increased price allowed the domestic industry in order to compensate for increased costs under NRA, two dollars would be put into the pockets of the Canadian industry, which then furnished two-thirds of the domestic consumption. His strictures on the proposal were seconded by Paul Patterson, representative of the Scripps-Howard papers, large purchasers of newsprint.

C. R. McMillen, the Canadian adviser to the NRA on paper codes, in a reply to Hanson's argument (February 7, 1934), paid his respects to the "legalistic" character of objections made by A.N.P.A. to the Supplemental Code and accused the publishers of being willing to condone destruction of the domestic newsprint industry by denying it NRA benefits, in order to guarantee to itself continued cheap paper through unrestricted competition. This refusal, he asserted, "is a suggestion that no patriotic publisher could make if he understood the facts . . ." His principal argument was directed toward preservation of the existing domestic industry, even at the cost of temporarily increased paper prices under NRA, as an insurance policy against complete removal of the industry abroad, resulting ultimately in much higher prices. He pointed out that any newsprint mill still surviving in the United States had given evidence of inherent vigor and economic soundness, and concluded: "The question is simple. Shall a strong and seasoned United States industry, already the victim of an uninterrupted ten-year decline in price, comprising the hardy survivors of that tremendous ordeal, be squeezed to a slow death by the concurrent pressure on the one hand of additional operating costs imposed by our Government in the cause of recovery, and on the other hand of cutthroat price cutting by a few, perhaps desperate, foreign mills?" Whatever the merits of the respective cases, the publishers' pressure was sufficient at the moment to prevent effectuation of the main objective of both original and Supplemental Codes, "a swap of maximum hours and minimum wages for cost protection; that is, a provision in one form or another about not selling below cost." [15]

Another experiment in the same direction met a similar fate. On April 3 the Paper Committee met with the Newsprint Code Authority in Washington upon invitation of Major George A. Berry, Division Administrator, to hear the latter's proposed solution. This would create a Newsprint Planning and Adjustment Board to replace the Code Authority, and would provide for publisher representation in fixing prices. It was drafted without the manufacturers' participation, was presented to General Johnson, and received his approval on condition that no minimum price be effective until set by the Board. It clearly indicated governmental deference to the voice of the press, since it marked "the first major departure in government code policy against consumer or labor voice in matters affecting the direct management of an industry." It called for a nine-man board, three from the industry, three from the press, one labor representative from the newsprint and one from the printing trades, and an impartial chairman to be appointed by General Johnson. Its acts were subject to his disapproval, and non-unanimous decisions were to become effective only with his consent. Since it was fundamentally a price-fixing scheme, the industry accepted it and the publishers rejected it at their Annual Convention on May 2.

President Howard Davis of the Publishers' Association, however, requested a second public hearing, which was set for August 3. Meantime Pickard had gone ahead with tentative plans for putting the April scheme into operation, on the strength of "scores" of letters from publishers supporting it. Chairman Rickard, in opening, indicated that the Code Authority found "some difficulty in understanding why it was deemed necessary to call this public hearing . . ." since the attitude of all parties was well known. It served as a vehicle for another vehement attack on the manufacturers by Hanson, who was seconded by Bainbridge Colby, who in 1917 had been one of the government prosecutors of the newsprint monopoly. In addition to previous avenues of attack, the latest proposal was opposed on the ground that it permitted the apportioning of paper among consumers and on the whole was tantamount to government control and so a danger to freedom of the press. Hanson stated that the "American Newspaper Publishers' Association wants no agency of the Government to be placed in a position to tell newspaper publishers of this country how much paper they may use in the production of their newspapers, from whom they must buy it and how much they shall pay for it.

"This board cannot be created. I say this advisedly . . ." This seems to have marked the end of formal action in the matter prior to the Schechter case decision in May, 1935, in spite of various pressures on the Administration to take action to relieve the industry. It is not unlikely that the bitter fight between the publishers and the Administration over the Newspaper Code, a matter which lies outside the province of this study, may have rendered the latter wary of forcing a showdown in an issue where the organs of public opinion would have been marshaled in force against a policy already under heavy fire.[16]

The "official" history of the Newsprint Code, written by the Deputy Administrator, reflects in considerable measure the industry's dissatisfaction with the Government's do-nothing policy:

"The only other critical comment which the Deputy's Office wishes to add concerns itself with the lack of desire on the part of NRA, or the President, to help this Industry out of its difficulties. Just what the basis of this attitude was, is not known, but it is strongly suspected that the attitude of the Newspaper Publishers Association was a very strong element in spite of the fact that many of the smaller and Mid-Western publishers were in favor of the stabilization proposal of the Industry. Every attempt on the part of the Newsprint Industry toward price stabilization remained unsuccessful in view of the strong opposition of the large newspaper publishers who took the attitude that the domestic industry was not fit to survive.

"The ultimate results of the lack of such an Industry in the United States and the utter dependence of the newspaper publishers on foreign manufacturers not controlled by any Constitution or Supreme Court was apparently lost sight of in the immediate object of holding down Newsprint prices to a level ruinous both to the domestic and Canadian producers." [17]

The conclusions of Edward R. Jones, in charge of a preliminary study of the operations of the industry under NRA, written in 1936, may well serve as a terminal summary of this period of newsprint history:

"The Newsprint Industry probably emerged from the code period in no better condition than it entered it. This was due to the fact that there was no improvement in the price situation and the industry was still at the mercy of its customers. This situation could not have been remedied by the code without resort to Section 3e of the Act, which proved to be contrary to the policy of the Administration . . .

"The relationship between the Administration and the industries was usually pleasant and harmonious. The Newsprint Industry was definitely disappointed and disillusioned by the Administration's failure to grant it tariff protection from foreign, chiefly Canadian, producers. As the opposition of the publishers to the proposals of the Newsprint Code Authority created a situation of a delicate and inflamable [*sic*] nature, the refusal of the Administration to take any steps toward raising the price of newsprint still appears to have been the wisest and safest course . . .

"In conclusion it is difficult to state just what was the effect of the codes themselves, and what part of the improvement in the industry has been due solely to general business conditions. Possibly the greatest impetus for the revival came in May and June, 1933 in anticipation of the benefits expected to accrue from N.R.A. This would tend to substantiate the belief that the greatest boon of N.R.A. in these industries was psychological. The industries did not suffer the expected setback following the Schechter Decision. Agitation for voluntary codes has been discontinued. There is a feeling among some informed individuals that the paper industries have gained all that they can gain from codes, that a continuance of the codal form of industrial control would not mean an improvement in business . . ."[18]

Turning back from American stabilization efforts to market trends, it should be noted that the tide of consumption turned toward the end of 1933 and that the first quarter of 1934 showed production up to 93 per cent of the corresponding period of 1929. This production, however, brought only 53 per cent as much as in 1929. With prices at the old $40 level the Canadian industry complained that the only gain was in cutting losses through a larger volume of production; the usual cry for a higher price resounded in the autumn of 1934. This was prevented by the action of the St. Lawrence Paper Company, a member of the Canadian Export Manufacturers' Association, in contracting with Scripps-Howard and Hearst for 1935 deliveries at the previous price. When the agreement was announced Premier Taschereau indicated that his Government could not tolerate "such complete disregard of the public interests . . ." and moved toward punitive measures which resulted in withdrawal of certain concessions as to stumpage dues and permission to cut undersize timber. This threat moved the Publishers' Association to threaten in turn: "Should Premier Taschereau and certain Canadian banks, by unusual restrictions imposed upon the St. Lawrence Paper Mills Company, succeed in establishing a precedent whereby contracts between Quebec mills and United States publishers may be arbitrarily vitiated, the Directors and the Newsprint Committee of the American Newspaper Publishers' Association will be compelled to advise its members to turn their attention immediately to other available and potential sources of supply." Taschereau countered by proposing to appeal to Dominion authorities to prevent exportation of paper at prices below production costs. This could be done under the recent Dominion Marketing Act permitting the central government to regulate prices of certain exports. The company stuck to its guns, however, even in the face of an attempt by International and others to raise the price to $42.50, and after considerable skirmishing the 1935 price remained unchanged.[19]

Conditions improved rapidly in 1935, and October production and sale of newsprint were at the highest levels in the history of the industry. So vigorously did this tendency operate that by December predictions were being made that a seller's market was in sight, with mills operating at 80 per cent capacity and the remaining 20 per cent not being immediately available. Price was the only disturbing aspect.

Here Quebec entered the picture with a measure permitting the Government to raise stumpage dues on Crown-land wood from $1.35 to $6.00 per cord, the lower rate to be applicable to companies agreeing to certain conditions on sales prices. The alternative was to be made effective by Order in Council at the discretion of the Government. The Publishers' Association recommended in reply to this that its members "place their commitments as far as possible with United States mills, with whose government they can deal directly, or with mills operating in foreign countries, whose governments have not threatened to interpose themselves on bona fide contracts." To which Premier Taschereau is said to have replied, "Pure bluff." The Great Northern Co. took the lead in setting 1935 prices, with an announcement in October of a rise of one dollar, the first effective price increase since 1923. This was a disappointment to the Canadian producers, but they were not yet in a sufficiently stable position to unite for a greater increase.[20]

This year also witnessed the first important impingement of the tariff on the newsprint situation since 1913. Secretary of State Cordell Hull's program of Reciprocal Trade Agreements, with its policy of whittling down the exorbitant Hawley-Smoot Tariff by reciprocal concessions to individual nations, generalized through the most-favored-nation clauses, was being applied to Canada during this year. An agreement with Sweden had already bound on the free list continued entries of wood pulp, and it appeared that the same favor would be extended to Canada. Such a policy applied to newsprint would, the manufacturers urged, subject the domestic industry to unlimited Canadian competition. Binding newsprint on the free list should therefore be accompanied by a quota system applied to Canada and any other supplying country, on such terms as to permit complete utilization of the domestic machinery and expansion of plant capacity when demand again put pressure upon supply. This favor was not granted, for when the agreement was published late in the year it was found that both wood pulp and newsprint were bound on the free list for the duration of the agreement.[21]

A year of transition followed in 1936. While the Canadian industry was still clearing away the debris of depression (four of the five major producers were still in receivership), Dominion and provincial authorities moved to prevent a recurrence of previous disasters. Consumption outspeeded production to a point where demand began to approach supply. The interventionist attitude of the Provinces betokened a situation which might make price increases easier of achievement. Under all these circumstances the publishers' pressure was unequal to the task of preventing higher prices for 1937. April saw Ontario follow Quebec's example in legislation giving the Government power to charge five times the regular stumpage dues, plus a fine of $1000 per day for conducting operations which were detrimental to the public interest. The Dominion Marketing Act was also amended so as to bring newsprint definitely within its provisions. This led the Paper Committee to warn the Publishers' Association that "the time is near when United States publishers who may purchase Canadian newsprint will not have to deal alone with the manufacturer of their choice, but with a coalition of the Canadian Government and of the Canadian manufacturers . . ." and to repeat its 1935 advice to deal where possible with other than Canadian mills. By April 11 Peter Heenan, Ontario's Minister of Lands and Forests, was informing manufacturers of the provincial decision, taken after consultation with Quebec, that stability in the industry would be promoted by prorating of tonnage among the mills, and warning them not to commit themselves to contracts prior to July 1, 1936. He continued: "The government is asking the industry itself to put its house in order . . ." [22]

Under these circumstances the signs pointed to price increases, with a note of warning that they should not be too great, lest untoward developments ensue. In May the *Paper Trade Journal* quoted from a report of John Stadler, a consulting engineer involved in the reorganization of Price Bros., agreeing with other authorities "that newsprint at more than $45 per ton would encourage the development of newsprint manufacture in the southern part of the United States . . ." Publishers therefore received, almost with a note of relief as if they had been spared something much worse, the Great Northern's announcement on August 3 that the 1937 price would be increased only $1.50 (to $42.50) per ton. This "assured an orderly advance in the price of newsprint and a stable market . . ." and "was widely hailed by publishers as being a fair advance which they could afford to pay without hardship to the publishing industry." Per contra, the Canadians felt that a march had been stolen on them. The second half of the year saw the market move definitely from the buyer's side to the seller's, and operators were pictured as being worried over how to keep production up to demand.[23]

All signs pointed to a new boom in 1937, accompanied by many of the circumstances which had previously made boom periods the prelude to disaster. Last-quarter operations in 1936 had been at 91 per cent of capacity, only 2 per cent below the estimated maximum for the industry as a whole. In mid-February Lord Rothermere cabled Canadian manufacturers: "Hope your confreres fully recognize that the improvement in pulp and paper is only at the initial stage. From sources of information at my disposal, it is a certainty, barring a war, pulp and newsprint industries will, within two years, be confronting a shortage that may easily become permanent. There is now no room for weak-kneed negotiations for supplies to publishers or others except at prices much beyond those prevailing at the present moment . . . The newsprint industry in particular is on the threshold of prosperity beyond anything it has experienced before." Charles Vining, President of the Newsprint Association of Canada, told the Canadian Club of Montreal on February 8 that money would soon be needed to provide new productive capacity for paper. C. L. Sibley, veteran Canadian correspondent of the *Paper Trade Journal*, noted during the same month that "every newsprint unit in Canada which can be operated on an efficient basis . . . is working to capacity . . . The price trend is upward, and the market is rapidly developing symptoms of being a sellers' market, after being for seven lean years a buyers' market . . ." And on March 19 International announced a price increase of $7.50 ($50) per ton for 1938, to be followed promptly by most of the Canadian mills.[24]

Under these circumstances the Publishers' Association would normally have launched a full-dress offensive. Instead, it confined itself to a mildly hopeful statement that since the Great Northern had not yet announced its price, there was still a possibility of moderating Canadian demands. Together with this came a warning to eschew the new form of contract being offered, betokening renewed confidence on the part of the mills, abolishing the interlocking provisions which had been useful to the publishers by permitting one price-cutting mill to set the figure for large segments of the industry. In August a "recession" appeared and developed strength until in mid-October paper stocks broke badly on the Montreal Stock Exchange. At almost the same moment the Great Northern announced a $48 price for 1938. A crisis impended. Would the Great Northern price break the market, or would the International, in combination with the smoothly cooperating provincial authorities, be able to maintain the $50 price? The general abandonment of the interlocking contract aided the Canadian producers, as did the firmly held provincial attitude opposed to price-cutting, and they persisted in their price in the face of lessened consumption, large stocks on hand, and the momentarily unfavorable position of the industry. Instead of speeding production and engaging in a frenzied hunt for business to keep the wheels turning, the leading Canadian companies cut to a five-day week, tailoring production to probable demand. The $50 price was also maintained through 1939 and announced for 1940, in which year the Great Northern price went up to $49. In other words, intra-industrial co-operation, backed by governmental policy, had enabled the manufacturers to weather a period of economic difficulty which in other days would probably have enabled publishers' pressure to force prices down.[25]

This practical example of the value of production control and political manipulation in flattening the curves of the business cycle left successive Presidents of the American Paper and Pulp Association pondering in their annual reports on the problem of the relation of the government to business. Frank J. Sensenbrenner announced in 1937 that "Industry quite generally seems to view with favor the business principles laid down in the National Industrial Recovery Act . . ." In the light of the boom of 1937 he concluded that "the [paper] industry appears to be moving irresistibly toward a catastrophe similar to that which occurred in the newsprint industry within the last ten years." Two years later D. C. Everest presented to the Association its reply to a questionnaire sent to all trade associations requesting their opinion on questions of supply and demand: "we have had ample proof in the paper industry that no matter how well the individual companies may be armed with facts concerning the economic status of the industry at any given moment, and their own relative importance in and dependence upon the industry trend, and no matter how farsighted their individual management may be, these individual company efforts are wholly inadequate to stem the occasional downward rush toward economic fatality.

Nor can such individual action steady the seasonal and cyclical fluctuations in production which create instability to labor and capital. Neither of these phenomena benefit the public interest, and the Association experience over the years seems to indicate that a program rigorously restricted to the limitations of the Anti-trust Laws is not sufficient to protect the broad public interest that lies in an economically sound paper and pulp industry." With this contrast between Canadian practice and American wishful thinking this study may well close, before the abnormalities of another war period present other and more complex variables.[26]

The foregoing story has witnessed a shift from complete local supply of the market to a situation wherein the major portion of the commodity came from Canada. The development of policy has thus taken place under the impetus of increasing demand, faced by a relative decline in the native supply. It has been complicated by the alert desire of producers of Canadian wood, pulp, and paper (often financed extravagantly by American funds) to obtain for themselves an ever-increasing share of the profits accruing from the business; complicated, too, by the nature of Dominion-provincial relations which lodged control of forest resources largely in the hands of the latter. Against this shifting background the factor of supply and demand has been influenced further by domestic tariff policy, by occasional efforts of producers to tailor production so as to raise prices, by recurring periods of sudden heavy demand, and by subsequent entry of large increments of capital into the industry.

The net result has been a series of pendulum swings which it has been the object of the foregoing account to examine. The narrative has indicated how successive periods (usually brief) of high prices have been followed in order by publishers' attacks upon manufacturers, by large capital investment, and by much longer periods of lowered prices. These successive swings have for decades keyed publisher-manufacturer relations to a pitch of apparently permanent antagonism. This has arisen partly from the naturally competitive position of the two parties, partly from recurring crises which have aggravated this competition, and partly from policies deliberately adopted on both sides and inevitably exacerbating the "normal" hostility. Such developments as John Norris' crusade for free newsprint, for example, hardly inspired manufacturers to think well of publishers; by the same token, recurrent efforts to raise prices by combination drew no expressions of endearment from the opposite side of the fence. The practical problem of the future would seem to resemble that of the past: to maintain prices at a point where both interests may live at peace with fair profits.

This happy solution has not hitherto been realized. The writer approached this study with slight knowledge and few preconceptions; he has pursued it as objectively as his capabilities permit. He believes that both parties share the responsibility for failure to arrive at a solution. Discounting, however, manufacturers' desire for large dividends on occasionally swollen capital, it is his judgment that over the years the major responsibility for a lack of equilibrium should be laid at the door of the publishers, whose aggressive leadership and unique position for influencing public policy have given them striking advantages over the manufacturers. Some optimism for the future seems warranted, however. The later chapters of this account have indicated recurring periods of easier relationships, when intelligent understanding succeeded earlier bitterness. As these conclusions are set down, informed leaders of both groups have indicated belief that a live-and-let-live attitude seems to be developing. If the foregoing story possesses any utilitarian value aside from its exposition of historical developments, it should be as a signpost pointing hopefully in that direction.

NOTES

CHAPTER I

1. *Tariff Hearings before the Committee on Ways and Means, First Session, Fifty-Third Congress* (Washington, 1893), *House Miscellaneous Document* 43, 53d Congress, 1st Session, pp. 1047–49; *Notes on Tariff Revision, Prepared for the Use of the Committee on Ways and Means of the House of Representatives* (Washington, 1909), *House Document* 1503, 60th Congress, 2d Session, p. 524. *The Paper Trade Journal* (New York and Chicago, 1872 ff.), LXII (March 23, 1916 ff.), carries a series of articles covering the history of paper making in the United States. (Volumes I–XXXVIII inclusive are paged consecutively; subsequent volumes page each issue. Citations will be by date and page through volume XXXVIII, by date only in case of later volumes.)

2. *Pulp and Paper Investigation Hearings* (6 vol.; Washington, 1909), *House Document* 1502, 60th Congress, 2d Session, pp. 1093–95; *Reciprocity with Canada: Hearings before the Committee on Finance of the United States Senate Sixty-Second Congress on H. R. 4412 An Act to Promote Reciprocal Trade Relations with the Dominion of Canada and for Other Purposes* (Washington, 1911), *Senate Document* 56, 62d Congress, 1st Session, pp. 1097–99; *Tariff Information Surveys on the Articles in Paragraph 322 of the Tariff Act of 1913 and Related Articles in Other Paragraphs* (Washington, 1921), pp. 15–17; *United States Tariff Comission: Summary of Tariff Information, 1929, on Tariff Act of 1922* (Washington, 1929), p. 2439; George A. Prochaska, Jr., *The Pulp and Paper Industry* (Typewritten: Washington, n.d.), *Records of the National Recovery Administration*, The National Archives, pp. 18–21, 44–5; R. S. Kellogg, *The Story of News Print Paper* (New York: News Print Service Bureau, 1936), pp. 5–21.

3. The matter was stated succinctly by Mr. R. S. Kellogg, one of the veteran observers of the newsprint scene, when he wrote: "The publisher must get his white paper at a price which, taken with all his other production costs, totals enough less than his receipts from circulation and advertising so that he can profitably continue in the publishing business . . . The newsprint maker must sell his products for a price that will not only pay his direct out-of-pocket cost, but which will also adequately provide for maintenance of raw material supply, depreciation

of plant and obsolescence of equipment in addition to return for the use of capital. If he fails for long to get such a price, he ceases to be a paper manufacturer . . ." (Quoted in *Paper Trade Journal*, CIII (Nov. 12, 1936).)

CHAPTER II

1. Daily papers published in the United States increased from 971 to 2,226 between 1880 and 1900, and weeklies and semiweeklies from under nine thousand to almost fourteen thousand. Arthur Meier Schlesinger, *The Rise of the City, 1878–1898* (New York: Macmillan, 1933), p. 185.

2. The name was changed in 1883 to the American Paper Manufacturers' Association, and again in 1897 to the American Paper and Pulp Association in order to admit pulp manufacturers to membership. *Paper Trade Journal*, XXVI (October 16, 1897), pp. 49–51; E. R. Jones, *Paper Industry Study* (Typewritten: Washington, 1936), *Records of the National Recovery Administration*, The National Archives, pp. 360–62.

3. Some emphasis on this early effort to balance production and consumption may not be amiss in view of the later insistence of its leaders upon the purely social character of the Association. The difficulties of the manufacturers are pointed up by the fact that Canada was made a "slaughter market" in 1878, as indicated by Canadian complaints a decade later. *Paper Trade Journal*, XVI (April 2, 1887), p. 187.

4. *Ibid.*, IX (Jan. 3, 1880), p. 1, (Feb. 21, 1880), p. 57; *The New York Times* (New York, 1851 ff.), Mar. 13, 1880. The boom lasted from September, 1879 to July, 1880. On the influence of the boom in stimulating new production, cf. *Paper Trade Journal*, XXX (Feb. 15, 1900, Supplement), p. 4.

5. *The Congressional Globe* (Washington, 1833 ff.), 46th Congress, 2d Session, pp. 653, 765, 1043, 1062, 1230, 1231, 1234, 1385, 1386.

6. *Paper Trade Journal*, IX (Feb. 21, 1880), p. 57; N. Y. *Times*, Mar. 13, 1880.

7. United States tariff legislation is conveniently collected in *Tariff Acts Passed by the Congress of the United States from 1789 to 1897, Including All Acts, Resolutions, and Proclamations Modifying or Changing Those Acts* (Washington, 1898), *House Document* 562, 55th Congress, 2d Session.

8. Boutwell's ruling is found in *Synopsis of Sundry Decisions*

Rendered by the Treasury Department under the Tariff and Other Acts, During the Year Ending December 31, 1872 (Washington, 1873), p. 215. Cf. also N. Y. *Times*, Mar. 8, 9, 13, 1880.

9. N. Y. *Times*, Mar. 13, 14, 1880; Allen Johnson & Dumas Malone, editors, *Dictionary of American Biography* (21 vol.; New York: Scribner's, 1928–1944), XII, p. 641. An inveterate raconteur, Miller retold the story of his appearance before the committee many times, with an airy disregard for dates but with sufficient detail to establish his importance in the episode. Cf. *The Paper World* (Holyoke and Springfield, Mass., 1880 ff.), IX (Aug., 1888). This monthly journal paged each issue separately. Citations will be by volume and month. *Paper Trade Journal*, XXVII (Feb. 19, 1898), p. 172.

10. It might be noted parenthetically that this was one of the few clear-cut victories won by the manufacturers at congressional hands. N. Y. *Times*, Mar. 10, 17, 24, 25, 26, 31, Apr. 6, 14, 16, 23, 24, 29, May 2, 14, 1880; *Paper Trade Journal*, IX (Mar. 13, 1880), p. 84, (Mar. 20, 1880), p. 92, (Mar. 27, 1880), p. 100, (Apr. 17, 1880), p. 124. James A. Garfield, an opponent of the Wood bill, claimed to have received five thousand copies of newspapers containing an editorial blast circularized to the country press supporting Wood's proposal.

11. *Paper Trade Journal*, XXVI (Oct. 16, 1897), pp. 51–3.

12. *Ibid.*, XVIII (Aug. 3, 1889), p. 603.

13. *Ibid.*, XXIII (Jan. 6, 1894), p. 3; XXIV (Mar. 30, 1895), p. 322, XXV (Jan. 4, 1896), p. 5; *American Newspaper Publishers' Association, Committee on Paper, Bulletin* 326, May 11, 1895. The Association publishes several series of bulletins on different matters of interest to its members. Material on newsprint is likely to appear in any of them. Since all the bulletins are numbered consecutively, without regard to series, it seems simplest to cite by number, date, and page when page is given.

14. *Paper Trade Journal*, XXV (Dec. 5, 1896), p. 1000.

15. *Ibid.*, XI (Dec. 2, 1882), p. 585. The Civil War opened with newsprint dutied at 30 per cent ad valorem under the Act of March 3, 1863, which also introduced the classification of "unsized" printing paper, which included newsprint. This level of duty was maintained through successive revisions until that of 1883. *House Document* 562, 55th Congress, 2d Session, *passim; Globe*, 42d Congress, 2d Session, pp. 3511, 3908–11. Newsprint was excepted from the 10 per cent horizontal reduction of 1872,

16. *House Document* 562, 55th Congress, 2d Session, pp. 297, 307–

8; *Paper World*, VIII (Feb., 1887), IX (Aug., 1888); *Tariff Hearings before the Committee on Ways and Means, Second Session, Fifty-Fourth Congress, House Document* 338 (2 vol.; Washington, 1897), p. 1764. Reminiscing of 1883 before the Dingley hearings of 1896, he quoted himself as having said: "we do not care to have any more protection, so as to avoid friction between the newspaper publishers and the paper manufacturers."

17. *Paper Trade Journal*, XVII (Mar. 3, 1888), p. 148, (June 30, 1888), p. 456, (July 28, 1888), p. 533, XXVI (Oct. 16, 1897), p. 53; *The Congressional Record* (Washington, 1874 ff.), 50th Congress, 1st Session, p. 9276; *ibid.*, 2d Session, p. 698. The restoration of the duty on pulp seems to have been due to the effort of those interested in chemical pulp; the Act of 1883 made no distinction between the two types.

18. *Paper Trade Journal*, XIX (Jan. 11, 1890), p. 30, (Mar. 15, 1890), p. 230; *Revision of the Tariff: Hearings before the Committee on Ways and Means, Fifty-First Congress, First Session, 1889–1890* (Washington, 1890), *House Miscellaneous Document* 176, pp. 717–26; *To Reduce the Revenue and Equalize Duties on Imports, and for Other Purposes, House Report* 1466, 51st Congress, 1st Session (April 16, 1890), p. 12. Little mechanical pulp was being imported at this time because the low prices resulting from sharp domestic competition made importation unprofitable.

19. While the bill was pending before the Senate, Warner Miller told the annual convention of the paper manufacturers that "we have undoubtedly a productive capacity of from 33⅓ to 50 per cent above the actual consuming power of the country . . ." *Paper Trade Journal*, XXIII (July 28, 1894), pp. 707, 710.

20. *Ibid.*, p. 700; N. Y. *Times*, June 19, 1894; *Record*, 53d Congress, 2d Session, pp. 6440–42; *Replies to Tariff Inquiries: Schedule M. Pulp, Papers, and Books. Bulletin No. 54, Part II. Committee on Finance, United States Senate. Senate Report* 513, 53d Congress, 2d Session (July 10, 1894), pp. 11–30. The publishers' association mildly counselled its membership to write to Washington in an effort to secure removal of the wood-pulp duty, but did not exert itself unduly in this direction. A.N.P.A. *Bulletin* No. 237 (Jan. 4, 1894).

CHAPTER III

1. *Paper Trade Journal*, XXVI (Jan. 2, 1897), p. 8. They seem to have contemplated asking for an increase from $1.20 to $1.67 per ton

on mechanical pulp. *House Document* 1502, 60th Congress, 2d Session, p. 13.

2. *Paper Trade Journal,* XXVI (Jan. 9, 1897), p. 28; *House Document* 338, 54th Congress, 2d Session, pp. 1753–67, carries the committee hearings on the newsprint aspects of the Dingley Bill. Lengthy examination of Norris' career leaves the author unable to be categorical about his motivation. It appears to be compounded of low-tariff sentiment, a very practical desire to secure cheap newsprint for his employers, the *World* and later the *Times,* and on occasion not entirely devoid of straight vindictiveness. At this stage of the story, despite his insistence that he spoke only for himself, he may have had one eye on Joseph Pulitzer, his publisher, who was credited by a shrewd observer of the newspaper scene as having done "more to injure the news paper manufacturing business than any other publisher in this country, by the methods he forced upon the manufacturers whenever he called for bids on his big contract for white paper.

"Every time this contract was renewed by the manufacturer Pulitzer would make a lot of new conditions that would have to be accepted by the manufacturer before he could receive the contract. The World contract . . . was the prime factor in driving down the price of paper every year much faster than the manufacturers were able to cheapen the cost of production. The upshot of it all was that Mr. Pulitzer simply secured his white paper away below cost of manufacturing, and of course the other large publishers were compelled to demand the same low rates . . ." The same observer also quoted Norris as asserting that "he didn't give a continental darn what the price of news paper was, or what it would ever be, so long as the New York *World* purchased its paper cheaper than any other publisher in New York." *The Paper Mill and Wood Pulp News* (New York, 1876 ff.), XXIII (Apr. 14, 1898), XXIV (Oct. 19, 1899). Cited subsequently as *Paper Mill.*

3. The Association was founded in 1887 and had from time to time manifested a desultory interest in the newsprint problem, without making it a major issue. Its incorporation in 1897 and the injection of the Norris drive placed it in a position to become an aggressive factor. *Report of Proceedings of the Eleventh Annual Convention of the American Newspaper Publishers' Association Held at the Waldorf-Astoria, New York, February 16th, 17th and 18th, 1897* (New York, 1888 ff.), pp. 41–2. Printed under various titles, these annual reports are bound together in the office of the Association. Cited subsequently as A.N.P.A. *Report,* 1897, etc. The Association's articles of incorporation (Feb. 19,

1897) are printed in *Senate Document* 56, 62d Congress, 1st Session, pp. 1141–2.

4. A leading article in the *Paper Trade Journal*, XXVI (Mar. 6, 1897), p. 185, rehearsed the evil plight to which the industry had been brought by overproduction and discounted the wisdom of competitive prices and cultivation of the export trade as remedies, insisting that curtailment of output (i.e., combination) was the most desirable plan.

5. March 31. *Record*, 55th Congress, 1st Session, p. 557.

6. In addition to Norris' comment, above, cf. *Paper Trade Journal*, XXIV (Dec. 28, 1895), p. 1174, XXV (Nov. 28, 1896), p. 980.

7. *Ibid.*, XXII (Apr. 29, 1893), p. 374, XXV, *passim*.

8. *Ibid.*, XXVI (Apr. 10, 1897), p. 295, (May 1, 1897), pp. 352, 358; Joan V. M. Foster, "Reciprocity and the Joint High Commission of 1898–9," *The Canadian Historical Association: Report of the Annual Meeting Held at Montreal May 25–26, 1939, with Historical Papers* (Toronto: University of Toronto Press, 1939, pp. 87–98), pp. 87–8; L. Ethan Ellis, *Reciprocity 1911: A Study in Canadian-American Relations* (New Haven: Yale University Press, 1939), p. 5.

9. Laurier was still standing firm, as far as public information went, as late as May 21; the shift took place before June 8. *Paper Trade Journal*, *XXVI* (May 22, 1897), p. 417, (June 6, 1910), pp. 492, 498.

10. *Ibid.* (June 26, 1897), p. 508.

11. On the subsequent story see *Record*, 55th Congress, 1st Session, pp. 1864–5, 2499, 2702, 2705, 2709, 2780–3, 2787, 2909–10; *House Document* 1502, 60th Congress, 2d Session, pp. 475–9; N. Y. *Times*, July 22, 1897.

12. In a debate in the House on March 4, 1908, Gilbert M. Hitchcock, then a Representative from Nebraska, made the statements summarized in this sentence, basing them on his own experience as a publisher in Omaha and upon the testimony of Norris, Miller, and Russell in the Dingley hearings. Sereno E. Payne and John Dalzell, in reply, tried to show that the average price in 1897 was $2.00 per hundredweight. *Record*, 60th Congress, 1st Session, pp. 2906–7. Cf. also *House Document* 1502, 60th Congress, 2d Session, p. 15.

13. *Record*, 55th Congress, 1st Session, p. 2781. He also stated that the suggestion for the retaliatory proviso on paper was made to the committee by the House managers. The proceedings of the committee were not bound or preserved.

14. There is surprisingly little evidence of A.N.P.A. activity in connection with this legislation. Its paper committee issued at least one

appeal to publishers to urge their Congressmen to put groundwood on the free list. *Paper Trade Journal*, XXVI (Apr. 24, 1897), p. 332.

15. Statements of Vice-President G. C. Sherman to the annual convention of the American Paper and Pulp Association, Feb. 16, 1898. *Ibid.*, XXVII (Feb. 19, 1898), p. 143; *Paper Mill*, XXII (Apr. 14, 1898).

16. *Paper Mill, XXIII* (Feb. 3, 1898); *Paper Trade Journal*, XXVI (Sept. 4, 1897), p. 705, XXVII (Jan. 1, 1898), p. 4, (Feb. 5, 1898), pp. 101, 104, 123 (The *World* comment is reprinted in this issue), XLVI (Feb. 6, 1908); *United States Tariff Commission: Tariff Information Surveys on the Articles in Paragraph 322 of the Tariff Act of 1913 and Related Articles in Other Paragraphs: Printing Paper* (Washington, 1923), pp. 12–3. Cited subsequently as U. S. Tariff Commission, *Tariff Information*, 1923.

17. It should be noted that the trade journals speak quite matter-of-factly about trusts and combinations among the various branches of the business at this period.

18. A.N.P.A. *Report*, 1898, pp. 34–5. Norris was again made chairman. From the tone of Bryant's remarks it would appear that the meeting was a sincere attempt to conciliate the publishers. Warner Miller's statement to the mid-winter meeting of the Paper and Pulp Association a few days earlier was couched in firm language, but not excessive in its demands: "gentlemen, all we ask is for a six per cent dividend, and we are going to have it . . . that is something we have never enjoyed." *Paper Mill*, XXIII (Feb. 17, 1898).

19. *Paper Trade Journal*, XXVII (May 7, 1898), p. 377; *Paper Mill*, XXIII, *passim.*

20. *Paper Mill*, XXIII (July-Sept., 1898), *passim*, especially Aug. 11, 1898.

21. *Ibid.*, Sept. 22, 1898.

22. *Ibid.*, Dec. 15, 1898.

23. N. Y. *Times*, Sept. 2, 1898; *Paper Mill*, XXIV (Jan. 26, 1899), (Feb. 2, 1899); *Paper Trade Journal*, XXVII (Dec. 24, 1898), pp. 1038, 1042; A.N.P.A. *Report*, 1899, pp. 8–9. Norris' first two briefs and Miller's statement of January 7, 1899, are reprinted in *House Document* 1502, 60th Congress, 2d Session, pp. 746–8, 1221–5, 1258 ff. In view of oft-repeated charges that the International had taken in obsolete mills, as frequently denied by its spokesmen, the following contemporary comment is of some interest: "we must also admit that there were hulks among the news paper mills, and that was one reason why the

news paper manufacturers were so long in bringing about the news paper syndicate . . ." *Paper Mill*, XXIII (Dec. 1, 1898).

24. *Paper Trade Journal*, XXIX (Nov. 23, 1899), p. 820, XLVI (Feb. 6, 1908).

25. *Ibid.*, XXIX (July 13, 1899), p. 199, (July 20, 1899), p. 244, (Nov. 9, 1899), p. 764, (Dec. 7, 1899), p. 874; *Paper Mill*, XXIV (July 6, Sept. 21, Dec. 7, 1899).

26. By autumn the Great Northern Paper Co., a new organization not affiliated with the trust, was offering inducements to buyers in order to break into the field. The new competition introduced by it and by other newcomers broke the temporary price control of the International and inaugurated another period of declining prices lasting into 1906. *Paper Trade Journal*, XXIX (Sept. 7, 1899), p. 458, XXX (Feb. 8, 1900), pp. 167, 178, 180, (Feb. 22, 1900), p. 244, XXXI (Oct. 18, 1900), p. 485, XLVI (Feb. 6, 1908); A.N.P.A. *Bulletin*, No. 692 (Jan. 15, 1900), pp. 7–8; A.N.P.A. *Report*, 1900, pp. 9–26; *News-Print Paper Industry: Letter from the Federal Trade Commission Transmitting Pursuant to a Senate Resolution of April 24, 1916, the Final Report of the Commission Relative to the News-Print Paper Industry in the United States, Senate Document* 49, 65th Congress, 1st Session (June 3, 1917), pp. 23–4.

27. *Paper Trade Journal*, XXX (June 7, 1900), p. 715, XLVI (Feb. 6, 1908); *Light on the Print Paper Situation. Being an Address Delivered by Lincoln B. Palmer . . . before the New York Associated Dailies at Albany, New York, January 23, 1917* (pamphlet; New York: A.N.P.A., 1917), p. 5. The trade journals are filled with talk of combination in all fields of the industry between 1900 and 1902.

28. It should be noted that the lands held in fee could still export pulpwood; the ratio between fee and Crown lands varied widely from Province to Province. The prohibition was announced early in the year, to take effect on May 1, 1900. *Paper Trade Journal*, XXX (Jan. 18, 1900), pp. 71, 84, (Feb. 15, 1900), Supplement, p. 7; *Reciprocity with Canada: Compilation of 1911, Senate Document* 80, 62d Congress, 1st Session, pp. 4915–9, prints the Canadian provincial legislation in full.

29. *Senate Document* 49, 65th Congress, 1st Session, pp. 23–4; *Paper Trade Journal*, XXXII (Apr. 18, 1901), pp. 485, 496, 502, (May 23, 1901), pp. 645–6, XXXVIII (Feb. 18, 1904), pp. 283–4, (Apr. 21, 1904), p. 576, XL (Feb. 9, 1905), p. 79; *House Document* 1502, 60th Congress, 2d Session, pp. 1242, 1247–54, 1298. An inter-

view with Chisholm appearing in *The Brooklyn Daily Eagle,* April 2, 1902, amplified his views. *Ibid.,* pp. 1225–7.

30. A.N.P.A. *Report,* 1904, pp. 30–6. A resolution authorized acceptance of contributions up to one hundred thousand dollars for a war chest. The Lilley Resolution was never passed, but the Judiciary Committee to which it was referred held hearings on April 5 and 13 which elicited considerable information. The hearings do not appear in the documents of the 58th Congress, but are printed in the Mann Committee hearings of 1908, *House Document* 1502, 60th Congress, 2d Session, pp. 1229–1302. Prior to introduction of the Lilley Resolution the publishers had asked Payne for a hearing on removal of the wood-pulp tariff and had been rebuffed. Shortly before the April hearings Edward Rosewater, a publisher of Omaha, Nebraska, handed President Theodore Roosevelt a memorandum urging investigation of the trust by the Department of Commerce and Labor, and prosecution if the information so gathered should warrant action. Roosevelt's reception of this overture was said not to be "thoroughly sympathetic . . ." N. Y. *Times,* Mar. 8, 1904; *House Document* 1502, pp. 1245–6. For a sketch of Ridder, cf. *Dictionary of American Biography,* XV, pp. 590–1.

31. Lilley seems to have introduced his resolution, modeled after a previous one attacking the beef trust, without consulting the A.N.P.A., and as the result of a local situation.

32. A.N.P.A. *Report,* 1905, p. 38; *Paper Trade Journal,* XXXVIII (Apr. 28, 1904), p. 603, XXXIX (Sept. 29, 1904) (beginning with Volume XXXIX, July, 1904 ff., this journal is paged by issues instead of continuously for the year as previously. It will subsequently be cited by volume and date), (Dec. 29, 1904). An account of this prosecution, the details of which do not forward the present story, will be found in David Bryn-Jones, *Frank B. Kellogg: A Biography* (New York: G. P. Putnam's Sons, 1937), pp. 45–8.

33. *House Document* 1502, 60th Congress, 2d Session, pp. 699–700; *Paper Trade Journal,* XLI (Dec. 7, 1905), XLII (Jan. 4, 1906), XLIII (Dec. 13, 1906), XLVI (Feb. 6, 1908). An official of the International testified that average gross receipts per ton of sales dropped from $42.52 in 1901 to $39.90 in 1906. *Senate Document* 49, 65th Congress, 1st Session, p. 24.

34. Though the shortage was acute by May and continued during the summer, the price held steady during the first half of the year. *House Document* 1502, 60th Congress, 2d Session, pp. 248, 2981; *Paper Trade Journal,* XLIV (May 16, 1907), XLV (Dec. 5, 1907).

The shortage was aggravated by low water and strikes, designed to induce the mills to adopt the three-tour (shift) system. *Ibid., passim.*

35. *Paper Trade Journal,* XLIV (Feb. 7, 1907) and *passim,* XLV (July 18, 1907) and *passim,* XLVI (Jan. 2, Feb. 6, 1908); *House Document* 1502, 60th Congress, 2d Session, pp. 1733, 2969–81; *Senate Document* 56, 52d Congress, 1st Session, p. 1160; Palmer, *op. cit.,* p. 6; *Tariff Hearings before the Committee on Ways and Means of the House of Representatives, Sixtieth Congress,* 1908–1909, *House Document* 1505, 60th Congress, 2d Session (9 vols., paged continuously: Washington, 1909), p. 5914.

36. *House Document* 1502, 60th Congress, 2d Session, pp. 1026–30, 1078–98, 1140–1.

37. *Ibid.,* pp. 171–2; *Paper Trade Journal,* XLV (Sept. 12, 1907); *New-York Tribune* (New York, 1841 ff.), Sept. 19, 1907.

38. A letter from Ridder's paper manufacturer seems to show, however, that the *Staats-Zeitung* contract had not been closed as late as October 2. *House Document* 1502, 60th Congress, 2d Session, pp. 1966–7. Ridder's account is in *Senate Document* 56, 62nd Congress, 1st Session, p. 1261.

39. *The Fourth Estate,* XIV (New York, 1894 ff.), (Sept. 14, 21, 28, Oct. 5, Nov. 2, 1907). Norris' proposals contained instructions to a paper committee enlarged from three to nine to enlighten the President and Congress in order:

"First, that the authority of existing statutes for repression of trade combinations may be invoked;

"Second, that the defiance of recent judicial action prohibiting participation in such a combination by certain Western mills may be punished, and

"Third, that the President may be put in possession of information which shall equip him to advise Congress of the abuse of its tariff favors by papermakers."

As a final directive a resolution declared "That it is the sense of this meeting that the duty on printing paper, wood pulp and all material entering into the manufacture of printing paper should be repealed." A.N.P.A. *Report,* 1908, *Appendix,* pp. 80–94.

The greater emphasis on the tariff approach may have been due to an earlier statement of Attorney General Charles J. Bonaparte that the Department of Justice was already involved in seven anti-trust cases. Memorandum of an interview in the summer of 1907, *Paper Trade Journal,* XLVI (Mar. 5, 1908). For further comment, cf. *ibid.,* XLV

(Sept. 19, 26, 1907). One observer pointed out that the Dingley tariff, in effect since 1897, had not prevented fluctuations in the price of paper, concluding rather perspicaciously that "the tariff is only remotely, if at all, the cause of the present high price of print paper."

40. To John Norris, November 13, 1907, printed in *Record*, 60th Congress, 1st Session, p. 2986. The evidence thus requested went to Bonaparte February 10, 1908, but was not sent to publishers until March 4.

41. *Paper Trade Journal*, XLVI (Mar. 5, 1908); N. Y. *Tribune*, Nov. 8, 1907; *Fourth Estate*, XIV (Nov. 16, 1907); *House Document* 1502, 60th Congress, 2d Session, pp. 1323–4.

42. Roosevelt's rapid retrenchment and shift to conservation may be explained by pressure from the American Paper and Pulp Association, by the advice of Chief Forester Gifford Pinchot, by his innate political sagacity, or by a combination of these factors. By November 11 he was writing to David S. Cowles, head of the A.P.P.A.: "I am very firmly of the belief that wood pulp and forest products should not pay any duty. Our supply of timber is being exhausted altogether too rapidly in this country, and the exhaustion should be checked in every possible way instead of stimulated . . ." *Theodore Roosevelt Papers* (The Library of Congress). Two days later he wrote Senator William P. Frye of Maine in similar vein. *Ibid.*

The implications of the message regarding future American inroads upon their raw materials were not lost upon Canadians. For text of the message and editorial comment, cf. *Record*, 60th Congress, 1st Session, pp. 76, 1631; *Paper Trade Journal*, XLV (Nov. 14, Dec. 5, 1907), XLVI (Jan. 2, 1908), XLVII (Nov. 5, 1908); *Fourth Estate*, XIV (Nov. 16, 23, Dec. 7, 1907).

CHAPTER IV

1. The six volumes of the Mann Committee hearings, *House Document* 1502, 60th Congress, 2d Session, have found frequent place in documenting earlier chapters. They delved into all phases of production and consumption, and their compilation made Chairman James R. Mann the recognized congressional authority on the paper question for the next decade. For a sketch of Mann, one of the most useful legislators of his generation, cf. *Dictionary of American Biography*, XII, p. 244.

2. According to Norris this information had been submitted in October, 1907; it was circularized to the publishers under date of March 4,

1908, and read into *The Congressional Record* (60th Congress, 1st Session, pp. 2986–7) on March 6. *House Document* 1505, 60th Congress, 2d Session, p. 5917. It was answered seriatim by Albert H. Walker in *Paper Trade Journal*, XLVI (Mar. 12, 1908). Ridder was by this time President of the A.N.P.A.

3. *House Document* 1502, 60th Congress, 2d Session, p. 211; A.N.P.A. *Bulletin*, No. 1788 (Mar. 7, 1908), pp. 121–2, 1793 (Mar. 16, 1908), pp. 139–52.

4. *Record*, 60th Congress, 1st Session, pp. 2850, 3854; *Fourth Estate*, XV (Mar. 28, 1908); A.N.P.A. *Report*, 1908, p. 68. Canadian reaction was vigorous. A Canadian publisher told his colleagues in the A.N.P.A. that Roosevelt's message was "one of the most ludicrous statements that was ever put forth by any President or monarch" with its suggestion that Canadian forests should be devastated while those below the border recuperated from recent overcutting. *Ibid.*, pp. 66–7. The pulp and paper section of the Canadian Manufacturers' Association urged immediate prohibition of pulpwood exports in case the United States removed the duty on pulp. *House Document* 1502, 60th Congress, 2d Session, pp. 1602–3.

5. N. Y. *Tribune*, Apr. 3, 1908; *Record*, 60th Congress, 1st Session, pp. 4338, 4512–3; *Letter from the Attorney-General, Transmitting a Response to the Inquiry of the House as to Whether or not any Proceedings Have Been Taken to Prosecute the International Paper Company or Related Corporations for Alleged Violations of Federal Law, House Document* 860, 60th Congress, 1st Session, pp. 1–2; *Letter from the Secretary of Commerce and Labor, Transmitting a Response to the Inquiry of the House as to Investigations into the Management of the International Paper Company and other Corporations, House Document* 867, 60th Congress, 1st Session, p. 1. The President indicated his sympathetic interest in the inquiry by instructing Bonaparte to start preparing his reply several days before the resolution was passed. (Letter to Bonaparte, Apr. 3, 1908; *Roosevelt Papers.*)

6. *Paper Trade Journal*, XLVI (Apr. 23, 1908). The manufacturers were in Washington in force by this time, denying monopoly and insisting that prices had gone up much less than costs. The A.P.P.A. had meantime circularized its membership urging counterpressure on Congress lest the duty be repealed in spite of Cannon's efforts. *Ibid.*

7. A.N.P.A. *Report*, 1908, p. 20; *Record*, 60th Congress, 1st Session, pp. 4976, 4994, 5024–33, 66th Congress, 2d Session, p. 4342.

8. A.N.P.A. *Report*, 1908, pp. 21–5, 61–71; *Senate Document* 56,

62d Congress, 1st Session, pp. 1225–6; *Paper Trade Journal*, XLVI (Apr. 23, 1908).

9. *House Document* 1502, 60th Congress, 1st Session, pp. 222–3, 832; *Pulp and Paper Investigation, House Report* 1786, 60th Congress, 1st Session, pp. 1–18; *Record, ibid.*, p. 7153; *Fourth Estate*, XV (June 6, 1908), (Oct. 17, 1908); *House Document* 1505, 60th Congress, 2d Session, p. 5900; *House Document* 562, 55th Congress, 2d Session, p. 553. Norris supported this reciprocity proposal in the autumn of 1908.

10. *House Document* 1502, 60th Congress, 2d Session, pp. 2018–22; *Paper Trade Journal*, XLVI (June 18, 1908), XLVII (July 2, 1908). This journal asserted that his salary was underwritten by Adolph Ochs, Victor Lawson, Medill McCormick, Seitz, and Ridder, all publishers of metropolitan journals. Ridder's proposal called for contributions according to tonnage of newsprint consumed.

11. *House Document* 1502, 60th Congress, 2d Session, pp. 2028–30; *Fourth Estate*, XV (July 4, 1908). Bryan successfully resisted the manufacturers' request to oppose a free paper plank. A.N.P.A. *Bulletin*, No. 1851 (July 24, 1908), pp. 406–7.

12. It should be noted that the A.P.P.A. included all branches of the industry, including news. *Paper Trade Journal*, XLVI (Feb. 6, 1908), XLVII (July 30, Oct. 7, 1908); *Senate Document* 56, 62d Congress, 1st Session, pp. 1023–5.

13. *House Document* 1502, 60th Congress, 2d Session, p. 3. Reference has already been made to this voluminous record. In the following account reference is to these volumes unless otherwise indicated, and page citations will be held to a minimum.

14. *Ibid.*, p. 38.

15. *Ibid.*, pp. 1348–50.

16. Mann wrote in mid-July that though the majority of publishers were not sufficiently interested to reply, probably most of those seriously affected by increased paper costs had done so. *Ibid.*, pp. 2023–5.

17. *Ibid.*, p. 818. The facts bear out trade journal charges of reluctance of publishers to appear. *Paper Trade Journal*, XLVI (May 7, 21, 28, 1908). A request for information sent to 931 manufacturers brought 172 returns, representing 220 plants.

18. *Fourth Estate*, XV (June 27, 1908); *Paper Trade Journal*, XLVI, June 4, 1908); *House Document* 1502, 60th Congress, 2d Session, pp. 1303–32, 1557–8.

19. *House Report* 1786, 60th Congress, 1st Session, pp. 1–18.

20. *Paper Trade Journal*, XLVII (Nov. 26, 1908); N. Y. *Tribune*,

Nov. 22, 1908; *Fourth Estate,* XV (Nov. 28, 1908); *House Document* 1505, 60th Congress, 2d Session, pp. 5879–6056 contains the text of the hearings.

21. He declared that the principal users of spruce had bought over twelve thousand square miles of timber tracts in Quebec alone, with the International controlling seven thousand, or four and one-half million acres. *House Document* 1505, 60th Congress, 2d Session, p. 5904. This process of hedging against exhaustion of American forests by acquisition of Canadian timber limits had been going on for many years. The International was reported to have increased its holdings 44 per cent to a total of four million, one hundred and five thousand acres in the fourteen months prior to January, 1908. *Paper Trade Journal,* XLVI (Jan. 30, 1908).

22. *House Document* 1502, 60th Congress, 2d Session, pp. 3314–9.

23. It will be remembered that Ontario had in 1900 prohibited the exportation of pulpwood cut from Crown lands. Quebec manipulated her stumpage charges so as to exact twenty-five cents more per cord on pulpwood exported from Crown lands than on such wood pulped in the Province. This had been ruled an export tax, subjecting Crown-land wood from Quebec to the countervailing provisions of the Dingley Act.

24. *Record,* 61st Congress, 1st Session, p. 991; *Paper Trade Journal,* XLVIII (Mar. 18, 1909); *Reciprocity with Canada: Hearings before the Committee on Ways and Means of the House of Representatives* 61st Congress, 3d Session on H.R. 32216 (Washington, 1911), p. 170 (No document number was assigned to this title. Cited subsequently as *Hearings, Ways and Means,* 61st Congress, 3d Session); *Reciprocity with Canada: Hearings before the Committee on Finance of the United States Senate on H.R. 32216 An Act to Promote Reciprocal Trade Relations with the Dominion of Canada and for Other Purposes, Senate Document 834,* 61st Congress, 1st Session, p. 154. President William Howard Taft aptly characterized the Mann Report in a letter to Melville E. Stone, August 4, 1909, saying that it "was not a report as to a difference of conditions but was a recommendation of a diplomatic proposition to Canada to change conditions in Canada so that the paper makers of this country could stand $2, and by offering to Canadian manufacturers the opportunity to bring their paper in at [$2] to induce this change of condition . . ." *William Howard Taft Papers* (The Library of Congress).

25. *Paper Trade Journal,* XLVIII (Feb. 25, Mar. 11, 1909); *House Document* 1505, 60th Congress, 2d Session, pp. 8267–73.

26. *Record*, 61st Congress, 1st Session, p. 189. Taft's correspondence during the later stages of the debate refers several times to Payne's feeling that the $2.00 rate on newsprint, as carried in his bill, was too low to protect the industry adequately.

The reader has doubtless noted that chemical pulp and higher-priced papers have not been mentioned in connection with the Mann Report or the Payne Bill. This is because of the fact that the main interest of the present study is in cheap newsprint and the mechanical pulp which is its chief component.

27. Mann's speech, *ibid.*, pp. 645–54; other remarks, pp. 708, 881, 894, 934–8, 974–5; *Paper Trade Journal*, XLVIII (Mar. 25, Apr. 1, 1909).

28. A.N.P.A. *Report*, 1909, pp. 42–5; N. Y. *Tribune*, Apr. 7–13, 1909.

29. *Paper Trade Journal*, XLVIII (June 10, 17, 1909); *Senate Document* 56, 62d Congress, 2d Session, pp. 1226–7.

30. *Record*, 61st Congress, 1st Session, pp. 3390–3407, 3416–39; N. Y. *Tribune*, June 18–9, 1909.

31. *Record*, 61st Congress, 1st Session, pp. 3455–68, 3478–83.

32. *Ibid.*, pp. 3489–92, 3706, 3790–1, 3860; N. Y. *Tribune*, June 26, 1909.

33. *Ibid.*, p. 4636; Ellis, *op. cit.*, pp. 31–2. The Conference Committee originally set the surtax rate at $4.00, but a printer's error reduced it to $2.00, where it remained, since correction would have involved returning the bill to conference. N. Y. *Tribune*, Aug. 1, 1909.

34. *Record*, 61st Congress, 1st Session, pp. 4693–4; *Paper Trade Journal*, XLVIII (July 22, Aug. 5, 1909); N. Y. *Tribune*, July 27–29, 31, 1909. In the light of the publishers' hullabaloo over the Payne-Aldrich legislation and the reciprocity fiasco of 1911 Taft wrote rather ruefully, "I realize now, though, that I made one mistake; I ought to have made as strong a point on paper as I did on hides . . . I believe that if we could have stuck to the $2.00 duty of the House bill, with the condition attached of free raw material from Canada, we should have done the right thing . . ." (To Francis E. Leupp, Nov. 23, 1911. *Taft Papers.*) The tactics of the press annoyed him at the time, and he wrote to William Dudley Foulke on July 15: "I am not a high-tariff man, I am a low-tariff man; but I am in favor of a little justice and not of yellow journalism gone mad in order to accomplish some little personal profit for the proprietors of newspapers." Cf. also letters to Charles P. Taft

(July 13), W. H. H. Miller (July 13), Mrs. Taft (July 17, 25), H. V. Jones (Aug. 6), and Payne to Taft (Nov. 19, 1909), *ibid.*

35. The evidence at hand does not warrant a categorical statement, but there seems little doubt that Canadian assurances to this or a similar effect were secured. The late George F. Steele told the writer that he attended a conference at which a number of publishers agreed among themselves to a scaling down of duties over a period of years, in return for free access to Canadian wood. McCormick went from this conference to Ottawa, where he saw Laurier and Gouin, who agreed to give access to both fee and Crown-land wood in return for lowered duties. This information, said Steele, was conveyed to Mann. I have been unable to place this story exactly in the sequence of events. Cf. also *Paper Trade Journal*, XLIX (Sept. 2, 1909).

36. *Record*, 61st Congress, 1st Session, pp. 4730–3; N. Y. *Tribune*, Aug. 1, 1909.

37. *Paper Trade Journal*, XLIX (Aug. 5, Sept. 2, 1909); A.N.P.A. *Bulletin*, 2037 (Aug. 3, 1909), pp. 545–6, 2093 (Sept. 3, 1909), pp. 597–8; Ellis, *op. cit.*, pp. 33–4. The actual duty on paper from Quebec was $6.10 because of a thirty-five-cent countervailing levy occasioned by Quebec's export tax on logs.

CHAPTER V

1. *Survey of Pulp Woods on the Public Domain* (Washington, 1920), *Senate Document* 234, 66th Congress, 2d Session, pp. 5–6; U. S. Tariff Commission, *Tariff Information*, 1923, pp. 37–9. Meantime few new machines were being installed in the States, and new Canadian mills brought five hundred daily tons into the market between 1910 and 1916. *Senate Document* 49, 65th Congress, 1st Session, pp. 24–5.

2. *Record*, 61st Congress, 2d Session, p. 8; N. Y. *Tribune*, Dec. 7, 1909; *Paper Trade Journal*, XLIX (Nov. 29, Dec. 9, 23, 1909). Medill McCormick quoted Cannon as saying that "he would see us in hell before he would even let us circulate a petition among the members for a conference." *Ibid.* (Oct. 28, 1909).

3. A.N.P.A. *Bulletin*, No. 2066 (Sept. 27, 1909), p. 719, No. 2083 (Oct. 30), pp. 787–8, No. 2099 (Dec. 4), p. 859.

4. Ellis, *op. cit.*, covers the general reciprocity story of 1910–1911; such parts of the present story as are not specifically documented are drawn from this account. The present more detailed account of the news-

print aspects should be viewed in proper perspective in the larger framework.

5. *Paper Trade Journal*, L (Jan. 6, 13, Feb. 10, 1910); A.N.P.A. *Bulletin*, No. 2133 (Feb. 1, 1910), p. 75, No. 2154 (Mar. 19, 1910), p. 194.

6. A.N.P.A. *Bulletin*, No. 2154 (Mar. 19, 1910), p. 193; *Paper Trade Journal*, L (Mar. 31, Apr. 7, 14, 1910). An editorial in this latter journal aptly characterized the situation: "In the Payne-Aldrich act the publishers did not profit, neither did the paper men, the paper and pulp schedules being left in such shape as to please no one. The maximum tariff failed to frighten the Canadians into letting us have free pulp wood, so the whole tariff revision scheme fell flat . . ." One immediate result was a tremendous stimulus to investment in the Canadian paper business. It was reported that by July, 1911, fifty-three millions of British and Canadian capital had been so invested; statistics of similar American investments were not available, though they must have been large. *Ibid.*, LIII (Aug. 3, 1911).

7. A.N.P.A. *Report*, 1910, pp. 30–1; Ridder to Taft, April 28. *Taft Papers*. A last-minute effort was evidently made through Laurier to persuade Gouin to ease the situation, but he refused. N. Y. *Tribune*, Apr. 28, 1910.

8. Memorandum in the *Taft Papers*.

9. A.N.P.A. *Bulletin*, No. 2209 (June 9, 1910), p. 517; *Paper Trade Journal*, L (July 7, 1910); *Newfoundland Tariff Negotiations*. EXCEPTIONALLY CONFIDENTIAL. TO BE FILED AS A CONFIDENTIAL DOCUMENT AND ISSUED ONLY UPON THE WRITTEN ORDER OF THE SECRETARY OF STATE (printed pamphlet in the *Philander C. Knox Papers* (The Library of Congress), pp. 6–8).

10. It should perhaps be noted at this point that the Treasury Department ordered collectors to stop imposing countervailing duties of twenty-five and thirty-five cents, respectively, upon imports of pulp and paper made from Quebec's Crown-land wood after May 1, when the export prohibition became effective. This was on the ground that a complete embargo put an end to the discrimination formerly practiced in the export levy. This put Quebec's exports on the same duty basis as those of Ontario. *Paper Trade Journal*, L (May 12, 1910), LI (Aug. 4, 1910); A.N.P.A. *Bulletin*, No. 2191 (May 10, 1910), p. 440, No. 2251 (Aug. 6, 1910), p. 696.

11. *Daily Consular and Trade Reports* (Washington, 1903 ff.) Aug. 8, Oct. 26, 1910; Pepper to C. W. Norton, Aug. 15, 1910, *Taft Papers*;

Senate Document 56, 62d Congress, 1st Session, p. 1007; *Canadian Tariff Negotiations.* EXCEPTIONALLY CONFIDENTIAL. TO BE FILED AS A CONFIDENTIAL DOCUMENT AND ISSUED ONLY UPON THE WRITTEN ORDER OF THE SECRETARY OF STATE (printed pamphlet in the *Knox Papers,* pp. 37–8). This pamphlet, cited subsequently as *Can. Tar. Negot.,* takes the story to November 18, 1910.

12. Quotations from Ellis, *op. cit.,* pp. 62, 65, 67. Cf. also Fielding's remarks in introducing the proposals in Parliament, *Paper Trade Journal,* LII (Feb. 2, 1911).

13. A.N.P.A. *Bulletin,* No. 2338 (Dec. 24, 1910), pp. 1104–5.

14. *Senate Document* 56, 62d Congress, 1st Session, p. 1223; A.N.P.A. *Bulletin,* No. 2361 (Jan. 28, 1911), p. 81. The agreement left paper made from Crown-land wood subject to the Payne-Aldrich levy of $3.75 plus the $2.00 surtax. It was intended, therefore, as Ridder pointed out, to influence holders of Crown-land limits to put pressure upon the Provinces to relax their export restrictions so as to participate in the advantages of the American market enjoyed by the holders of private lands.

15. Quoted, Ellis, *op. cit.,* p. 70.

16. *Hearings, Ways & Means,* 61st Congress, 3d Session, pp. 271–3; *Paper Trade Journal,* LII (Feb. 2, 1911); *United States Tariff Commission: Reciprocity with Canada: A Study of the Arrangement of 1911* (Washington, 1920), pp. 47–8, 69. Cited subsequently as U. S. Tariff Commission, *Reciprocity with Canada.*

17. *Record,* 61st Congress, 3d Session, pp. 1515–9, 1618; *Paper Trade Journal,* LIV (Feb. 15, 1912); *Reciprocity with Canada, House Report* 2150, 61st Congress, 3d Session, p. 1. McCall made no mention of this amendment in his report.

18. *Hearings, Ways & Means,* 61st Congress, 3d Session, *passim; Senate Document* 56, 62d Congress, 1st Session, pp. 1145–7, 1224. The Senate hearings are found in *Senate Document* 834, 61st Congress, 3d Session.

19. The Senate hearings are printed in *Senate Document* 56, 62d Congress, 1st Session. The Ridder-Simmons colloquy is found on p. 1315.

20. *Paper Trade Journal,* LIV (Feb. 15, 1912); *Pulp and News-Print Paper Industry, Senate Document* 31, 62d Congress, 1st Session, pp. 31–6.

21. *Paper Trade Journal,* LII (May 25, 1911); *Senate Document* 56, 62d Congress, 1st Session, pp. 1321–5, describes Root's discussion

of his amendment before the committee. Taft told of his connection with it in letters to Horace Taft (May 25) and St. Clair McKelway (June 13). *Taft Papers.*

22. A.N.P.A. *Bulletin*, No. 2518 (Sept. 28, 1911), p. 945, 2569 (Dec. 16), p. 1181; *Paper Trade Journal*, LIII (Aug. 3, 24, Sept. 7, 1911), LIV (Feb. 15, 1912).

23. *Paper Trade Journal*, LV (Nov. 7, 1912); A.N.P.A. *Bulletin*, No. 2533 (Oct. 21, 1911), p. 1021; A.N.P.A. *Report*, 1912, p. 24; *Record*, 62d Congress, 2d Session, pp. 3934, 6615, 10738; *Taft Papers*, June and July, 1912, contain a number of letters to the President urging a repealer.

24. U. S. Tariff Commission, *Reciprocity with Canada*, p. 56; A.N.P.A. *Bulletin*, No. 2598 (Jan. 27, 1912), pp. 73–5, 2902 (May 24, 1913), p. 511, 2945 (July 26, 1913), p. 675. *Taft Papers*, October, 1911—March, 1912, contain a considerable body of material on the executive aspects of this matter.

25. A.N.P.A. *Bulletin*, No. 2791 (Nov. 23, 1912), p. 1119; A.N.P.A. *Report*, 1913, p. 30; *Tariff Schedules. Hearings before the Committee on Ways and Means House of Representatives* (Washington, 1913), *House Document* 1447, 62d Congress, 3d Session, p. 4742; *Senate Document* 49, 65th Congress, 1st Session, p. 55.

26. U. S. Tariff Commission, *Reciprocity with Canada*, p. 49; A.N.P.A. *Bulletin*, No. 2817 (Jan. 4, 1913), p. 1; *Paper Trade Journal*, LV, Nov. 21, 1912); *House Document* 1447, 62d Congress, 3d Session, pp. 4748–51. The new regulation, affecting four companies—Laurentide, Price Bros., Belgo-Canadian and Wayagamack—became effective May 1, 1913.

27. *Senate Document* 234, 66th Congress, 2d Session, p. 7. U. S. Tariff Commission, *Tariff Information*, 1923, pp. 33–6, gives figures showing decisive Canadian advantage in cost of production between 1913 and 1916, ranging from $3.10 to $5.35 per ton. This advantage was due mainly to cheaper pulp, which in turn rested on low-cost wood.

28. The hearings, confined to a single afternoon and with each speaker limited to ten minutes unless granted more at the expense of another, are found in *House Document* 1447, 62d Congress, 3d Session, p. 4673 ff.

29. *Record*, 63d Congress, 1st Session, p. 1061; A.N.P.A. *Bulletin*, No. 2879 (Apr. 12, 1913), pp. 423–4. Finland, whose exports to the United States were then negligible, imposed export duties.

30. Desire to be rid of the expense connected with Norris' operations may have played its part also. Cf. A.N.P.A. *Report*, 1913, pp. 32–4.

31. *Record*, 63d Congress, 1st Session, pp. 1061–3, 1149–50, 1210, 3600, 3695–3703, 4342–7; *Paper Trade Journal*, LVI, June-Sept., *passim*, reports Norris' activities in thwarting the efforts of certain Democrats on the Finance Committee to retain some measure of retaliation.

32. A.N.P.A. *Bulletin*, No. 2983 (Oct. 13, 1913), pp. 827–8.

CHAPTER VI

1. U. S. Tariff Commission, *Reciprocity with Canada*, p. 50; *Ibid.*, *Tariff Information*, 1923, p. 25; *Paper Trade Journal*, LVIII (Feb. 19, 26, Mar. 16, May 14, 1914), LIX (July 9, 1914).

2. *Paper Trade Journal*, LIX (Aug. 13, 1914), LXI (Aug. 5, 1915), LXII (Feb. 17, 1916); A.N.P.A. *Bulletin*, No. 3164 (Aug. 15, 1914), p. 637; W. A. Averill, *Prices of Paper* (Pamphlet: Washington, 1919), pp. 7–8.

3. *Paper Trade Journal*, LVIII (Jan. 1, 1914), LX, *passim*, LXI (Sept. 23, 1915); A.N.P.A. *Bulletin*, No. 3273 (Mar. 6, 1915), p. 235, 3392 (Nov. 27, 1915), p. 621, 3400 (Dec. 18, 1915), p. 645; *Senate Document* 49, 65th Congress, 1st Session, pp. 40–2; E. O. Merchant, "The Government and the News-Print Paper Manufacturers." *Quarterly Journal of Economics*, XXXII (Feb., 1918), pp. 238–9.

4. Merchant, *op. cit.*, pp. 240–3; *Senate Document* 49, 65th Congress, 1st Session, pp. 80–1, 107, 113–4, 132; A.N.P.A. *Bulletin*, No. 3517 (Sept. 6, 1916), pp. 475–7.

5. Open market prices of roll paper in carload lots were generally under $2.35 per hundredweight in 1915; the minimum price for the third quarter of 1916 was $3.00, and by December 1 it had risen to $5.00. *Senate Document* 49, 65th Congress, 1st Session, p. 51.

6. A.N.P.A. *Bulletin*, 1916, *passim*; *Paper Trade Journal*, LXX (May 6, 1920).

7. *Senate Document* 49, 65th Congress, 1st Session, pp. 15–7; *Paper Trade Journal*, LXII (Apr. 27, May 4, 25, 1916). Whence came the stimulus for this mid-western drive is not clear. It was suggested at the time that an agency furnishing Oklahoma papers with "boiler plate" copy had raised the price, alleging increased paper costs, and so induced pressure upon Congress.

8. *Senate Document* 49, 65th Congress, 1st Session, pp. 16, 142–3; *Paper Trade Journal*, LXII (May 4, 1916). This journal editorialized as follows: "it should be put down in red ink that the daily newspaper publishers of the country have no grievance against the men who make their white paper. If they had they would have said so at the annual convention of the American Newspaper Publishers' Association, held in New York City last week. Instead of giving expression to any grievance the publishers listened attentively to proposals as to how they could cut down on their consumption of white paper . . ."

9. *Paper Trade Journal*, LXII (June 22, 1916), LXIII (July 13, 20, 27, 1916).

10. N. Y. *Times*, Aug. 2, 1916; A.N.P.A. *Bulletin*, No. 3647 (Apr. 28, 1917), pp. 361–2; *Paper Trade Journal*, LXIII (Aug. 3, 10, 1916).

11. *Paper Trade Journal*, LXIII (Sept. 21, 1916); A.N.P.A. *Bulletin*, No. 3506 (Aug. 19, 1916), p. 415, 3514 (September 2, 1916), p. 466; *Record*, 64th Congress, 1st Session, pp. 14011–2. For an explanation of this increased tempo, cf. note 40, chapter VI.

12. *Paper Trade Journal*, LXIII (Oct. 19, Nov. 2, 9, 1916); A.N.P.A. *Bulletin*, No. 3539 (Oct. 21, 1916), p. 561, 3557 (Nov. 25, 1916), p. 631, 3561 (Dec. 2, 1916), p. 646; *News-Print Paper Investigation*: *Reply of the Federal Trade Commission to Resolution No. 95 of the Senate*, *Senate Document* 61, 65th Congress, 1st Session, p. 5. The $65 price was a common figure for late-1916 contracts, though at least two producers refused to follow the others up the price ladder and contracted at $10 to $18 below the usual level. *Senate Document* 49, 65th Congress, 1st Session, p. 115.

13. *Paper Trade Journal*, LXIII (Dec. 7, 14, 21, 1916); A.N.P.A. *Bulletin*, No. 3569 (Dec. 16, 1916), p. 675, 3572 (Dec. 23, 1916), pp. 695–8, 3576 (Dec. 30, 1916), pp. 709–11; N. Y. *Times*, Dec. 13, 17, 1916.

14. *Paper Trade Journal*, LXIII (Dec. 18, 1916), LXIV (Jan. 4, 1917); *Senate Document* 61, 65th Congress, 1st Session, p. 6; N. Y. *Times*, Dec. 16, 30, 1916.

15. On the price situation cf. U. S. Tariff Commission, *Tariff Information*, 1923, p. 25; Averill, *op. cit.*, p. 9.

16. A.N.P.A. *Bulletin*, No. 3590 (Jan. 22, 1917), p. 41, 3599 (Feb. 5, 1917), p. 67; N. Y. *Times*, Jan. 5, 27, 1917; *Paper Trade Journal*, LXIV (Jan. 11, 1917); *Senate Document* 61, 65th Congress, 1st Session, p. 6.

17. *Paper Trade Journal*, LXIV (Feb. 15, 22, Mar. 1, 1917); N. Y. *Times*, Feb. 11, 15, 24, 26, 27, 1917; Merchant, *op. cit.*, p. 244.

18. N. Y. *Times*, Mar. 4, 1917; A.N.P.A. *Bulletin*, No. 3617 (Mar. 3, 1917), pp. 137–41; *Paper Trade Journal*, LXIV (Mar. 8, 1917); *News-Print Paper Industry: Letter from the Federal Trade Commission Transmitting in Response to a Senate Resolution of April 24, 1916, a Report Relative to an Investigation of the News-Print Paper Industry of the United States, Senate Document* 3, 65th Congress, Special Session of the Senate, pp. 3–12. The Commission was particularly severe in its strictures upon the N.P.M.A.: "prices were actually made in the industry without the operation of free competitive influences in their determination. By means of a trade association, organized ostensibly for a lawful purpose, conditions in the market were influenced in a very substantial degree and in a manner which sustained a price which would not be possible under conditions of free competition. Concert of action was made possible through this association in the matter of discouraging new production of news-print paper, in the division of customers, in the promotion of fear that the supply would not be equal to the demand, in disseminating propaganda justifying higher prices because of alleged higher costs, and in other ways." *Ibid.*, p. 6. The agreement was signed by the International, Abitibi Power & Paper Co. (Ltd.), Spanish River Pulp & Paper Mills (Ltd.), The Laurentide Co. (Ltd.), the Belgo-Canadian Pulp & Paper Co., The Northwest Paper Co., and Taggarts Paper Co. The Great Northern, a large American producer, had not been involved in the price inflation practiced by so many concerns.

19. Merchant, *op. cit.*, pp. 245–6; A.N.P.A. *Bulletin*, No. 3642 (Apr. 14, 1917), pp. 345–8; *Paper Trade Journal*, LXIV (Apr. 5, 1917), LXVI (Feb. 7, 1918); *Senate Document* 61, 65th Congress, 1st Session, pp. 6–7; *Senate Document* 49, 65th Congress, 1st Session, pp. 140–1. It should perhaps be noted that the A.N.P.A. Paper Committee objected to the indictments and secured a promise from the Department of Justice to put off prosecution of those indicted if they joined the arbitration scheme. A.N.P.A. *Bulletin*, No. 3647 (Apr. 28, 1917), p. 363. Those indicted were: George H. Mead, Philip T. Dodge, Edward W. Backus, George Cahoon, Jr., G. H. P. Gould, Alexander Smith, and F. J. Sensenbrenner. The first five were members of the N.P.M.A.'s Executive Committee, Smith was a Chicago banker prominent in underwriting paper mills, and Sensenbrenner had been active in organizing the Association. Four—Dodge, Mead, Smith, and Cahoon—were signatories of the Trade Commission proposal. Steele,

the Secretary, was not indicted, as he had given evidence before the grand jury.

20. A.N.P.A. *Bulletin,* No. 3662 (May 19, 1917), p. 429, 3676 (June 2, 1917), p. 526.

21. *Senate Document* 49, 65th Congress, 1st Session, pp. 11–3, 127–31.

22. N. Y. *Times,* June 14, July 28, 1917; A.N.P.A. *Bulletin,* No. 3680 (June 16, 1917), p. 549, 3690 (June 23, 1917), pp. 599–600, 3710 (Aug. 2, 1917), p. 665; *Paper Trade Journal,* LXIV (June 21, 28, 1917), LXV (July 12, 19, 26, Sept. 6, 1917), LXVI (Feb. 7, 1918). A number of editorial associations composed of smaller papers adopted resolutions supporting the Trade Commission proposals.

23. A.N.P.A. *Bulletin,* No. 3735 (Sept. 8, 1917), pp. 755–60.

24. N. Y. *Times,* Oct. 8, 9, 1917; *Record,* 65th Congress, 1st Session, pp. 7323, 7874; *Government Control and Regulation of Print-Paper Industry, Senate Report* 177, 65th Congress, 1st Session (submitted Oct. 6, 1917), pp. 1–11.

25. A.N.P.A. *Bulletin,* No. 3774 (Nov. 10, 1917), p. 919; *Paper Trade Journal,* LXV (Nov. 22, 1917); N. Y. *Times,* Nov. 9, 13, 16, 18, 24, 1917.

26. A.N.P.A. *Bulletin,* No. 3782 (Nov. 26, 1917), pp. 943–9, 3783 (Nov. 27, 1917), pp. 951–8, 3786 (Nov. 30, 1917), pp. 963–74; N. Y. *Times,* Nov. 27, 28, Dec. 13, 1917. Dodge, Mead, Cahoon and Backus paid $2500 each, Sensenbrenner $1000. Smith was in Europe on war work at the time of the settlement.

A letter allegedly sent by Steele to the defendants reflects the temper and tactics of the Association: "*we went into this proposition of advising the newspaper publishers that there was going to be a great shortage of newsprint paper next Fall* [*1916*], *not because we loved the publishers or wanted to do a benevolent, high and philanthropic thing, but because we felt it would produce such an effect on their minds that they would not hesitate to sign up contracts at high prices when times of renewal came around if they knew there was an actual shortage in supply. It was to serve our own purposes and to help ourselves that we took this ground with them.* I AM THOROUGHLY SATISFIED THIS ATTITUDE OF OURS HAS ACTUALLY CONTRIBUTED VERY LARGELY TO THE RESULT THAT THE NEWSPAPER PUBLISHERS NOW REALIZE THAT WE HAVE THEM FIRMLY IN OUR POWER AND THAT THERE IS NO USE OF THEIR SQUIRMING OR TWISTING AT ALL." Quoted in A.N.P.A. *Bulletin,* No. 3774 (Nov. 26, 1917), pp. 969–70.

27. *Paper Trade Journal,* LXV (Dec. 6, 20, 27, 1917); A.N.P.A.

Bulletin, No. 3812 (Dec. 29, 1917), pp. 1133–4; Merchant, *op. cit.*, p. 252.

28. U. S. Tariff Commission, *Tariff Information*, 1923, p. 25. Open market prices dropped slightly during the first quarter, perhaps under the influence of recent events, rose slightly in the second quarter, and held steady until the end of 1919.

29. *Record*, 65th Congress, 2d Session, pp. 662–89, 707–23, 758–9, 821–32, 875–88, 1922; N. Y. *Times*, Jan. 10, 12, 16, 1918; *Paper Trade Journal*, LXVI (Jan. 17, 24, Feb. 14, 1918).

30. A.N.P.A. *Bulletin*, No. 3827 (Jan. 26, 1918), p. 54, 3919 (June 21, 1918), p. 689, 3929 (July 17, 1918), p. 718, 3941 (Aug. 7, 1918), p. 763, 3971 (Oct. 4, 1918), pp. 865–6, 4012 (Dec. 12, 1918), pp. 965–8; *Paper Trade Journal*, LXVI (June 13, 1918), LXVIII (Feb. 6, 1919); N. Y. *Times*, June 5, 20, 1918.

31. An acute contemporary analysis of these developments, tending to exculpate the manufacturers and to blame publishers for their own predicament, is contained in an address delivered by W. J. Pape to the National Editorial Association on March 11, 1921. *Paper Trade Journal*, LXXII (Mar. 17, 1921).

32. U. S. Tariff Commission, *Tariff Information*, 1923, p. 17. Toward the end of the year it was asserted that business interests were budgeting more than necessary to advertising in order to lighten excess-profits taxes, advertising charges being deductible in computing these levies. This was denied with sufficient vehemence to lend considerable color to the accusation.

33. A.N.P.A. *Bulletin*, No. 4118 (Aug. 9, 1919), p. 323, 4121 (Aug. 16, 1919), p. 331, 4133 (Sept. 13, 1919), p. 369, 4148 (Oct. 25, 1919), p. 423, 4217 (Apr. 28, 1920), p. 229. Many contracts contained a new provision, reflecting the strong position of the manufacturers, providing for periodic price revisions during the year.

34. *Paper Trade Journal*, LXIX (Nov. 20, 1919); *Record*, 66th Congress, 1st Session, pp. 4012, 4235–6, *ibid.*, 2d Session, p. 100.

35. N. Y. *Times*, Apr. 30, May 14, 1920; *Paper Trade Journal*, LXXII (Mar. 17, Apr. 14, 1920); *Hearings before the Committee on Finance, United States Senate on the Proposed Tariff Act of 1921 (H.R. 7456)*, *Senate Document* 108, 67th Congress, 2d Session, p. 4880.

36. A.N.P.A. *Bulletin*, No. 4217 (Apr. 28, 1920), pp. 218, 227, 233, 4408 (May 17, 1921), p. 371.

37. *Senate Document* 108, 67th Congress, 2d Session, pp. 4880–1, 4907–9.

38. *Paper Trade Journal*, LXXII (Mar. 17, Apr. 14, 1921); N. Y.

Times, Apr. 9, 1920. The News Print Service Bureau was organized in January, 1918, following the dissolution of the Newsprint Manufacturers' Association in 1917 to take over the legitimate aspects of the latter's activities. It was soon placed under the direction of R. S. Kellogg, whose statistical studies proved of great value to the trade.

39. *Record*, 66th Congress, 2d Session, pp. 4337–45; *Distribution and Consumption of Print Paper in the United States: Letter from the Secretary of Commerce, Transmitting Report in Response to House Resolution 489 Regarding the Supply, Distribution, and Consumption of Print Paper in the United States, House Document* 696, 66th Congress, 2d Session, pp. 1–20.

40. *Newsprint Paper Industry, Hearings before Subcommittee Pursuant to S. Res. 164, Authorizing Committee on Manufactures to Investigate Newsprint Paper Industry, 1920* (Washington, 1920), pp. 13–6, 34, 61–3. Cited subsequently as *Manufacturing Comm. Hearings*. N. Y. *Times*, Apr. 30, 1920. Patterson laid the beginning of the trouble to the fact that the first action of the mill men, in the autumn of 1916, in prorating tonnage and raising prices, was made without taking the publishers into their confidence as to the seriousness of the situation. This, he argued, led to a defensive reaction and the assumption of a mistaken attitude of antagonism toward the publishers which ought not to be repeated in the present emergency. He concluded by stating that he felt that the contract price increases for 1920 were justifiable. Cf. also *Paper Trade Journal*, LXX (May 6, 1920).

41. *Paper Trade Journal*, LXX (May 6, 13, 1920); N. Y. *Times*, May 2, 6, 8, 11, 13, 1920; *Manufacturing Comm. Hearings, Secret* (a portion of these hearings were held privately to spare paper companies from divulging trade secrets), pp. 69–71, 112.

42. This document, *Senate Report* 662, 66th Congress, 2d Session, is not available in the regular document series. It was read into *The Congressional Record*, 70th Congress, 2d Session, pp. 5055–8, by Walsh.

43. *Paper Trade Journal*, LXVIII (May 1, 1919).

44. *Ibid.*, LXIX (Aug. 7, 1919).

45. *Record*, 66th Congress, 2d Session, pp. 3436–8, 3560–4; *Paper Mill*, XLIII (Feb. 7, 1920); N. Y. *Times*, Feb. 3, 1920; *Foreign Affairs Committee, House, Exportation of Pulp Wood from Canada to United States, Hearings on S.J. Res. 152, Authorizing the Appointment of Commission to Confer with Dominion Government or Provincial Governments of Quebec, Ontario, and New Brunswick as to Certain Restrictive Orders in Council of Said Provinces Relative to Exportation of

Pulpwood Therefrom to United States, Mar. 9—April 27, 1920 (Washington, 1920), pp. 5–84. Underwood commented to the House Committee on Foreign Affairs apropos Section 2: "I do not think a blind man can fail to see that that means that this commission shall report to the Congress what kind of embargo we shall lay against Canada."

46. N. Y. *Times*, Apr. 27, 1920; *Paper Mill*, XLIII (Mar. 13, 1920); *Paper Trade Journal*, LXX (Apr. 29, 1920). A Canadian paper man was quoted as saying: "Senator Underwood is speaking in the interests of one company, the International Paper Company." *Ibid.*, (May 6, 1920).

47. *Record*, 66th Congress, 2d Session, pp. 8439–40; *Papers Relating to the Foreign Relations of the United States, 1921* (Washington, 1870 ff.), I, pp. 302–11. Memorandum of May 27, 1920. The measure was looked on in Canada as a blackmailing scheme. *The Montreal Gazette* was quoted as calling it "an insolent and dishonest" proposal. *Paper Trade Journal*, LXX (June 3, 1920).

48. The end of the year found the Board of Directors and the Paper Committee of the A.N.P.A. meeting with the News Print Service Bureau in a session presided over by President Dodge of the International Paper Co. which set up a joint committee of ten to discuss mutual problems. John Norris, in his grave since 1914, must have stirred uneasily at this portent. A.N.P.A. *Bulletin*, No. 4408 (May 17, 1921), p. 367, reporting a meeting of November 19, 1920.

49. *Ibid.*, p. 367; *Newsprint Paper Industry: Letter from the Chairman of the Federal Trade Commission Transmitting, in Response to Senate Resolution 337 (70th Congress), A Report on Certain Phases of the Newsprint Paper Industry, Senate Document 214, Special Session of the Senate* (71st Congress; July 8, 1930), p. 109.

50. *Record*, 67th Congress, 1st Session, pp. 2694–5, 4499–4500, 4644; *Paper Trade Journal*, LXXII (May 26, 1921); A.N.P.A. *Bulletin*, No. 4610 (May 4, 1922), p. 357; *Foreign Relations*, 1921, pp. 299–311, 1923, pp. 494–501. A stout but unsuccessful attempt was made to levy 5 per cent ad valorem on chemical pulp, to the advantage of the few mills devoted exclusively to that manufacture.

CHAPTER VII

1. Jones, *op. cit.*, p. 80.

2. It should be noted that any impetus to new paper production makes itself felt in the market only after a lapse of about two years, it

taking that length of time to prepare the necessary mills and water power. By the same token, once under way, heightened production is apt to overlap a period of decreased consumption, resulting in unemployment or oversupply, or both.

3. *Senate Document* 214, 71st Congress, Special Session Senate, pp. 31–2; A.N.P.A. *Bulletin*, No. 4662 (July 28, 1922), p. 603, 4670 (Aug. 26, 1922), p. 645, 4678 (Sept. 8, 1922), p. 677, 4701 (Oct. 21, 1922), p. 783; *Paper Trade Journal*, CIII (Oct. 15, 1936).

4. *Paper Trade Journal*, LXXIV (Apr. 20, 27, 1922); *United States Tariff Commission: The Trade Agreement with Canada* (Washington, 1936), p. 3.

5. *Paper Trade Journal*, LXXVI (Feb. 22, May 24, June 28, 1923), LXXVII (July 5, 26, Oct. 30, Nov. 6, 1923), LXXX (Feb. 5, 1925). Senator George A. Moses told the A.P.P.A. early in 1925 that he had gone to Canada in 1923 to investigate the Royal Commission and had quickly satisfied himself that "the whole question had risen through skillful propaganda started by an extensive land owner who desired to get more money and who succeeded in making it a national problem." *Ibid.*, (Feb. 12, 1925). Cf. also N. Y. *Times*, July 6, 11, 13, Aug. 3, 15, 1923.

6. *Paper Trade Journal*, LXXVII (July 12, 19, 1923); N. Y. *Times*, July 16, 17, 1923; *Foreign Relations*, 1923, pp. 494–8.

7. For the Royal Commission, cf. *Paper Trade Journal*, LXXVII, LXXVIII, *passim*. On other developments covered in the foregoing paragraph, cf. *ibid.*, LXXVIII (Mar. 20, Apr. 17, 1924), LXXX (Jan. 22, 1925), LXXXII (Feb. 4, Mar. 4, 1926); N. Y. *Times*, Aug. 3, Oct. 7, 1923, Feb. 14, 1925.

8. *Paper Trade Journal*, LXXX (Jan. 15, Feb. 5, 1925); N. Y. *Times*, July 20, 1924, Feb. 2, 1925, Jan. 30, 1926.

9. *Paper Trade Journal*, LXXVIII (June 5, 1924), LXXIX (July 3, 1924); N. Y. *Times*, Mar. 7, 27, 1925.

10. *Paper Trade Journal*, LXXVIII (June 12, 1924), LXXX (Jan. 1, Feb. 5, Apr. 9, 1925), LXXXI (July 16, 1925), LXXXII (Feb. 4, 1926); N. Y. *Times*, Jan. 31, 1926; A.N.P.A. *Bulletin*, No. 5213 (Apr. 30, 1926), p. 233.

11. *Paper Trade Journal*, LXXXII, *passim*, details International's Canadian operations. For particular aspects, cf. *ibid.*, (Apr. 29, May 20, June 24, 1926), LXXXIII (July 29, Aug. 26, Nov. 18, Dec. 30, 1926), XCII (June 18, 1931); N. Y. *Times*, Jan. 28, 1927; A.N.P.A. *Bulle-*

tin, No. 5213 (Apr. 30, 1926), pp. 230–1, 5374 (May 5, 1927), p. 275.

12. *Paper Trade Journal,* LXXXIV (Jan. 20, 27, Feb. 3, 10, Mar. 3, 24, May 26, 1927); A.N.P.A. *Bulletin,* No. 5521 (May 3, 1928), p. 145; N. Y. *Times,* Jan. 16, 1927.

13. *Paper Trade Journal,* LXXXIV (May 5, 1927), LXXXV (Nov. 3, 1927); A.N.P.A. *Bulletin,* No. 5521 (May 3, 1928), p. 170; N. Y. *Times,* June 24, Oct. 25, Dec. 18, 1927; *Senate Document* 214, 71st Congress, Special Session Senate, pp. 36, 85.

14. *Paper Trade Journal,* LXXXVI (May 17, 24, June 7, 21, 1928), LXXXVII (Aug. 23, Sept. 13, 1928), LXXXVIII (Feb. 21, Mar. 7, 14, 1929); *Senate Document* 214, 71st Congress, Special Session Senate, pp. 36–46, 85–90 (This contains the best brief account available); A.N.P.A. *Bulletin,* No. 5521 (May 3, 1928), pp. 171–2, 5631 (May 9, 1929), p. 177; N. Y. *Times,* Oct., 1928, through Feb., 1929, *passim,* gives a running account of such phases of the negotiations as were disclosed to the public.

15. A complete file of the A.N.P.A. *Bulletin* was not available to the writer at this point in the narrative. The principal developments of policy of 1928–1930 are summarized or quoted in A.N.P.A. *Bulletin,* No. 5631 (May 9, 1929), pp. 177–216, from which the following account is taken unless otherwise indicated.

16. *Control of White-Paper Business. Hearings, 70th Congress, 2d Session, on S. Res. 292, to Investigate Activities of Groups of Foreign Citizens Controlling Supply of White Paper in United States, January 30, 1929,* pp. 1–5.

17. The situation was complicated by the fact that the International had loaned Thomason part of the purchase price of the *Journal.* The company in 1928 had embarked deliberately upon the practice of investing in newspapers as a means of securing a market for its output, but Graustein denied that the plan contemplated any effort to influence policy. *Senate Document* 214, 71st Congress, Special Session Senate, pp. 92–7.

CHAPTER VIII

1. *Paper Trade Journal,* LXXXIX (Sept. 5, 1929), XC (Feb. 20, 1930); *Senate Document* 214, 71st Congress, Special Session Senate, pp. 46–7.

2. N. Y. *Times*, Nov. 21, Dec. 9, 17, 1929; A.N.P.A. *Bulletin*, No. 5694 (Nov. 19, 1929), p. 525; *Paper Trade Journal*, LXXXIX (Nov. 28, 1929).

3. *Senate Document* 214, 71st Congress, Special Session Senate, pp. 46, 101–3; *Paper Trade Journal*, LXXXIX (Oct. 24, Dec. 5, 12, 19, 26, 1929); A.N.P.A. *Bulletin*, No. 5694 (Nov. 19, 1929), pp. 524–6, 5704 (Dec. 10, 1929), pp. 594–603, 5753 (May 14, 1930), pp. 160–2; N. Y. *Times*, Oct. 14, 16, Nov. 27, 28, 30, Dec. 3, 5, 9, 10, 13, 22, 31, 1929.

4. *Paper Trade Journal*, XCII (Feb. 5, 1931); A.N.P.A. *Bulletin*, No. 5753 (May 14, 1930), pp. 162–76.

5. *Paper Trade Journal*, XC (Jan. 16, 23, Feb. 6, 13, Mar. 20, 1930); N. Y. *Times*, Jan. 15, 1930.

6. *Paper Trade Journal*, XC (Apr. 3, May 22, June 19, 1930), XCI (Sept. 11, 25, Oct. 2, Nov. 6, 13, Dec. 4, 1930); N. Y. *Times*, Sept. 19, 1930; A.N.P.A. *Bulletin*, No. 5809 (Dec. 9, 1930), pp. 482–4.

7. *Paper Trade Journal*, XCII (Feb. 19, Apr. 23, May 21, 1931), XCIII (July 9, Dec. 10, 1931), XCIV (Feb. 18, Apr. 28, 1932); A.N.P.A. *Bulletin*, No. 5856 (May 6, 1931), pp. 222–4, 5919 (Nov. 21, 1931), pp. 503–4; N. Y. *Times*, Apr. 20, 22, May 16, Nov. 15, Dec. 2, 8, 1931. Canadian mills operated at sixty per cent capacity in 1931.

An example of the vast inflationary movement in the paper industry is found in the reorganization of Canada Power into the Consolidated Paper Corporation (with Anglo-Canadian reverting to its previous ownership) with reduction of capitalization from $103,832,266 to $52,627,596.

8. The origin of these difficulties is to be found to a considerable extent in the continued decline of consumption. The Paper Committee reported to the publishers in May, 1932, that the greatest decline in advertising lineage in the history of publishing had occurred since the beginning of the year. It warned, however, that publishers must not rest secure in the impression that the present buyer's market would endure indefinitely: "Desperate conditions usually result in desperate attempts at cure . . ." A.N.P.A. *Bulletin*, No. 5983 (May 19, 1932), pp. 193–4; *Paper Trade Journal*, XCV (Sept. 8, 22, 29, Nov. 3, Dec. 8, 1932); N. Y. *Times*, June 29, Sept. 15, 16, 18, 22, Oct. 18, 23, 26, Nov. 12, 18, Dec. 14, 1932.

9. *Paper Trade Journal*, XCVI (Feb. 16, 1933), XCVIII (Feb. 22,

1934); N. Y. *Times*, Apr. 18, 1933; A.N.P.A. *Bulletin*, No. 6111 (Apr. 28, 1933), pp. 268–9; John A. Guthrie, *The Newsprint Paper Industry: An Economic Analysis* (Cambridge: Harvard University Press, 1941), pp. 109–10.

10. *Paper Trade Journal*, XCIX (Sept. 27, 1934); Ralph V. Harlow, *The Growth of the United States* (New York: Henry Holt, 1943), II, pp. 534–6.

11. *Paper Trade Journal*, XCVII (July 20, Aug. 17, 24, Sept. 7, 14, 1933); N. Y. *Times*, July 18, Sept. 7, 1933; A.N.P.A. *Bulletin*, No. 6168 (Sept. 8, 1933), p. 503.

12. *Paper Trade Journal*, XCVII (Oct. 26, Nov. 2, 9, 23, 1933); N. Y. *Times*, Oct. 24, 25, Nov. 3, 1933.

13. *Paper Trade Journal*, XCVIII (Jan. 25, 1934); N. Y. *Times*, Jan. 19, 1934; Jones, *op. cit.*, pp. 395–400; A.N.P.A. *Bulletin*, No. 6266 (May 2, 1934), pp. 254–69, carries the story of Association policy through that date.

14. These statements, consisting of the original telegrams, letters, and editorial excerpts, are bound in a volume entitled *Newsprint Recommendations, Volume B-1*, in *Records of the National Recovery Administration*, The National Archives.

15. *Paper Trade Journal*, XCVIII (Feb. 8, Mar. 22, 1934); N. Y. *Times*, Jan. 19, Feb. 2, 3, 1934. The arguments of Hanson and Patterson (typewritten copies) are bound in *Newsprint Recommendations, Volume B*, in *Records of the National Recovery Administration*, The National Archives. McMillen's printed pamphlet, "Industrial Advisor's Report on Recommendation of Newsprint Code Authority . . ." is bound in *ibid., Volume A*.

16. *Paper Trade Journal*, XCIX (Aug. 9, 1934); N. Y. *Times*, Apr. 7, July 20, Aug. 1, 4, 1934; Letter of Berry to L. B. Palmer, April 12, 1934, *Newsprint Recommendations, Volume A*; Jones, *op. cit.*, pp. 401–3.

17. Quoted in Jones, *op. cit.*, p. 403. Jones himself comments: "There can be no doubt that what the industries expected to derive from the code was price stability and a guarantee of future profits . . . and . . . to obtain protection from foreign competition by resorting to Section 3e of the Act . . ."

18. *Ibid.*, pp. 425–7.

19. *Paper Trade Journal*, XCVIII (May 10, 24, 1934), XCIX (Oct. 18, 25, Nov. 8, 15, 22, 29, 1934), C (Apr. 4, 1935); A.N.P.A. *Bulle-*

tin, No. 6413 (May 7, 1935), pp. 302–3; N. Y. *Times*, Oct. 11, 14, 23, Nov. 6, 8, 14, 17, Dec. 20, 1934, Jan. 17, 24, 1935; Guthrie, *op. cit.*, pp. 98–9.

20. *Paper Trade Journal*, C (Apr. 18, May 16, 1935), CI (Nov. 28, Dec. 19, 1935), CII (Jan. 16, Feb. 6, 1936); A.N.P.A. *Bulletin*, No. 6413 (May 7, 1935), p. 304; N. Y. *Times*, Apr. 14, 27, May 1, 3, 11, 17, June 12, 1935; Guthrie, *op. cit.*, pp. 110–2. The Canadian industry operated throughout 1935 at 71.2% capacity.

21. *Paper Trade Journal*, CI (Aug. 8, Nov. 21, 1935); United States Tariff Commission, *The Trade Agreement with Canada, Report No. 111, Second Series* (Washington, 1936), pp. 5, 65–6.

22. *Paper Trade Journal*, CII (Feb. 20, Mar. 5, Apr. 30, 1936); A.N.P.A. *Bulletin*, No. 6580 (May 1, 1936), pp. 328–9, 338.

23. *Paper Trade Journal*, CII (May 7, 1936), CIII (Aug. 6, 13, Nov. 26, 1936); A.N.P.A. *Bulletin*, No. 6706 (Apr. 30, 1937), p. 315. As early as July, 1935, a United States Government report supported the possibilities of southern yellow pine for producing mechanical pulp. *National Pulp and Paper Requirements in Relation to Forest Conservation: Letter from the Secretary of Agriculture Transmitting in Response to Resolution No. 205 (73d Congress) a Report on National Pulp and Paper Requirements in Relation to Forest Conservation, Senate Document 115*, 74th Congress, 1st Session, p. 2.

24. *Paper Trade Journal*, CIV (Jan. 21, Feb. 4, 11, 18, 25, Mar. 25, Apr. 1, 1937); A.N.P.A. *Bulletin*, No. 6706 (Apr. 30, 1937), p. 310.

25. A.N.P.A. *Bulletin*, No. 6706 (Apr. 30, 1937), pp. 311, 318; *Paper Trade Journal*, CV (Oct. 21, 28, Dec. 9, 1937), CVI (Feb. 24, 1938).

26. *Paper Trade Journal*, CIV (Feb. 25, 1937), CVIII (Feb. 23, 1939).

BIBLIOGRAPHY

Averill, W. A. *Prices of Paper* (Pamphlet). Washington, 1919.

Bryn-Jones, David. *Frank B. Kellogg: A Biography*. New York: G. P. Putnam's Sons, 1937.

Bulletin of the American Newspaper Publishers' Association. Published in several series and numbered consecutively, citation is by number, date, and page, or by number and date when pagination is omitted.

Canadian Tariff Negotiations: EXCEPTIONALLY CONFIDENTIAL. TO BE FILED AS A CONFIDENTIAL DOCUMENT AND ISSUED ONLY UPON THE WRITTEN ORDER OF THE SECRETARY OF STATE. In *Philander C. Knox Papers*, Library of Congress.

The Congressional Globe. Washington, 1833 ff.

The Congressional Record. Washington, 1874 ff.

Daily Consular and Trade Reports. Washington, 1903 ff.

Distribution and Consumption of Print Paper in the United States: Letter from the Secretary of Commerce, transmitting Report in Response to House Resolution 489 Regarding the Supply, Distribution, and Consumption of Print Paper in the United States. House Document 696, Sixty-Sixth Congress, Second Session.

Ellis, L. Ethan. *Reciprocity 1911: A Study in Canadian-American Relations*. New Haven: Yale University Press, 1939.

Foreign affairs committee, house, exportation of pulpwood from Canada to United States, hearings on S. J. Res. 152, authorizing the appointment of commission to confer with Dominion government or provincial governments of Quebec, Ontario, and New Brunswick as to certain restrictive orders in council of said provinces relative to exportation of pulpwood therefrom to United States, March 9—April 27, 1920.

Foster, Joan V. M. "Reciprocity and the Joint High Commission of 1898–9," *The Canadian Historical Association: Report of the Annual Meeting Held at Montreal, May 25–26, 1939, with Historical Papers* (1939), pp. 87–98.

The Fourth Estate. New York (weekly), 1894 ff.

Government Control and Regulation of Print-Paper Industry. Senate Report 177, Sixty-Fifth Congress, First Session.

Guthrie, John A. *The Newsprint Paper Industry: An Economic Analysis.* Cambridge: The Harvard University Press, 1941.

Harlow, Ralph V. *The Growth of the United States,* Vol. II. New York: Henry Holt Co., 1943.

Hearings before the Committee on Finance, United States Senate on the Proposed Tariff Act of 1921 (H. R. 7456). Senate Document 108, Sixty-Seventh Congress, Second Session.

Industrial Advisor's Report on Recommendation of Newsprint Code Authority. Statement by C. R. McMillen, Advisor to the Industrial Advisory Board in Connection with the Hearing on Recommendations of Newsprint Code Authority under the Code of Fair Competition Relating to the Newsprint Industry. February 7, 1934. Printed pamphlet bound in *Newsprint Recommendations, Vol. A,* in *Records of the National Recovery Administration,* The National Archives, Washington.

Johnson, Allen, and Malone, Dumas (editors). *The Dictionary of American Biography.* 21 Vol. New York: Charles Scribner's Sons, 1928–1944.

Jones, Edward R. *Paper Industry Study. Department of Commerce, Office of National Recovery Administration.* Manuscript study of the operation of the newsprint industry under NRA in *Records of the National Recovery Administration,* The National Archives, Washington.

Kellogg, R. S. *The Story of News Print Paper.* New York: The News Print Service Bureau, 1936.

Letter from the Attorney-General, Transmitting a Response to the Inquiry of the House as to Whether or not any Proceedings Have been Taken to Prosecute the International Paper Company or Related Corporations for Alleged Violations of Federal Law. House Document 860, Sixtieth Congress, First Session.

Letter from the Secretary of Commerce and Labor, Transmitting a Response to the Inquiry of the House as to Investigations into the Management of the International Paper Company and other Corporations. House Document 867, Sixtieth Congress, First Session.

Merchant, E. O. "The Government and the News-Print Paper Manufacturers," *The Quarterly Journal of Economics,* XXXII (1918), pp. 238–56.

National Pulp and Paper Requirements in Relation to Forest Conservation: Letter from the Secretary of Agriculture Transmitting in Response to Resolution No. 205 (73d Congress) a Report on National Pulp and Paper Requirements in Relation to Forest Conservation. Senate Document 115, Seventy-Fourth Congress, First Session.

Newfoundland Tariff Negotiations. EXCEPTIONALLY CONFIDENTIAL. TO BE FILED AS A CONFIDENTIAL DOCUMENT AND ISSUED ONLY UPON THE WRITTEN ORDER OF THE SECRETARY OF STATE. In *Philander C. Knox Papers,* Library of Congress.

Newsprint paper industry, hearings before subcommittee pursuant to S. Res. 164, authorizing Committee on Manufactures to investigate newsprint paper industry, 1920. No document number assigned.

Newsprint Paper Industry: Letter from the Chairman of the Federal Trade Commission Transmitting, in Response to Senate Resolution 337 (70th Congress), A Report on Certain Phases of the Newsprint Paper Industry. Senate Document 214, Seventy-First Congress, Special Session of the Senate.

News-Print Paper Industry: Letter from the Federal Trade Commission Transmitting in Response to a Senate Resolution of April 24, 1916, a Report Relative to an Investigation of the News-Print Paper Industry of the United States. Senate Document 3, Sixty-Fifth Congress, Special Session of the Senate. (A preliminary report)

News-Print Paper Industry: Letter from the Federal Trade Commission Transmitting Pursuant to a Senate Resolution of April 24, 1916, the Final Report of the Commission Relative to the News-Print Paper Industry in the United States. Senate Document 49, Sixty-Fifth Congress, First Session.

News-Print Paper Investigation: Reply of the Federal Trade Commission to Resolution No. 95 of the Senate. Senate Document 61, Sixty-Fifth Congress, First Session.

Newsprint Recommendations, Volume A, B, B-1. In *Records of the National Recovery Administration,* The National Archives, Washington.

The New York Times. New York, 1851 ff.

New-York Tribune. New York, 1841 ff.

Notes on Tariff Revision, Prepared for the Use of the Committee on Ways and Means of the House of Representatives. House Document 1503, Sixtieth Congress, Second Session.

Palmer, Lincoln B. *Light on the Print Paper Situation. Being an Address Delivered by Lincoln B. Palmer . . . before the New York Associated Dailies at Albany, New York, January 23, 1917.* (Pamphlet) New York, 1917.

The Paper Mill and Wood Pulp News. New York (weekly), 1876 ff.

The Paper Trade Journal. New York and Chicago (weekly), 1872 ff.

The Paper World. Springfield, Mass. (monthly), 1880 ff.

Proceedings of the Convention of Newspaper Proprietors Held at the City of Rochester, N. Y. on Wednesday and Thursday, Feb. 16, 17, 1887. Manuscript minutes of the first convention of the American Newspaper Publishers' Association, on file in the New York office of the Association.

Prochaska, George A., Jr. *The Pulp and Paper Industry.* Manuscript study in *Records of the National Recovery Administration,* The National Archives, Washington.

Pulp and News-Print Paper Industry. Senate Document 31, Sixty-Second Congress, First Session.

Pulp and Paper Investigation. House Report 1786, Sixtieth Congress, First Session.

Pulp and Paper Investigation Hearings. 6 Vol. *House Document* 1502, Sixtieth Congress, Second Session.

Reciprocity with Canada. House Report 2150, Sixty-First Congress, Third Session.

Reciprocity with Canada: Compilation of 1911. Senate Document 80, Sixty-Second Congress, First Session.

Reciprocity with Canada: Hearings before the Committee on Finance of the United States Senate Sixty-Second Congress on H. R. 4412 An Act to Promote Reciprocal Trade Relations with the Dominion of Canada and for Other Purposes. Senate Document 56, Sixty-Second Congress, First Session.

Reciprocity with Canada: Hearings before the Committee on Ways and Means of the House of Representatives 61st Congress, 3d Session on H. R. 33216. No document number assigned.

Reciprocity with Canada: Hearings before the Committee on Finance of the United States Senate on H. R. 33216 An Act to Promote Reciprocal Trade Relations with the Dominion of Canada and for Other Purposes. Senate Document 834, Sixty-First Congress, Third Session.

To Reduce the Revenue and Equalize the Duty on Imports, and for Other Purposes. House Report 1466, Fifty-First Congress, First Session.

Replies to Tariff Inquiries: Schedule M. Pulp, Papers, and Books. Bulletin No. 54, Part II. Committee on Finance, United States Senate. Senate Report 513, Part 2, Fifty-Third Congress, Second Session.

Report of Proceedings of the Twelfth Annual Convention of the American Newspaper Publishers' Association Held at the Waldorf-Astoria, New York, February 16th, 17th and 18th, 1898. New York, 1898. The Association's annual reports are published under this or a similar title.

Revision of the Tariff: Hearings before the Committee on Ways and Means, Fifty-First Congress, First Session, 1889–90. House Miscellaneous Document 176, Fifty-First Congress, First Session.

Schlesinger, Arthur Meier. *The Rise of the City, 1878–1898.* New York: The Macmillan Co., 1933.

Survey of Pulp Woods on the Public Domain: A Letter from the Secretary of Agriculture to the Chairman of the Senate Committee on Agriculture and Forestry upon the Merits of the Bill (S. 3555) Authorizing the Secretary of Agriculture to Make a Survey of Pulp Woods on the Public Domain and to Prepare a Plan for the Reforestation of Pulp-Wood lands and appropriating the sum of $1,000,000 for these Purposes. Senate Document 234, Sixty-Sixth Congress, Second Session.

Synopsis of Sundry Decisions Rendered by the Treasury Department under the Tariff and Other Acts, During the Year Ending December 31, 1872. Washington, 1873.

Tariff Acts Passed by the Congress of the United States from 1789 to 1897, Including All Acts, Resolutions, and Proclamations Modifying or Changing Those Acts. House Document 562, Fifty-Fifth Congress, Second Session.

Tariff Hearings before the Committee on Ways and Means. First Session, Fifty-Third Congress. House Miscellaneous Document 43, Fifty-Third Congress, First Session.

Tariff Hearings before the Committee on Ways and Means. Second Session, Fifty-Fourth Congress. 1896–97. 2 Vol. *House Document* 338, Fifty-Fourth Congress, Second Session.

Tariff Hearings before the Committee on Ways and Means of the House of Representatives, Sixtieth Congress, 1908–1909. 9 Vol. *House Document* 1505 Sixtieth Congress, Second Session.

Tariff Information Surveys on the Articles in Paragraph 322 of the Tariff Act of 1913 and Related Articles in Other Paragraphs. Washington, 1921.

Tariff Schedules. Hearings before the Committee on Ways and Means House of Representatives. House Document 1447, Sixty-Second Congress, Third Session.

The Theodore Roosevelt Papers. The Library of Congress.

The William Howard Taft Papers. The Library of Congress.

United States Tariff Commission. Reciprocity with Canada: A Study of the Arrangement of 1911. Washington, 1920.

United States Tariff Commission. Summary of Tariff Information, 1929, on Tariff of 1922. Washington, 1929.

United States Tariff Commission. Tariff Information Surveys on the Articles in Paragraph 322 of the Tariff Act of 1913 and Related Articles in Other Paragraphs. Printing Paper. Washington, 1923.

United States Tariff Commission. The Trade Agreement with Canada. Report No. 111 Second Series. Washington, 1936.

INDEX

Abitibi Power and Paper Co., Ltd., 133, 144, 193
Addystone Pipe Case, 33
Adler, E. P., 137, 139, 147
Agriculture, Department of, 113
Alaska, 113
Aldrich, Nelson W., 59–63
Allen, Loren, 14
Allison, William B., 23
American Newspaper Publishers' Association, 8, 18, 20, 30, 36, 38, 40, 42–5, 49, 50, 59, 60, 67, 72, 74, 75, 81, 82, 84, 85, 87, 88, 91–100, 105–7, 110, 114–6, 122, 124, 126, 132, 134, 136–9, 143–6, 149, 150, 155, 157–62, 164, 165, 167, 168, 171, 174–8, 180, 183, 184, 191–7, 200
American Paper and Pulp Association, 45, 46, 50, 59, 128, 169, 170, 173, 178, 183, 184, 198
American Paper Makers' Association, 11, 14
American Paper Manufacturers' Association, 173
American Press Association, 117
American Protective Tariff League, 81
Anglo-Canadian Pulp and Paper Co., Ltd., 134–6, 200
Ansberry, T. T., 98
Anti-trust laws and newsprint, 7, 8, 32, 36–8, 41, 72, 90, 92, 99–102, 104, 107, 118, 139, 140, 159, 170. *See also*: Clayton Act; Combination and monopoly in manufacture and sale of newsprint; Federal Trade Commission; and Sherman Act.
Associated Press, 34, 36, 48

Backus, Edward W., 104, 193, 194
Baldwin, H. E., 29
Baltimore American, The, 115
Baltimore Sun, The, 117
Barnjum, Frank J. D., 127, 128, 198
Beaverbrook, Lord, 152
Beck, James M., 34
Belgo-Canadian Pulp and Paper Co., 61, 149, 190, 193
Berry, Major George A., 160
Bonaparte, Charles J., 36, 39, 41, 181–3
Boutwell, George S., 12, 173
British Columbia, 85, 86
Brompton Pulp and Paper Co., Ltd., 133–6
Brooks, Erastus, 12, 13
Brown, Elon R., 86
Brown, Norris, 60, 61, 63
Bryan, William Jennings, 45, 178, 184
Burbank, A. N., 41, 51
Butler, E. H., 144, 145

Cahoon, George, Jr., 193, 194
Canada, Department of External Affairs, 122, 127
Canada, newsprint policy. *See* Newsprint, Canadian policy.
Canada, pulpwood exportation restrictions. *See* Pulpwood, Canadian export restrictions.
Canada, reciprocity with. *See* Reciprocity, Canadian.
Canada, removal of paper and pulp industry to, 6, 20–4, 26–9, 51–5, 57, 58, 61, 69, 70, 75, 84, 88–90, 119, 125, 127, 131, 185, 188
Canada, trade treaty with France, 72, 73
Canada Power and Paper Corporation, Ltd., 149, 150, 200

Canadian Club of Montreal, 168
Canadian Export Paper Co., Ltd., 133
Canadian Lumbermen's Association, 27
Canadian Manufacturers' Association, 183
Canadian Newsprint Co., 133, 134
Canadian Paper Sales Co., Ltd., 133
Canadian policy, newsprint. *See* Ferguson, G. Howard; International Paper Co.; Mergers in Canadian newsprint industry; Ontario, paper and pulpwood policy; Price of newsprint; Quebec, paper and pulpwood policy; Royal Commission to investigate Canadian newsprint affairs; and Taschereau, L. A.
Canadian production control, 132, 133, 135, 136, 138, 140, 142, 143, 145–53
Canadian Pulp and Paper Association, 130, 131
Canadian sales methods, 133
Cannon, Joseph G., 41–4, 60, 70, 71, 183, 187
Chandler, W. G., 144, 146, 147, 151
Chicago Journal, The, 137
Chicago Tribune, The, 36
Chisholm, Hugh J., 26, 30, 32, 180
Clayton Act, 159
Cleveland, Grover, 15
Code of Fair Competition, 154, 156, 157, 160, 162
Colby, Bainbridge, 102, 161
Colver, William B., 109
Combination and monopoly in manufacture and sale of newsprint, 7, 8, 10, 14, 19, 20, 24, 25, 29–32, 34, 37–9, 41–3, 46–54, 56, 93–6, 99–102, 104, 107, 114, 117, 118, 139, 140, 158, 161, 177–9, 181, 193. *See also* Mergers in Canadian industry.
Commerce, Secretary of, 116
Commerce and Labor, Department of, 31, 32, 41, 105, 180
Conservation of newsprint and pulpwood, 37, 38, 53–7, 127, 129, 183
Consolidated Paper Corp., 200
Converting mill, 4, 5
Corporations, Bureau of, 41
Corporations, Commissioner of, 74
Cost of production, 59–61, 66, 83, 98, 101, 103, 111, 155, 157, 158, 164, 190
Cowles, David S., 43, 45, 47, 50, 53, 182
Crown lands, wood and paper products from, 5, 67, 73, 75, 86, 112, 119–22, 165, 179, 185, 188, 189

Dalzell, John, 177
Davenport Times, The, 137
Davis, Howard, 161
Democratic platform of 1908, 45
Depression, 140, 145
Digester, 4
Dingley Tariff, newsprint and wood pulp aspects, 20–4, 28, 29, 44, 175–8, 182
Dodge, Philip T., 91, 95, 101, 130, 193, 194, 197
Dominion Marketing Act, 164, 166
Donovan, William J., 140

Election of 1910, 71, 76
Election of 1912, 85, 86
Election of 1932, 140
Emergency Tariff Act, 126
Everest, D. C., 169

Federal Trade Commission, 94–111, 118, 193, 194
Federal Trade Commission Act, 159
Ferguson, G. Howard, 135, 136, 142–4
Fiber and manila pool, 39, 40

Fielding, William S., 22, 77, 189
Finnish newsprint, 152, 190
Fletcher, Duncan U., 96
Fordney-McCumber Tariff, 123, 126, 127
Foulke, William Dudley, 186
Fourdrinier paper machine, 5
France, trade treaty with Canada, 72, 73
Frye, William P., 17, 61, 65, 182

Gallinger, Jacob H., 17, 61
Garfield, James A., 174
Gaylord, E. K., 139
General Paper Co., 29–33, 180
George H. Mead Co., Ltd., 115, 133
Glass, F. P., 95, 96, 101, 102, 105, 116, 139, 140, 147
Gold standard, 152
Gouin, Sir Lomer, 60, 67, 71, 73, 187, 188
Gould, G. H. P., 104, 107, 193
Graustein, A. R., 130, 131, 136, 138, 139, 143–5, 156, 199
Great Northern Paper Co., 30–2, 107, 165, 167–9, 179, 193
Gregory, T. W., 99, 108
Groundwood pulp. *See* Wood pulp, mechanical.

Hale, Eugene, 60, 61, 65
Hamilton Spectator, The, 147
Hamlin, Condé, 30, 33
Hammond, W. S., 87
Hanson, Elisha, 155, 158–61
Harding, Warren G., 123
Hardwick, Thomas W., 110
Hartford Courant, The, 115
Harvester Trust, 104
Haskell, W. E., 121
Hastings, Arthur C., 45, 47, 53, 54, 56, 57, 79, 86, 118
Hawley-Smoot Tariff, 165
Hearst, William Randolph, 117, 125, 134, 149
Hearst press, 115, 133, 164
Heenan, Peter, 166
Heney, Francis J., 102, 103
Hitchcock, Gilbert M., 177
Hotaling, H. C., 122
Houde, Camillien, 148
Howard, Roy, 106
Hudson Falls, N. Y., 47
Hughes, Charles E., 128, 129
Hull, Cordell, 165
Hurlbut, William N., 133
Hurley, E. N., 97
Hutchins, W. S., 29
Hyman, Mark, 102

Industrial Commission, 30
Insurgents, and tariff and reciprocity, 71, 81, 84
Integrated paper mill, 5
"International Fair Play," 119, 120
International Paper Co., 9, 14, 18, 24–6, 29, 31–5, 41, 47, 48, 50, 51, 59, 71, 74, 87, 90–2, 95, 97, 101, 106, 121, 130, 134–9, 141, 143–5, 147–50, 152, 153, 157, 164, 168, 178–80, 185, 193, 197–9
International Paper Co. of Canada, Ltd., 125, 130, 131

Johnson, General Hugh S., 155, 156, 160
Joint High Commission, 26–8
Joliet News, The, 29
Jones, Edward R., 162, 163, 201
Jones, George, 12, 13
Jones, H. V., 187
Justice, Department of, 33, 34, 37, 99–102, 104, 181, 193

Kellogg, Frank B., 34, 108
Kellogg, R. S., 158, 172, 196
Ker, F. I., 147
King, William Lyon Mackenzie, 128
Knight case, 14
Knox, Philander C., 77–80

LaFollette, Robert M., 61, 62, 65, 116
Laurentide Paper Co., 133, 149, 190
Laurier, Sir Wilfrid, 21, 22, 177, 187, 188
Lawson, Victor, 184
Leupp, Francis E., 186
Lever Food Control Act, 118
Liberty Loan, 112
Lilley, George L., resolution on price of newsprint, 31, 32, 180
Location tickets, 75
Lodge, Henry Cabot, 88
Lyman, Chester W., 32, 47, 51, 53, 59, 71, 117

McCall, Samuel W., 80, 189
McCall Bill, 80, 81
McCormick, Medill, 36, 48, 49, 184, 187
McIntyre, A. G., 97
McKelway, St. Clair, 190
McKinley Tariff, 16, 17
McMillen, Hugh R., 155, 159, 201
Mann, James R., 43, 44, 46–52, 58, 62, 65–8, 70, 88, 182, 184, 187
Mann Bill, 72, 74, 76, 78
Mann Committee, 39, 42–4, 46–63, 67, 68, 70, 72, 180, 182, 184, 185
Manufacture, process of, 3–5
Manufacturers, 6–8, 13–15, 18–20, 32, 50–2, 54, 55, 58, 79, 84–7, 90, 92–104, 107, 108, 111–3, 115, 117, 118, 121, 122, 146, 147, 149, 151, 154–60, 162–75, 183–5, 188, 193–6. *See also* American Paper and Pulp Association.
Manufactures, Committee on, 113, 116
Mead, George H., 193, 194
Mergers in Canadian industry, 133, 135, 145–7, 149–53, 166
Michigan League of Home Dailies, 158
Miller, Warner ("Wood-pulp"), 12, 13, 15, 20, 27, 28, 174, 175, 177, 178
Mills Tariff Bill, 15, 16, 175
Minnesota and Ontario Co., 150
Mongrel Tariff of 1883, 15, 175
Monopoly in manufacture and sale of newsprint. *See* Combination and monopoly in manufacture and sale of newsprint.
Moses, George A., 198
Most-favored-nations, 85, 165
Munsey, Frank, 117

National Editorial Association, 122, 195
National Industrial Recovery Act. *See* NIRA.
National Recovery Administration. *See* NRA.
New Brunswick, 132
New Deal. *See*: Code of Fair Competition; Johnson, General Hugh S.; Newsprint Code Authority; NIRA; NRA; and Supplemental Code.
Newfoundland, 75, 149
Newspaper and Magazine Paper Corporation, 133–9, 143
Newspaper Code, 161
Newsprint, definition of, 3
Newsprint Association of Canada, 168
Newsprint Code Authority, 154, 156–8, 160, 161, 163
Newsprint Conservation Committee, 126
Newsprint Export Manufacturers' Association, 156
Newsprint Institute of Canada, Ltd., 136, 141, 143–7, 149–51, 153, 199
Newsprint Manufacturers' Association, 93–5, 97, 104, 107, 108, 193, 196
Newsprint Manufacturers of the United States, 154–6
Newsprint Planning and Adjustment Board, 160
Newsprint Service Bureau, 115, 196, 197

New York Express, The, 12
New York Times, The, 12, 31, 44, 105, 117, 136, 176
New York World, The, 19, 25, 176
Nipigon Corporation, Ltd., 135
NIRA, 9, 140, 153, 154, 159, 169, 201
Norris, John, 18–21, 25–7, 30–3, 36, 37, 43, 44, 46–51, 53, 54, 58, 72, 75, 81, 86–9, 171, 176–8, 181, 182, 184, 185, 191, 197
North Carolina Publishers' Association, 99
Northcliffe, Lord, 106
Northern Securities Co., 34
Northwest Paper Co., 193
NRA, 154–9, 162, 163. *See also*: Code Authority; Code of Fair Competition; NIRA; and Supplemental Code.

Ochs, Adolph, 184
Ontario, paper and pulpwood policy, 29, 64, 67, 71, 73, 119, 120, 125, 126, 132, 135, 136, 140, 142, 143, 166, 168, 179, 185, 187–9. *See also*: Pulpwood, Canadian export restrictions; and Quebec, paper and pulpwood policy.
Overproduction, 10, 11, 13, 34, 70, 84, 123, 125, 130–4, 142, 177, 197, 198
Owen, Robert L., 94, 105, 191

Palmer, Lincoln B., 95
Panic of 1873, 11
Panic of 1907, 9, 34, 37, 39
Pape, W. J., 195
Paper Trade Journal, The, 13, 52, 56, 84, 92, 167, 168
Patterson, Paul, 117, 159, 196
Payne, Sereno E., 57, 58, 65, 79, 80, 177, 180, 185, 187
Payne-Aldrich Tariff, 46, 53, 55–69, 71–3, 84–6, 185, 186, 188
Penny press, 50
Pepper, Charles M., 74–6
Philadelphia North American, The, 97
Pickard, W. W., 157, 161
Pinchot, Gifford, 182
Powell River Paper Co., 153
Price, 7–11, 13, 14, 18–21, 26, 28–31, 34–9, 42, 45, 46, 48–52, 70, 74, 84, 85, 87, 89, 90, 92, 93–8, 100–3, 106–15, 117, 118, 123, 125, 126, 132–65, 167–9, 172, 173, 179, 180, 182, 192–6
Price, John H., 145–9
Price Brothers Paper Co., 133, 144, 145, 152, 167, 190
Print Paper Conservation, Committee on, 114
Production control. *See* Canadian production control.
Publishers' Buying Corporation, 115
Publishers' Press, 34
Pulitzer, Joseph, 176
Pulp, dried, 12
Pulpwood, Canadian export restrictions, 5, 6, 21, 22, 26–9, 35, 37, 44, 51–3, 55, 56, 61–7, 70–3, 75–9, 83, 85, 86, 88, 90, 112, 119, 120–2, 124, 128, 129, 179, 183. *See also*: Crown lands, pulp and paper products from; Ontario, paper and pulpwood policy; and Quebec, paper and pulpwood policy.
Pulpwood, supplies of, 113
Pulpwood, tariff on, 15, 37, 38, 47, 61, 63–7

Quebec, paper and pulpwood policy, 64, 66, 67, 71–3, 75, 85, 86, 119, 120, 125, 126, 129, 132, 135, 136, 140, 142, 143, 156, 164–6, 168, 185, 187–9

Reciprocal Trade Agreements, 165, 166
Reciprocity, Canadian-American, 22, 53, 56, 58, 69–87, 91, 177, 187, 189, 190

Red Cross, 112
Reed, James A., resolution on newsprint, 113, 116–9, 122
Rickard, Edgar, 157, 158, 161
Ricketts, Edwin D., 114
Ridder, Herman, 30, 39, 41–5, 48, 50, 51, 59, 72, 74, 75, 78, 82, 89, 181, 183, 184, 189
Riordon Paper Co., 130
Roosevelt, Franklin D., 156
Roosevelt, Theodore, 36, 37, 40, 45, 180, 182, 183
Root, Elihu, 83, 189
Root Amendment, 83, 189, 190
Rosewater, Edward, 180
Rothermere, Lord, 167
Royal Commission, 128–30, 198
Russell, William E., 12, 13, 20, 24, 177
Russo-Japanese War, 30

St. James, Court of, 121
St. Lawrence Paper Co., 164
St. Maurice Valley Co., 133, 144, 149
St. Maurice Valley Sales Corporation, Ltd., 133
St. Paul Pioneer Press, The, 30
St. Regis Paper Co., 133, 156
Scandinavian newsprint, 152
Schechter case, 161, 163
Scripps-Howard papers, 144, 153, 164
Seitz, Don C., 30–3, 51, 59, 81, 184
Sensenbrenner, Frank J., 169, 193, 194
Seward, William H., 29
Sherman, G. C., 178
Sherman Act. *See* Anti-trust laws.
Sibley, C. L., 168
Simmons, F. M., 82, 189
Sims, Thetus W., 49, 51
Smith, Alexander, 193, 194
Smith, Courtland, 117
Smith, Herbert Knox, 4
Smith, Marcus J., resolutions on newsprint, 105–10
Smoot, Reed, 59, 88, 109, 110
Spanish River Pulp and Paper Mills, Ltd., 193
Spanish-American War, 24
Spot market, 74, 92, 93, 95, 97, 112–5, 132
Spruce Falls Power and Paper Co., Ltd., 136
Staats-Zeitung, New Yorker, Die, 30, 181
Stadler, John, 167
Standard newsprint, 123
Steel trust, 104
Steele, George F., 93–6, 187, 193, 194
Stevens, Frederick C. (newsprint tariff bill), 40, 43, 44, 47, 53
Stokes, Henry W., 128
Stone, Melville E., 185
Stumpage dues, 148, 164–6, 185
Supplemental Code, 156–60
Supply and demand, 6–9, 10, 11, 13, 30, 34, 39, 54–6, 70, 74, 84, 85, 89, 92–6, 102, 103, 111–6, 125, 126, 131–4, 139, 140, 142–4, 147, 149, 151, 158, 163–70, 173, 180, 195, 197, 198, 200, 202

Taft, Charles P., 186
Taft, Horace, 190
Taft, Mrs. William Howard, 187
Taft, William Howard, 65, 67, 70–4, 82, 83, 85, 185, 186, 190
Taggarts Paper Co., 193
Tariff, 6, 8, 10, 11, 15–25, 28, 36–9, 41–71, 74, 85, 86, 123, 126, 127, 174–6, 181, 182, 185, 188, 190, 197. *See also* Reciprocity, Canadian-American.
Tariff Commission, 15, 70, 82, 127
Taschereau, L. A., 124, 129, 131, 135, 136, 142–5, 147, 148, 153, 156, 164, 165
Thomason, S. E., 137–40, 143, 199
Three Rivers, Que., 130
Todd, G. Carroll, 99
Townshend, Richard W., 13
Trade associations, 46
Trade Relations, Bureau of, 74

Underwood, Oscar, 82, 86, 197
Underwood Resolution, 119–24, 126
Underwood Tariff, 45, 69, 85–7, 190
United Press, 48, 106

Varner, H. E., 99
Versailles, Treaty of, 116
Vest, George G., 23
Vining, Charles, 168

Walker, Albert H., 183
Waller, Tom T., 32
Walsh, David I., 118
War of 1914–1918, 90, 91, 100, 103, 105, 106, 111
Washington Times, The, 29
Watson, James E., 113
Wayagamack Paper Co., 133, 149, 190
Weed, Thurlow, 29
Williams, John Sharp, 40
Wilson, Woodrow, 86, 109, 122
Wilson-Gorman Tariff, 16, 17, 175
Winona speech, 71
Wood, Fernando, 12, 13, 174
Wood pulp, chemical, 4, 49, 175, 186, 197
Wood pulp, importation, 5, 6
Wood pulp, mechanical, 4, 175, 185, 202
Wood pulp, sulphite, 4
Wood pulp, Swedish, 165
Wood pulp, tariff on, 5, 10–25, 37, 40, 45, 47, 49, 53, 55, 57, 60–7, 87, 88, 180, 183